EDENS ZERO

8

SOMEONE TO LOVE

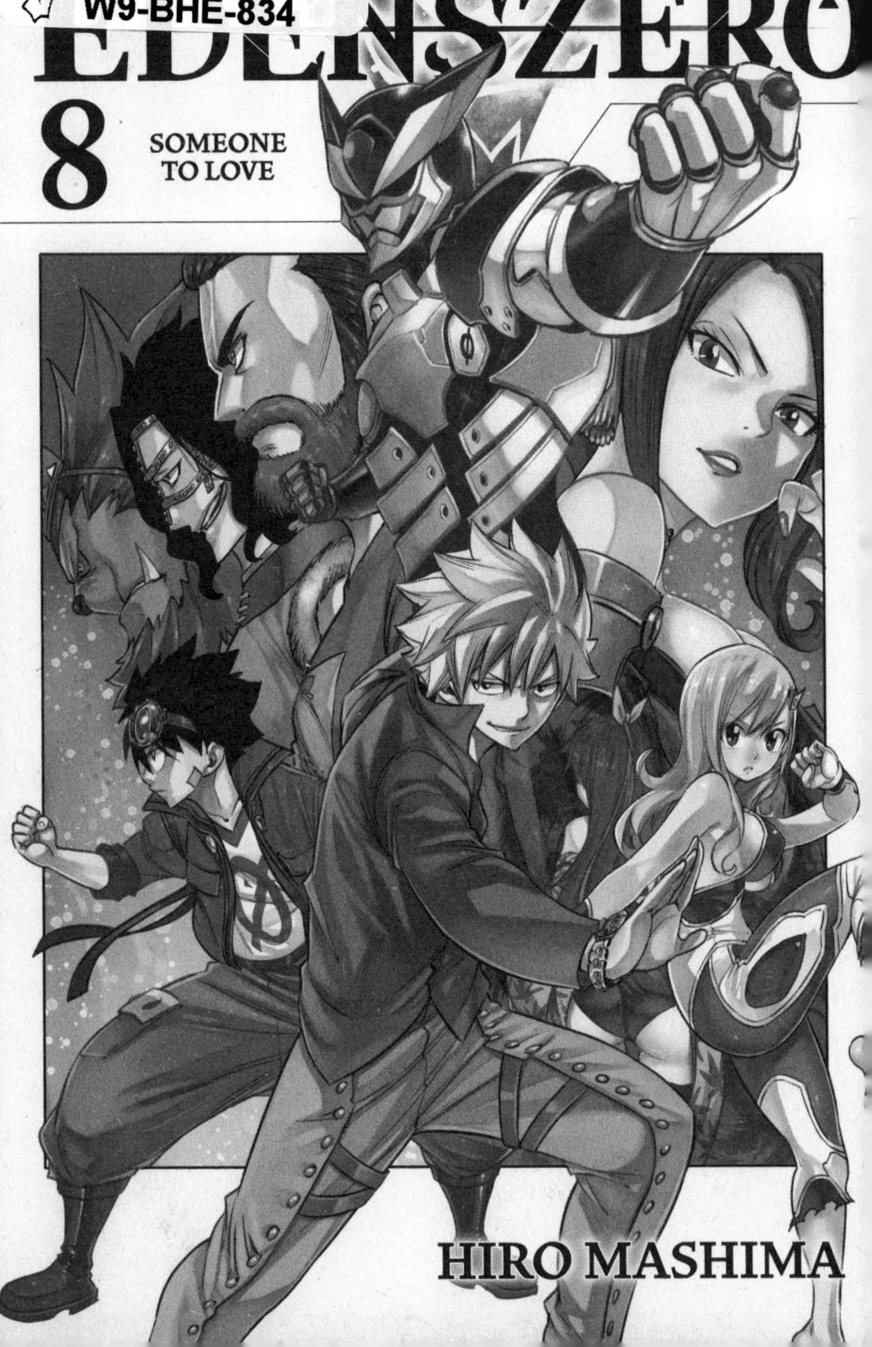

HIRO MASHIMA

EDENS ZERO 8 contents

EDENS ZERO

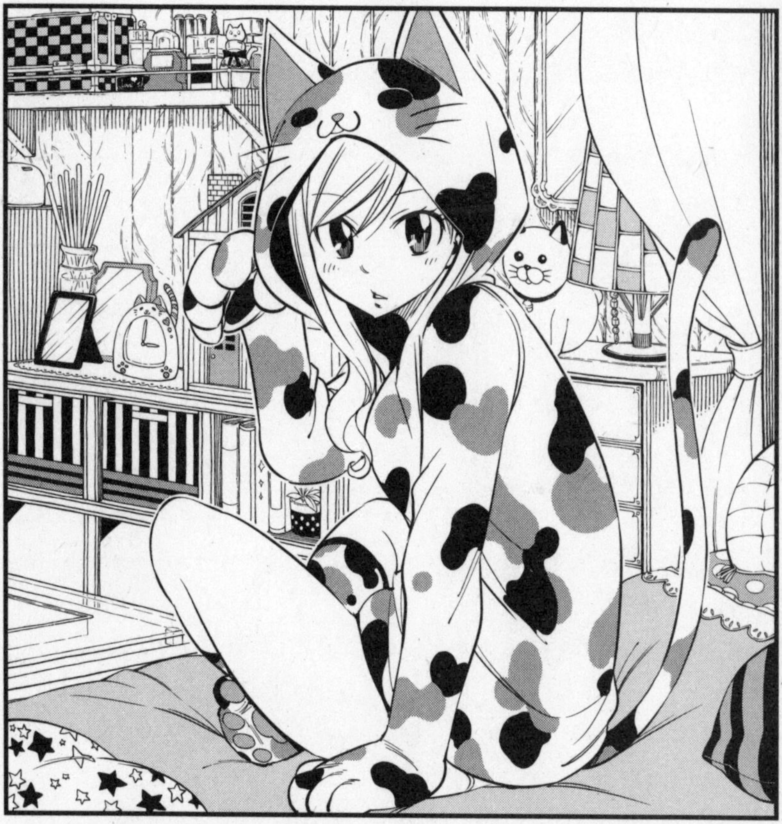

CHAPTER 60: UNTIL THE DAY IT TURNS TO STRENGTH

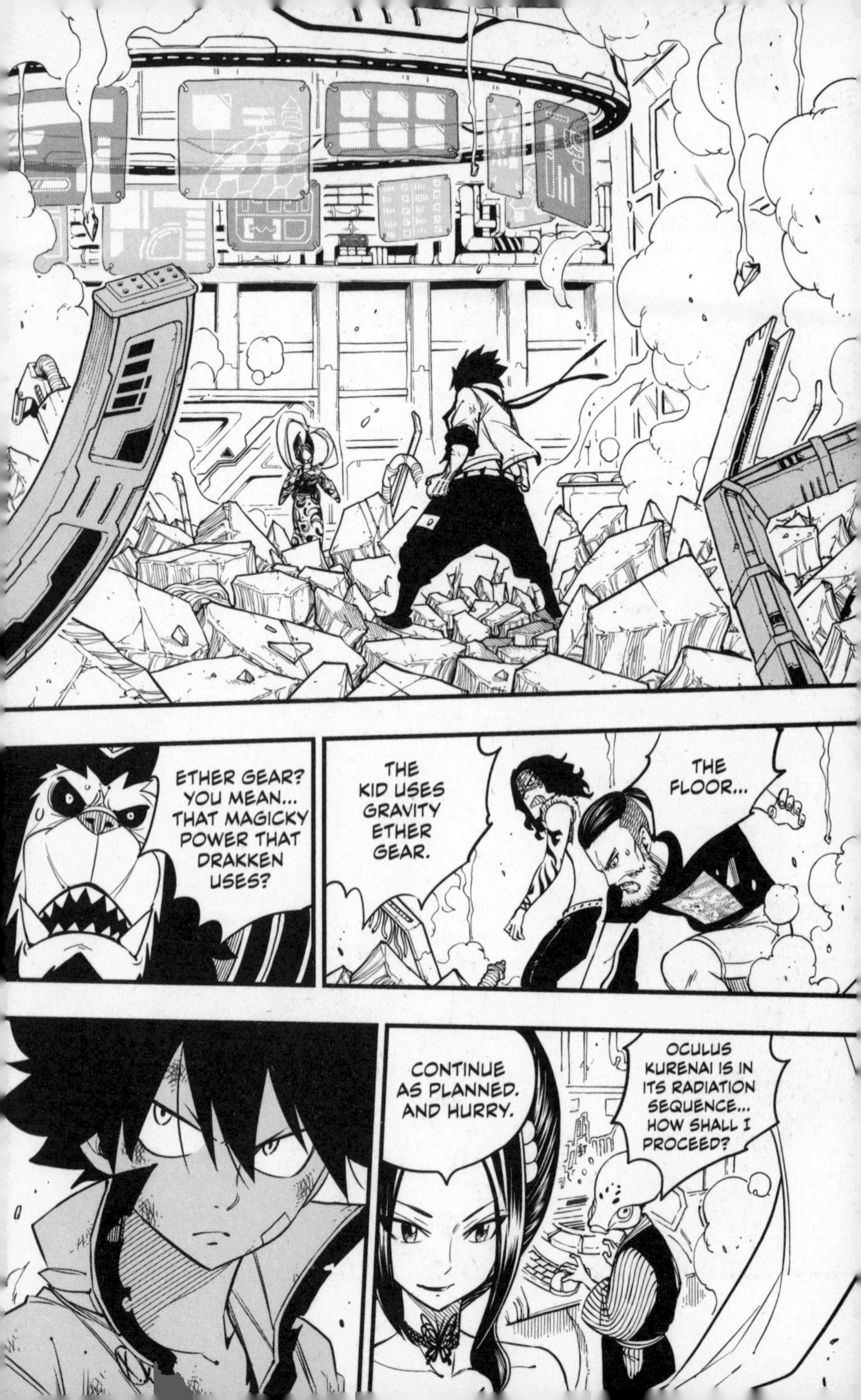
THE FLOOR...
THE KID USES GRAVITY ETHER GEAR.
ETHER GEAR? YOU MEAN... THAT MAGICKY POWER THAT DRAKKEN USES?
OCULUS KURENAI IS IN ITS RADIATION SEQUENCE... HOW SHALL I PROCEED?
CONTINUE AS PLANNED. AND HURRY.

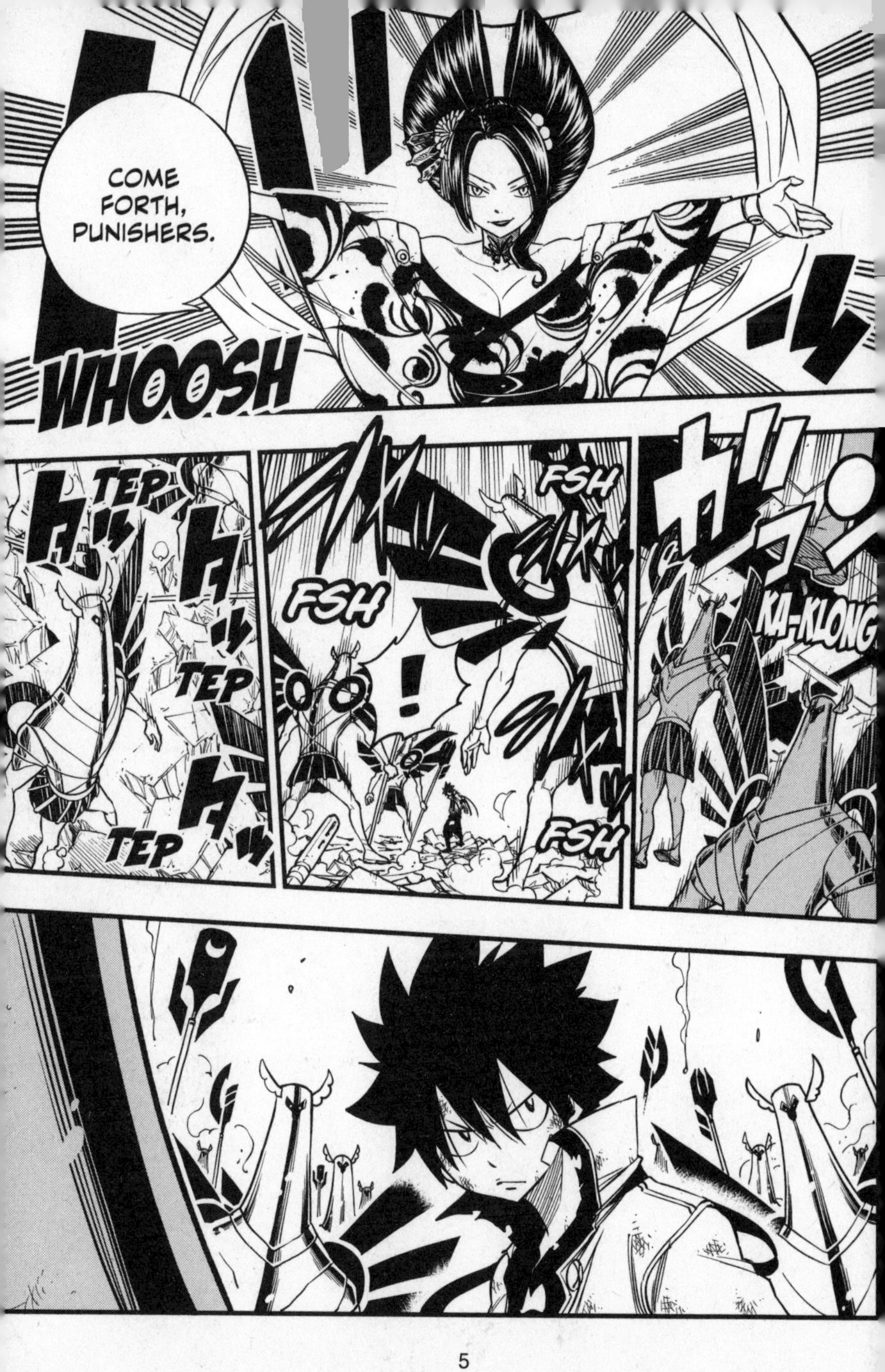
COME FORTH, PUNISHERS.
WHOOSH
KA-KLONG
FSH
FSH
!
FSH
TEP
TEP
TEP

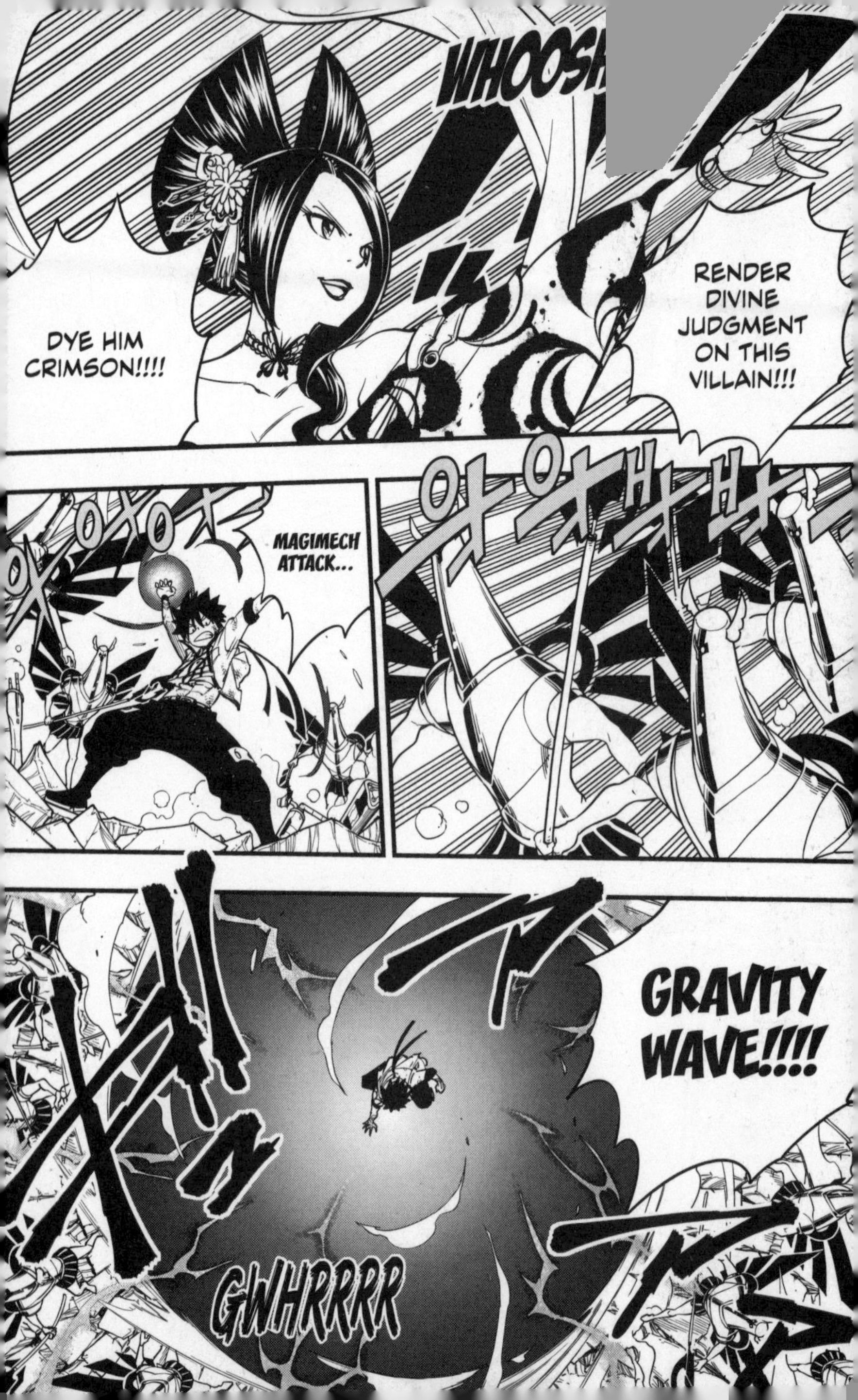
WHOOSH
RENDER DIVINE JUDGMENT ON THIS VILLAIN!!!
DYE HIM CRIMSON!!!!
MAGIMECH ATTACK...
GRAVITY WAVE!!!!
GWHRRRR

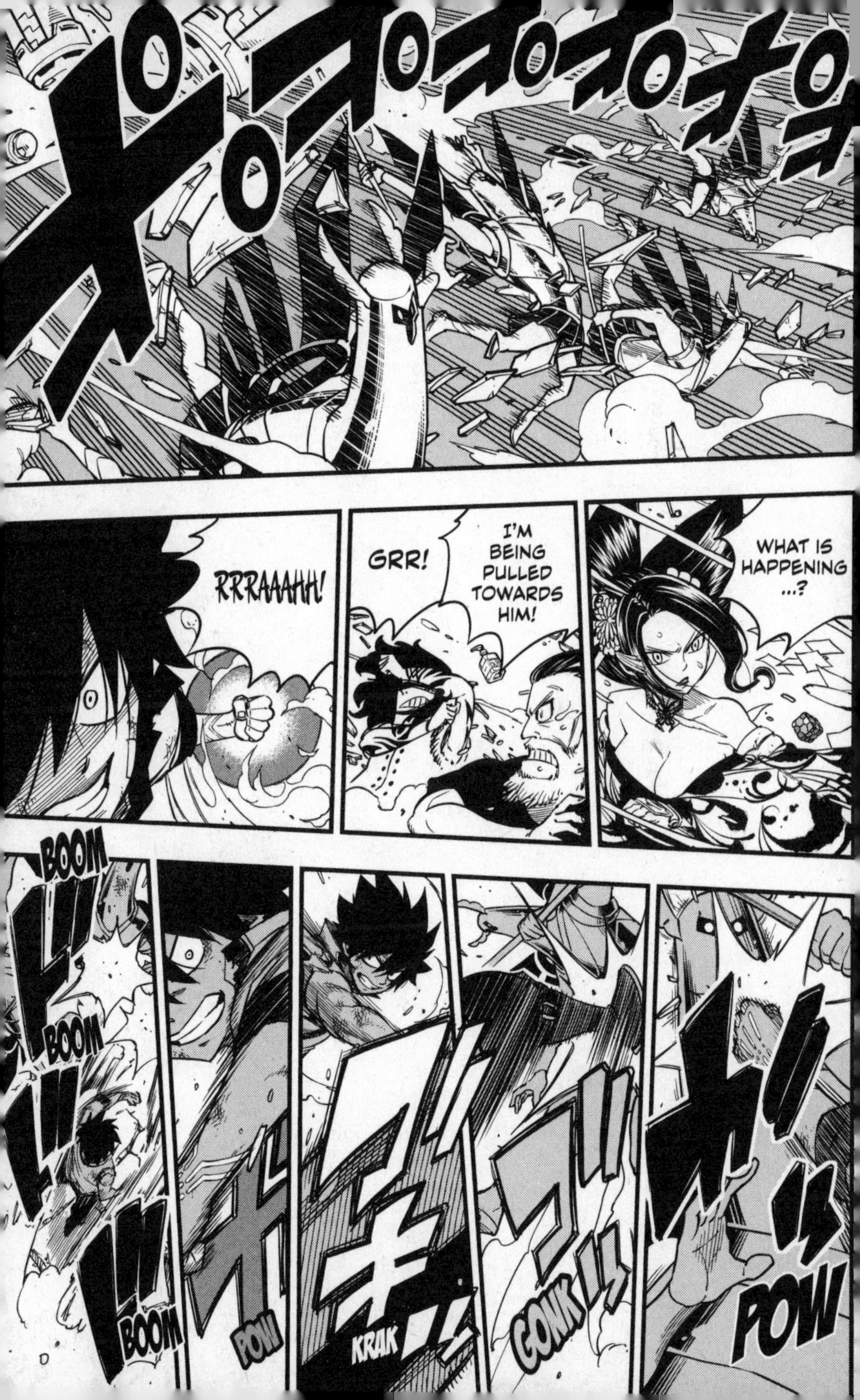
WHAT IS HAPPENING ...?
I'M BEING PULLED TOWARDS HIM!
GRR!
RRRAAAHH!
POW
GONK
KRAK
POW
BOOM
BOOM
BOOM

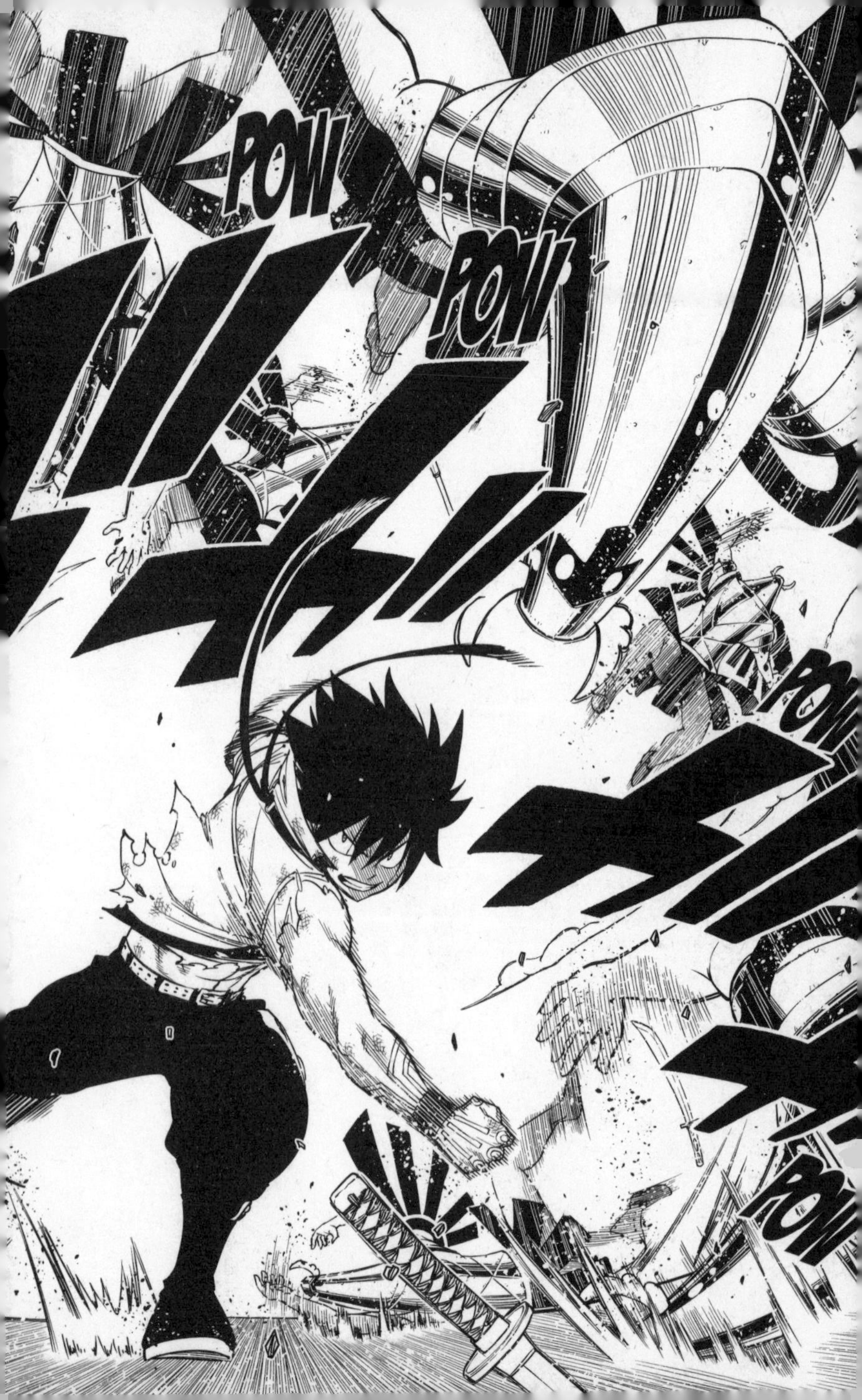
POW
POW
POW
POW

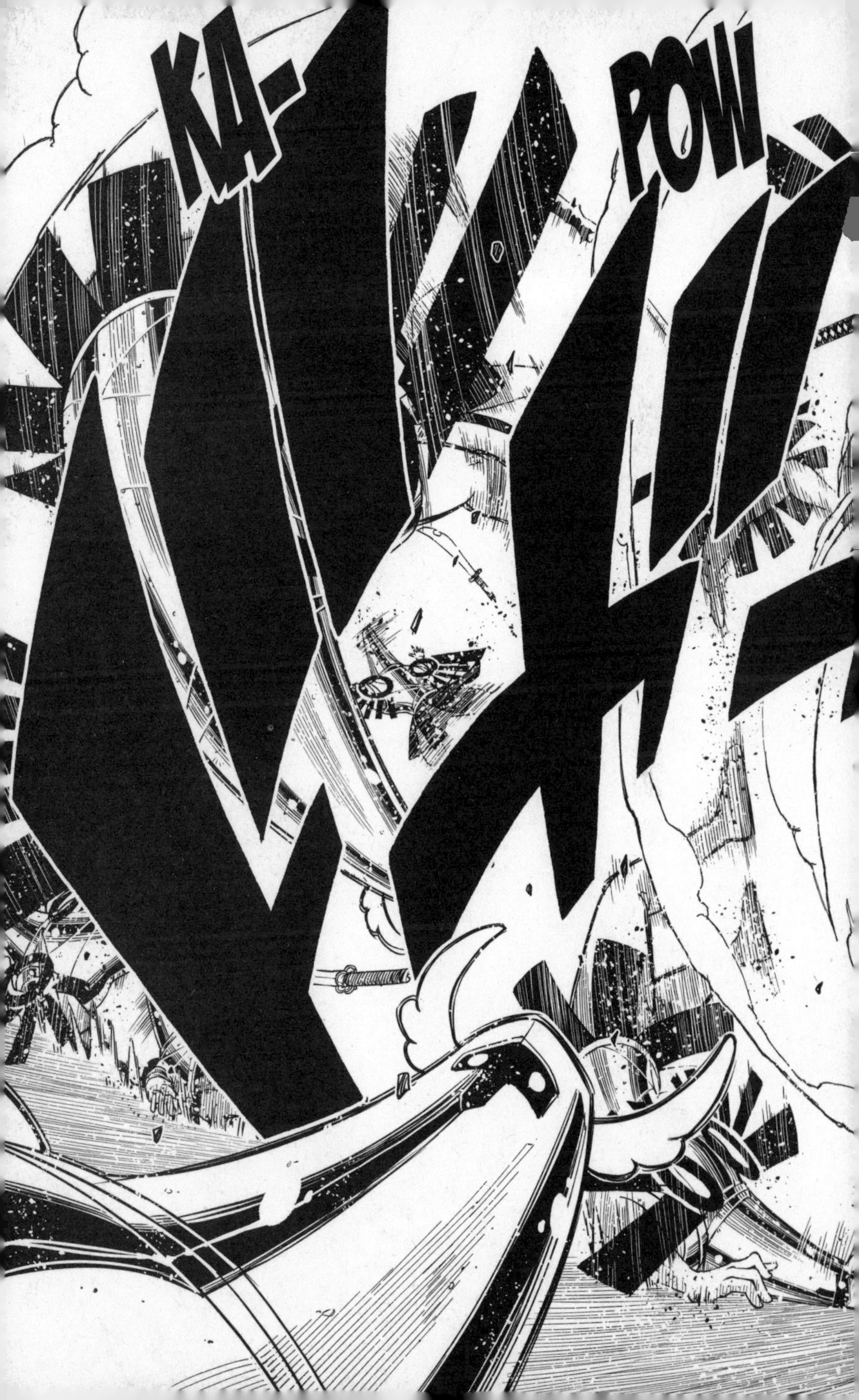
KA-
POW

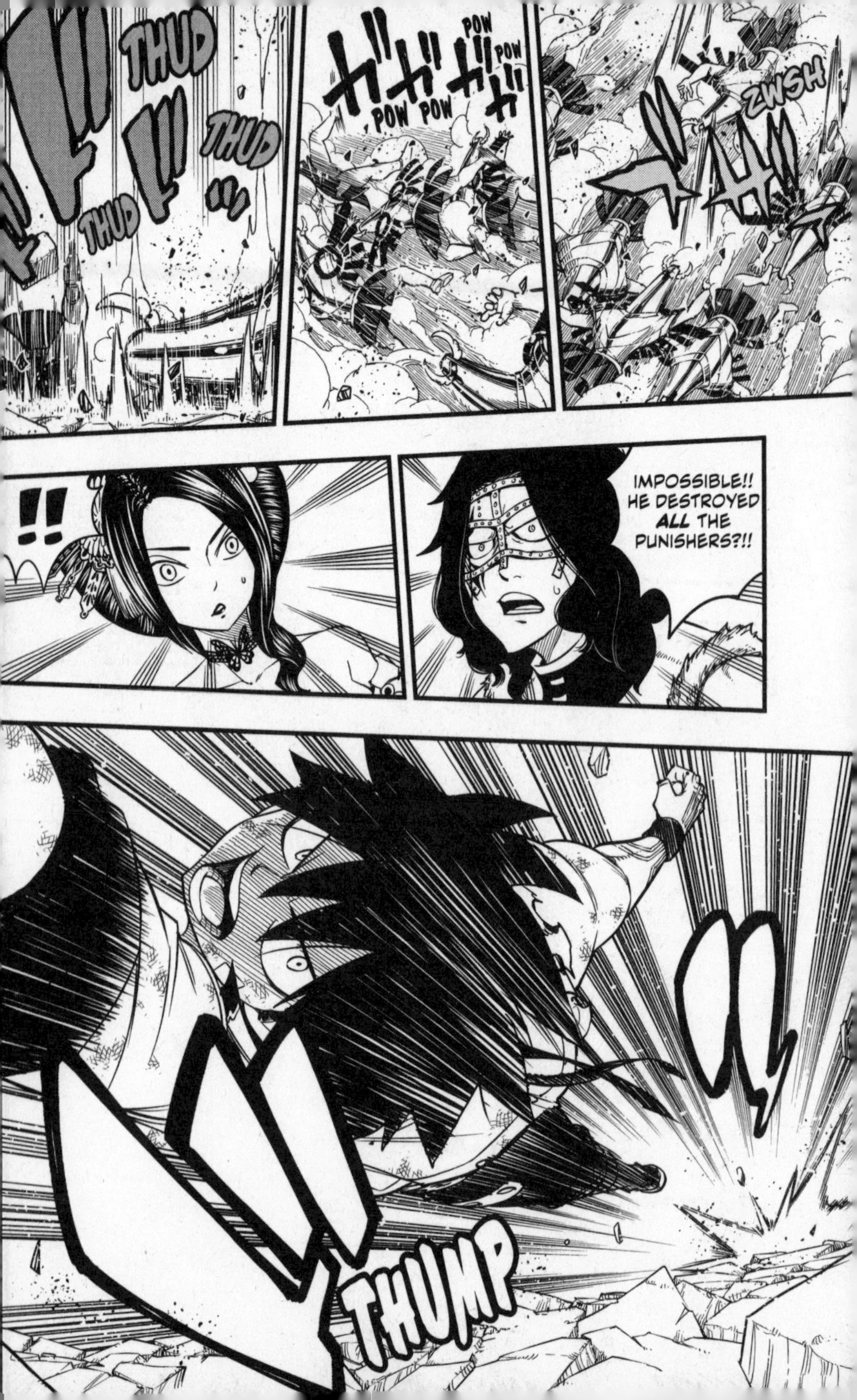
ZWSH
POW
POW
POW POW
THUD
THUD
THUD
IMPOSSIBLE!! HE DESTROYED ALL THE PUNISHERS?!!
!!
THUMP

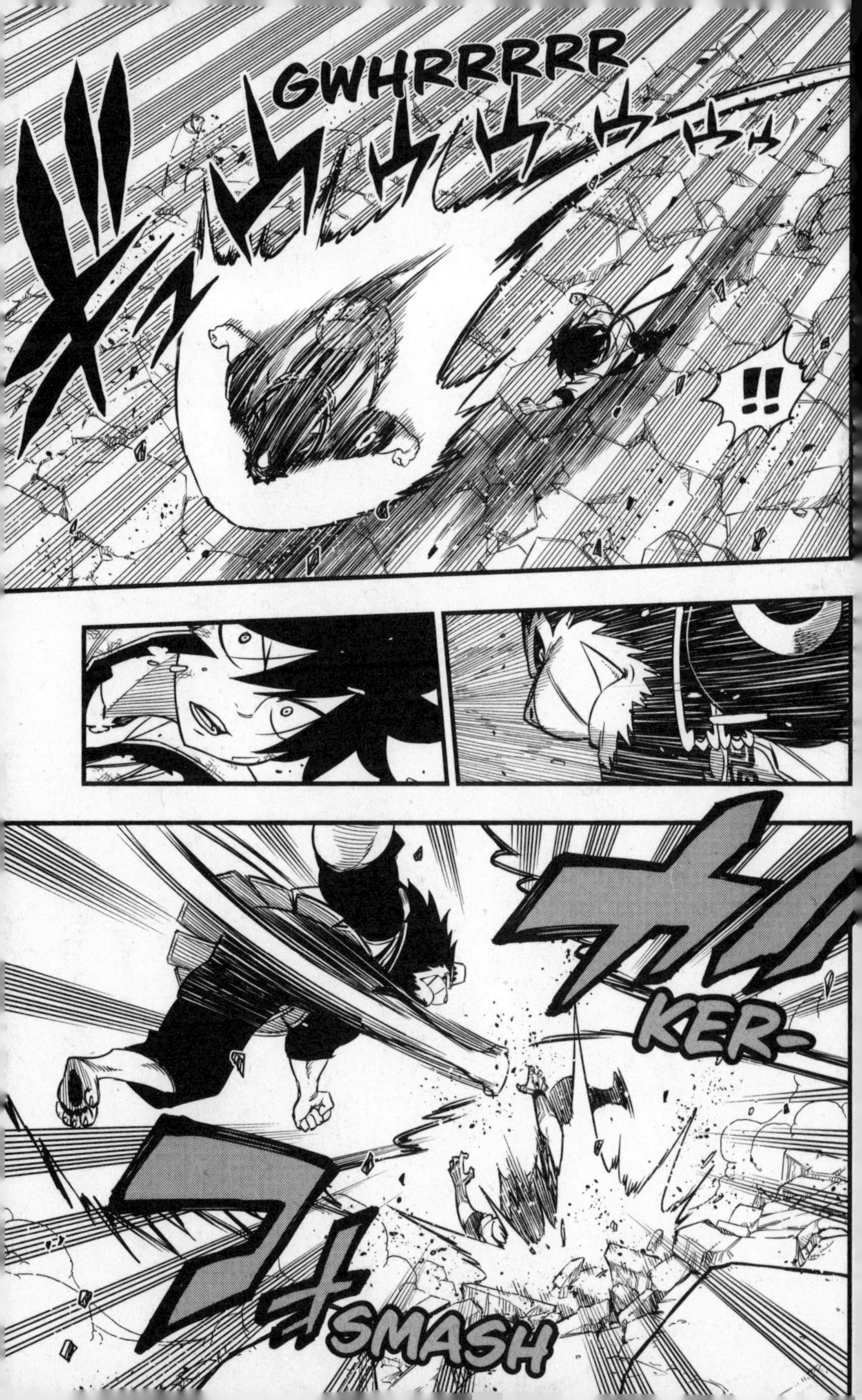
GWHRRRRR
!!
KER-
SMASH

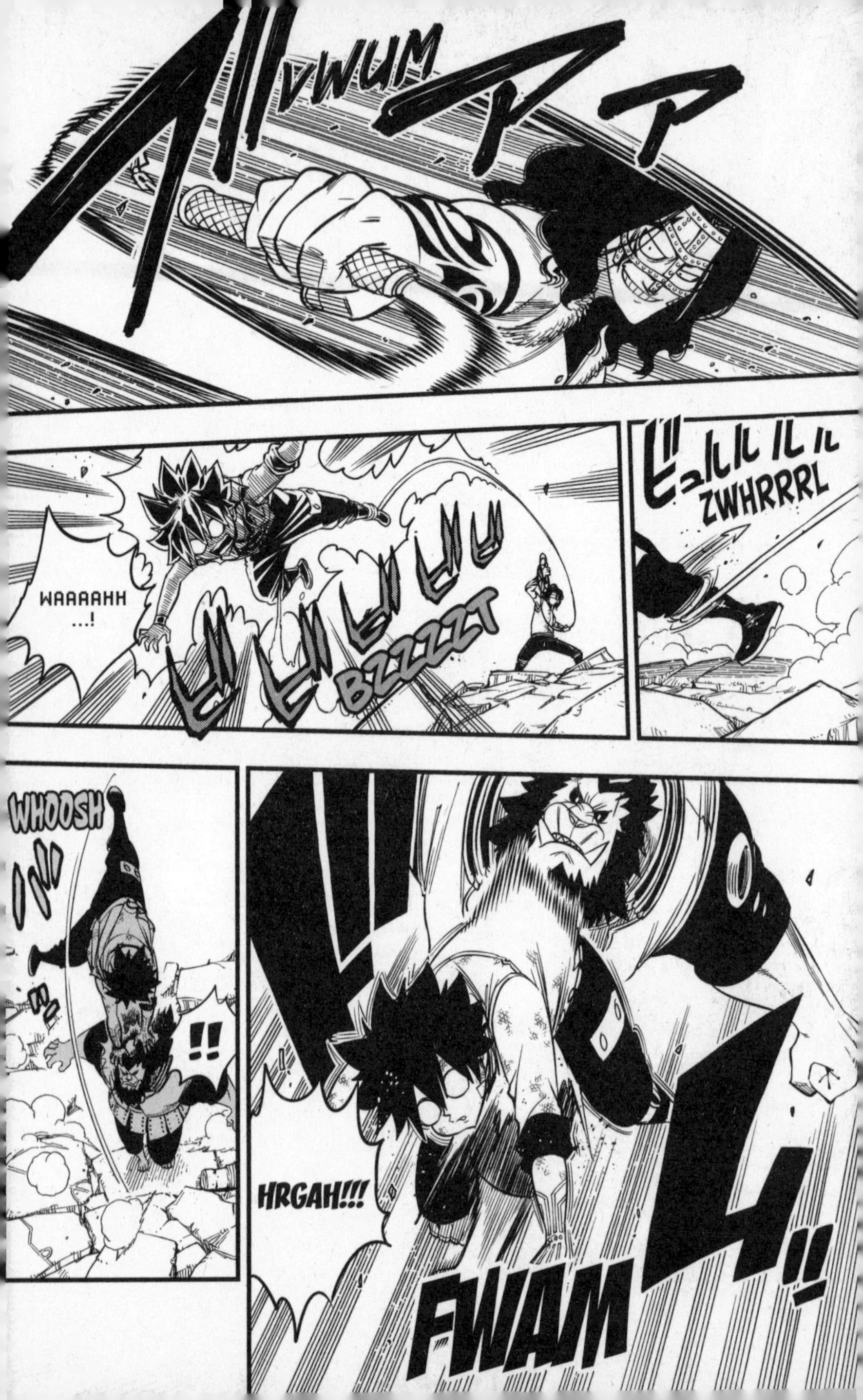
VWUM
ZWHRRRL
WAAAAHH ...!
BZZZZZT
HRGAH!!!
FWAM
WHOOSH
!!

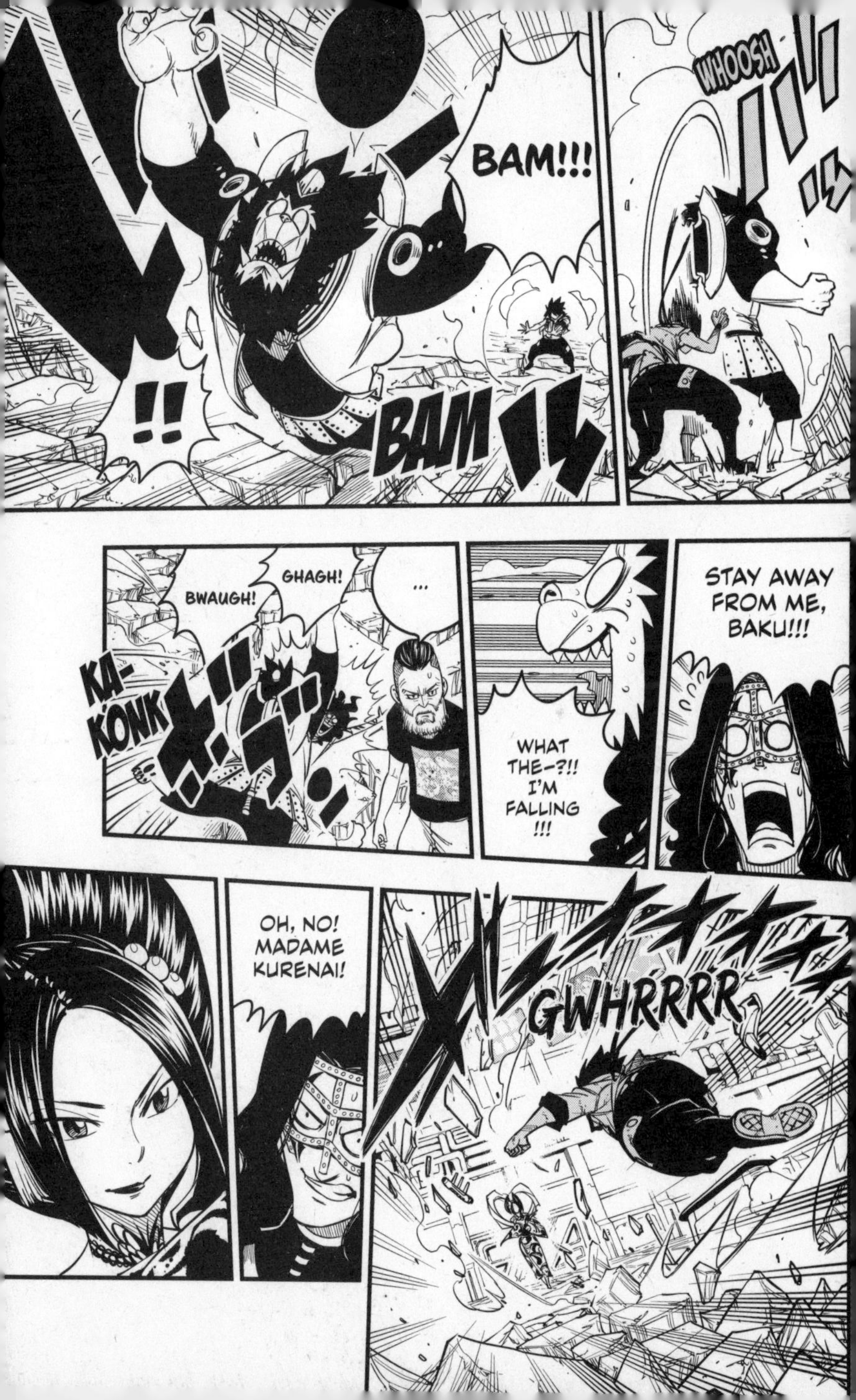
WHOOSH
BAM!!!
BAM
!!
STAY AWAY FROM ME, BAKU!!!
WHAT THE-?!! I'M FALLING !!!
...
GHAGH!
BWAUGH!
KA-KONK
GWHRRRR
OH, NO! MADAME KURENAI!

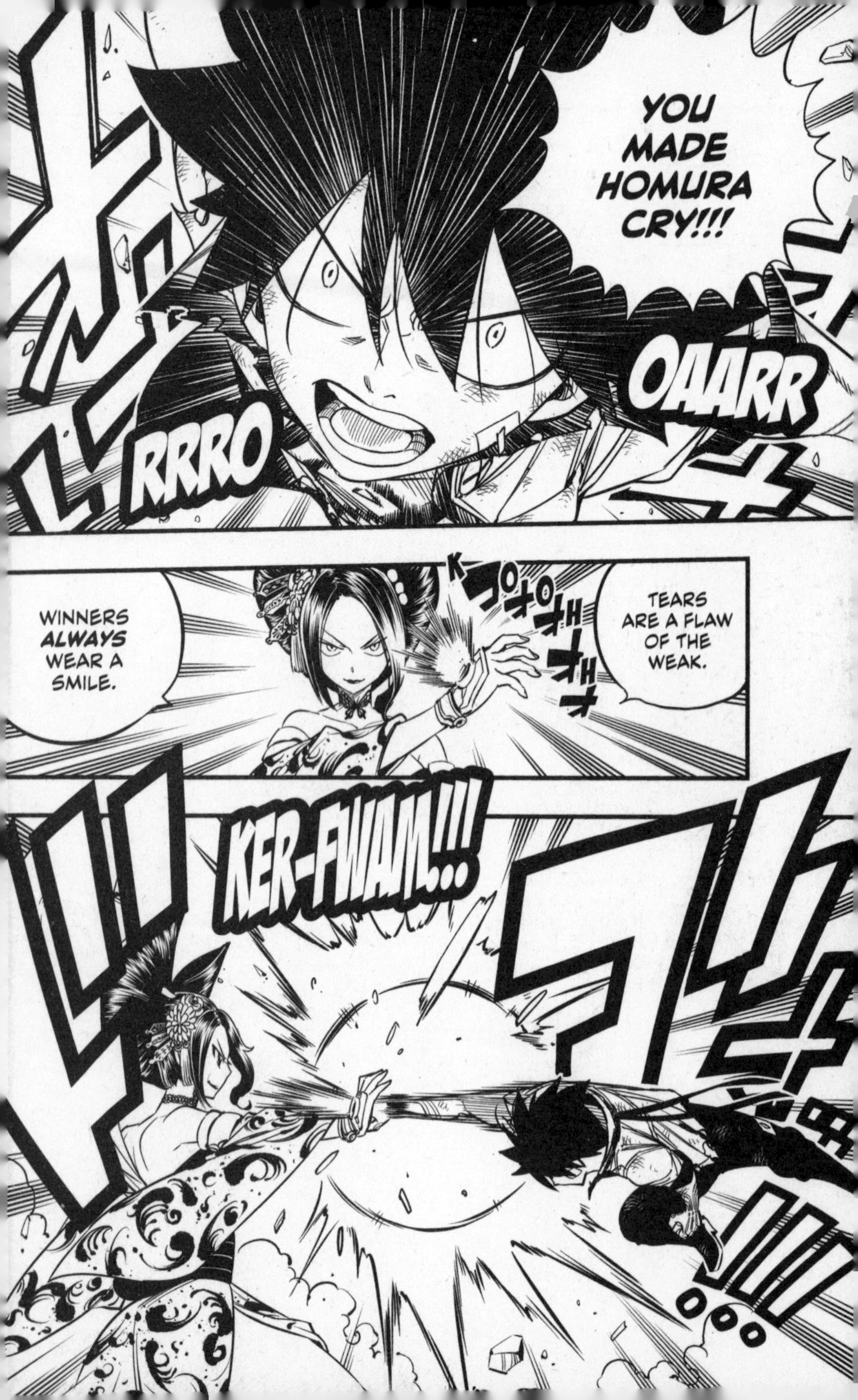
YOU MADE HOMURA CRY!!!
RRRO
OAAARR
TEARS ARE A FLAW OF THE WEAK.
WINNERS ALWAYS WEAR A SMILE.
KER-FWAM!!!

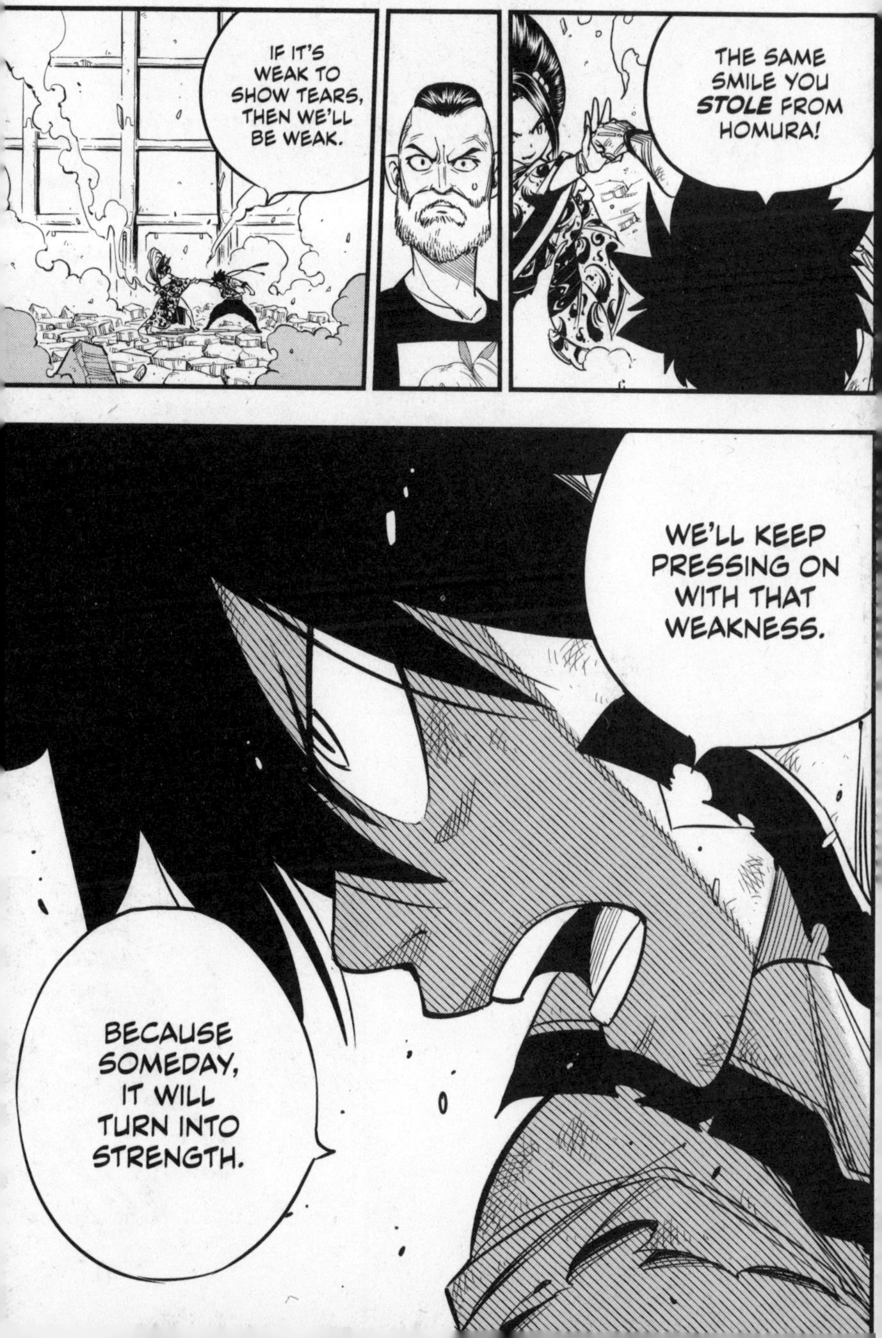
THE SAME SMILE YOU STOLE FROM HOMURA!
IF IT'S WEAK TO SHOW TEARS, THEN WE'LL BE WEAK.
WE'LL KEEP PRESSING ON WITH THAT WEAKNESS.
BECAUSE SOMEDAY, IT WILL TURN INTO STRENGTH.

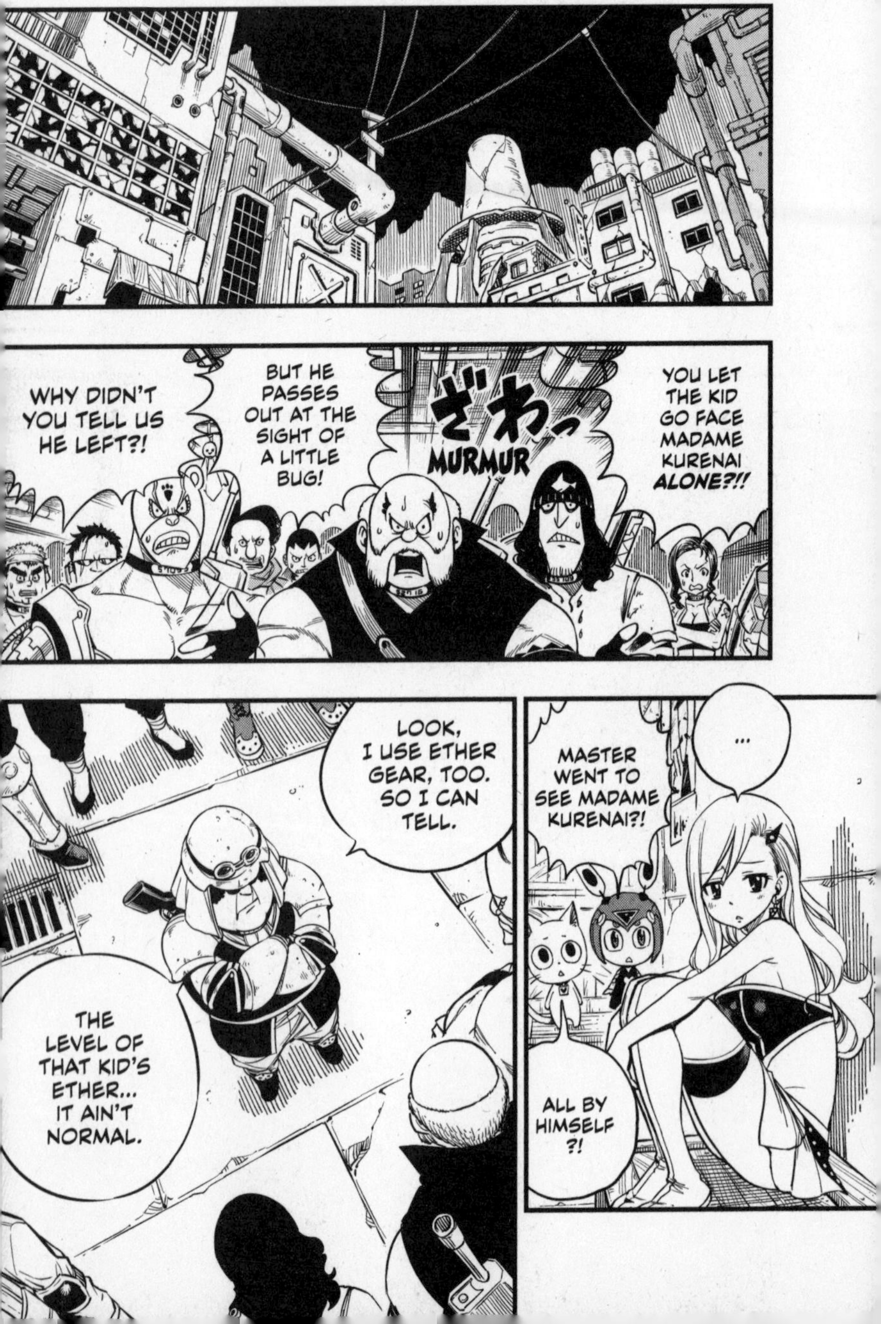
YOU LET THE KID GO FACE MADAME KURENAI ALONE?!!
ざわっ
MURMUR
BUT HE PASSES OUT AT THE SIGHT OF A LITTLE BUG!
WHY DIDN'T YOU TELL US HE LEFT?!
...
MASTER WENT TO SEE MADAME KURENAI?!
ALL BY HIMSELF ?!
LOOK, I USE ETHER GEAR, TOO. SO I CAN TELL.
THE LEVEL OF THAT KID'S ETHER... IT AIN'T NORMAL.

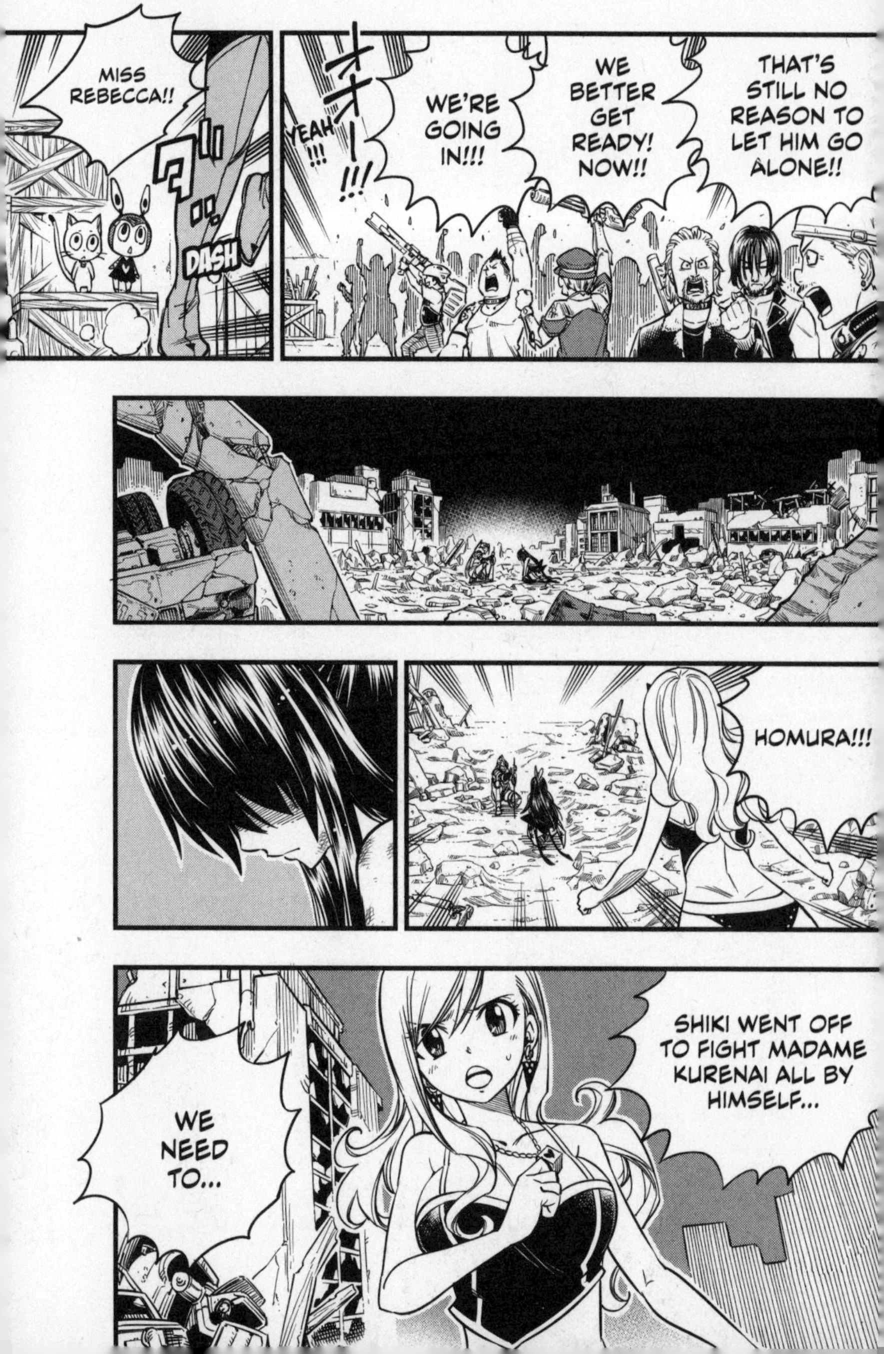
THAT'S STILL NO REASON TO LET HIM GO ALONE!!
WE BETTER GET READY! NOW!!
WE'RE GOING IN!!!
YEAH!!!
MISS REBECCA!!
DASH
HOMURA!!!
SHIKI WENT OFF TO FIGHT MADAME KURENAI ALL BY HIMSELF...
WE NEED TO...

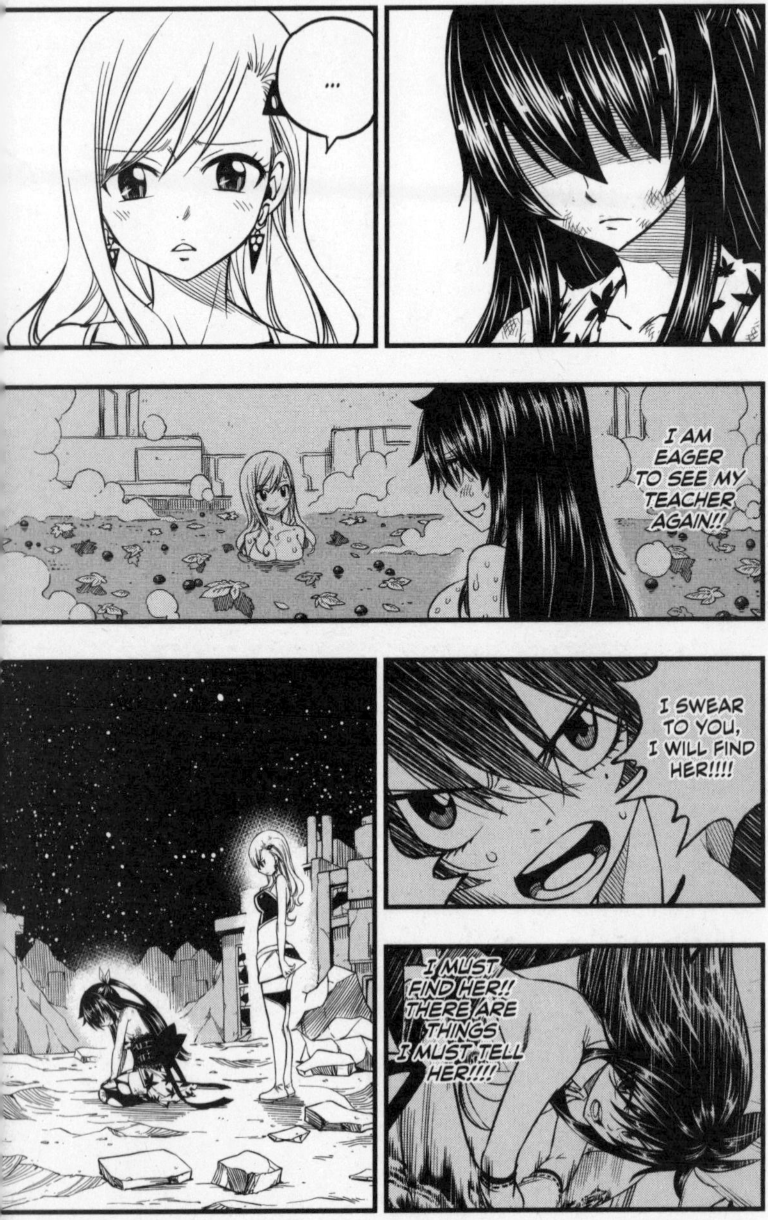
...
I AM EAGER TO SEE MY TEACHER AGAIN!!
I SWEAR TO YOU, I WILL FIND HER!!!!
I MUST FIND HER!! THERE ARE THINGS I MUST TELL HER!!!!

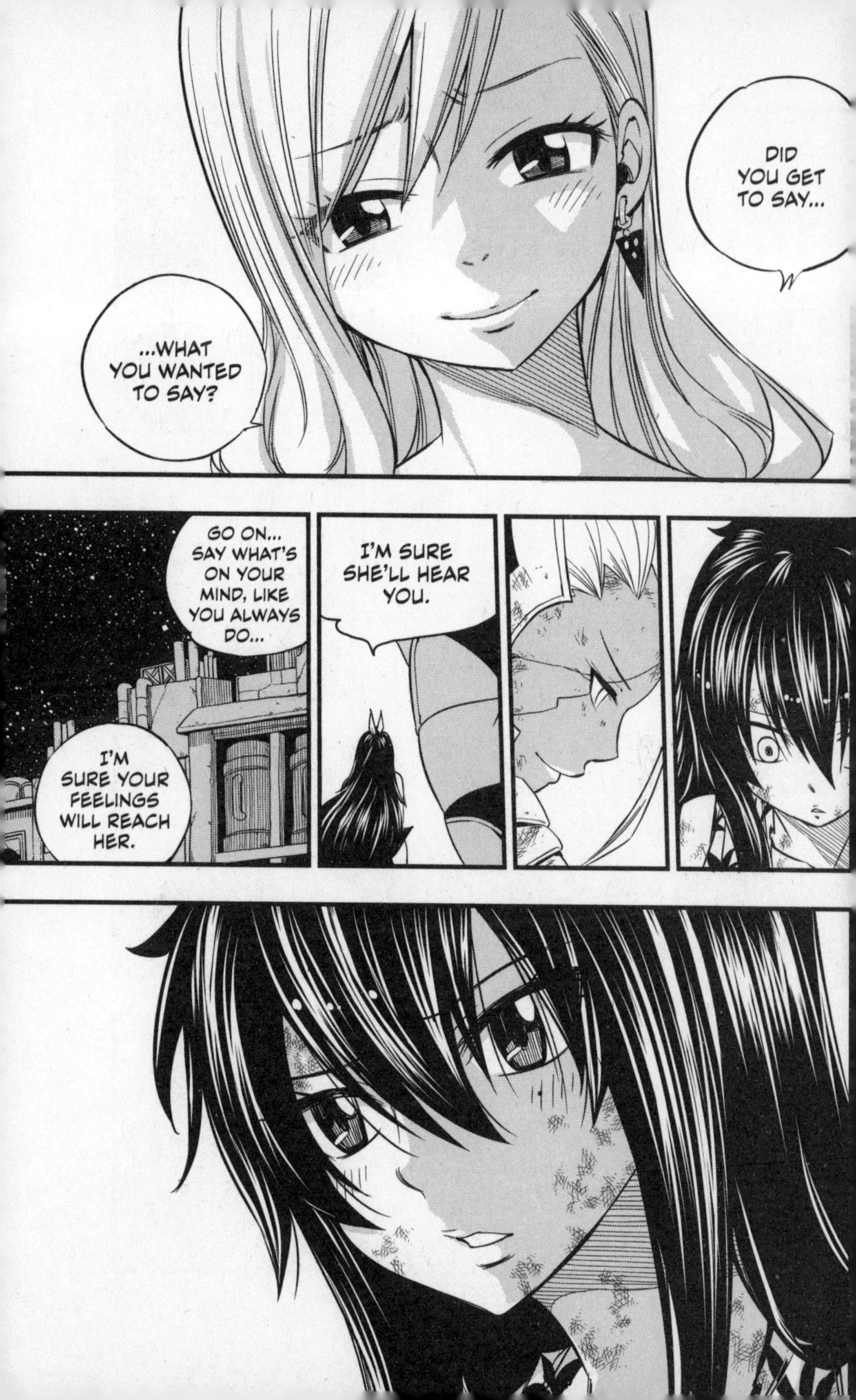
DID YOU GET TO SAY...
...WHAT YOU WANTED TO SAY?
I'M SURE SHE'LL HEAR YOU.
GO ON... SAY WHAT'S ON YOUR MIND, LIKE YOU ALWAYS DO...
I'M SURE YOUR FEELINGS WILL REACH HER.

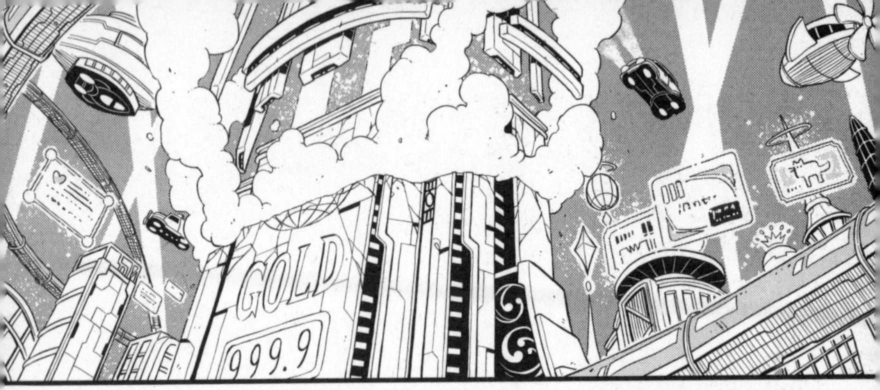
GOLD
999.9

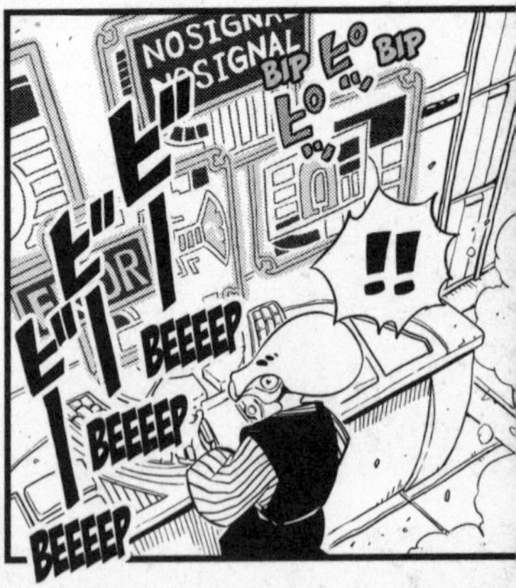
NOSIGNAL
NOSIGNAL
BIP BIP
!!
BEEEEP
BEEEEP
BEEEEP

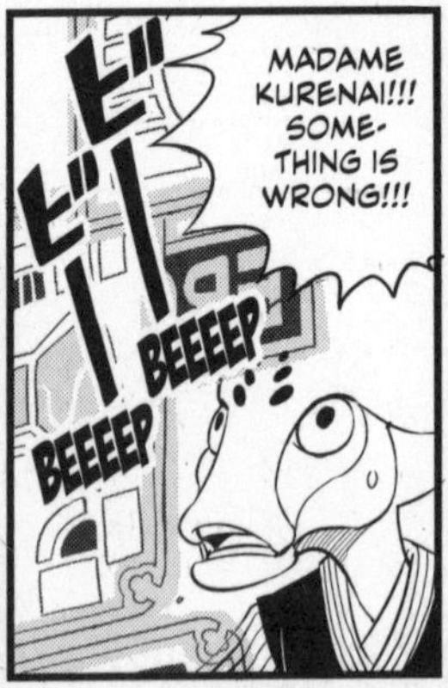
MADAME KURENAI!!! SOMETHING IS WRONG!!!
BEEEEP
BEEEEP

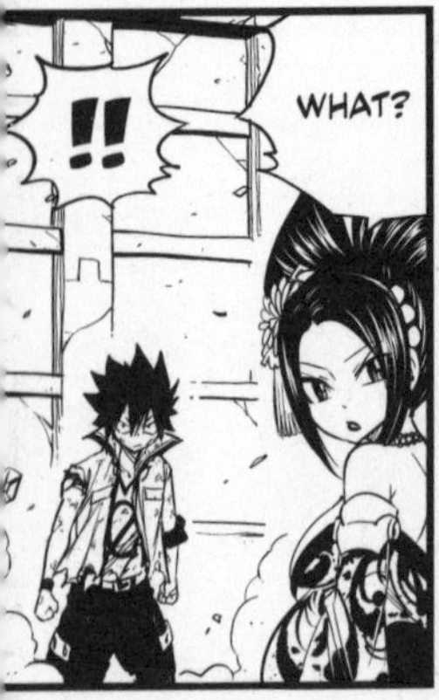
WHAT?
!!

Satellite: Kurenai

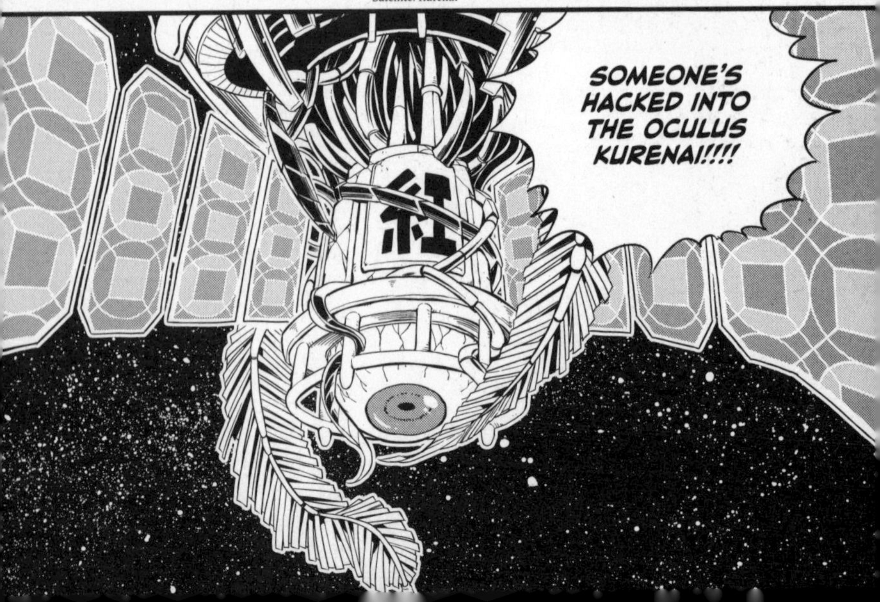
SOMEONE'S HACKED INTO THE OCULUS KURENAI!!!!
紅

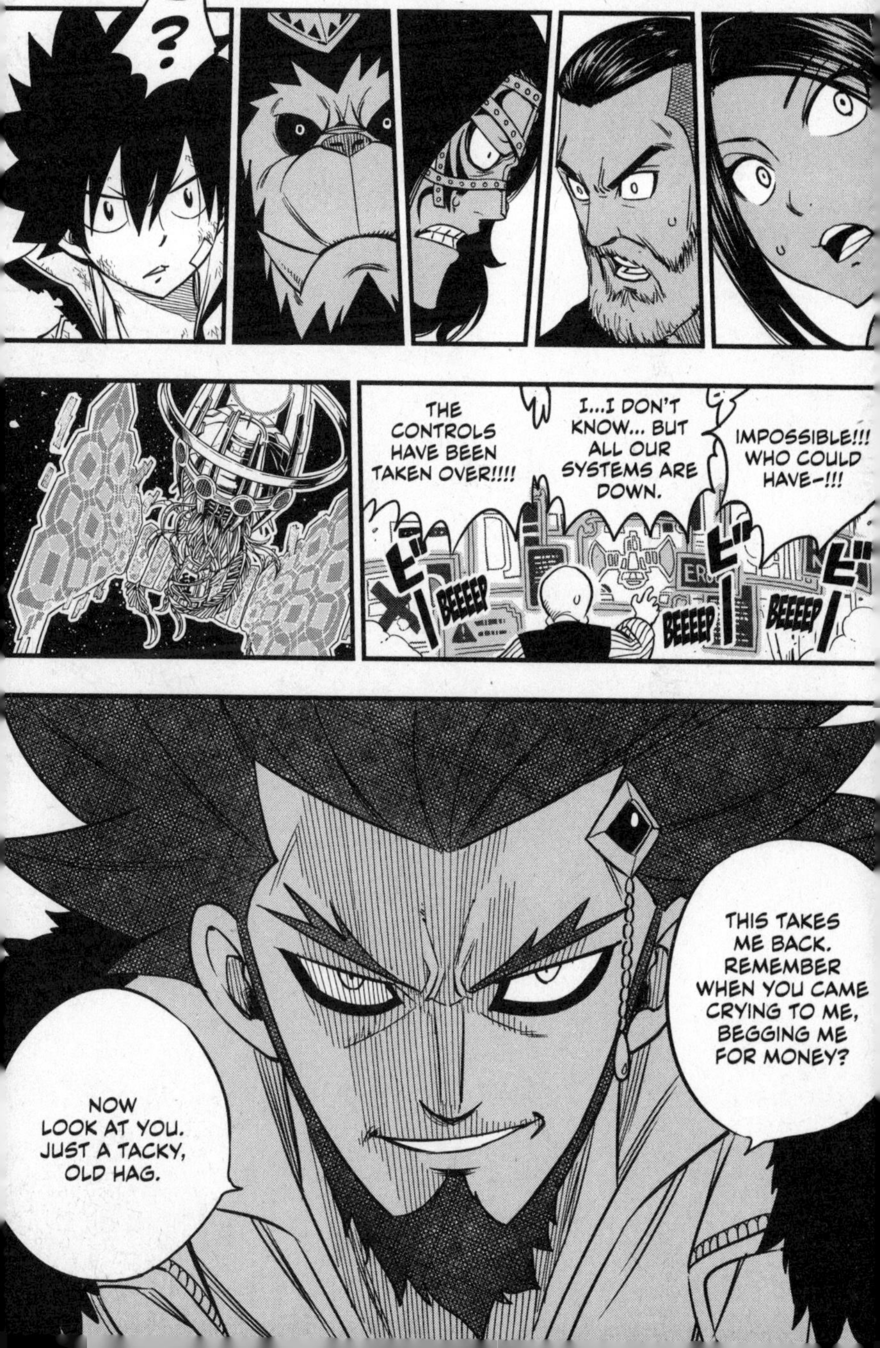
?
IMPOSSIBLE!!! WHO COULD HAVE-!!!
I...I DON'T KNOW... BUT ALL OUR SYSTEMS ARE DOWN.
THE CONTROLS HAVE BEEN TAKEN OVER!!!!
BEEEEP
BEEEEP
BEEEEP
THIS TAKES ME BACK. REMEMBER WHEN YOU CAME CRYING TO ME, BEGGING ME FOR MONEY?
NOW LOOK AT YOU. JUST A TACKY, OLD HAG.

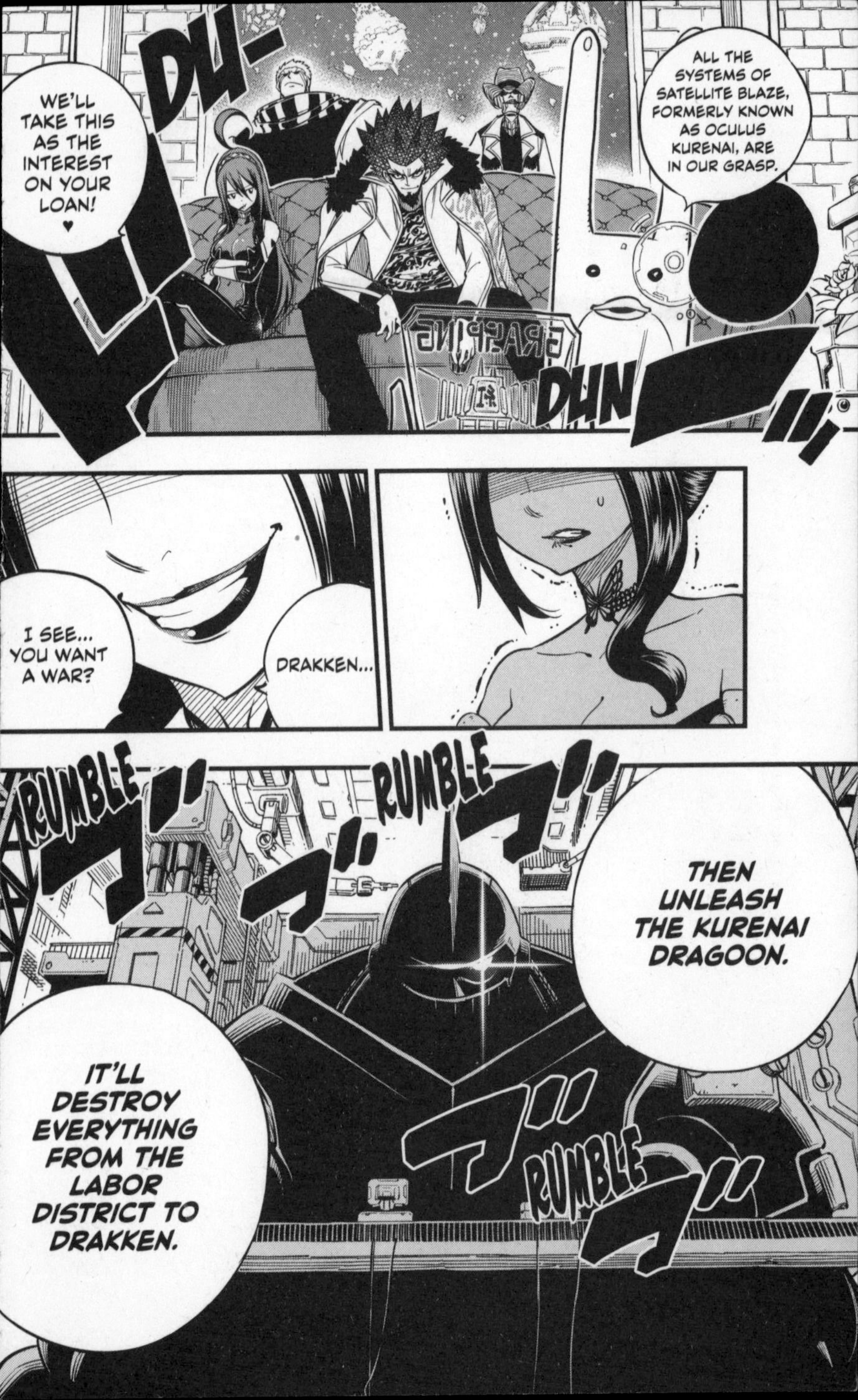
ALL THE SYSTEMS OF SATELLITE BLAZE, FORMERLY KNOWN AS OCULUS KURENAI, ARE IN OUR GRASP.
WE'LL TAKE THIS AS THE INTEREST ON YOUR LOAN! ♥
DU-
DUN
DRAKKEN...
I SEE... YOU WANT A WAR?
RUMBLE
RUMBLE
THEN UNLEASH THE KURENAI DRAGOON.
IT'LL DESTROY EVERYTHING FROM THE LABOR DISTRICT TO DRAKKEN.
RUMBLE

EDENS ZERO

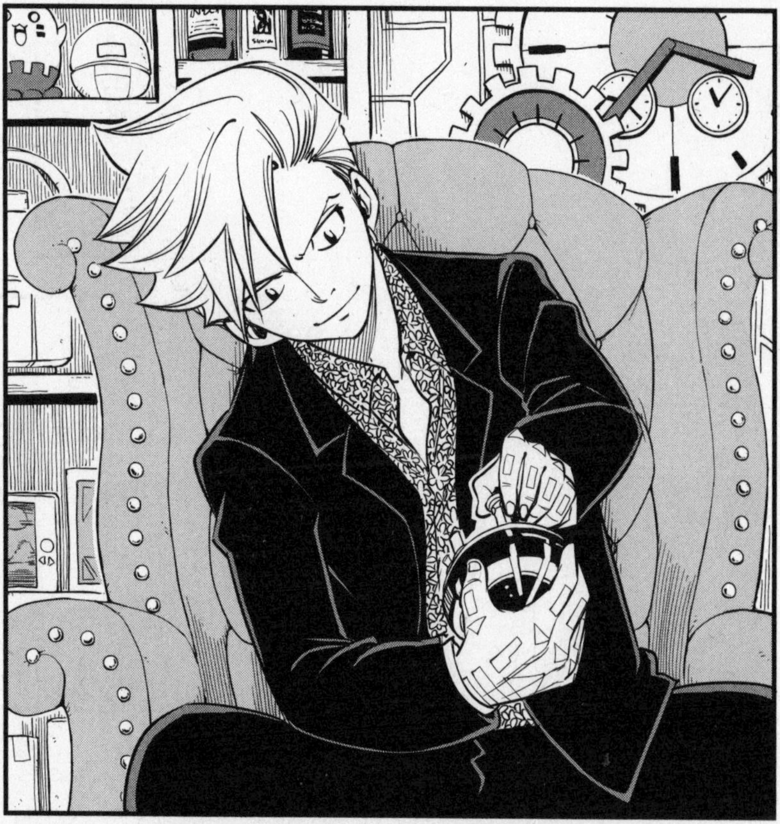

CHAPTER 61: ENTER ARSENAL

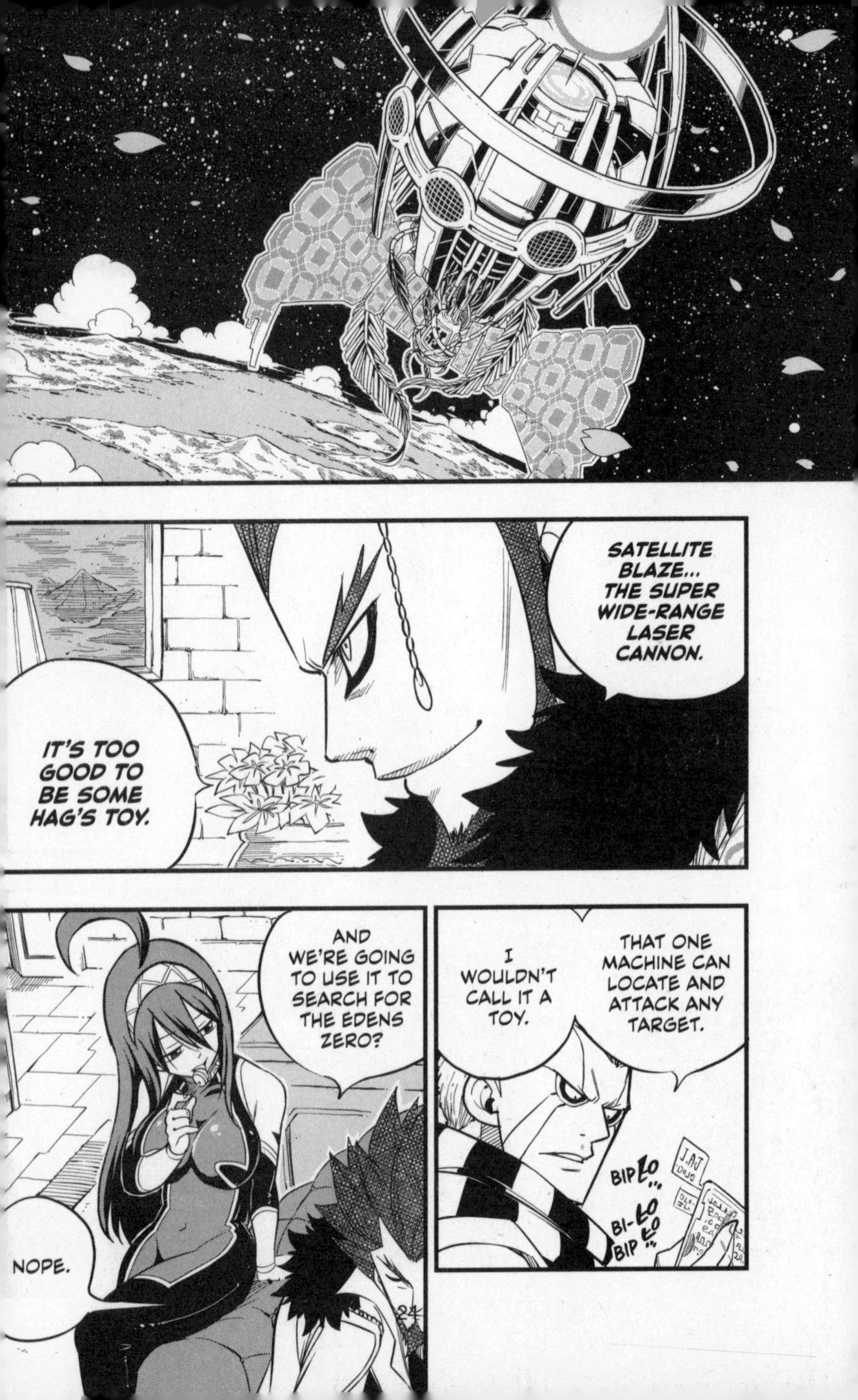
SATELLITE BLAZE... THE SUPER WIDE-RANGE LASER CANNON.
IT'S TOO GOOD TO BE SOME HAG'S TOY.
THAT ONE MACHINE CAN LOCATE AND ATTACK ANY TARGET.
I WOULDN'T CALL IT A TOY.
BIP...
BI-BIP...
AND WE'RE GOING TO USE IT TO SEARCH FOR THE EDENS ZERO?
NOPE.

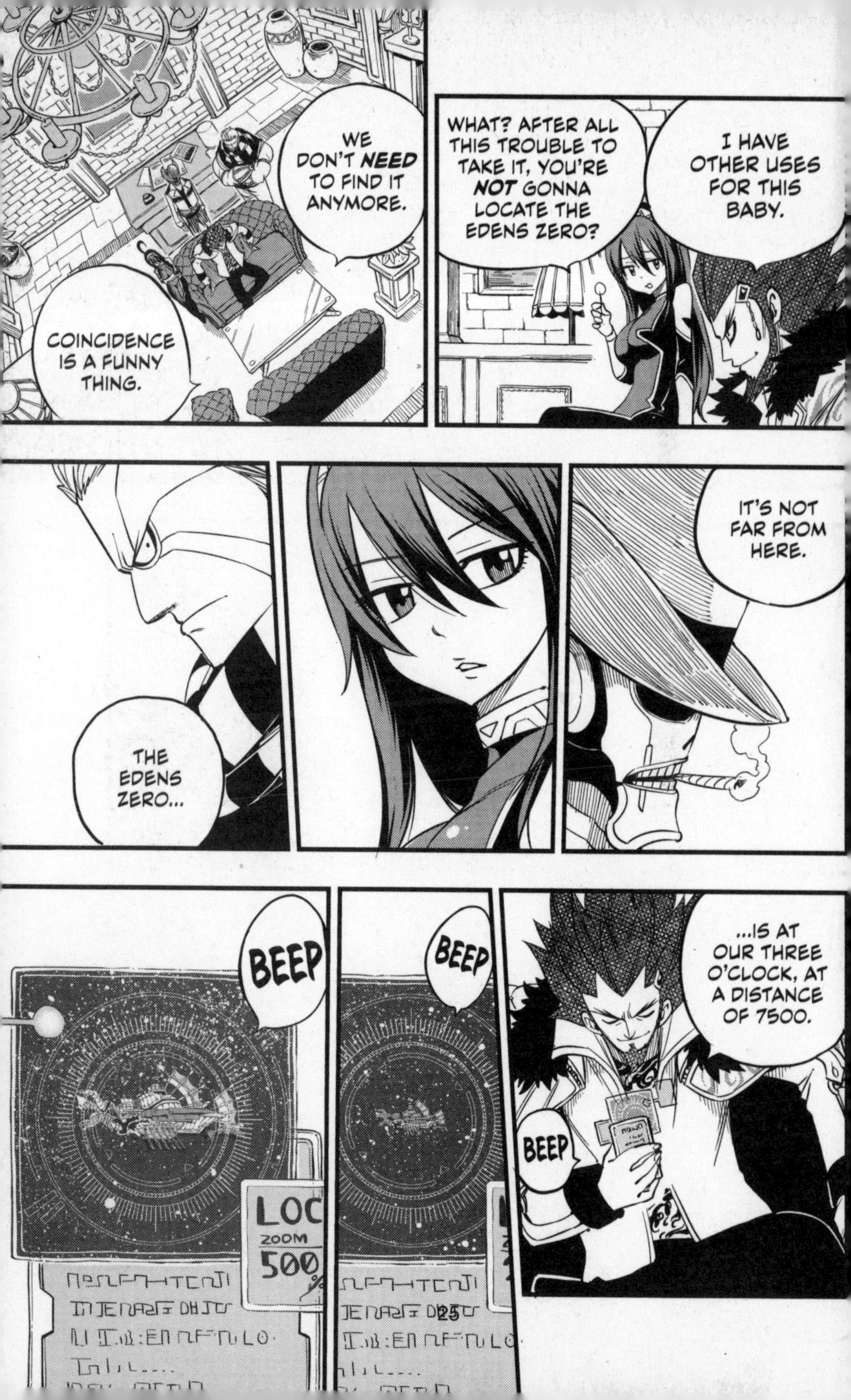
I HAVE OTHER USES FOR THIS BABY.
WHAT? AFTER ALL THIS TROUBLE TO TAKE IT, YOU'RE ***NOT*** GONNA LOCATE THE EDENS ZERO?
WE DON'T ***NEED*** TO FIND IT ANYMORE.
COINCIDENCE IS A FUNNY THING.
IT'S NOT FAR FROM HERE.
THE EDENS ZERO...
...IS AT OUR THREE O'CLOCK, AT A DISTANCE OF 7500.
BEEP
BEEP
BEEP
LOC
ZOOM
500

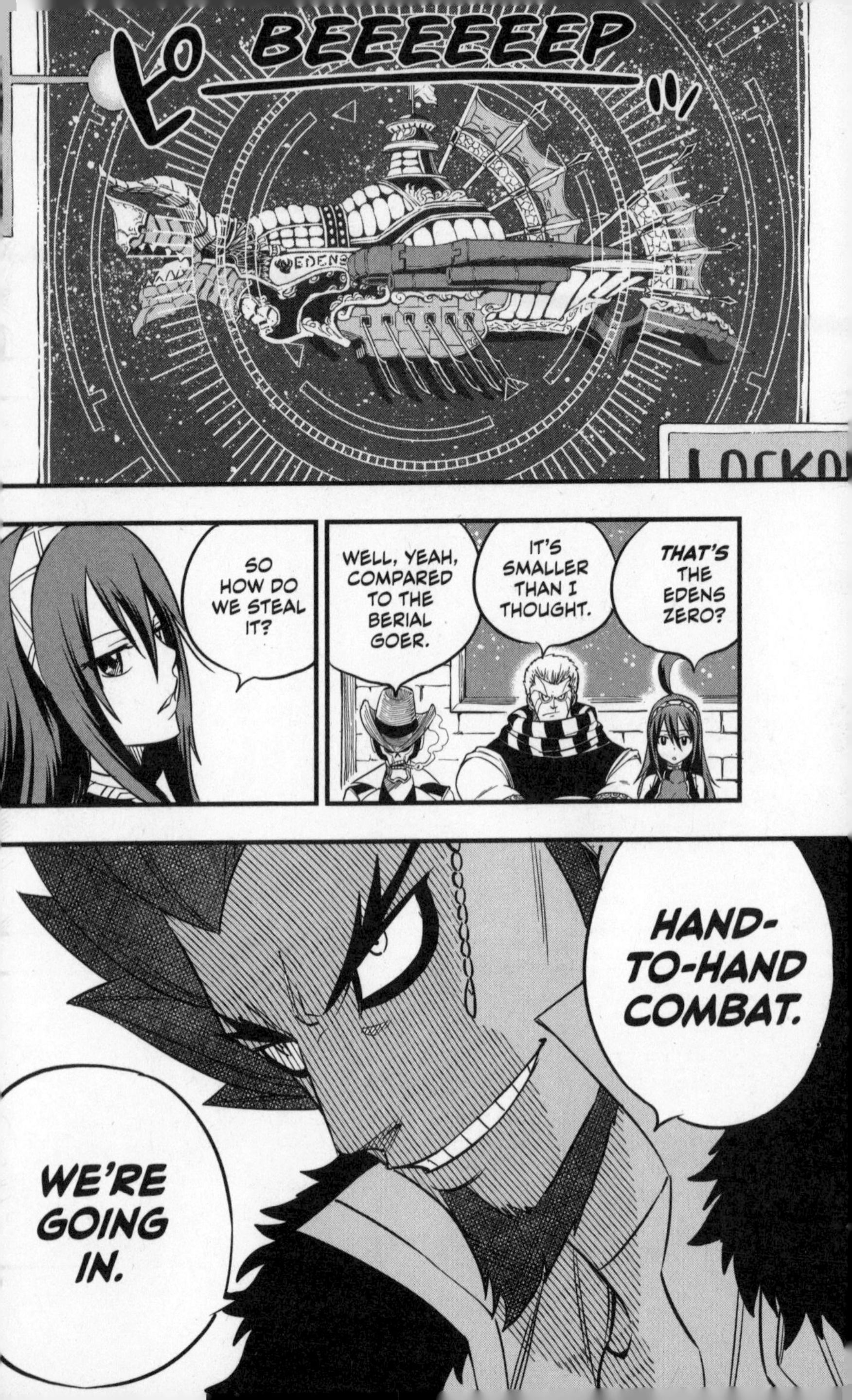
BEEEEEEEP
EDENS
THAT'S THE EDENS ZERO?
IT'S SMALLER THAN I THOUGHT.
WELL, YEAH, COMPARED TO THE BERIAL GOER.
SO HOW DO WE STEAL IT?
HAND-TO-HAND COMBAT.
WE'RE GOING IN.

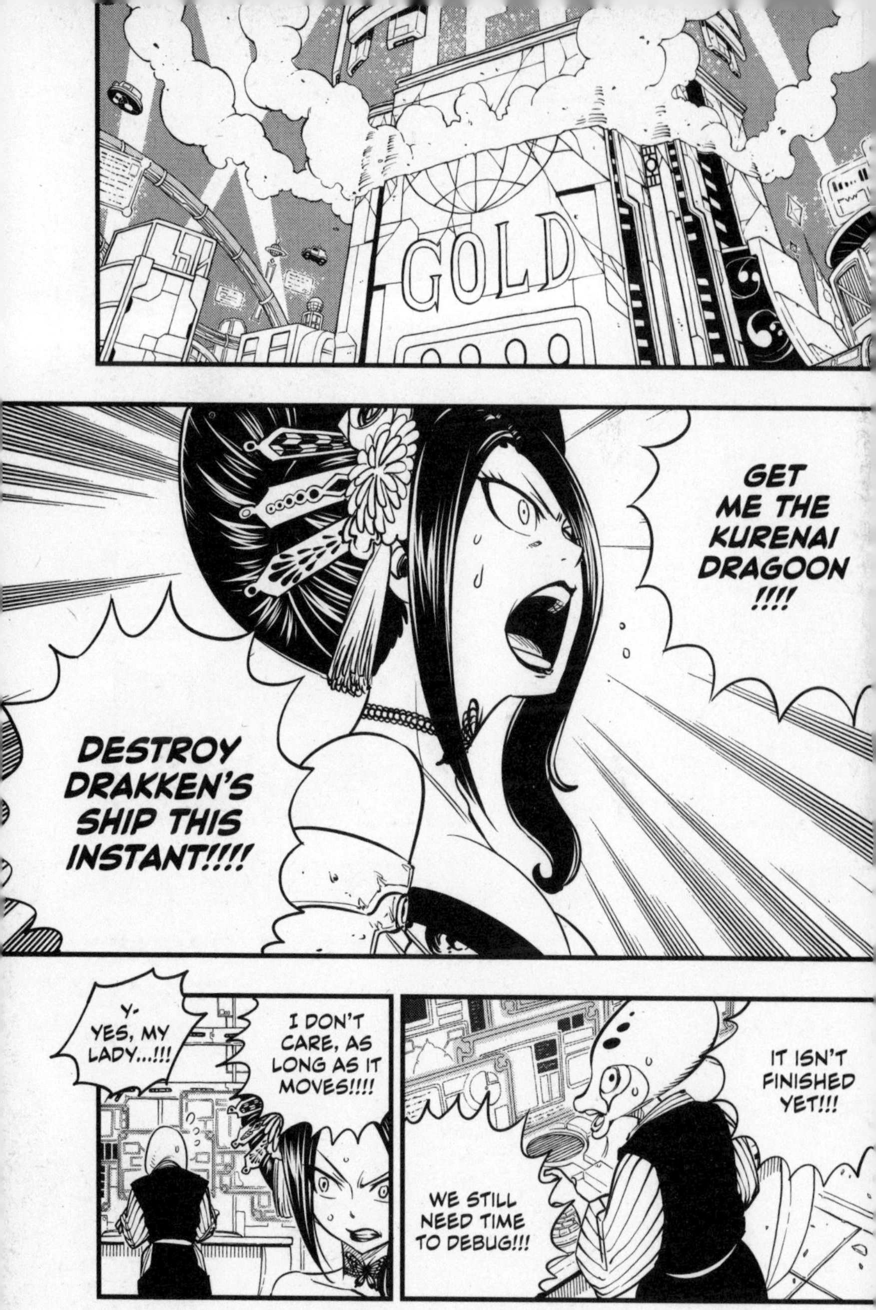
GOLD
GET ME THE KURENAI DRAGOON!!!!
DESTROY DRAKKEN'S SHIP THIS INSTANT!!!!
IT ISN'T FINISHED YET!!!
WE STILL NEED TIME TO DEBUG!!!
I DON'T CARE, AS LONG AS IT MOVES!!!!
Y-YES, MY LADY...!!!

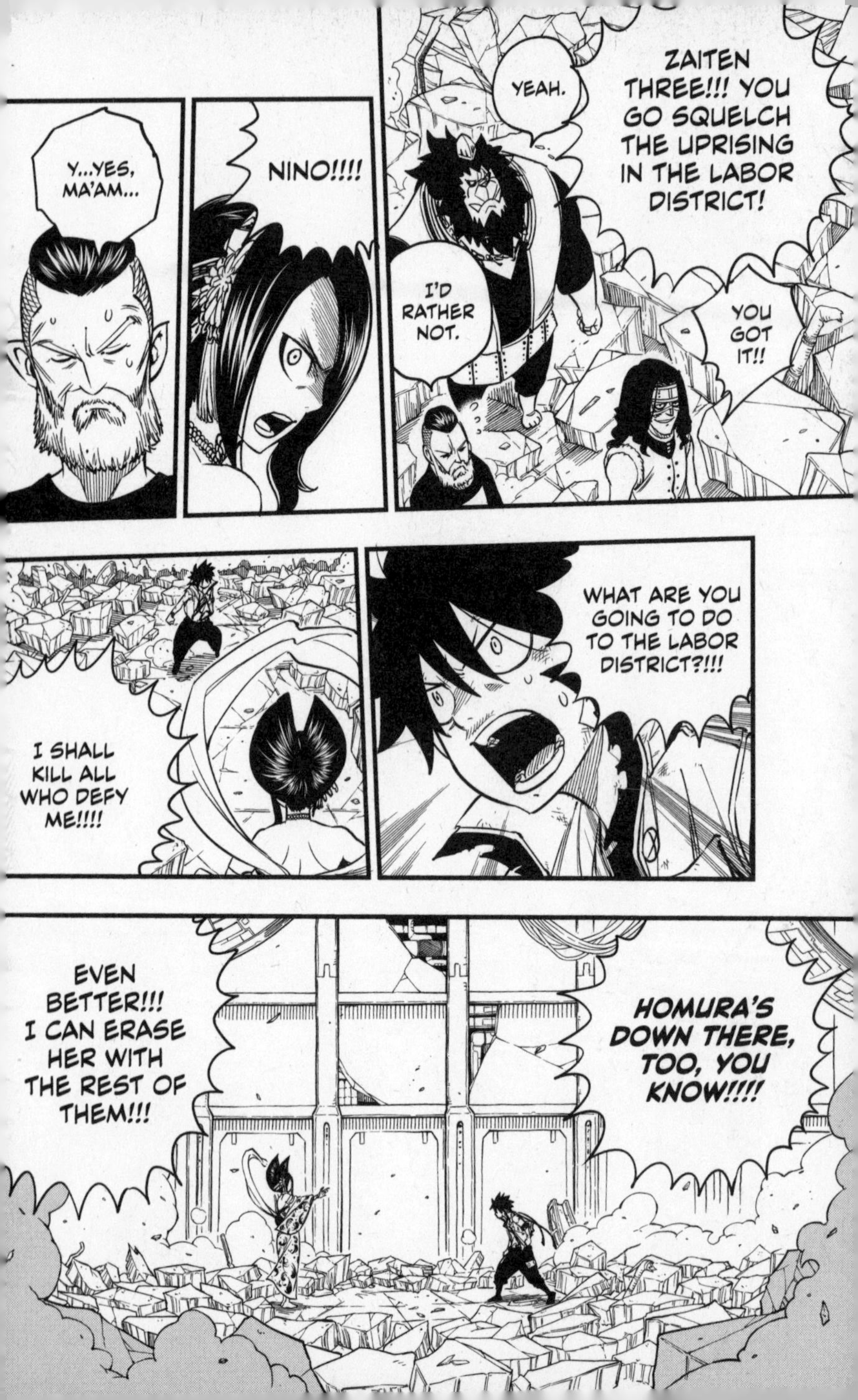
ZAITEN THREE!!! YOU GO SQUELCH THE UPRISING IN THE LABOR DISTRICT!
YEAH.
YOU GOT IT!!
I'D RATHER NOT.
NINO!!!!
Y...YES, MA'AM...
WHAT ARE YOU GOING TO DO TO THE LABOR DISTRICT?!!!
I SHALL KILL ALL WHO DEFY ME!!!!
HOMURA'S DOWN THERE, TOO, YOU KNOW!!!!
EVEN BETTER!!! I CAN ERASE HER WITH THE REST OF THEM!!!

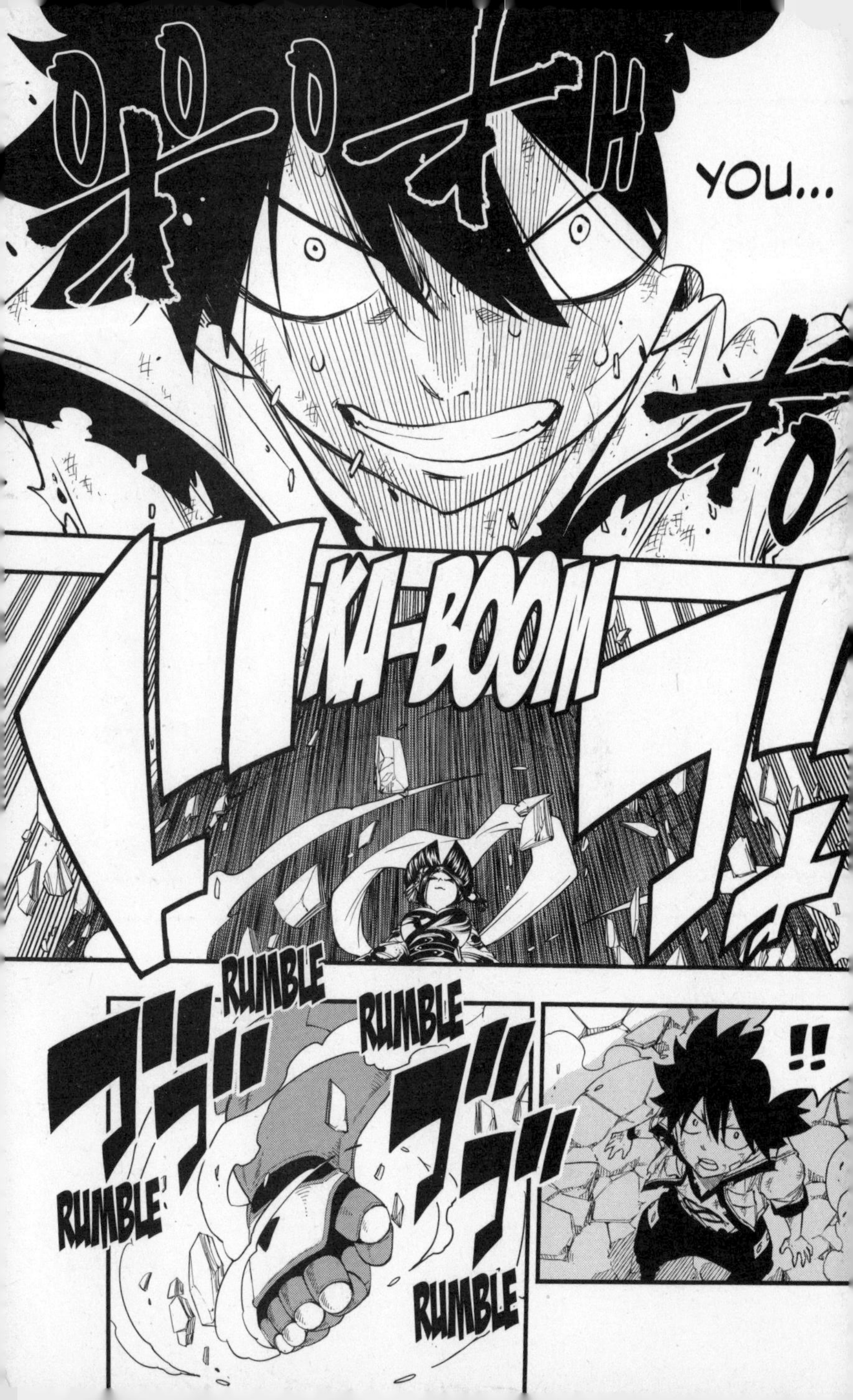
YOU...
OOOH
KA-BOOM
!!
RUMBLE
RUMBLE
RUMBLE
RUMBLE

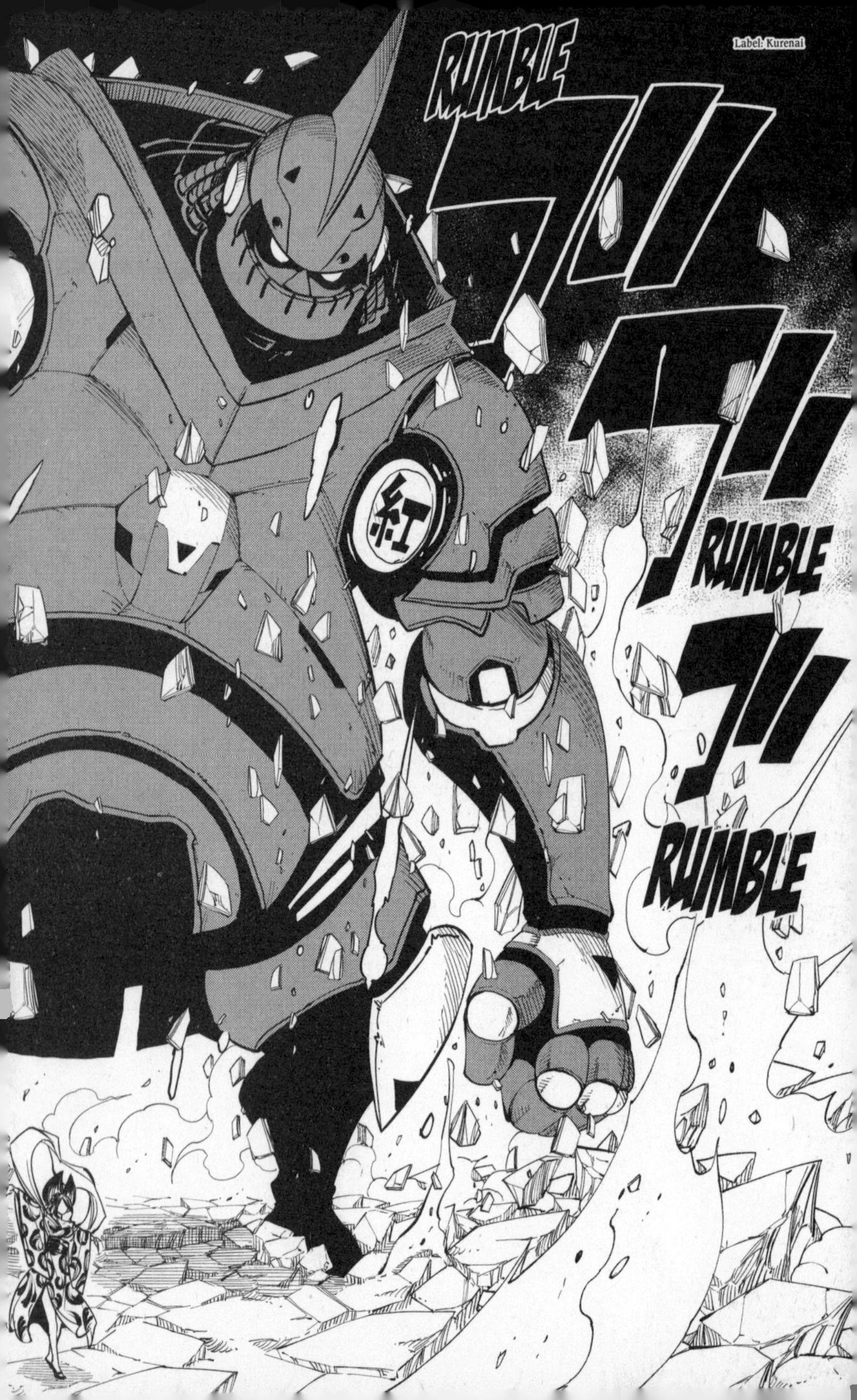
Label: Kurenai
RUMBLE
RUMBLE
RUMBLE
紅

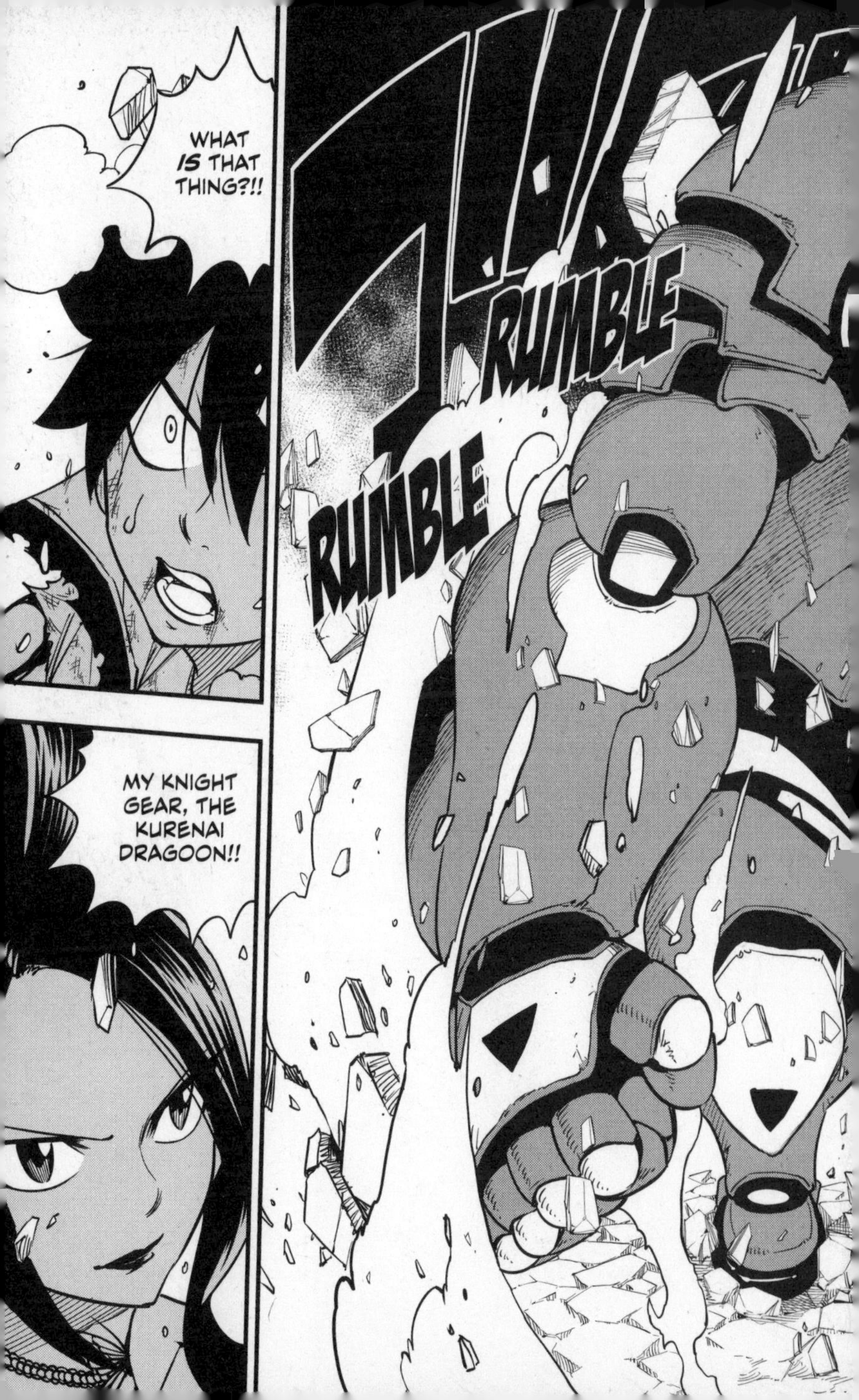
RUMBLE
RUMBLE
WHAT IS THAT THING?!!
MY KNIGHT GEAR, THE KURENAI DRAGOON!!

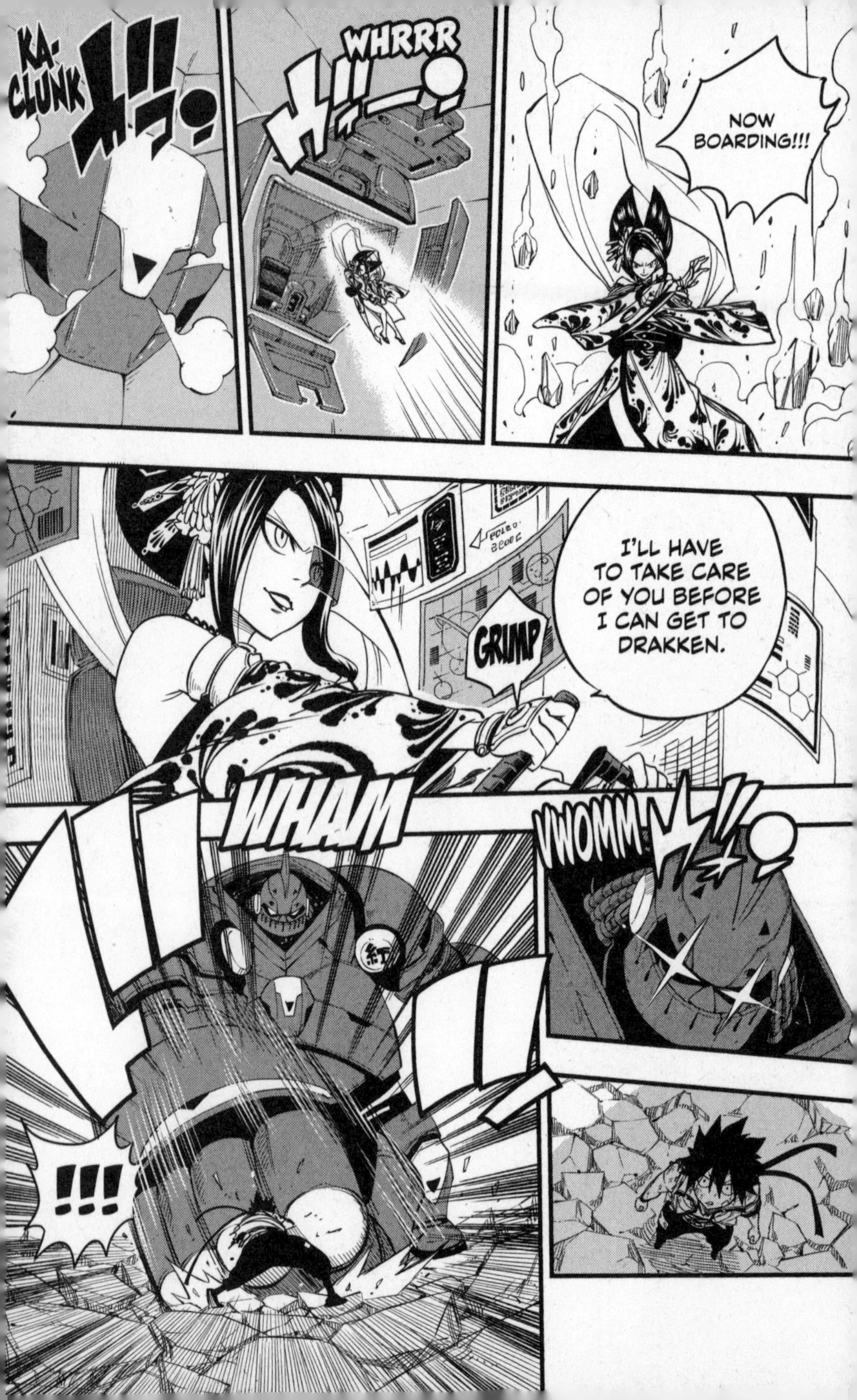
NOW BOARDING!!!
WHRRR
KA-CLUNK
I'LL HAVE TO TAKE CARE OF YOU BEFORE I CAN GET TO DRAKKEN.
GRUMP
VWOMM
WHAM
!!!

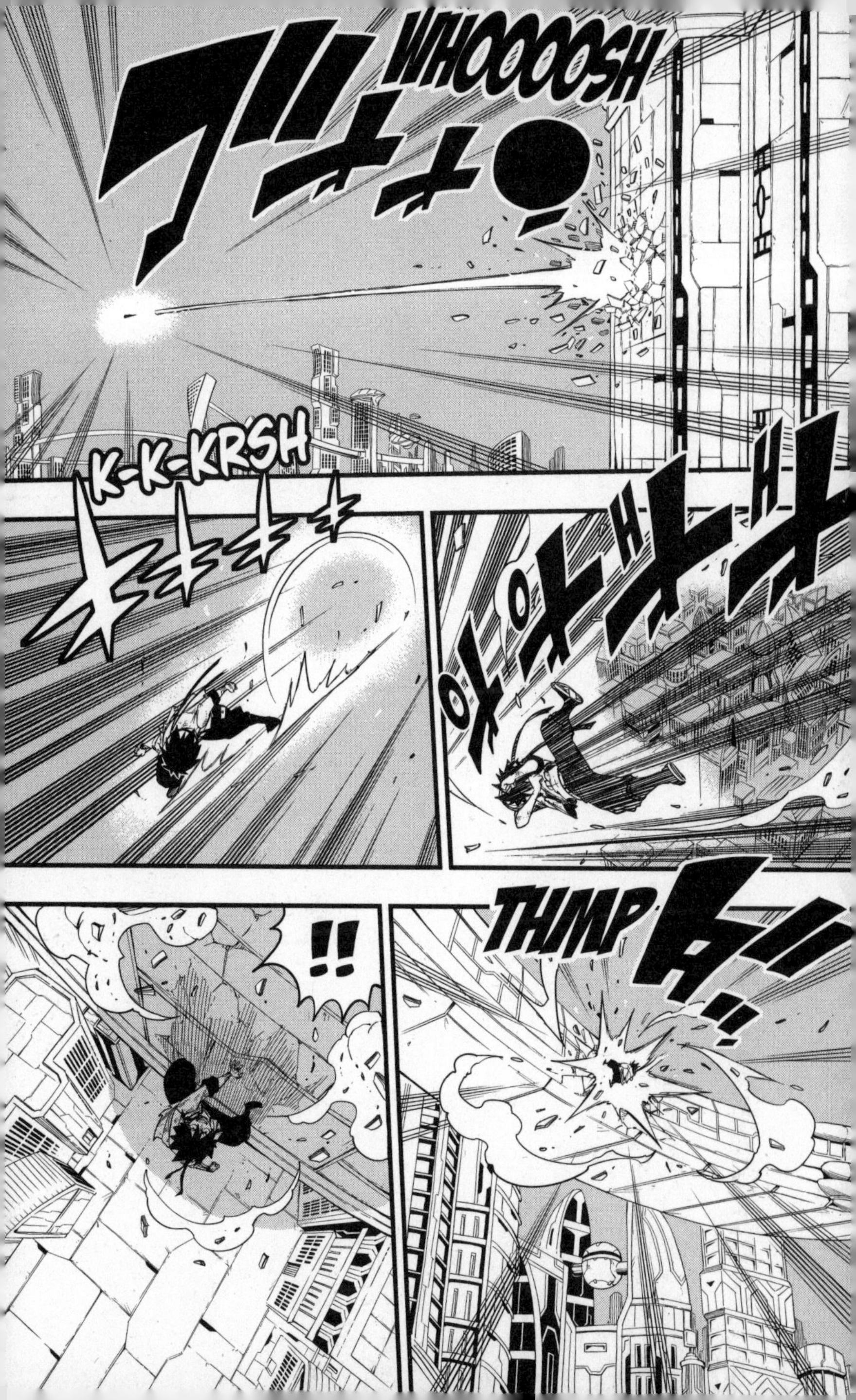
WHOOOOSH
K-K-KRSH
THMP
!!

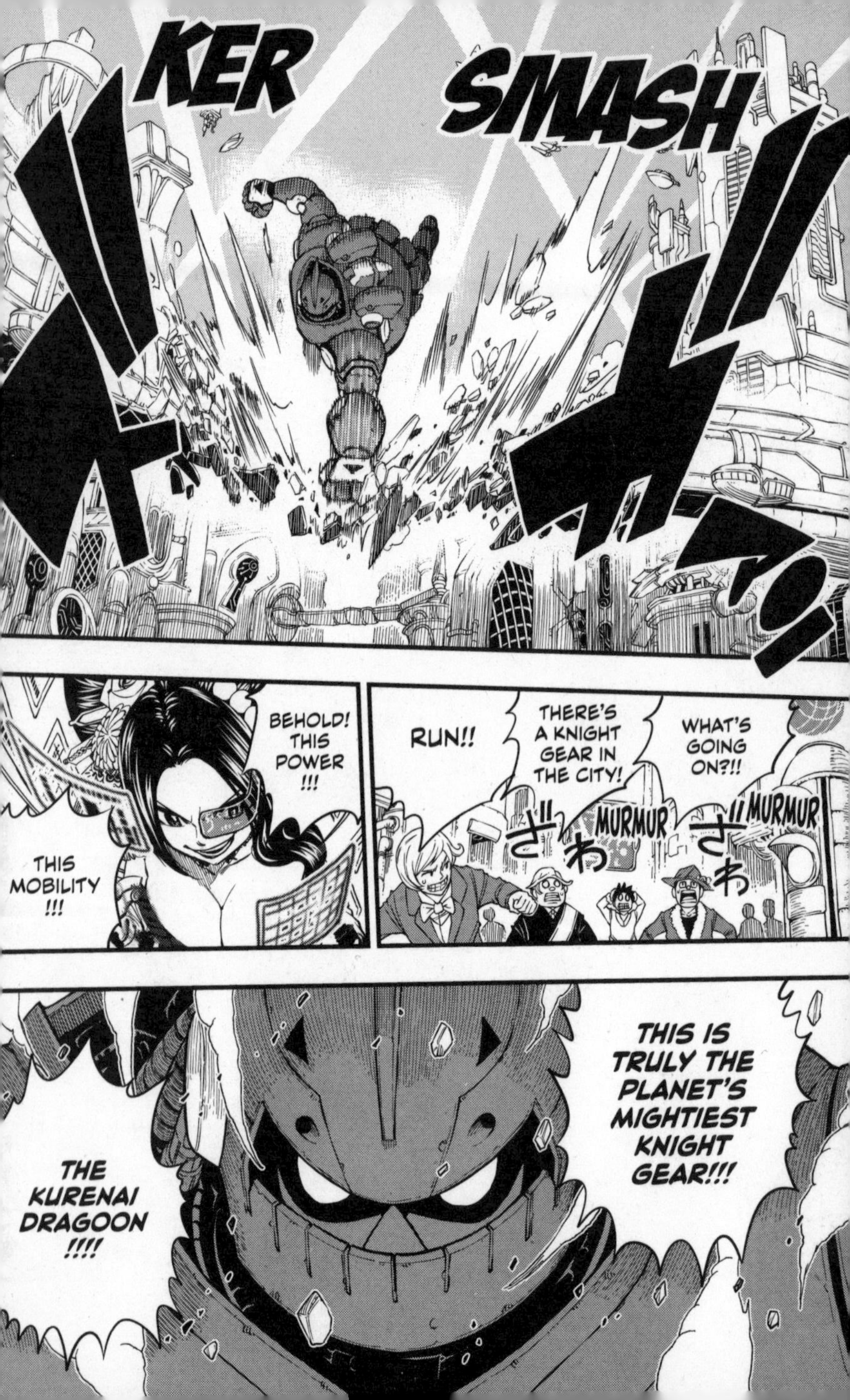
KER SMASH
WHAT'S GOING ON?!!
THERE'S A KNIGHT GEAR IN THE CITY!
RUN!!
ざわ MURMUR
ざわ MURMUR
BEHOLD! THIS POWER!!!
THIS MOBILITY!!!
THIS IS TRULY THE PLANET'S MIGHTIEST KNIGHT GEAR!!!
THE KURENAI DRAGOON!!!!

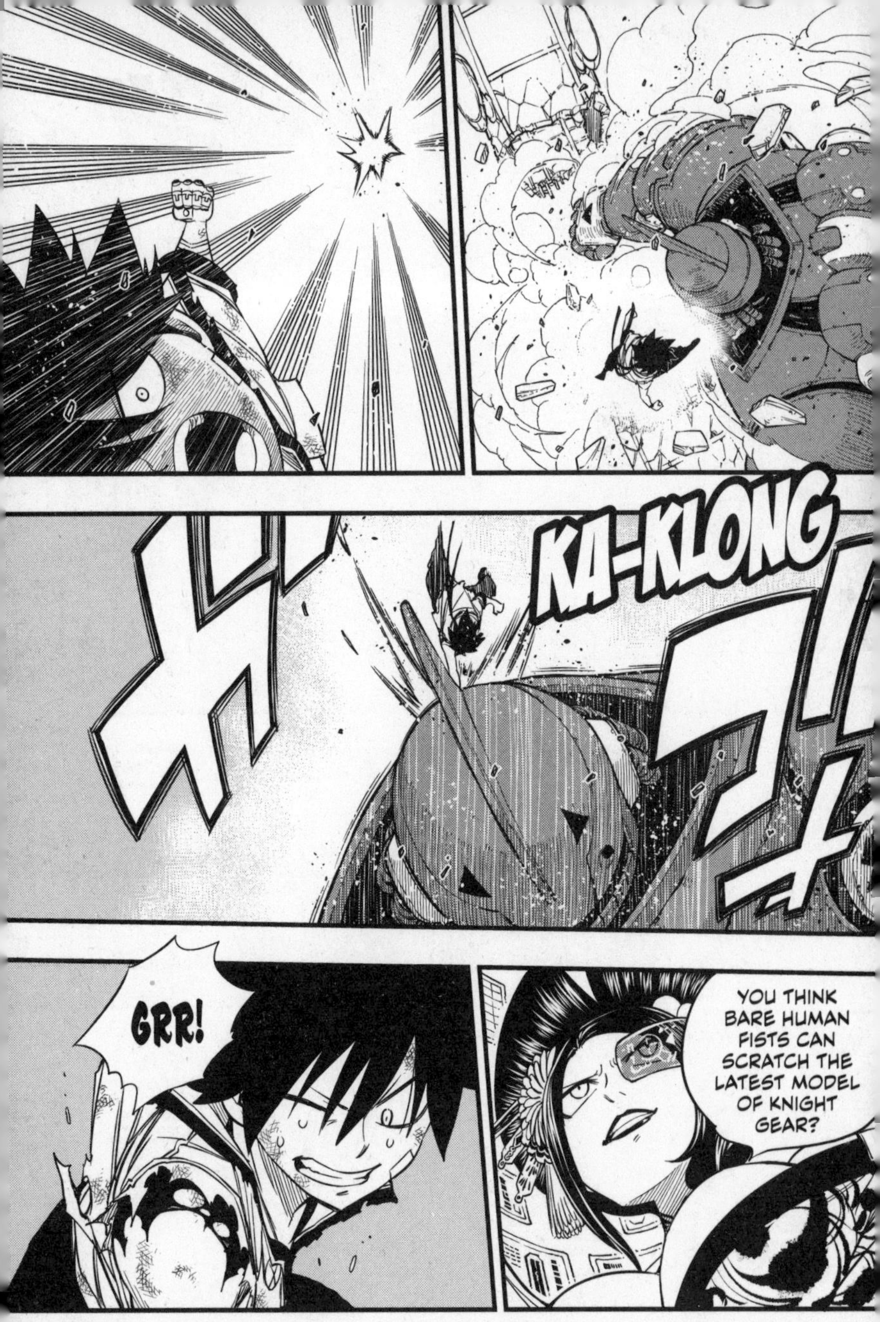
KA-KLONG
YOU THINK BARE HUMAN FISTS CAN SCRATCH THE LATEST MODEL OF KNIGHT GEAR?
GRR!

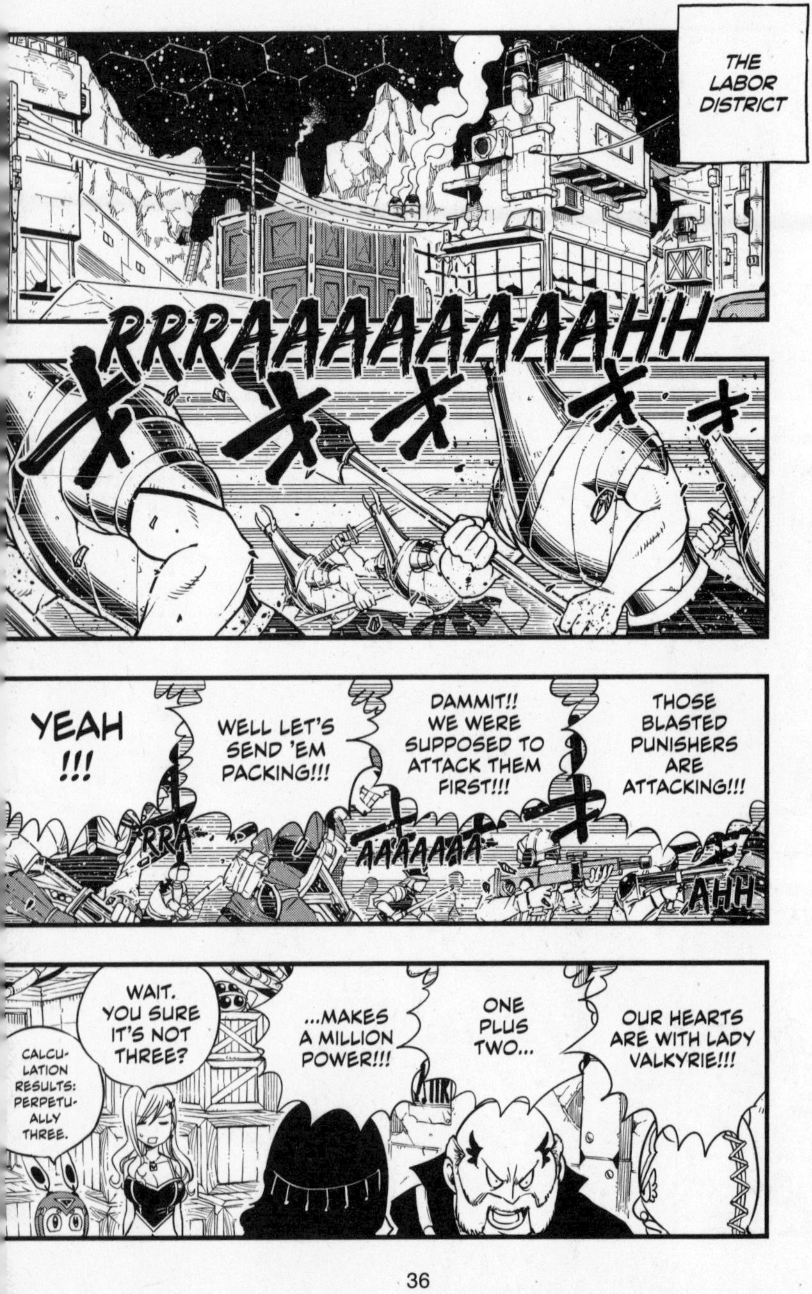
THE LABOR DISTRICT
RRRAAAAAAAAAAHH
THOSE BLASTED PUNISHERS ARE ATTACKING!!!
DAMMIT!! WE WERE SUPPOSED TO ATTACK THEM FIRST!!!
WELL LET'S SEND 'EM PACKING!!!
YEAH !!!
RRA
AAAAAAA
AHH
OUR HEARTS ARE WITH LADY VALKYRIE!!!
ONE PLUS TWO...
...MAKES A MILLION POWER!!!
WAIT. YOU SURE IT'S NOT THREE?
CALCU-LATION RESULTS: PERPETU-ALLY THREE.

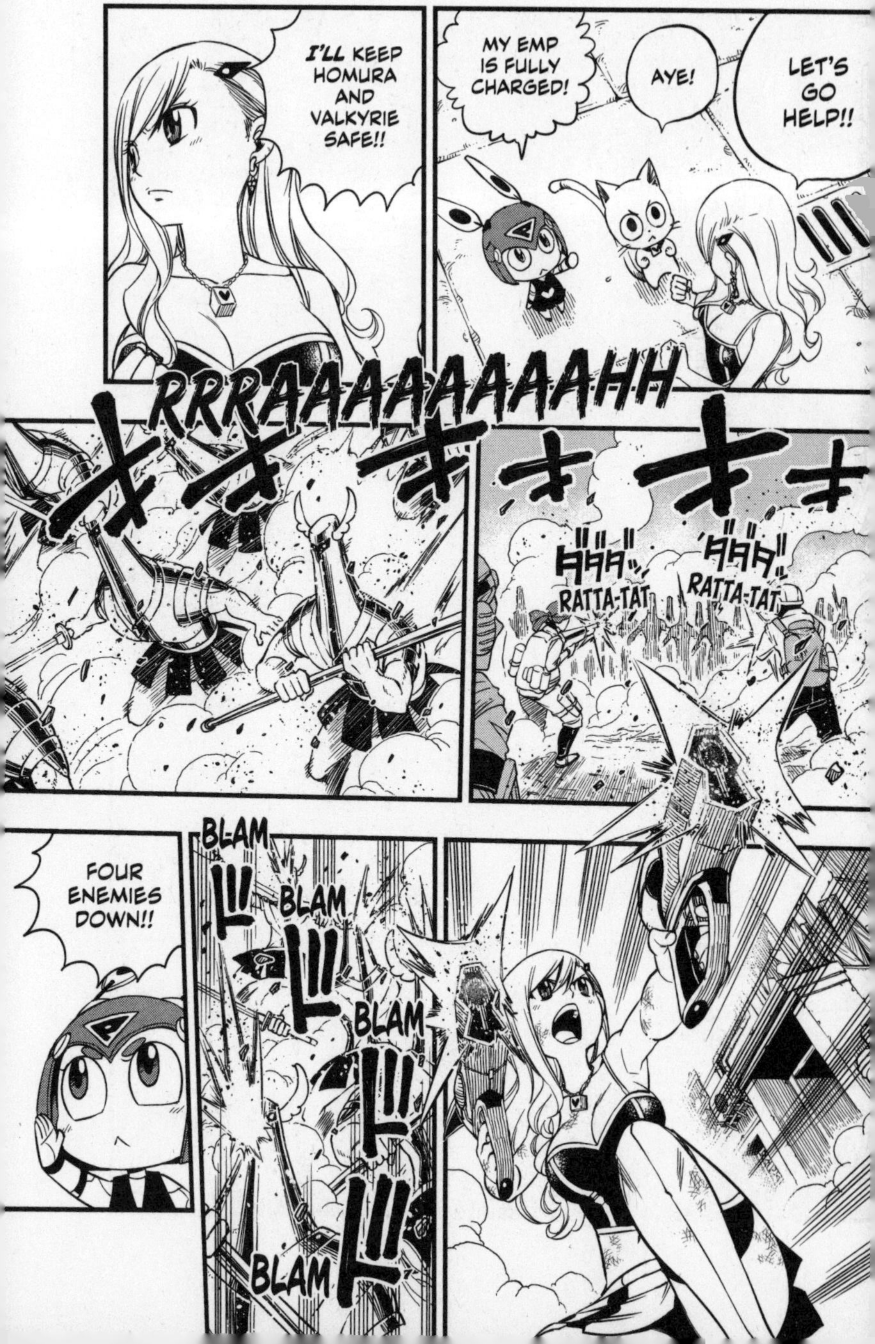
LET'S GO HELP!!
AYE!
MY EMP IS FULLY CHARGED!
I'LL KEEP HOMURA AND VALKYRIE SAFE!!
RRRAAAAAAAAAAHH
RATTA-TAT
RATTA-TAT
BLAM
BLAM
BLAM
BLAM
FOUR ENEMIES DOWN!!

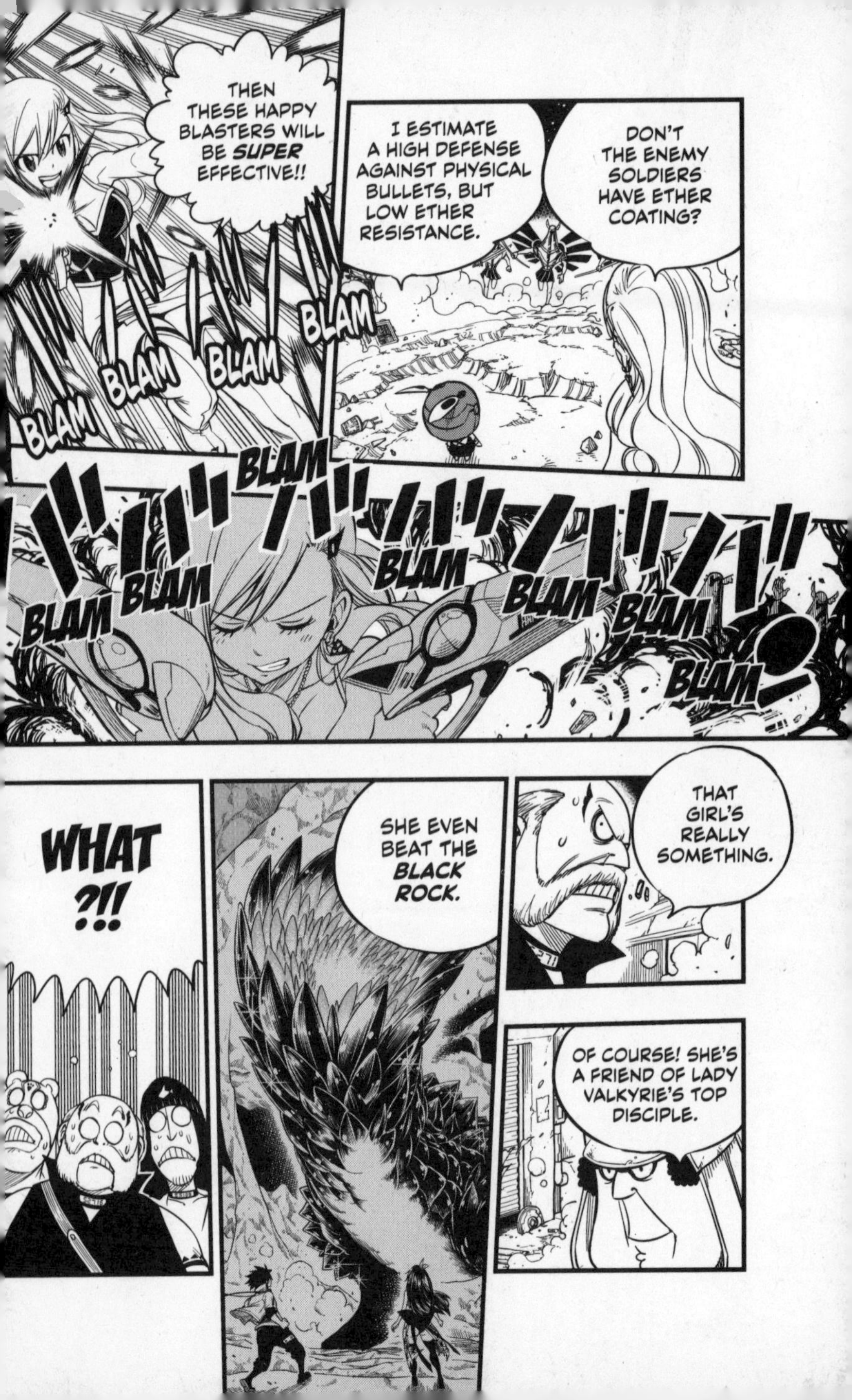

DON'T THE ENEMY SOLDIERS HAVE ETHER COATING?
I ESTIMATE A HIGH DEFENSE AGAINST PHYSICAL BULLETS, BUT LOW ETHER RESISTANCE.
THEN THESE HAPPY BLASTERS WILL BE *SUPER* EFFECTIVE!!
BLAM
BLAM
BLAM
BLAM
BLAM
BLAM
BLAM
BLAM
BLAM
BLAM
BLAM
BLAM
THAT GIRL'S REALLY SOMETHING.
OF COURSE! SHE'S A FRIEND OF LADY VALKYRIE'S TOP DISCIPLE.
SHE EVEN BEAT THE *BLACK ROCK*.
WHAT ?!!

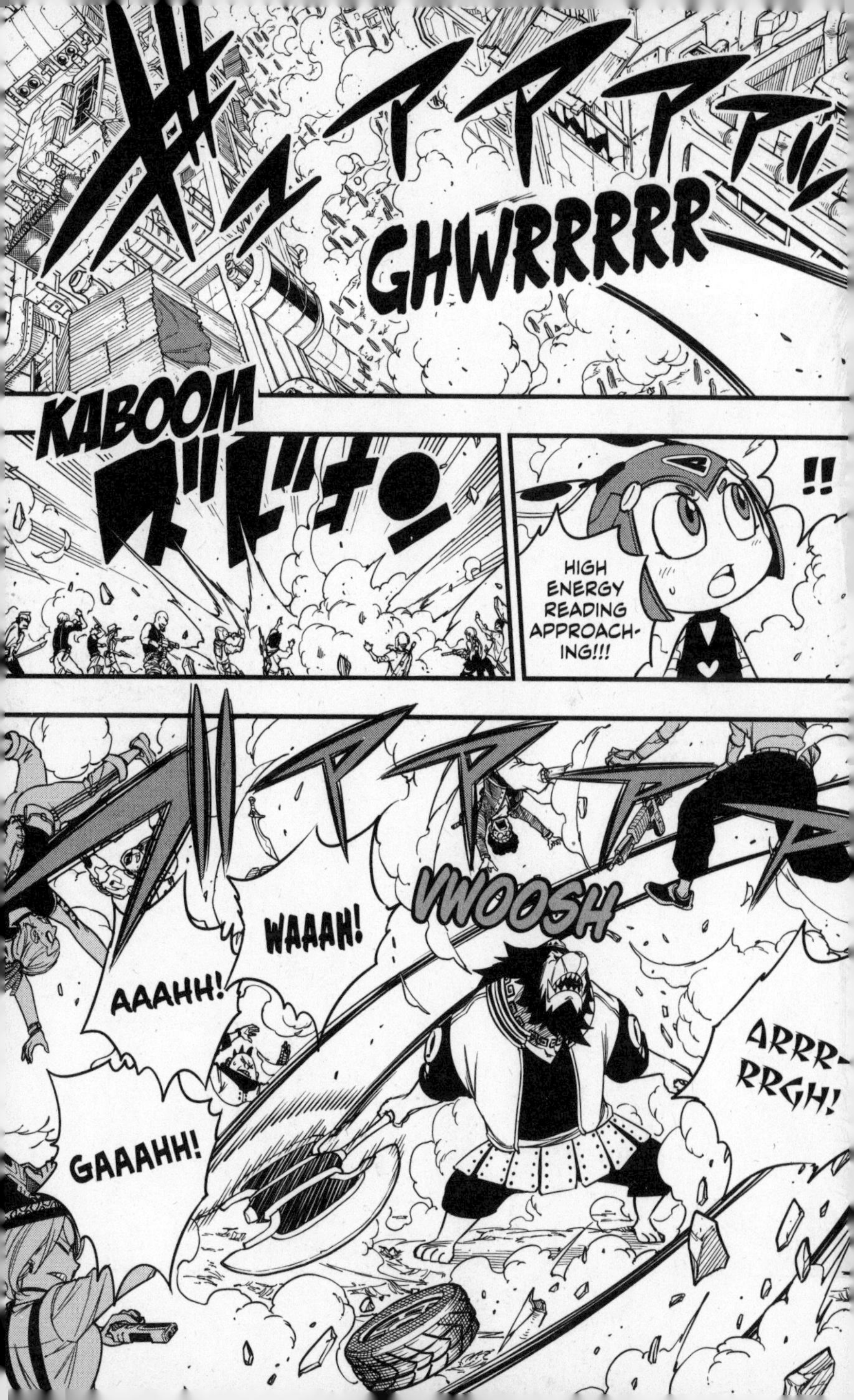
GHWRRRRR
!!
HIGH ENERGY READING APPROACH-ING!!!
KABOOM
VWOOSH
ARRRR-RRGH!
WAAAH!
AAAHH!
GAAAHH!

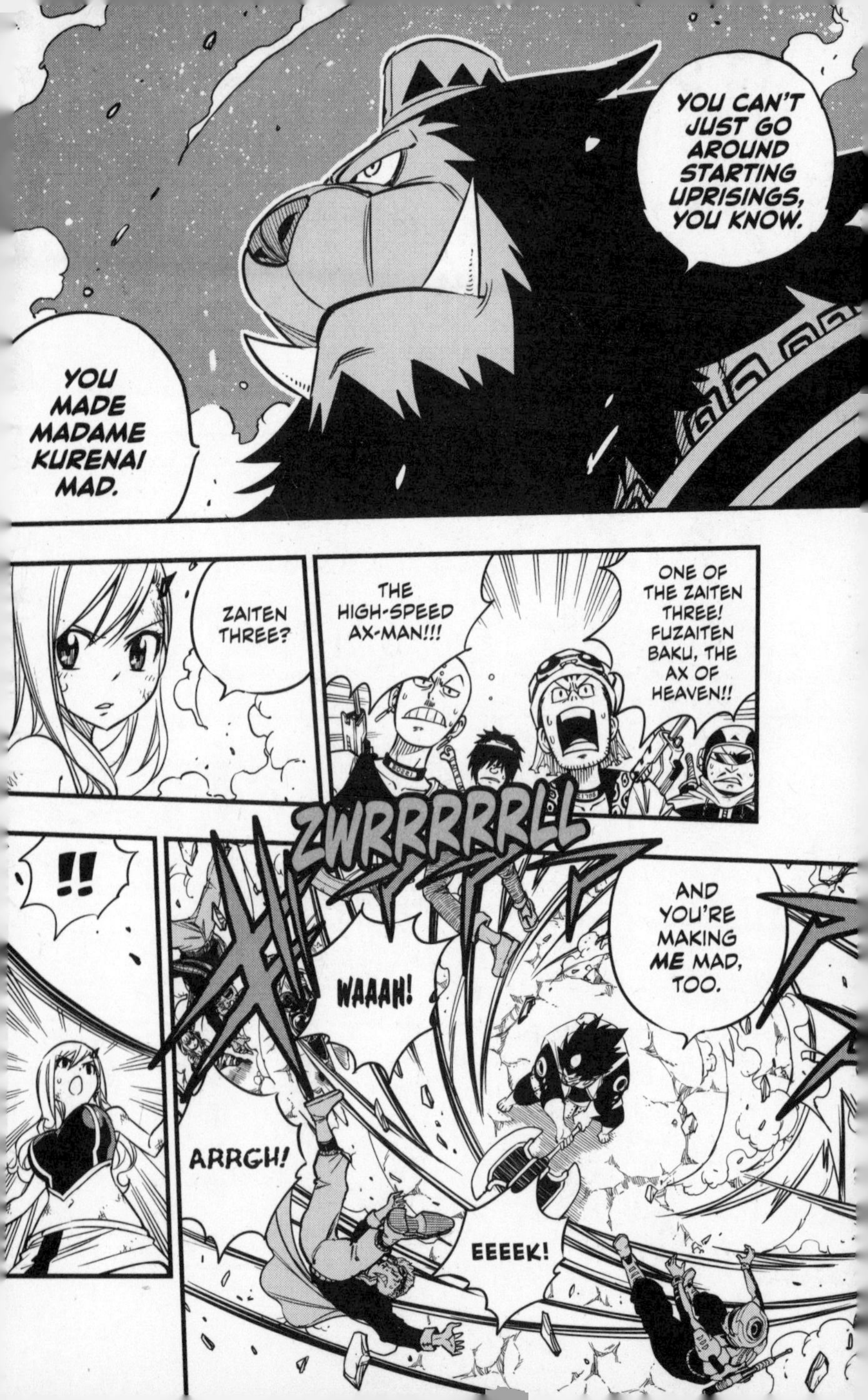
YOU CAN'T JUST GO AROUND STARTING UPRISINGS, YOU KNOW.
YOU MADE MADAME KURENAI MAD.
ONE OF THE ZAITEN THREE! FUZAITEN BAKU, THE AX OF HEAVEN!!
THE HIGH-SPEED AX-MAN!!!
ZAITEN THREE?
ZWRRRRRLL
AND YOU'RE MAKING ME MAD, TOO.
WAAAH!
ARRGH!
EEEEK!
!!

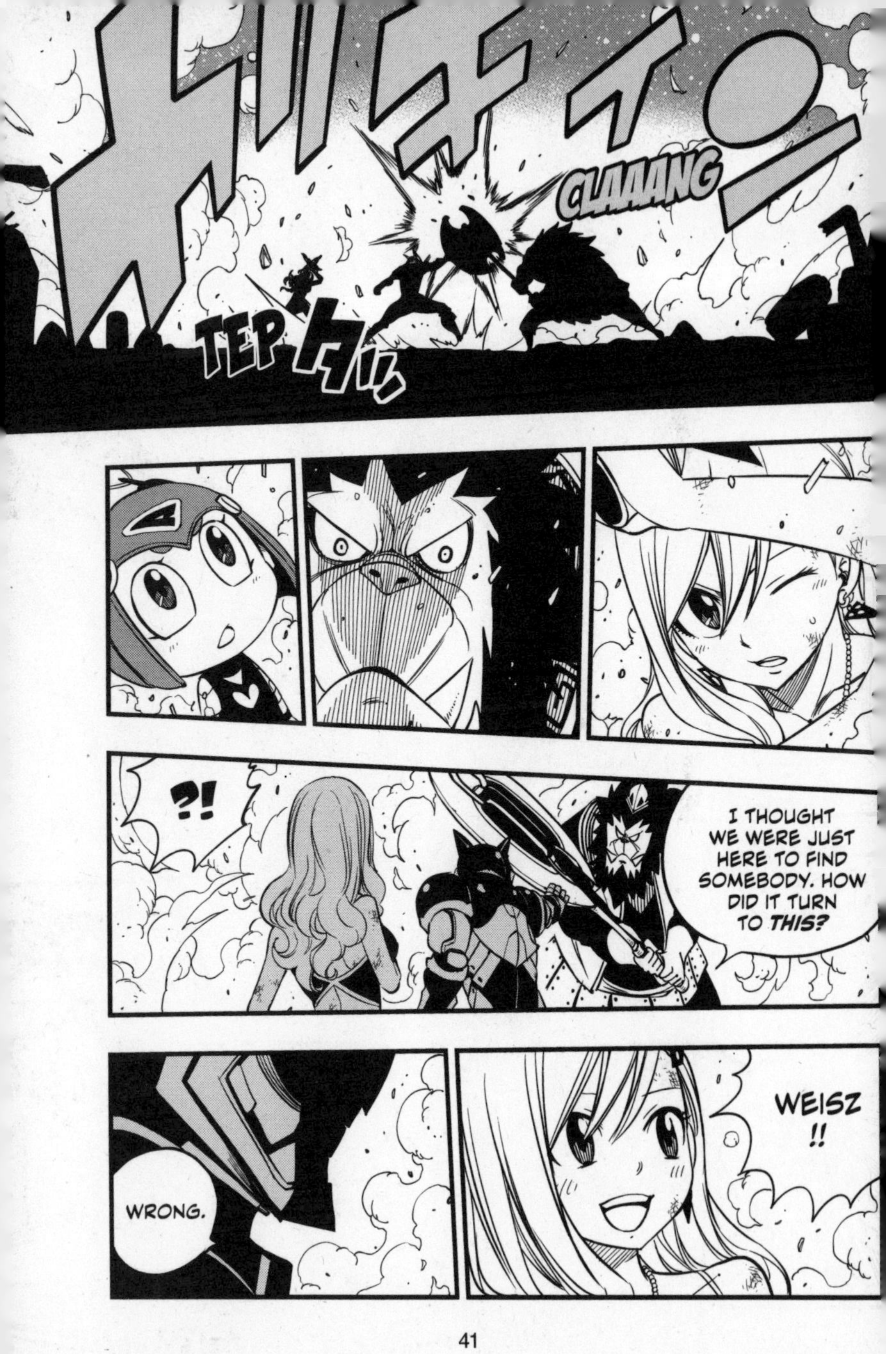
CLAAANG
TEP
I THOUGHT WE WERE JUST HERE TO FIND SOMEBODY. HOW DID IT TURN TO *THIS?*
?!
WEISZ !!
WRONG.

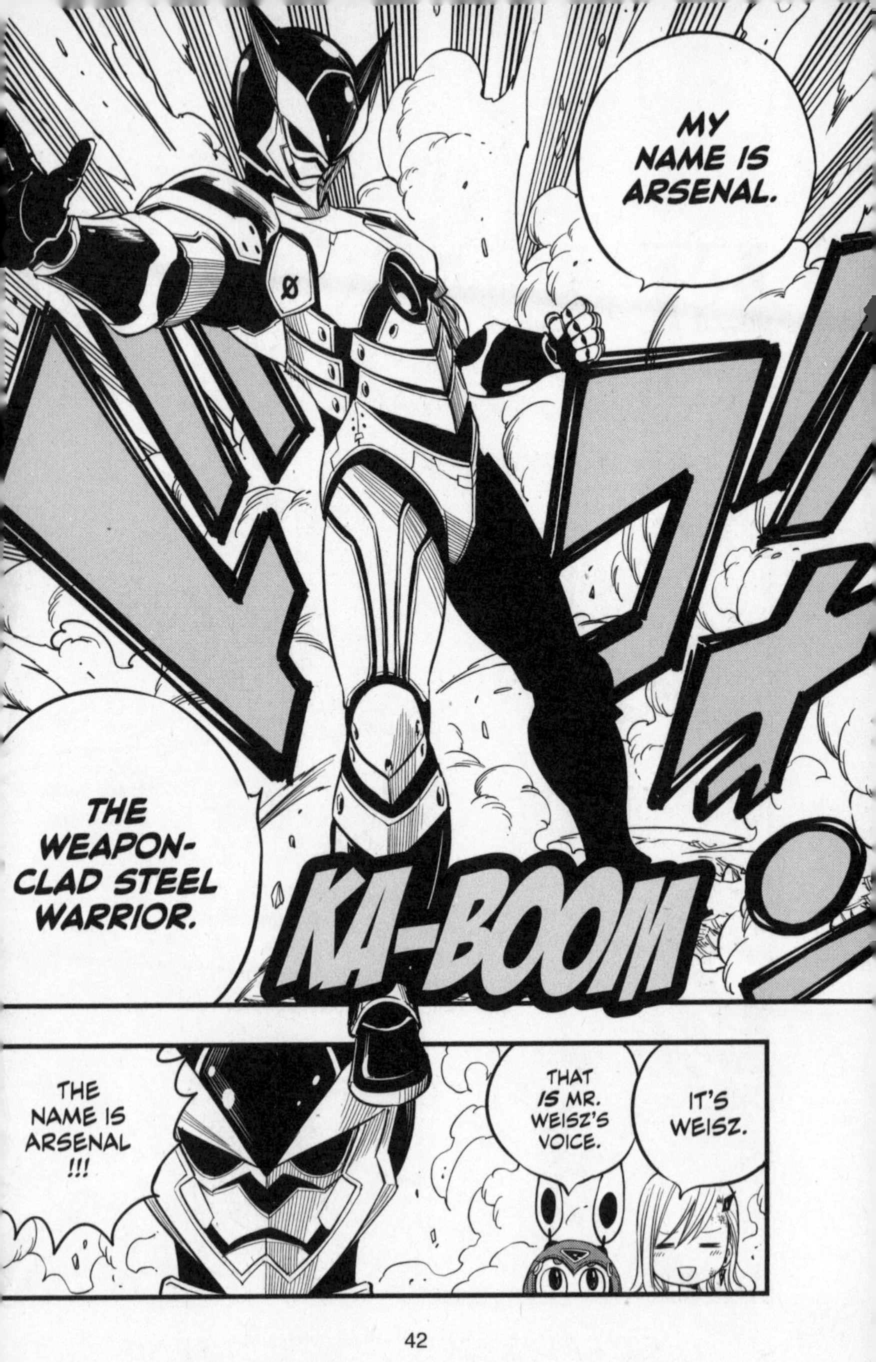
MY NAME IS ARSENAL.
THE WEAPON-CLAD STEEL WARRIOR.
KA-BOOM
IT'S WEISZ.
THAT *IS* MR. WEISZ'S VOICE.
THE NAME IS ARSENAL !!!

EDENS ZERO

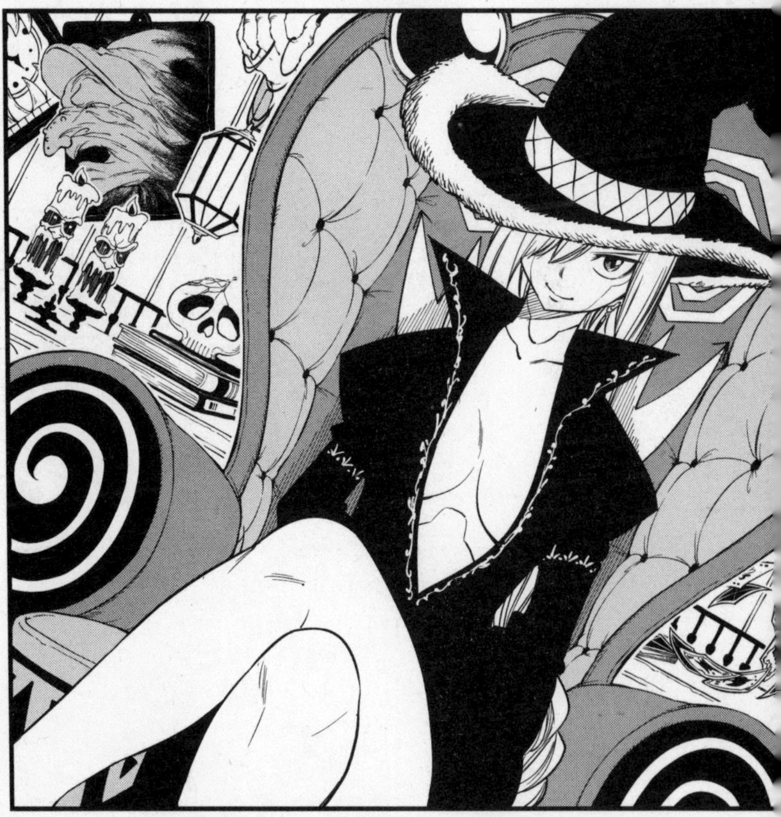

CHAPTER 62: THE LEGEND OF ME

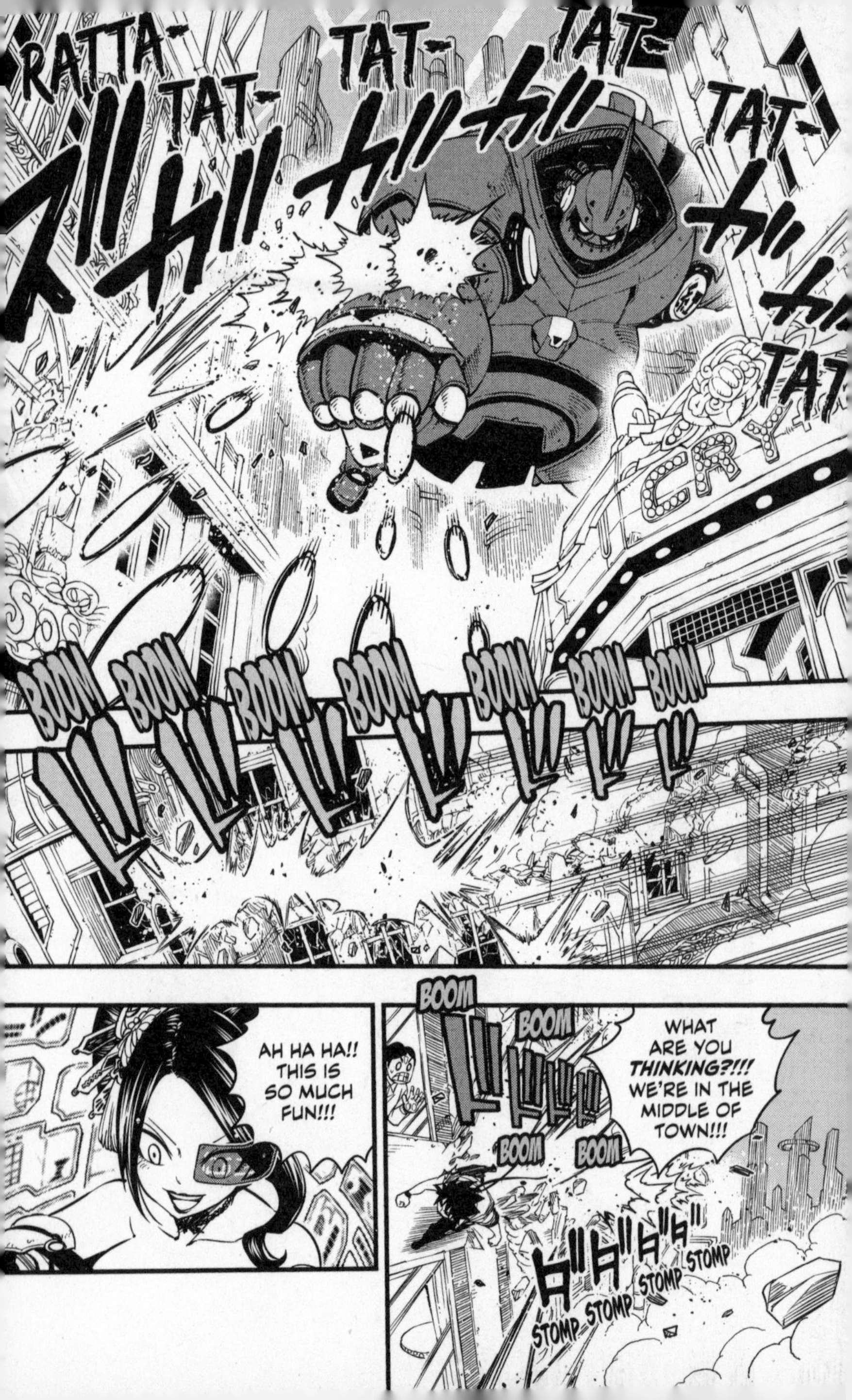
RATTA- TAT- TAT- TAT- TAT- TAT
CRY
BOOM BOOM BOOM BOOM BOOM BOOM BOOM
BOOM BOOM
WHAT ARE YOU *THINKING?!!!* WE'RE IN THE MIDDLE OF TOWN!!!
BOOM BOOM
STOMP STOMP STOMP STOMP
AH HA HA!! THIS IS SO MUCH FUN!!!

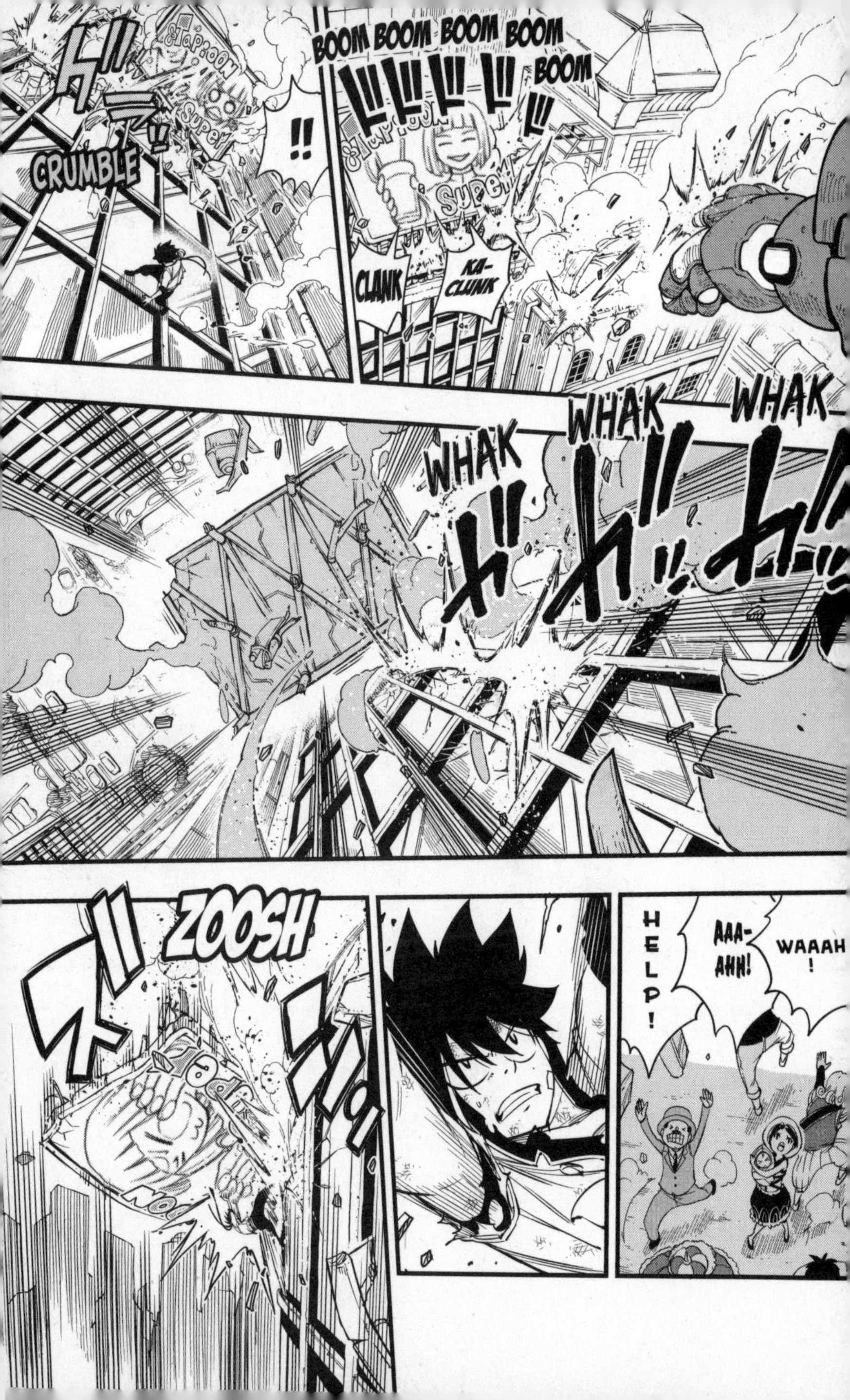
BOOM BOOM BOOM BOOM
BOOM
KA-CLUNK
CLANK
!!
CRUMBLE
WHAK
WHAK
WHAK
WAAAH!
AAA-AHH!
HELP!
ZOOSH

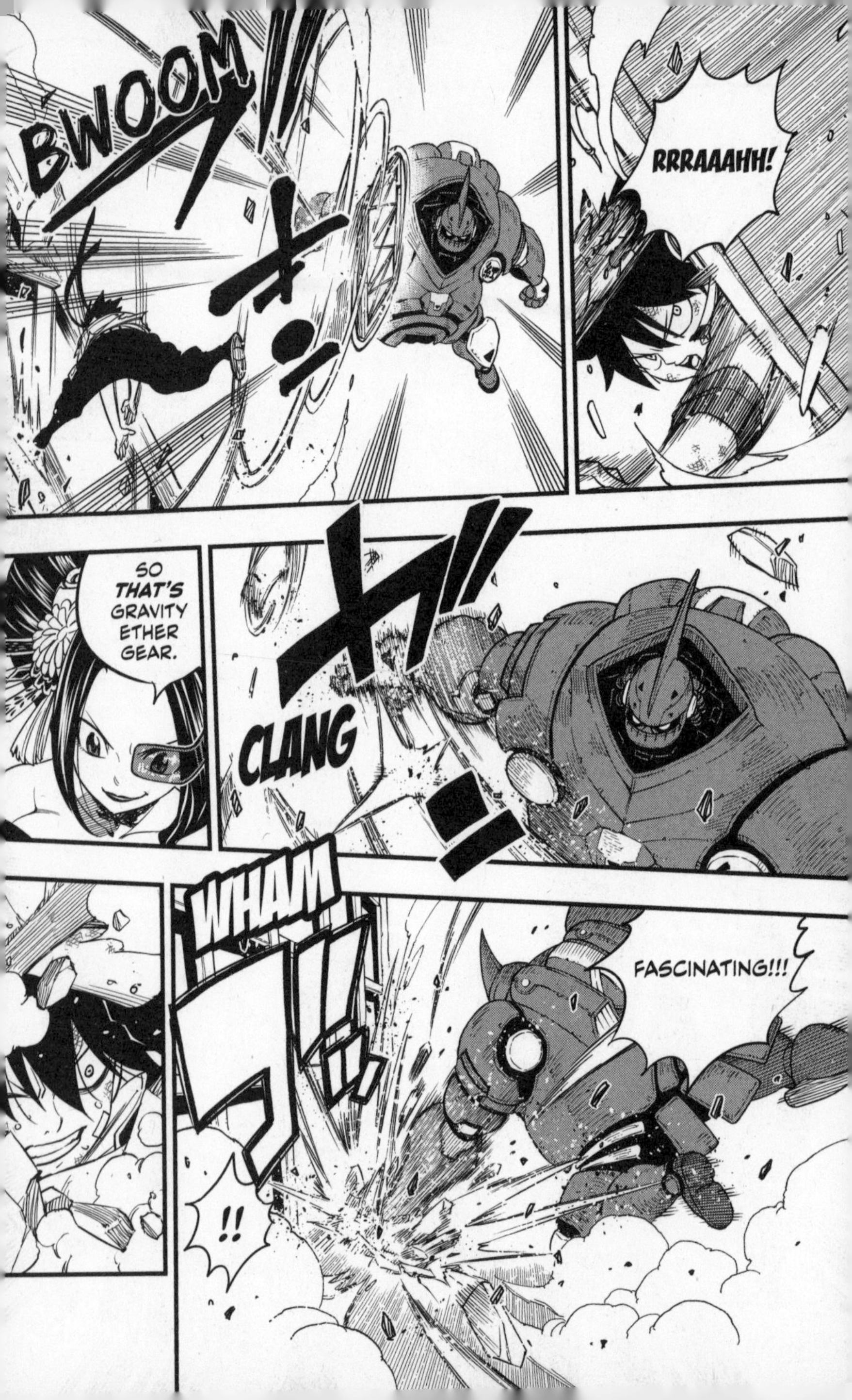
RRRAAAHH!
BWOOM
CLANG
SO *THAT'S* GRAVITY ETHER GEAR.
WHAM
FASCINATING!!!
!!

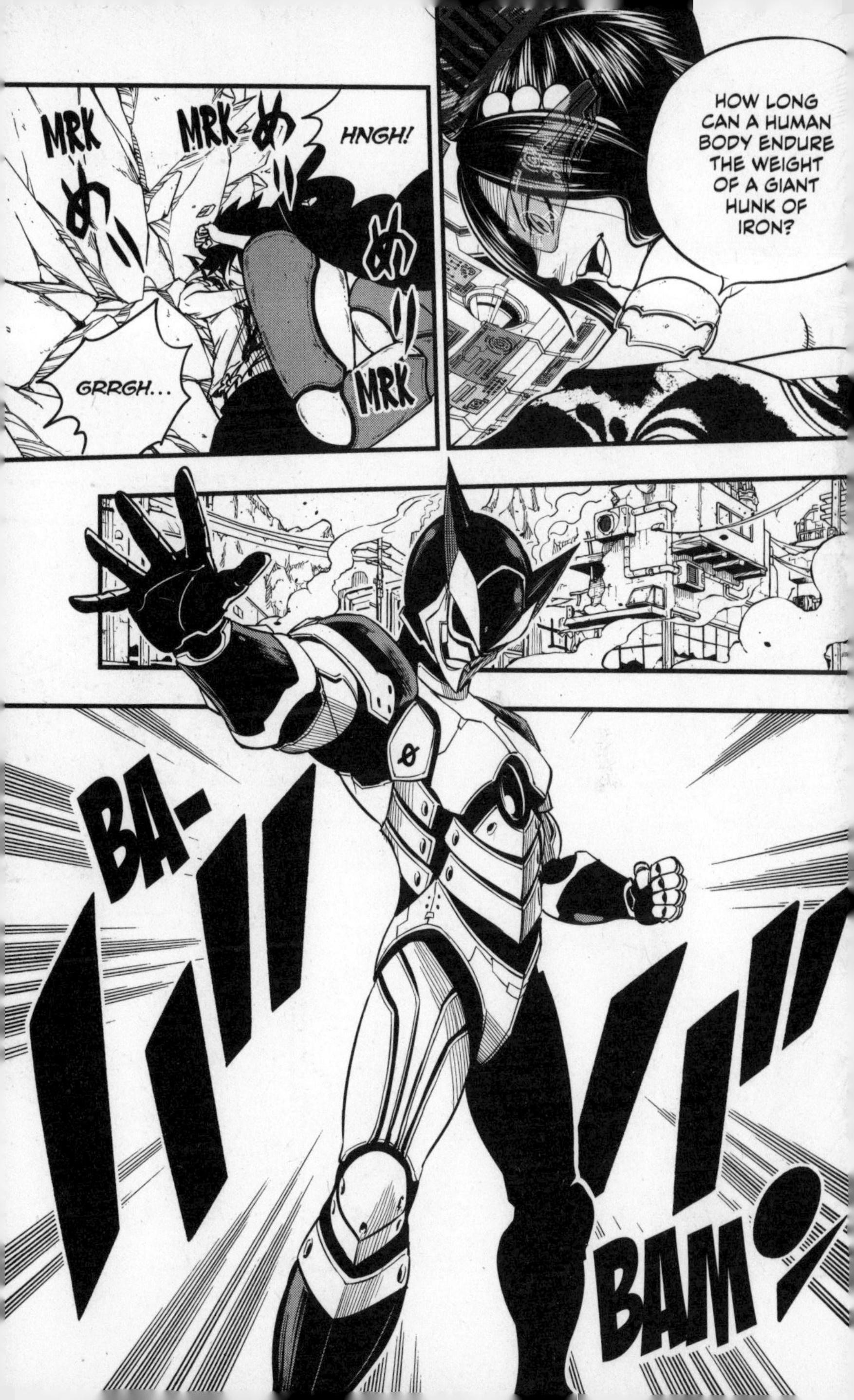
HOW LONG CAN A HUMAN BODY ENDURE THE WEIGHT OF A GIANT HUNK OF IRON?
HNGH!
MRK
MRK
MRK
GRRGH...
BA-
BAM

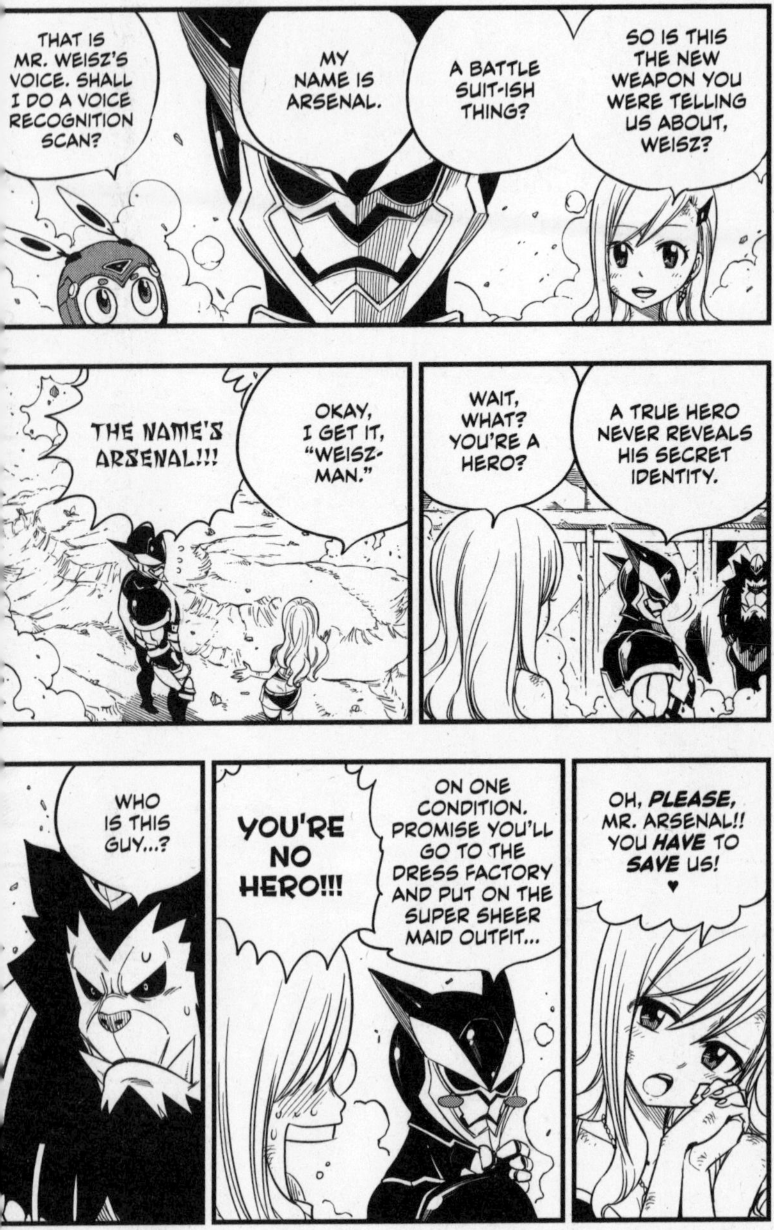
SO IS THIS THE NEW WEAPON YOU WERE TELLING US ABOUT, WEISZ?
A BATTLE SUIT-ISH THING?
MY NAME IS ARSENAL.
THAT IS MR. WEISZ'S VOICE. SHALL I DO A VOICE RECOGNITION SCAN?
A TRUE HERO NEVER REVEALS HIS SECRET IDENTITY.
WAIT, WHAT? YOU'RE A HERO?
OKAY, I GET IT, "WEISZ-MAN."
THE NAME'S ARSENAL!!!
OH, ***PLEASE***, MR. ARSENAL!! YOU ***HAVE*** TO ***SAVE*** US! ♥
ON ONE CONDITION. PROMISE YOU'LL GO TO THE DRESS FACTORY AND PUT ON THE SUPER SHEER MAID OUTFIT...
YOU'RE NO HERO!!!
WHO IS THIS GUY...?

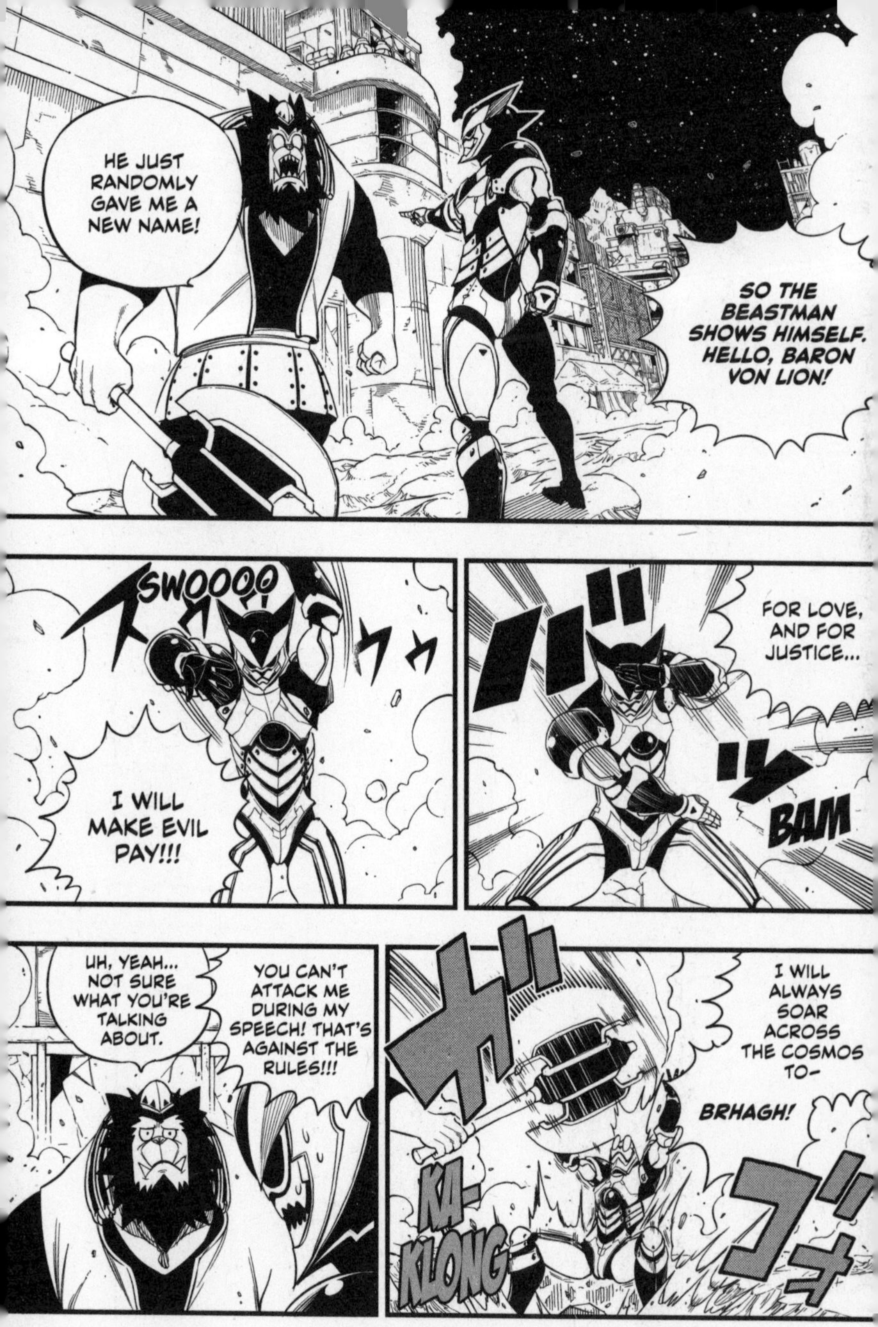
SO THE BEASTMAN SHOWS HIMSELF. HELLO, BARON VON LION!
HE JUST RANDOMLY GAVE ME A NEW NAME!
FOR LOVE, AND FOR JUSTICE...
BAM
SWOOOO
I WILL MAKE EVIL PAY!!!
I WILL ALWAYS SOAR ACROSS THE COSMOS TO-
BRHAGH!
KA-KLONG
YOU CAN'T ATTACK ME DURING MY SPEECH! THAT'S AGAINST THE RULES!!!
UH, YEAH... NOT SURE WHAT YOU'RE TALKING ABOUT.

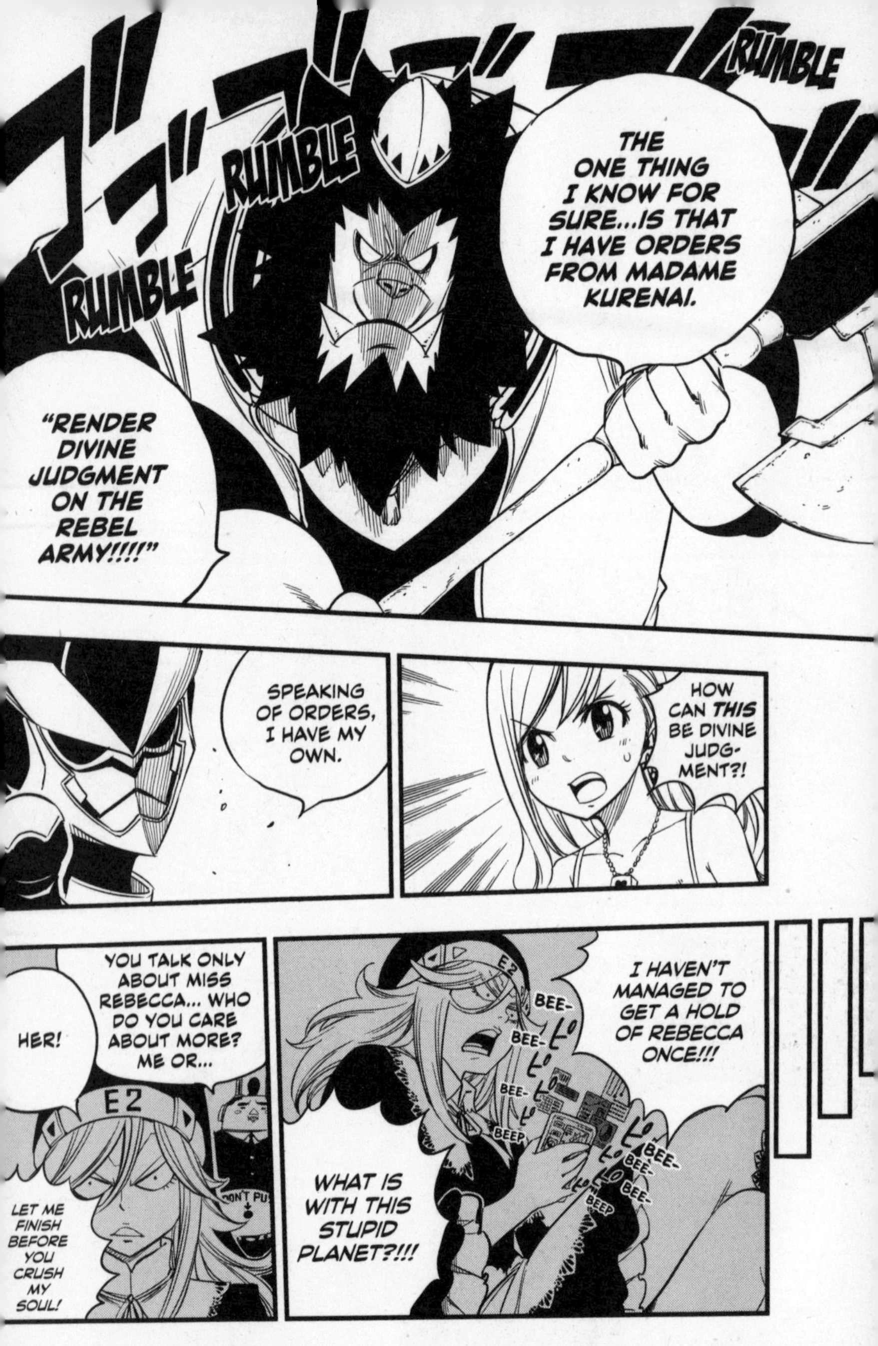
RUMBLE
RUMBLE
RUMBLE
THE ONE THING I KNOW FOR SURE...IS THAT I HAVE ORDERS FROM MADAME KURENAI.
"RENDER DIVINE JUDGMENT ON THE REBEL ARMY!!!!"
HOW CAN *THIS* BE DIVINE JUDG-MENT?!
SPEAKING OF ORDERS, I HAVE MY OWN.
I HAVEN'T MANAGED TO GET A HOLD OF REBECCA ONCE!!!
BEE- BEE- BEE- BEEP
BEE- BEE- BEE- BEEP
WHAT IS WITH THIS STUPID PLANET?!!!
YOU TALK ONLY ABOUT MISS REBECCA... WHO DO YOU CARE ABOUT MORE? ME OR...
HER!
LET ME FINISH BEFORE YOU CRUSH MY SOUL!

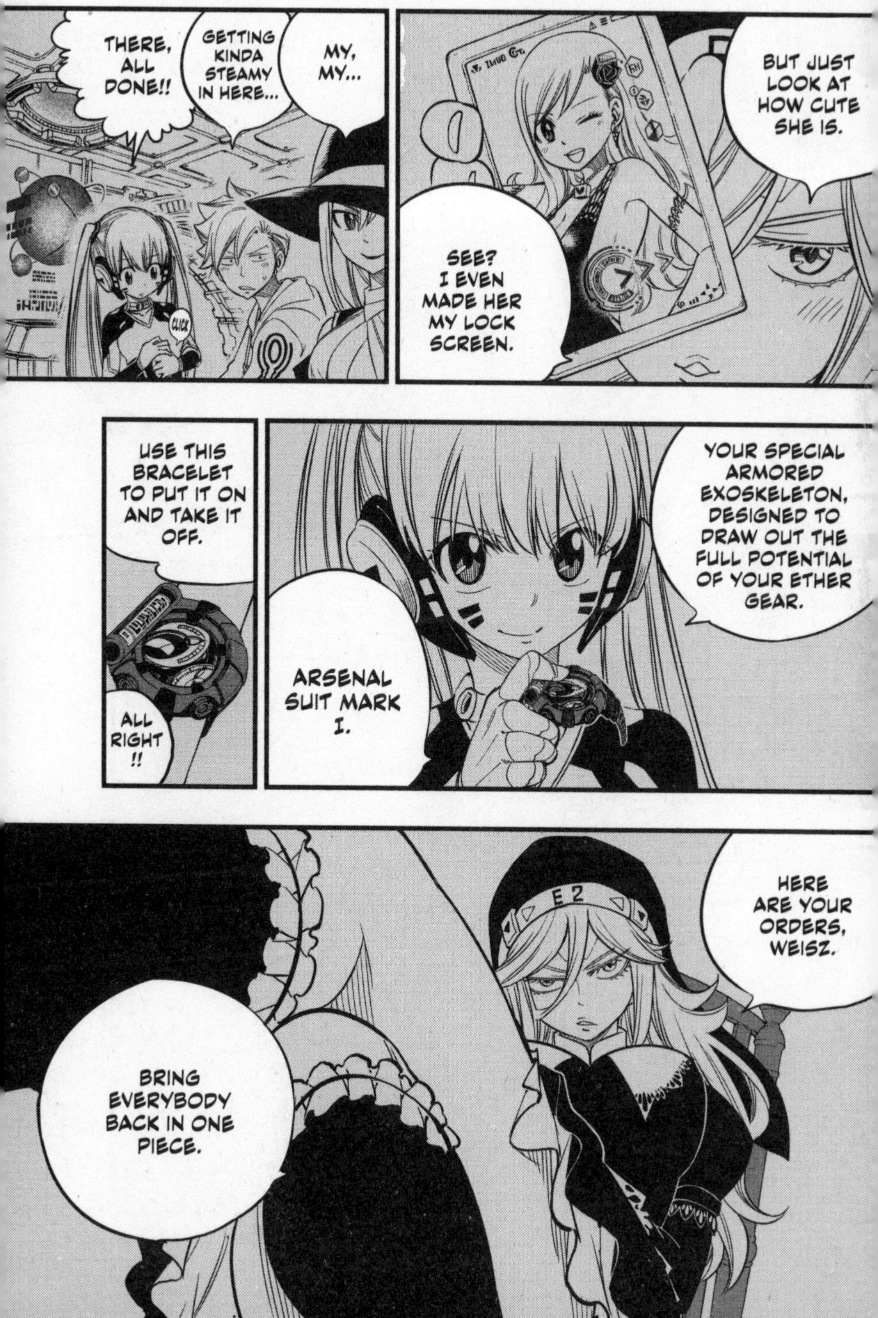
BUT JUST LOOK AT HOW CUTE SHE IS.
SEE? I EVEN MADE HER MY LOCK SCREEN.
MY, MY...
GETTING KINDA STEAMY IN HERE...
THERE, ALL DONE!!
CLICK
YOUR SPECIAL ARMORED EXOSKELETON, DESIGNED TO DRAW OUT THE FULL POTENTIAL OF YOUR ETHER GEAR.
ARSENAL SUIT MARK I.
USE THIS BRACELET TO PUT IT ON AND TAKE IT OFF.
ALL RIGHT !!
HERE ARE YOUR ORDERS, WEISZ.
BRING EVERYBODY BACK IN ONE PIECE.

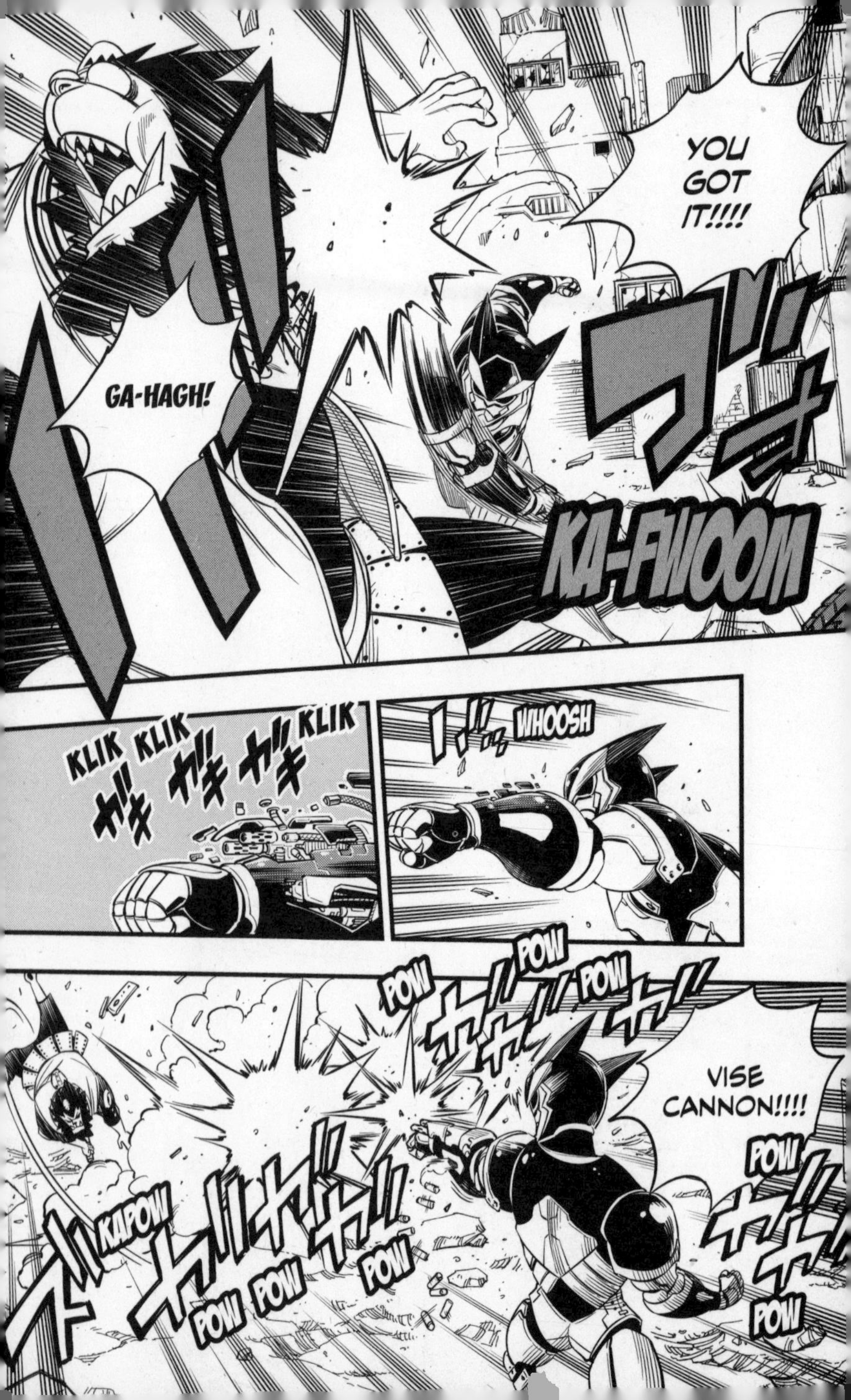
YOU GOT IT!!!!
KA-FWOOM
GA-HAGH!
WHOOSH
KLIK KLIK KLIK
POW
POW
POW
VISE CANNON!!!!
POW
POW
POW
POW
POW
KAPOW

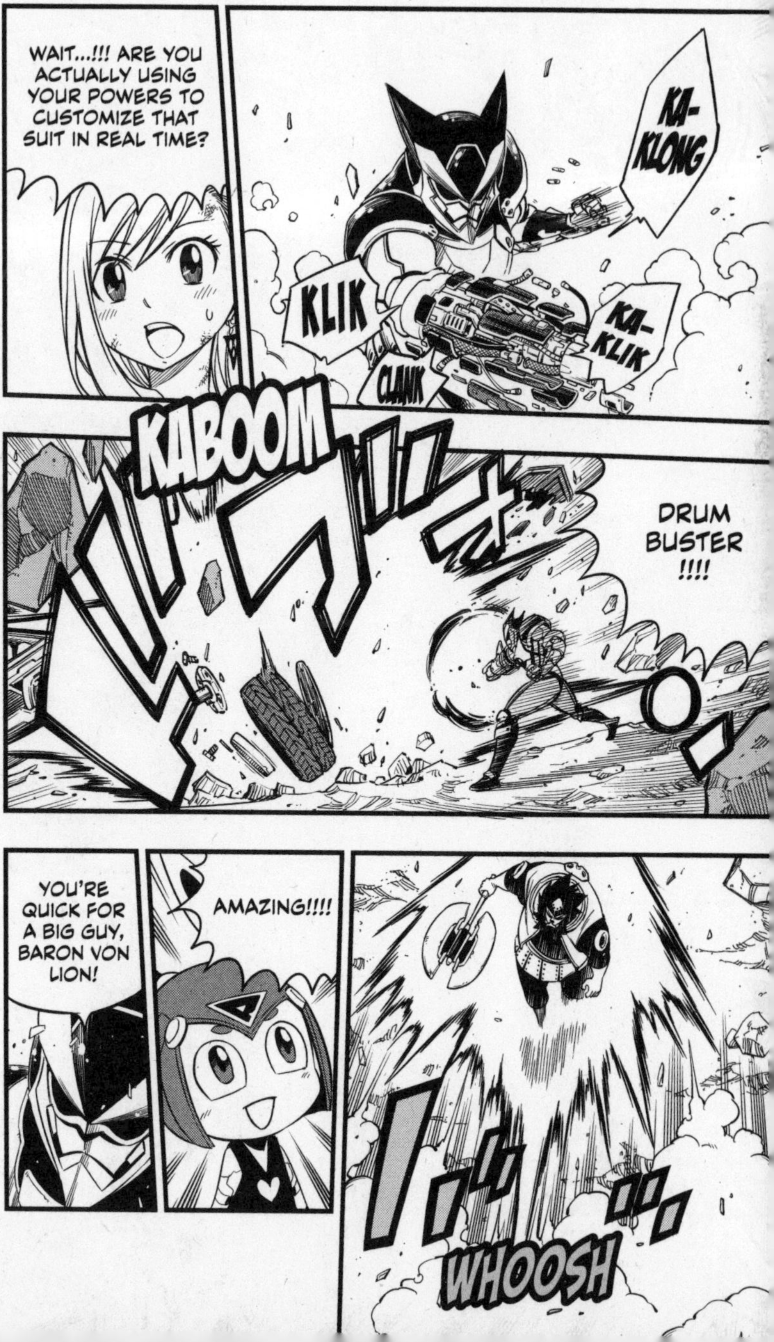
KA-
KLONG
KA-
KLIK
KLIK
CLANK
WAIT...!!! ARE YOU ACTUALLY USING YOUR POWERS TO CUSTOMIZE THAT SUIT IN REAL TIME?
DRUM BUSTER !!!!
KABOOM
WHOOSH
AMAZING!!!!
YOU'RE QUICK FOR A BIG GUY, BARON VON LION!

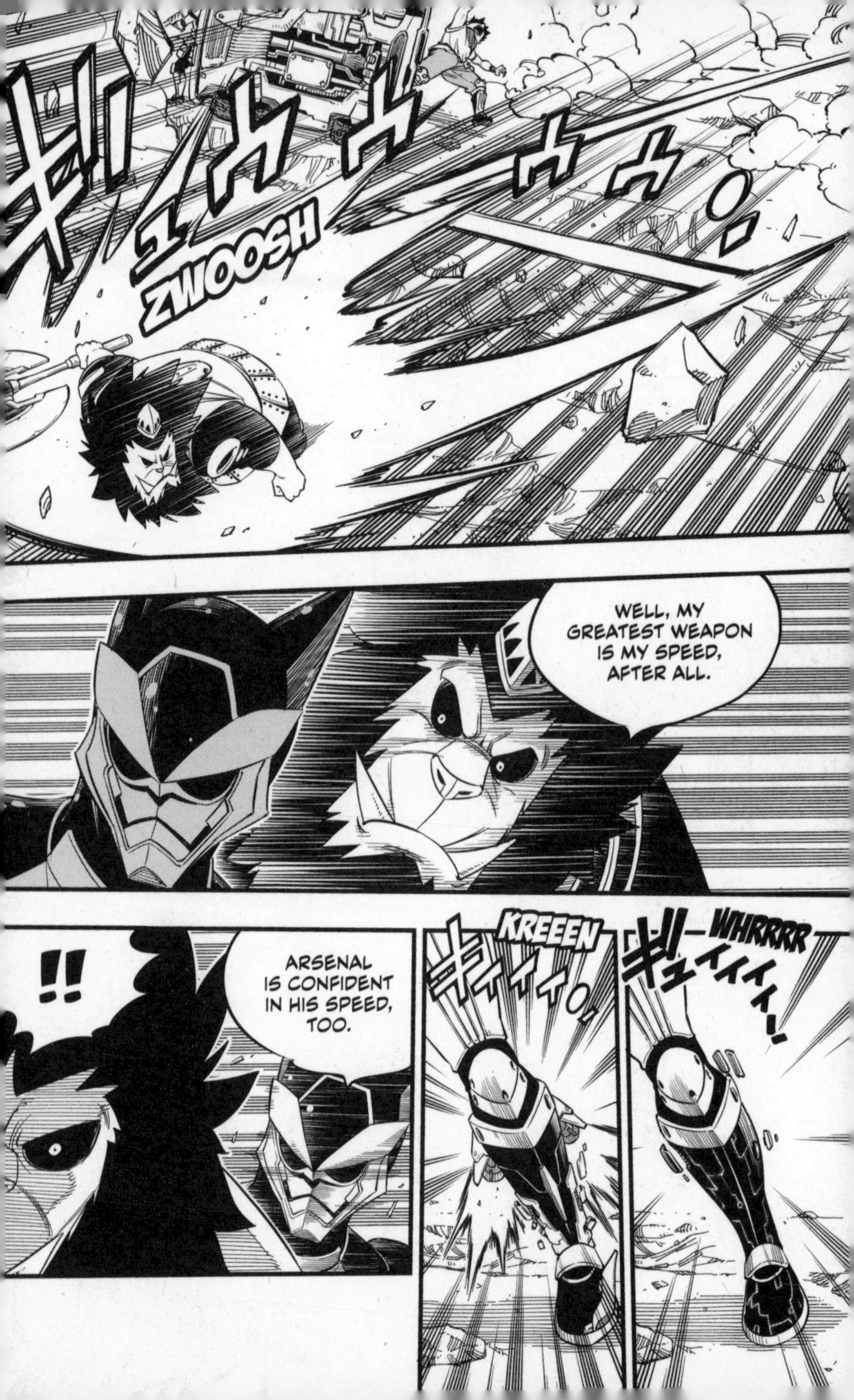
ZWOOSH
WELL, MY GREATEST WEAPON IS MY SPEED, AFTER ALL.
WHRRRR
KREEEN
ARSENAL IS CONFIDENT IN HIS SPEED, TOO.
!!

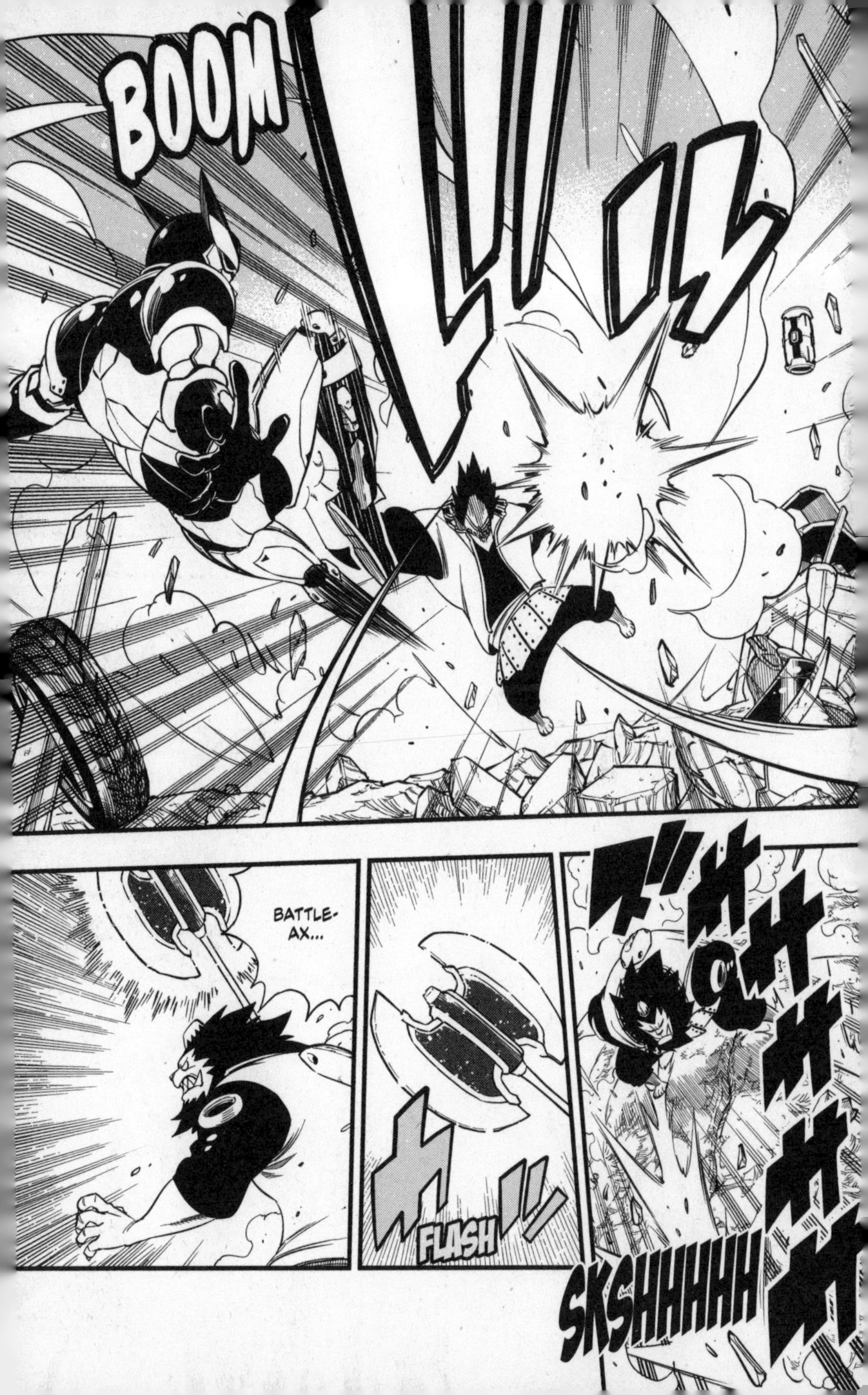
BOOM
SKSHHHHH
FLASH
BATTLE-AX...

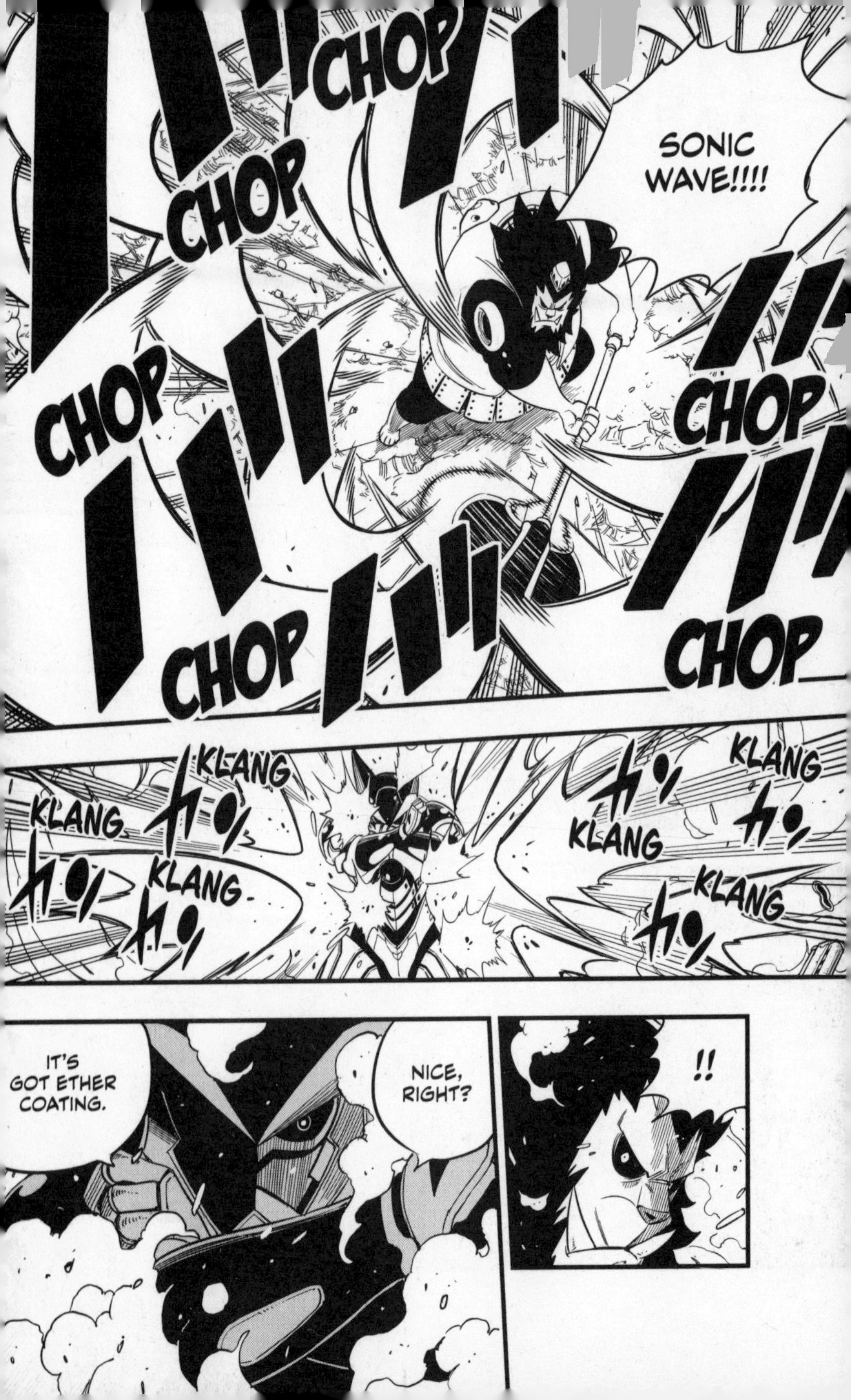
SONIC WAVE!!!!
CHOP
CHOP
CHOP
CHOP
CHOP
CHOP
CHOP
KLANG
KLANG
KLANG
KLANG
KLANG
KLANG
!!
IT'S GOT ETHER COATING.
NICE, RIGHT?

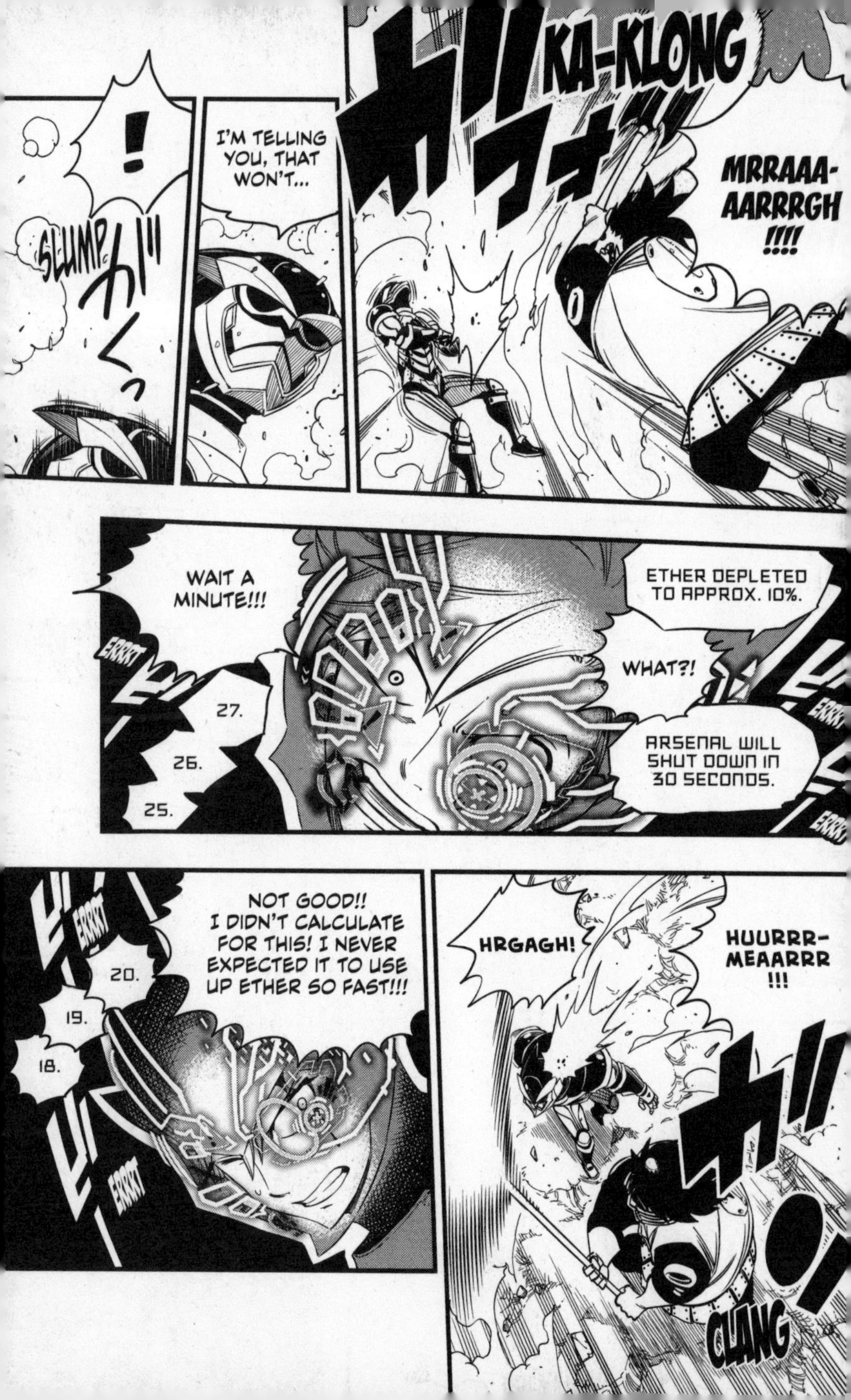
KA-KLONG
MRRAAA-AARRRGH!!!!
I'M TELLING YOU, THAT WON'T...
!
SLUMP
ETHER DEPLETED TO APPROX. 10%.
WHAT?!
ARSENAL WILL SHUT DOWN IN 30 SECONDS.
ERRRT
WAIT A MINUTE!!!
ERRRT
27.
26.
25.
ERRRT
HUURRR-MEAARRR!!!
HRGAGH!
CLANG
NOT GOOD!! I DIDN'T CALCULATE FOR THIS! I NEVER EXPECTED IT TO USE UP ETHER SO FAST!!!
ERRRT
20.
19.
18.
ERRRT

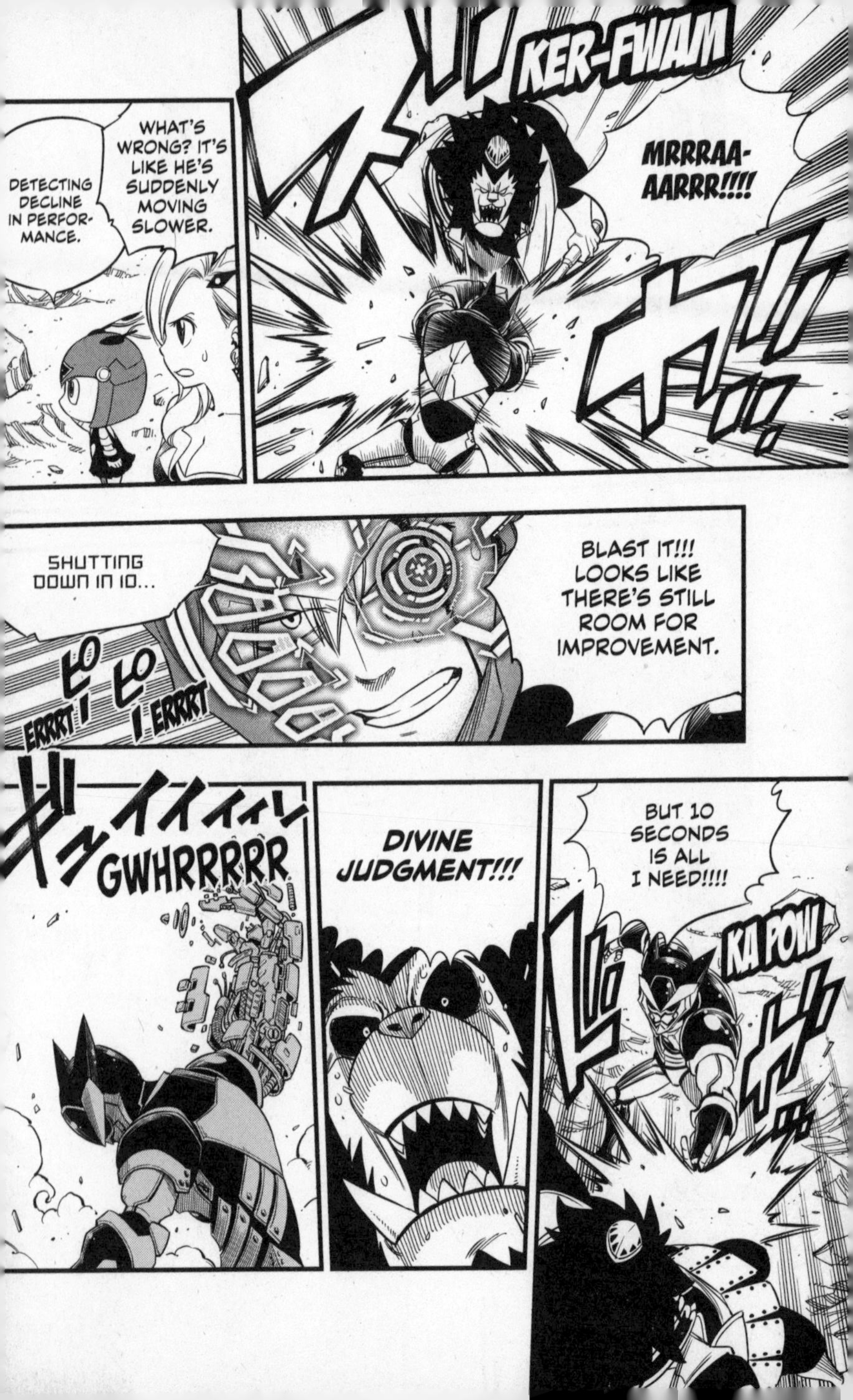
KER-FWAM
MRRRAA-AARRR!!!!
WHAT'S WRONG? IT'S LIKE HE'S SUDDENLY MOVING SLOWER.
DETECTING DECLINE IN PERFORMANCE.
BLAST IT!!! LOOKS LIKE THERE'S STILL ROOM FOR IMPROVEMENT.
SHUTTING DOWN IN 10...
ERRRT
ERRRT
BUT 10 SECONDS IS ALL I NEED!!!!
KA POW
DIVINE JUDGMENT!!!
GWHRRRRR

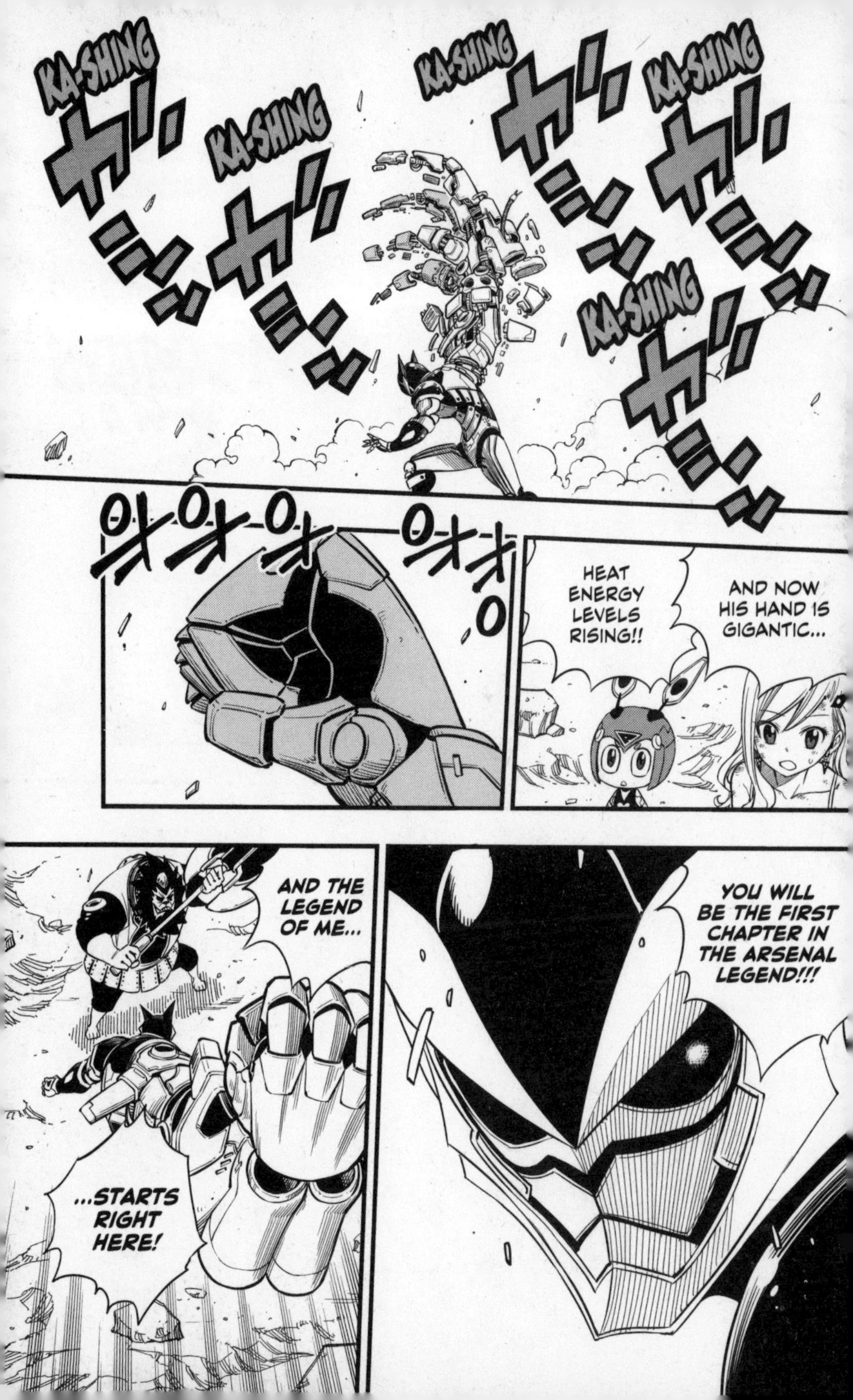
KA-SHING
KA-SHING
KA-SHING
KA-SHING
KA-SHING
AND NOW HIS HAND IS GIGANTIC...
HEAT ENERGY LEVELS RISING!!
YOU WILL BE THE FIRST CHAPTER IN THE ARSENAL LEGEND!!!
AND THE LEGEND OF ME...
...STARTS RIGHT HERE!

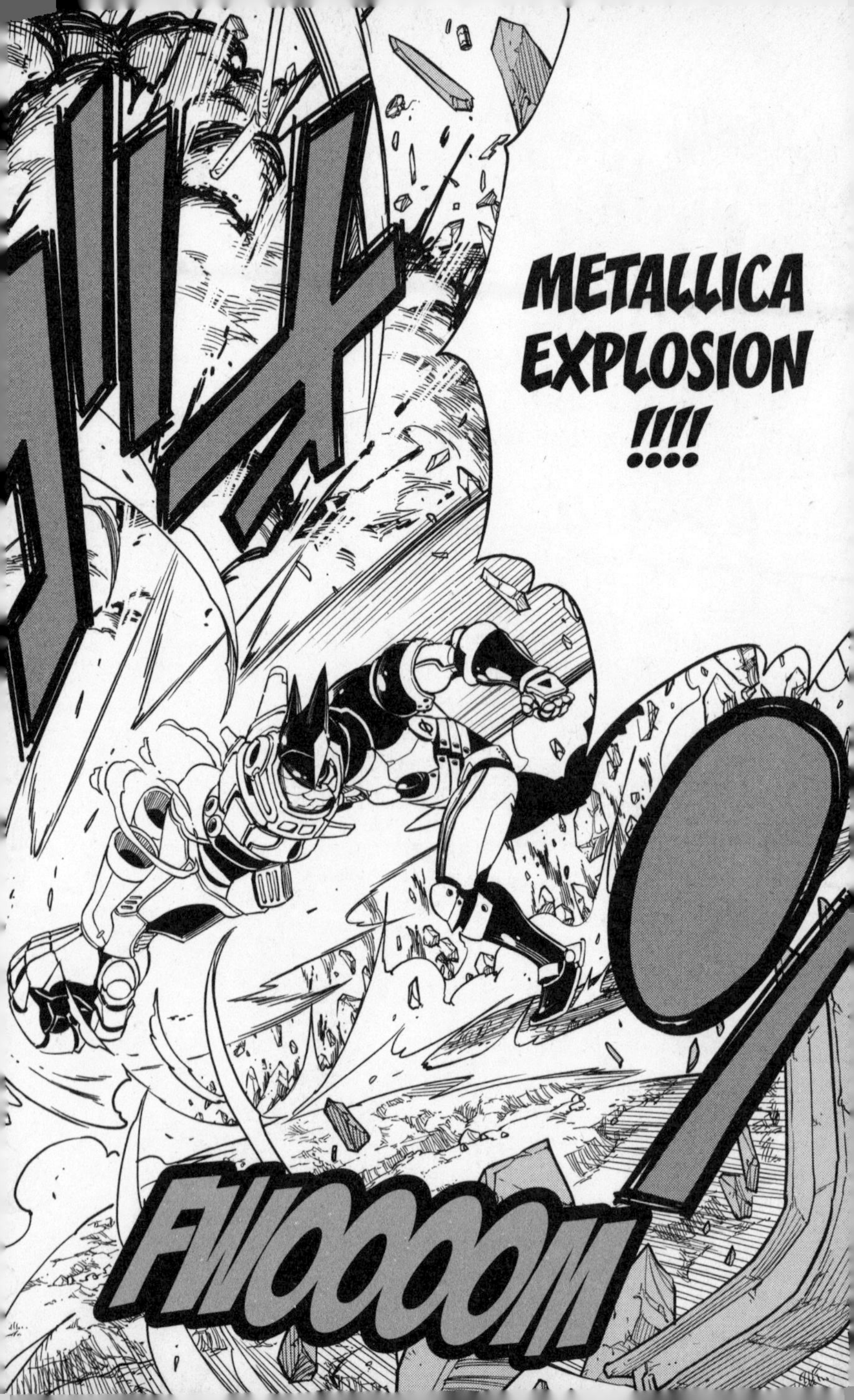
METALLICA EXPLOSION !!!!
FWOOOOM

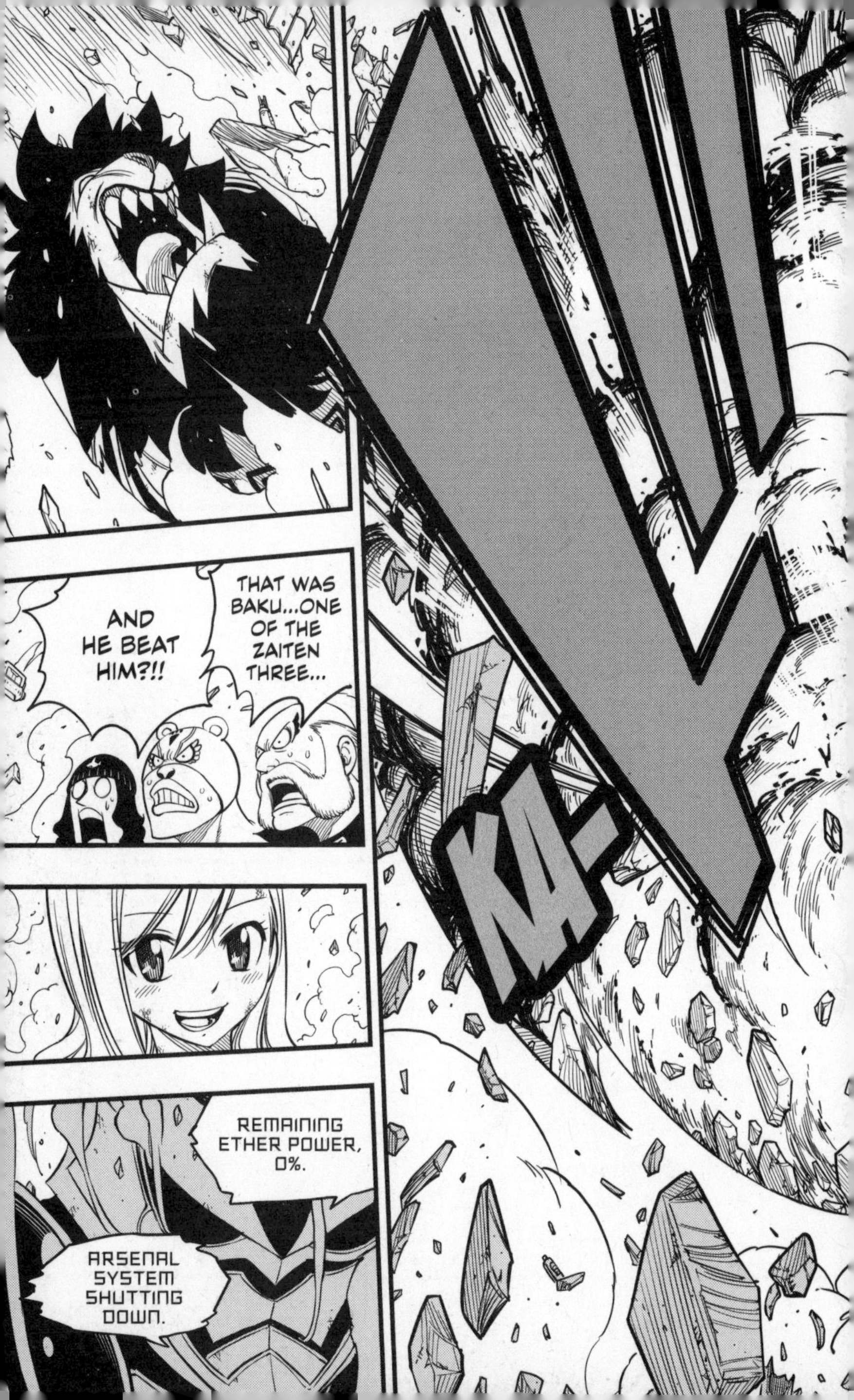
KA-
THAT WAS BAKU...ONE OF THE ZAITEN THREE...
AND HE BEAT HIM?!!
REMAINING ETHER POWER, 0%.
ARSENAL SYSTEM SHUTTING DOWN.

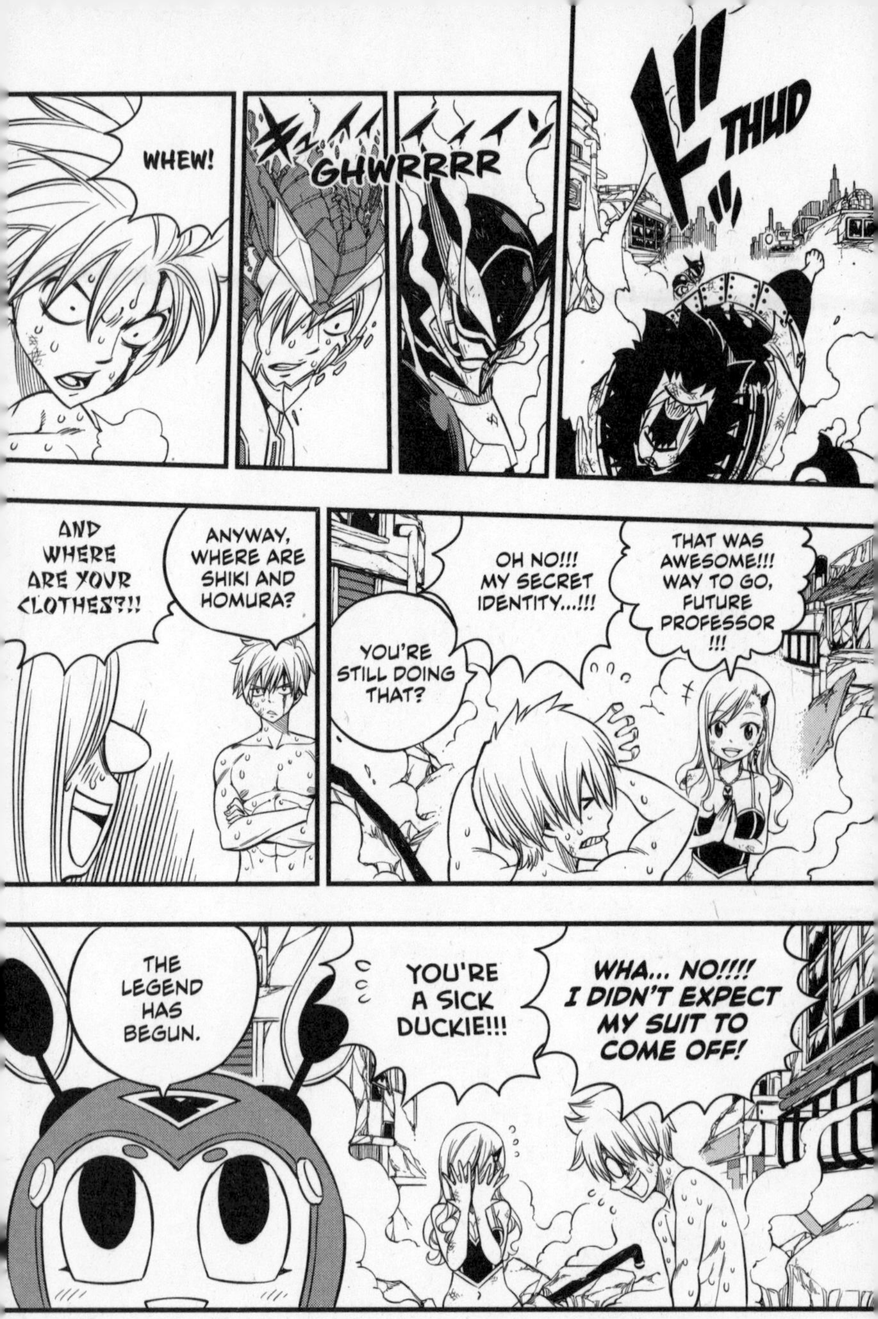
THUD
GHWRRRR
WHEW!
THAT WAS AWESOME!!! WAY TO GO, FUTURE PROFESSOR!!!
OH NO!!! MY SECRET IDENTITY...!!!
YOU'RE STILL DOING THAT?
ANYWAY, WHERE ARE SHIKI AND HOMURA?
AND WHERE ARE YOUR CLOTHES?!!
WHA... NO!!!! I DIDN'T EXPECT MY SUIT TO COME OFF!
YOU'RE A SICK DUCKIE!!!
THE LEGEND HAS BEGUN.

EDENS ZERO

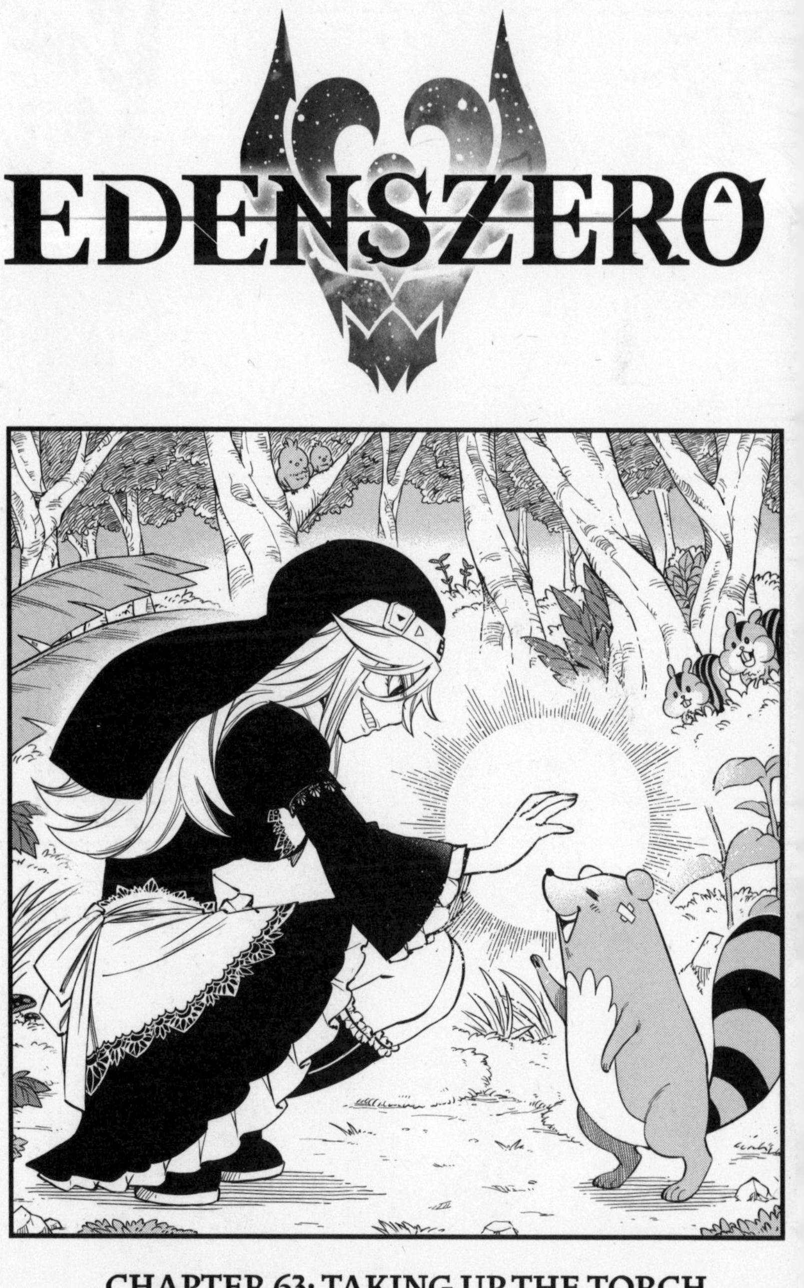

CHAPTER 63: TAKING UP THE TORCH

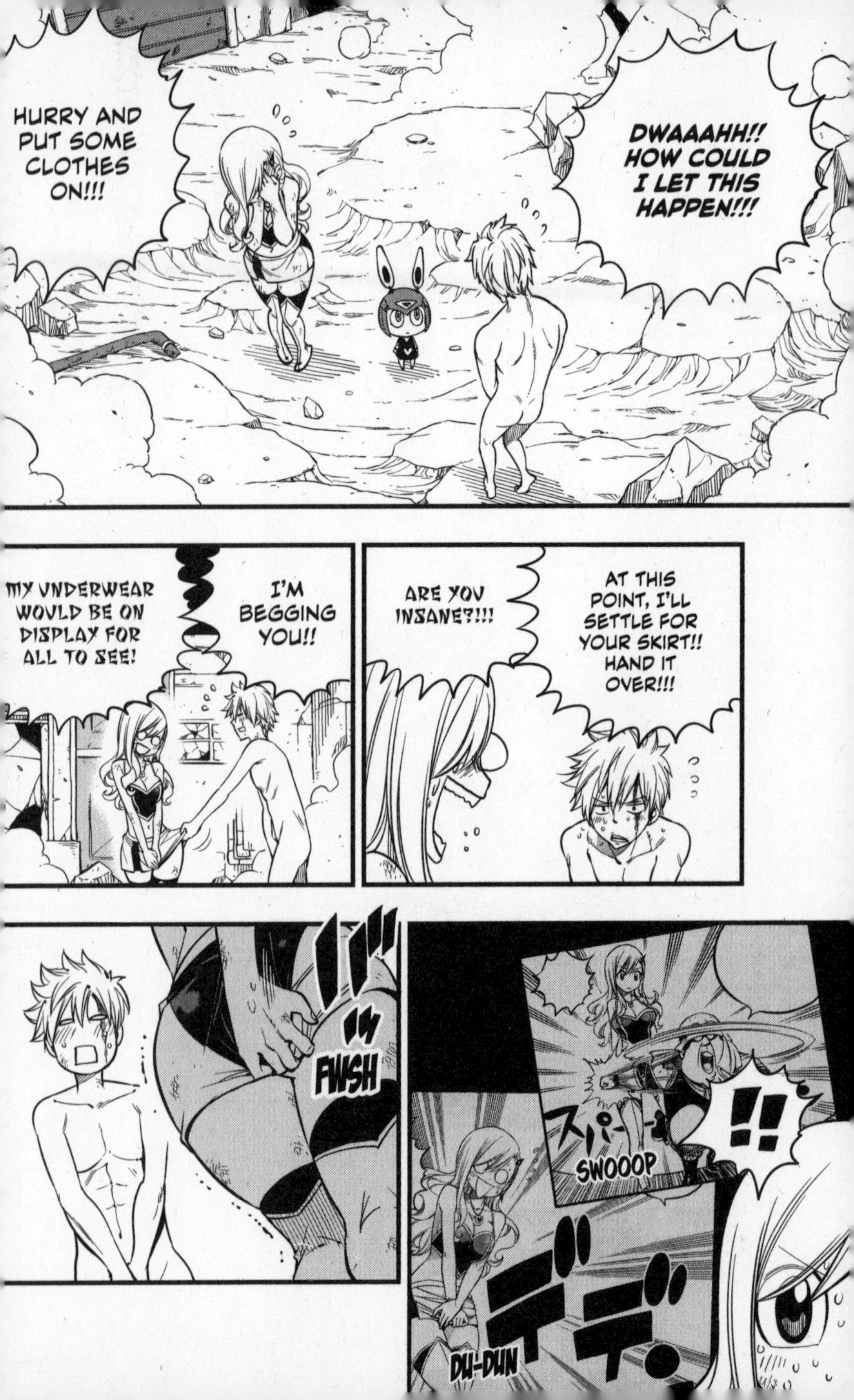
DWAAAHH!! HOW COULD I LET THIS HAPPEN!!!
HURRY AND PUT SOME CLOTHES ON!!!
AT THIS POINT, I'LL SETTLE FOR YOUR SKIRT!! HAND IT OVER!!!
ARE YOU INSANE?!!!
I'M BEGGING YOU!!
MY UNDERWEAR WOULD BE ON DISPLAY FOR ALL TO SEE!
!!
SWOOOP
DU-DUN
FWSH

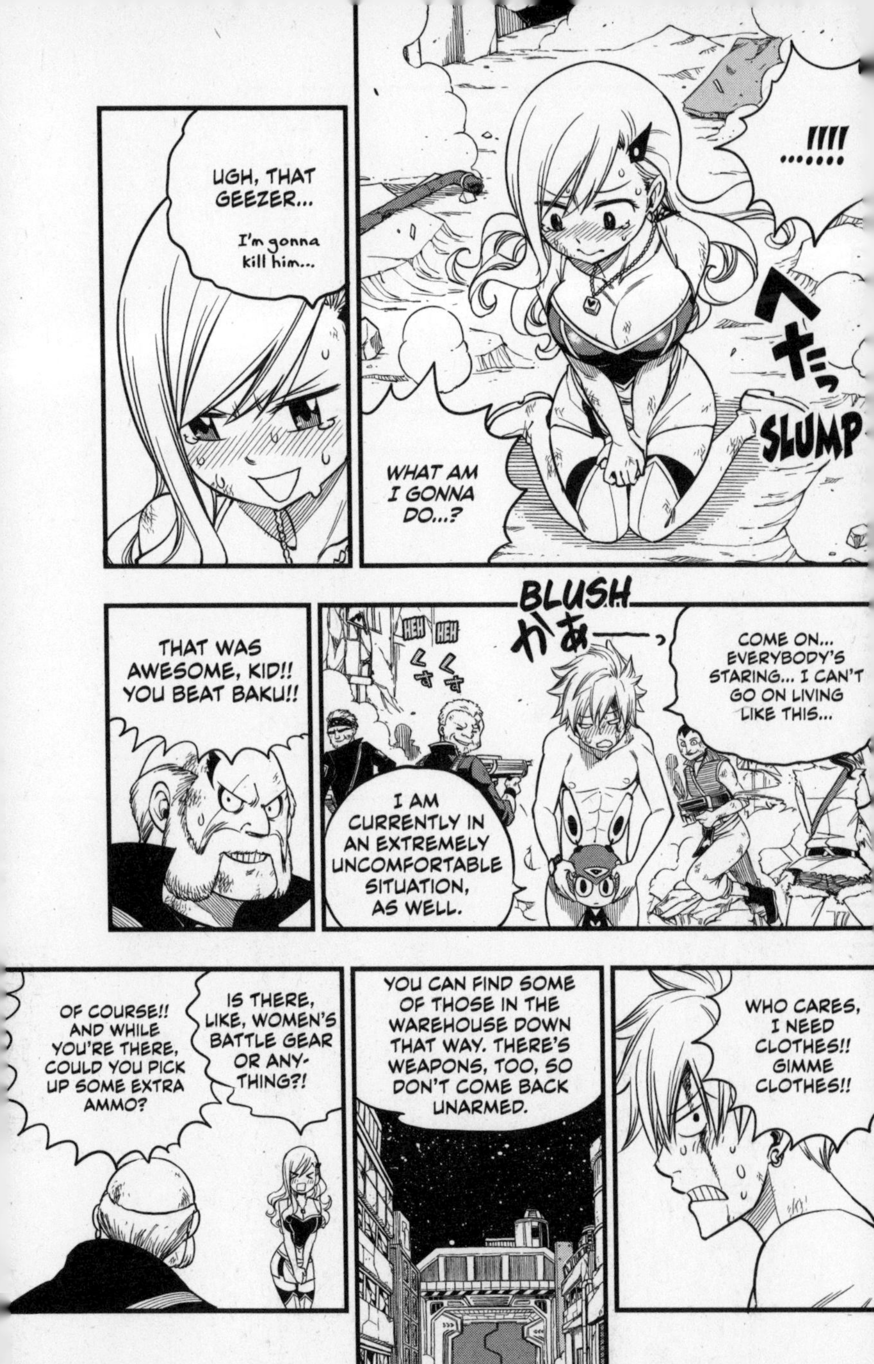
....!!!!
へたっ
SLUMP
WHAT AM I GONNA DO...?
UGH, THAT GEEZER...
I'm gonna kill him...
BLUSH
かあーっ
HEH HEH
くすくす
COME ON... EVERYBODY'S STARING... I CAN'T GO ON LIVING LIKE THIS...
I AM CURRENTLY IN AN EXTREMELY UNCOMFORTABLE SITUATION, AS WELL.
THAT WAS AWESOME, KID!! YOU BEAT BAKU!!
WHO CARES, I NEED CLOTHES!! GIMME CLOTHES!!
YOU CAN FIND SOME OF THOSE IN THE WAREHOUSE DOWN THAT WAY. THERE'S WEAPONS, TOO, SO DON'T COME BACK UNARMED.
IS THERE, LIKE, WOMEN'S BATTLE GEAR OR ANY-THING?!
OF COURSE!! AND WHILE YOU'RE THERE, COULD YOU PICK UP SOME EXTRA AMMO?

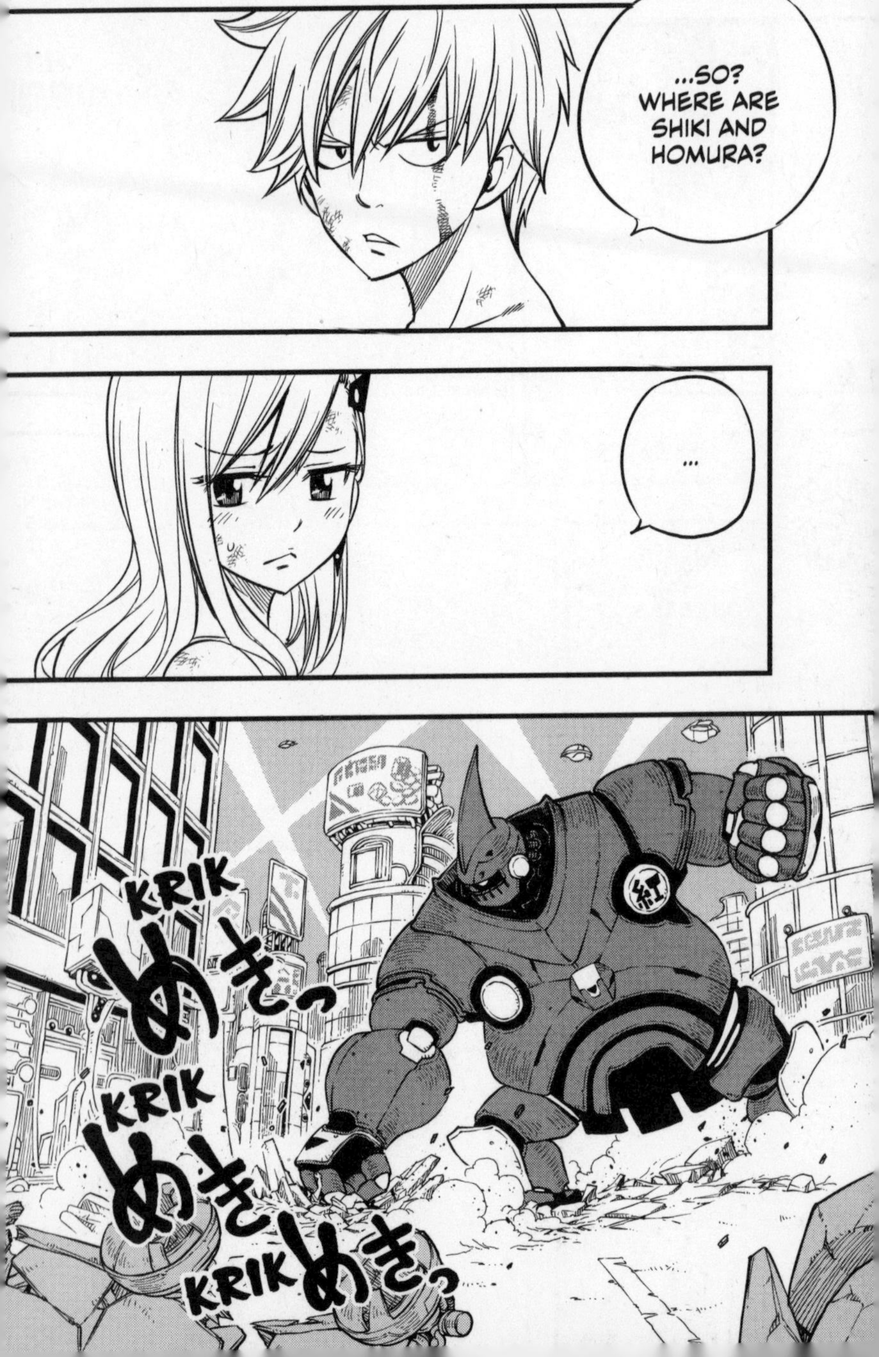
...SO? WHERE ARE SHIKI AND HOMURA?
...
KRIK
めきっ
KRIK
めき
KRIK
めきっ

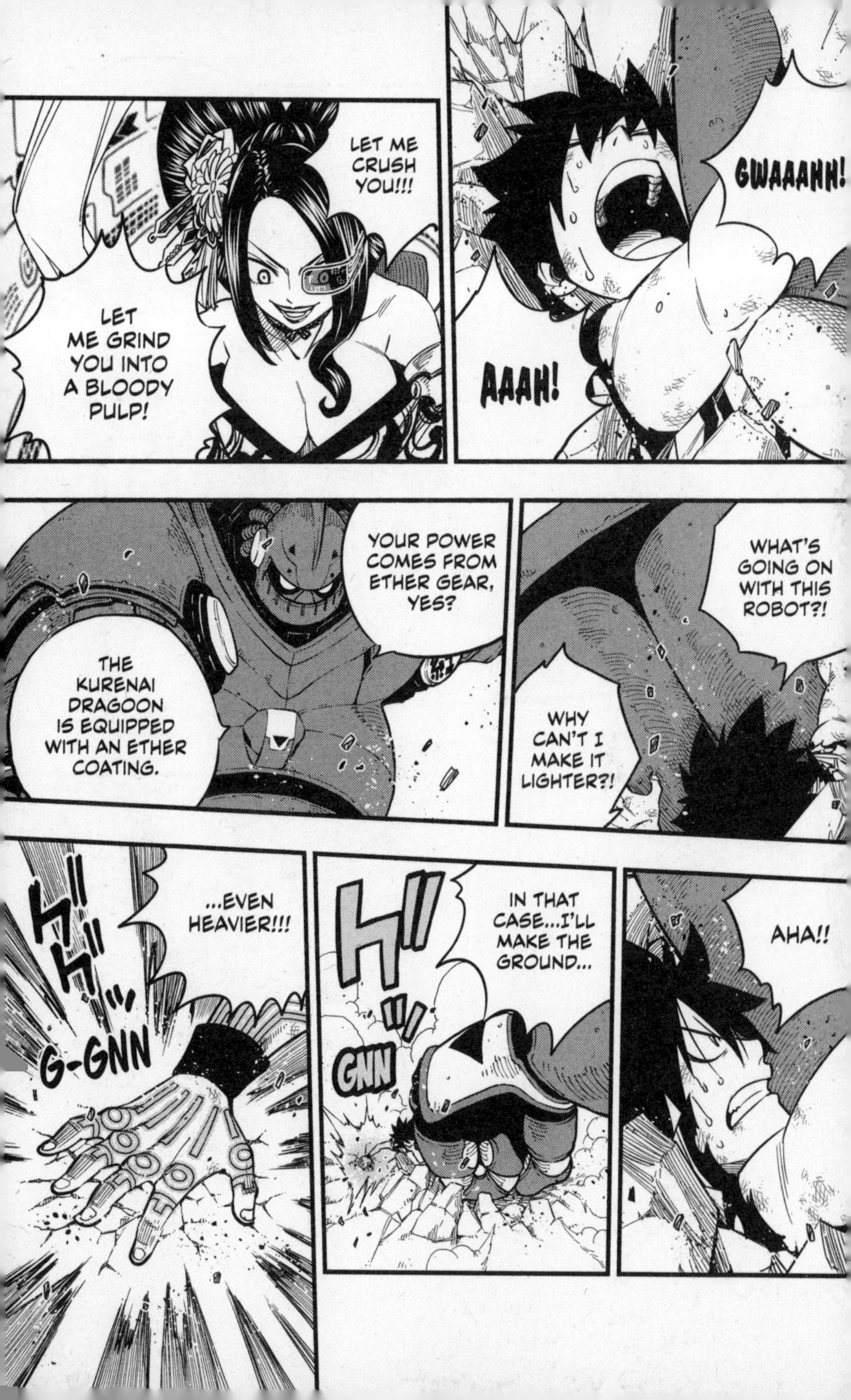
GWAAAHH!
AAAH!
LET ME CRUSH YOU!!!
LET ME GRIND YOU INTO A BLOODY PULP!
WHAT'S GOING ON WITH THIS ROBOT?!
WHY CAN'T I MAKE IT LIGHTER?!
YOUR POWER COMES FROM ETHER GEAR, YES?
THE KURENAI DRAGOON IS EQUIPPED WITH AN ETHER COATING.
AHA!!
IN THAT CASE...I'LL MAKE THE GROUND...
GNN
...EVEN HEAVIER!!!
G-GNN

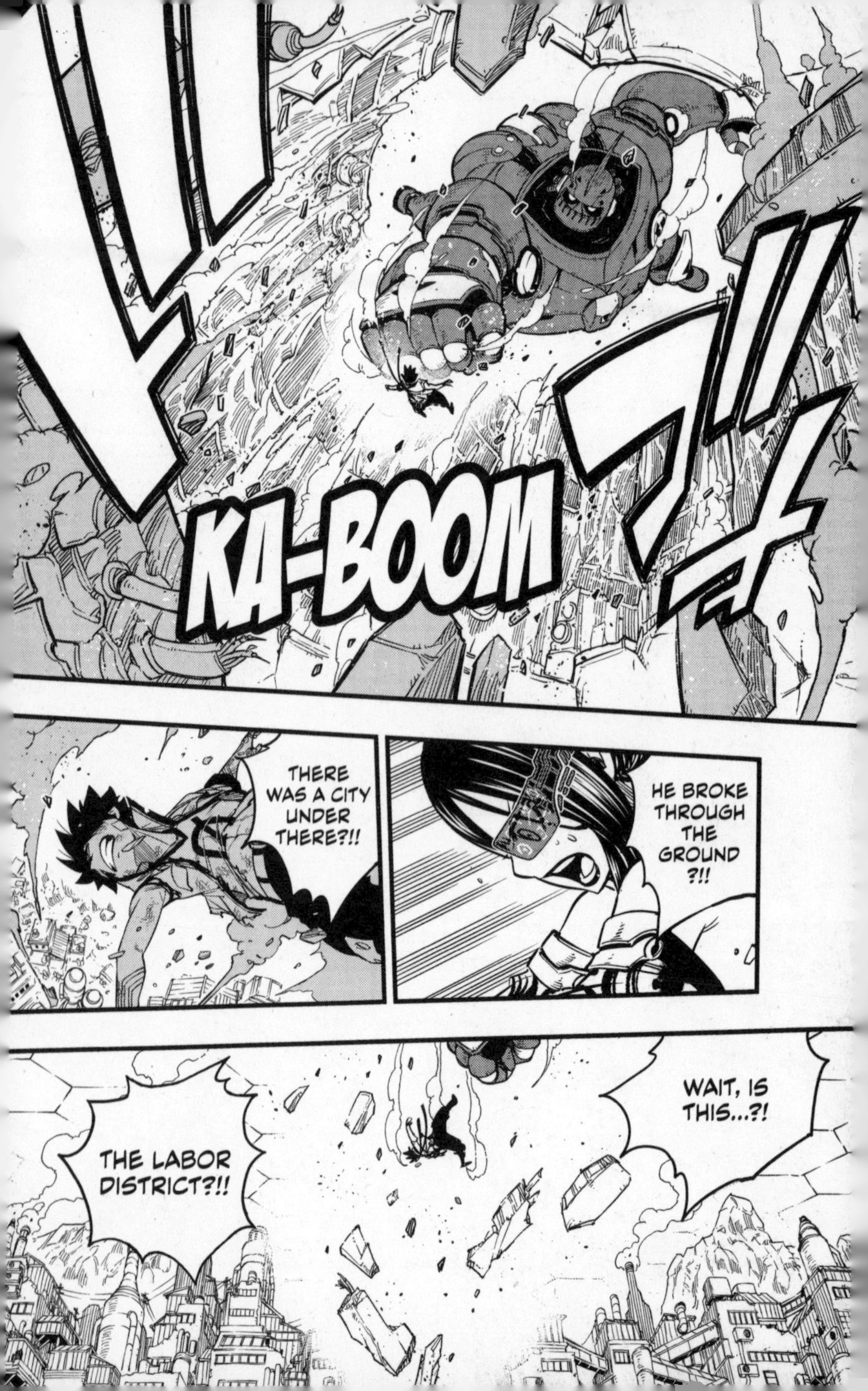
KA-BOOM
HE BROKE THROUGH THE GROUND ?!!
THERE WAS A CITY UNDER THERE?!!
WAIT, IS THIS...?!
THE LABOR DISTRICT?!!

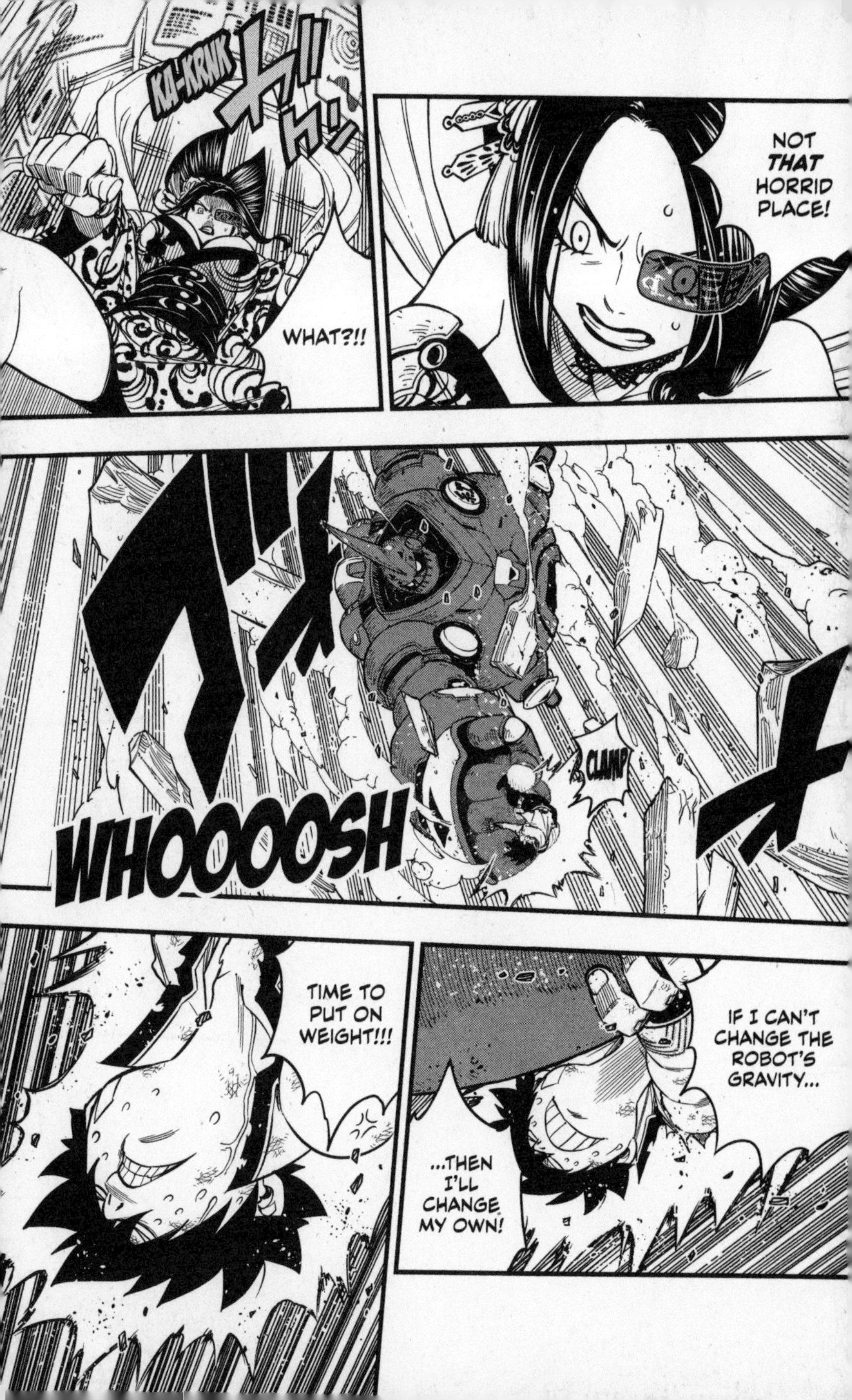
NOT *THAT* HORRID PLACE!
KA-KRNK
WHAT?!!
CLAMP
WHOOOOSH
IF I CAN'T CHANGE THE ROBOT'S GRAVITY...
...THEN I'LL CHANGE MY OWN!
TIME TO PUT ON WEIGHT!!!

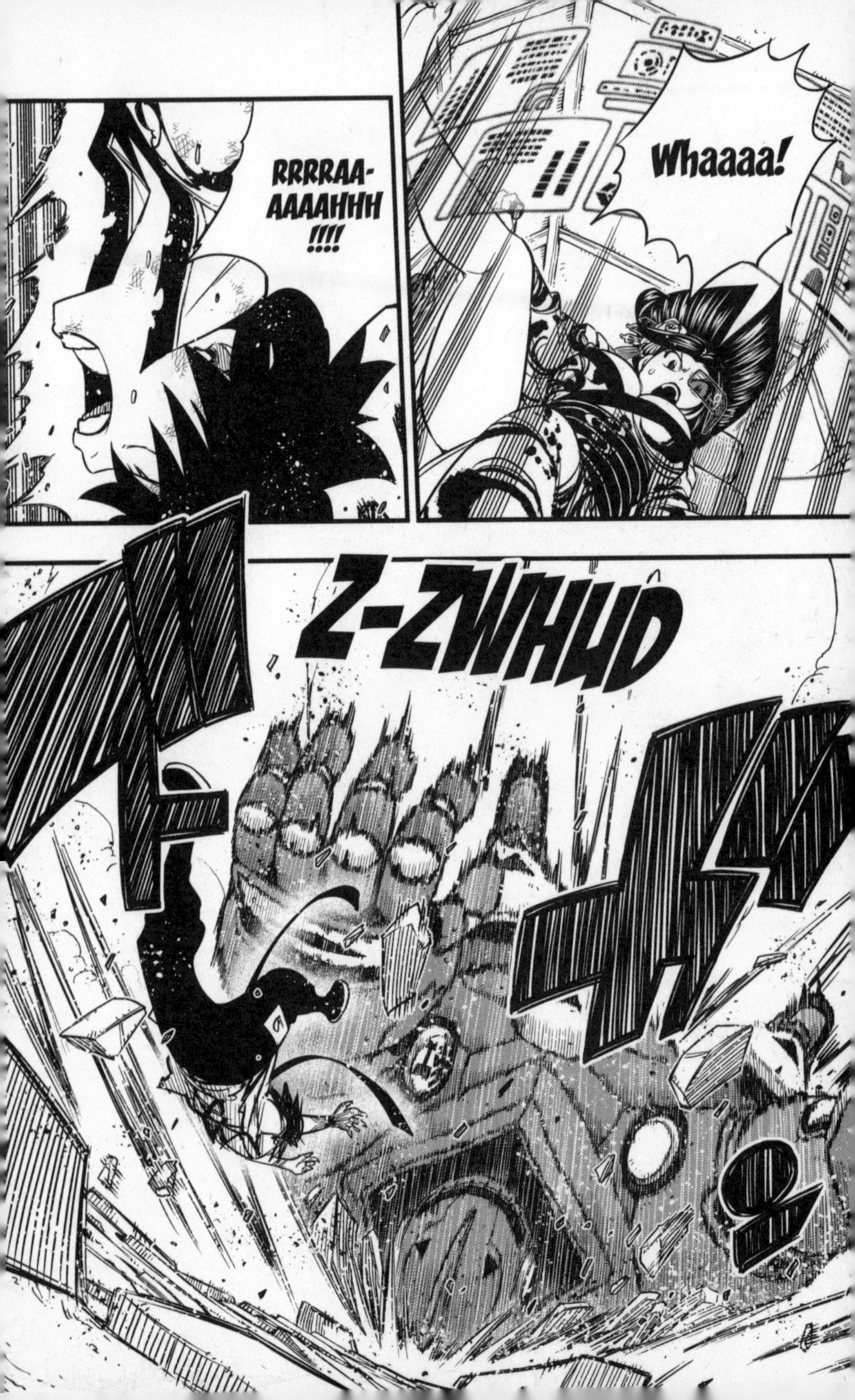
Whaaaa!
RRRRAA-AAAAHHH!!!!
Z-ZWHUD

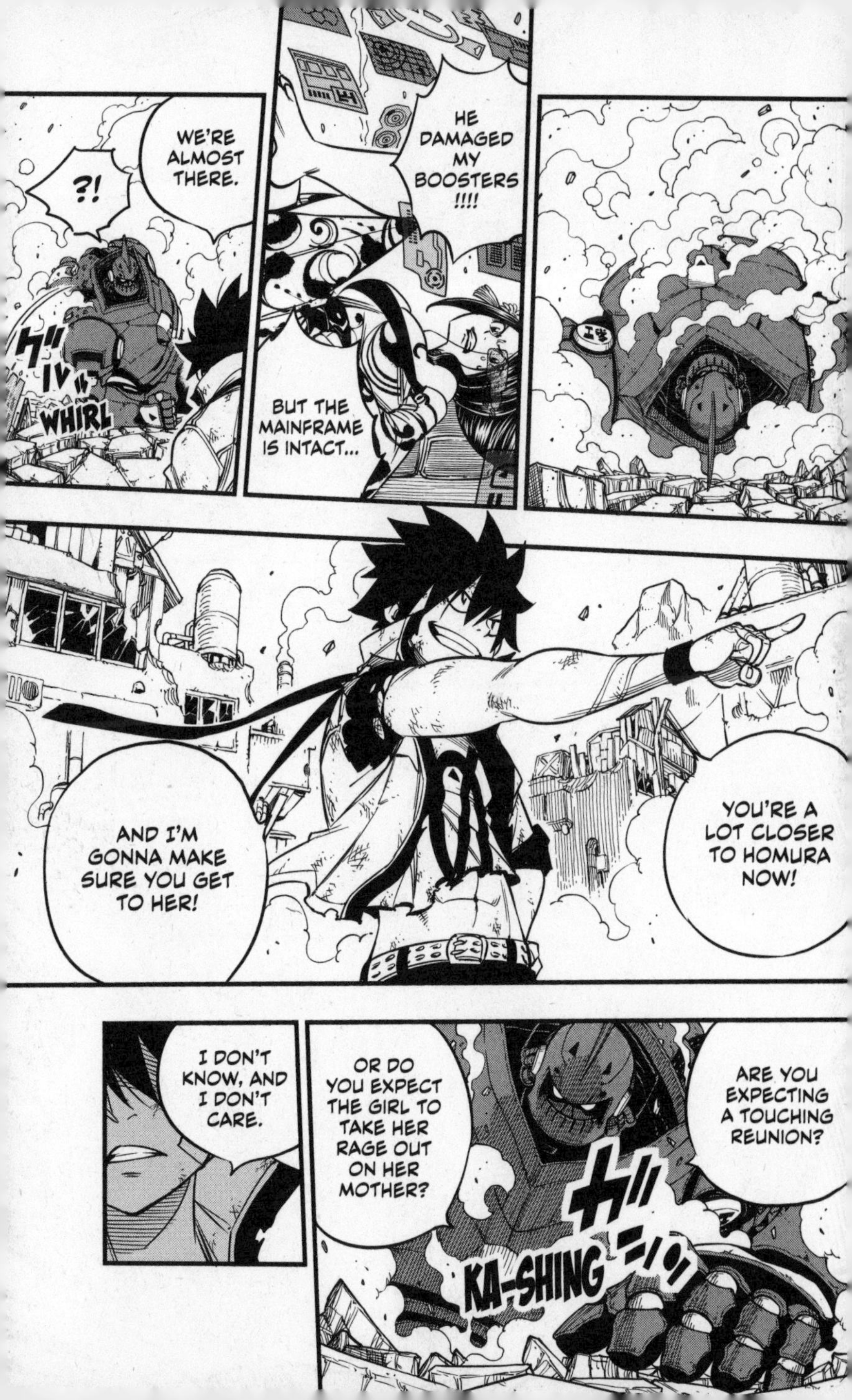
HE DAMAGED MY BOOSTERS !!!!
BUT THE MAINFRAME IS INTACT...
WE'RE ALMOST THERE.
?!
WHIRL
YOU'RE A LOT CLOSER TO HOMURA NOW!
AND I'M GONNA MAKE SURE YOU GET TO HER!
ARE YOU EXPECTING A TOUCHING REUNION?
OR DO YOU EXPECT THE GIRL TO TAKE HER RAGE OUT ON HER MOTHER?
KA-SHING
I DON'T KNOW, AND I DON'T CARE.

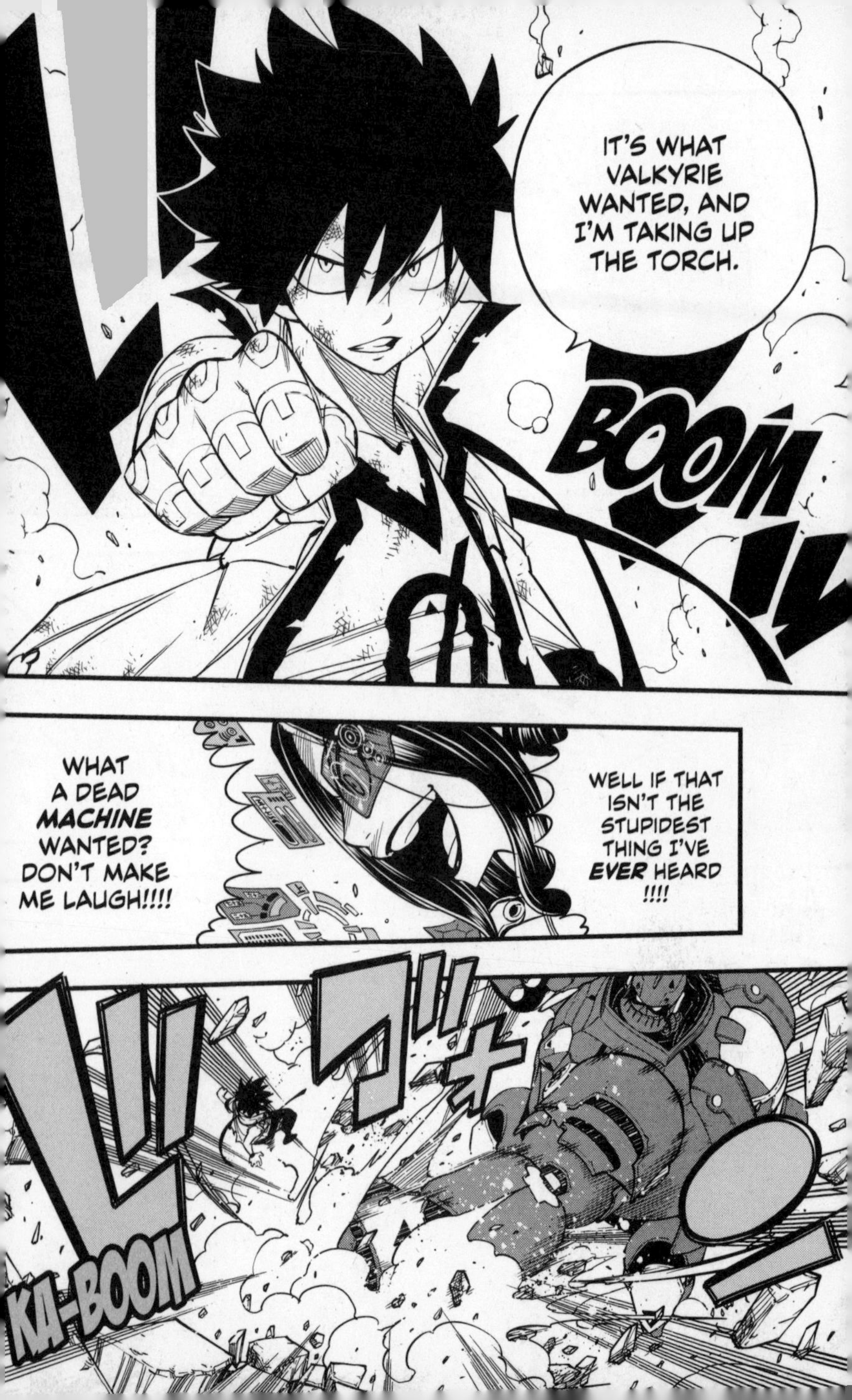
IT'S WHAT VALKYRIE WANTED, AND I'M TAKING UP THE TORCH.
BOOM
WELL IF THAT ISN'T THE STUPIDEST THING I'VE EVER HEARD !!!!
WHAT A DEAD MACHINE WANTED? DON'T MAKE ME LAUGH!!!!
KA-BOOM

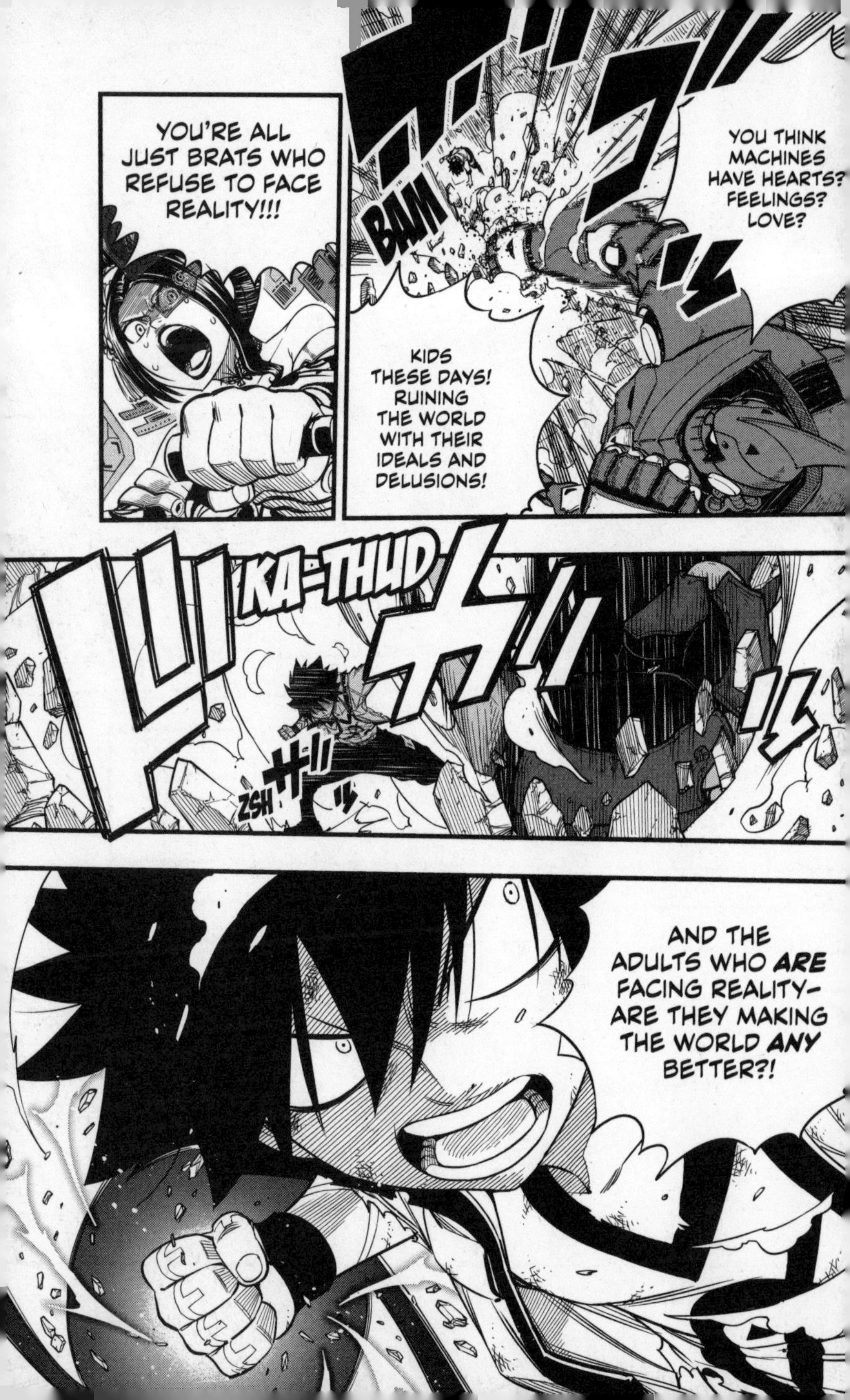
YOU THINK MACHINES HAVE HEARTS? FEELINGS? LOVE?
BAM
KIDS THESE DAYS! RUINING THE WORLD WITH THEIR IDEALS AND DELUSIONS!
YOU'RE ALL JUST BRATS WHO REFUSE TO FACE REALITY!!!
KA-THUD
ZSH
AND THE ADULTS WHO **ARE** FACING REALITY- ARE THEY MAKING THE WORLD **ANY** BETTER?!

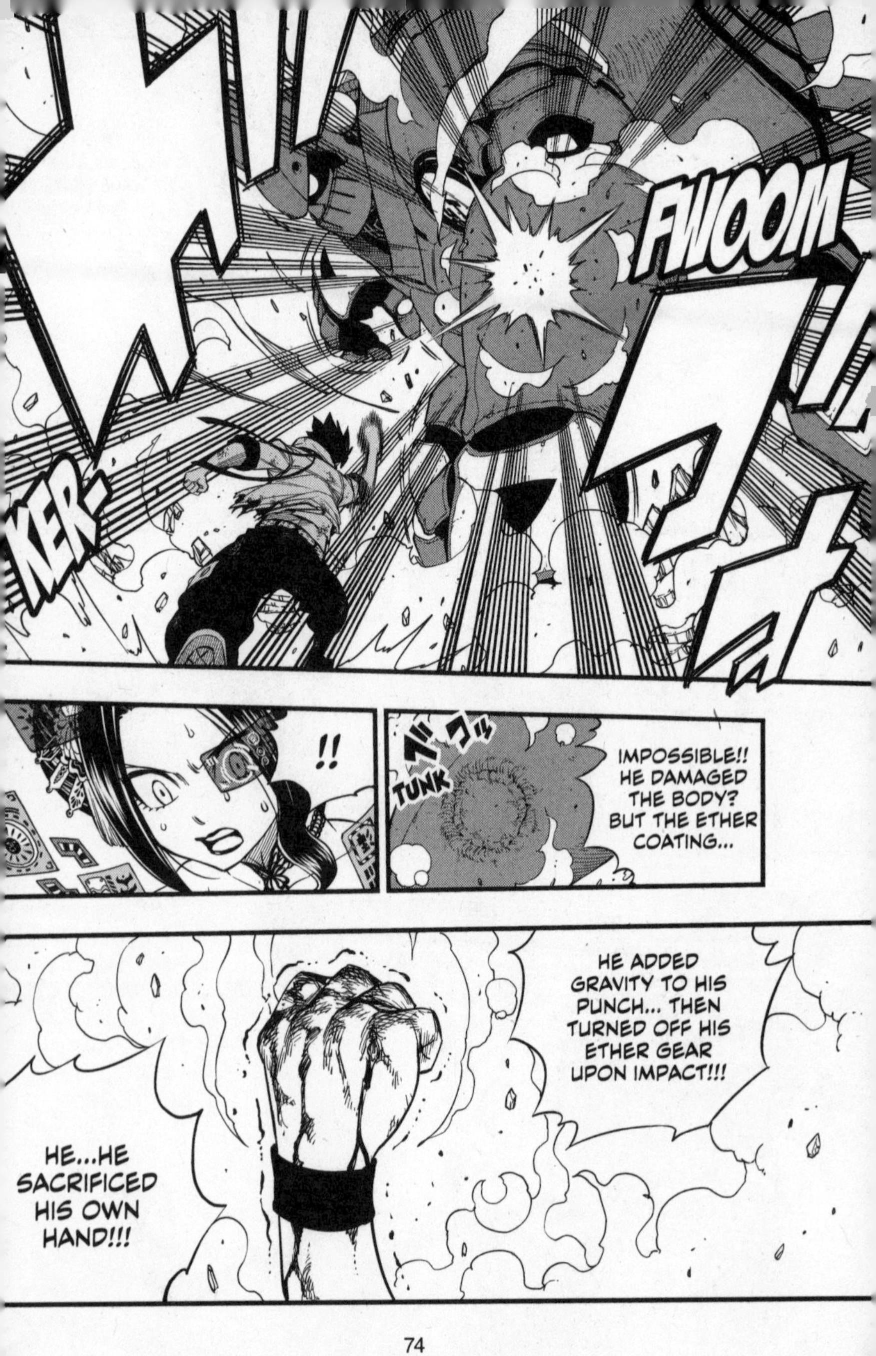
FWOOM
KER-
TUNK
IMPOSSIBLE!! HE DAMAGED THE BODY? BUT THE ETHER COATING...
!!
HE ADDED GRAVITY TO HIS PUNCH... THEN TURNED OFF HIS ETHER GEAR UPON IMPACT!!!
HE...HE SACRIFICED HIS OWN HAND!!!

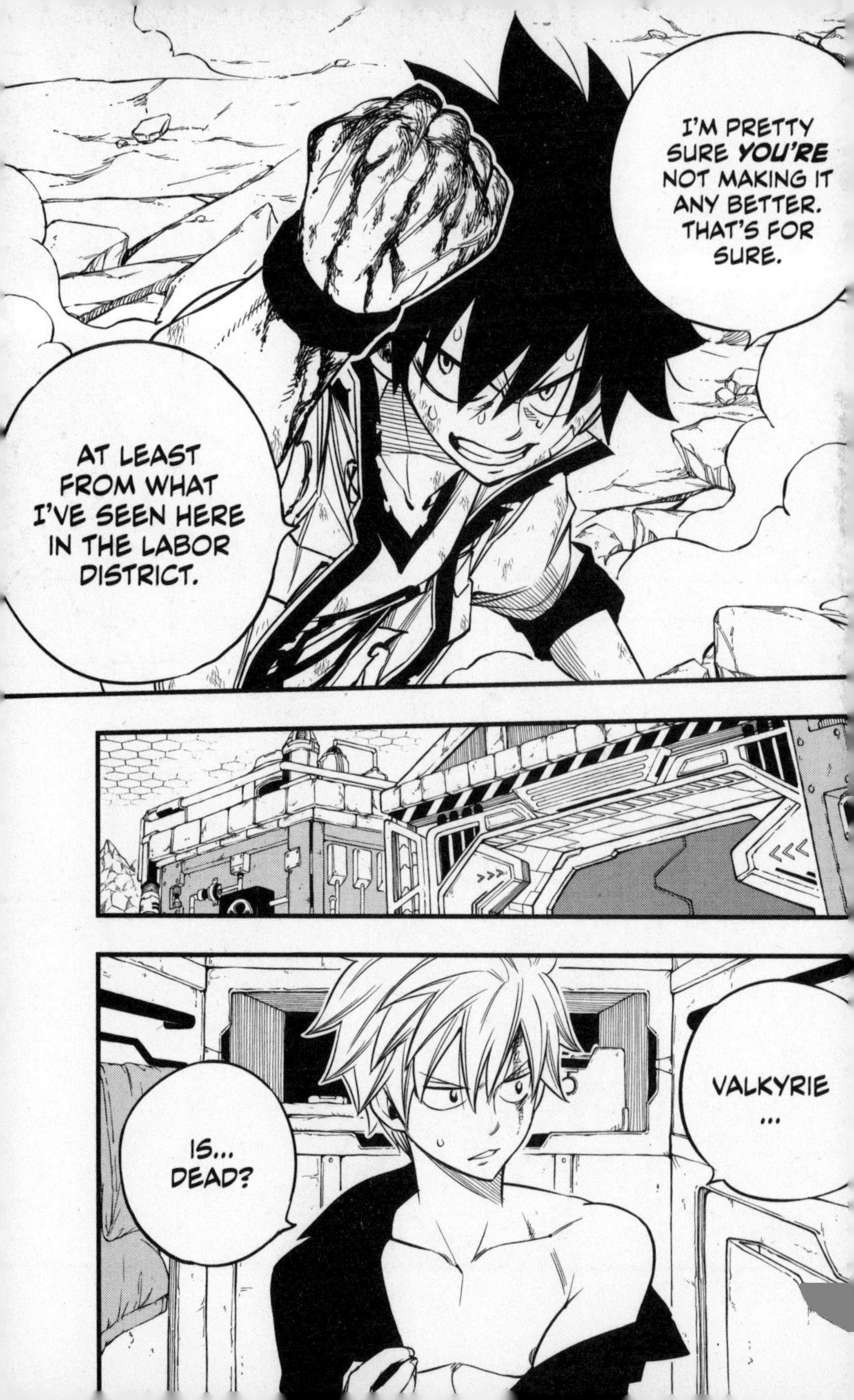
I'M PRETTY SURE ***YOU'RE*** NOT MAKING IT ANY BETTER. THAT'S FOR SURE.
AT LEAST FROM WHAT I'VE SEEN HERE IN THE LABOR DISTRICT.
VALKYRIE ...
IS... DEAD?

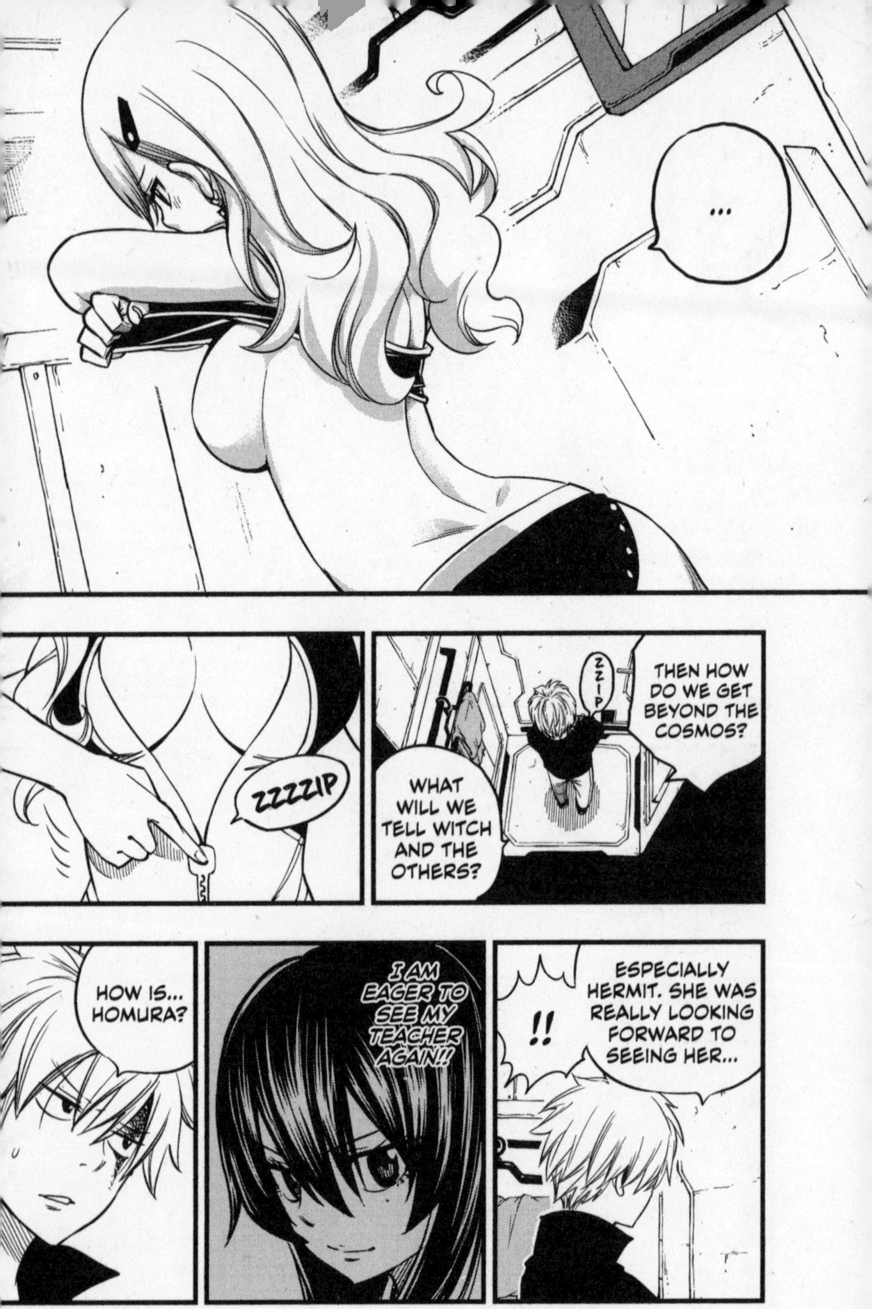
...
ZZIP
THEN HOW DO WE GET BEYOND THE COSMOS?
WHAT WILL WE TELL WITCH AND THE OTHERS?
ZZZZIP
ESPECIALLY HERMIT. SHE WAS REALLY LOOKING FORWARD TO SEEING HER...
!!
I AM EAGER TO SEE MY TEACHER AGAIN!!
HOW IS... HOMURA?

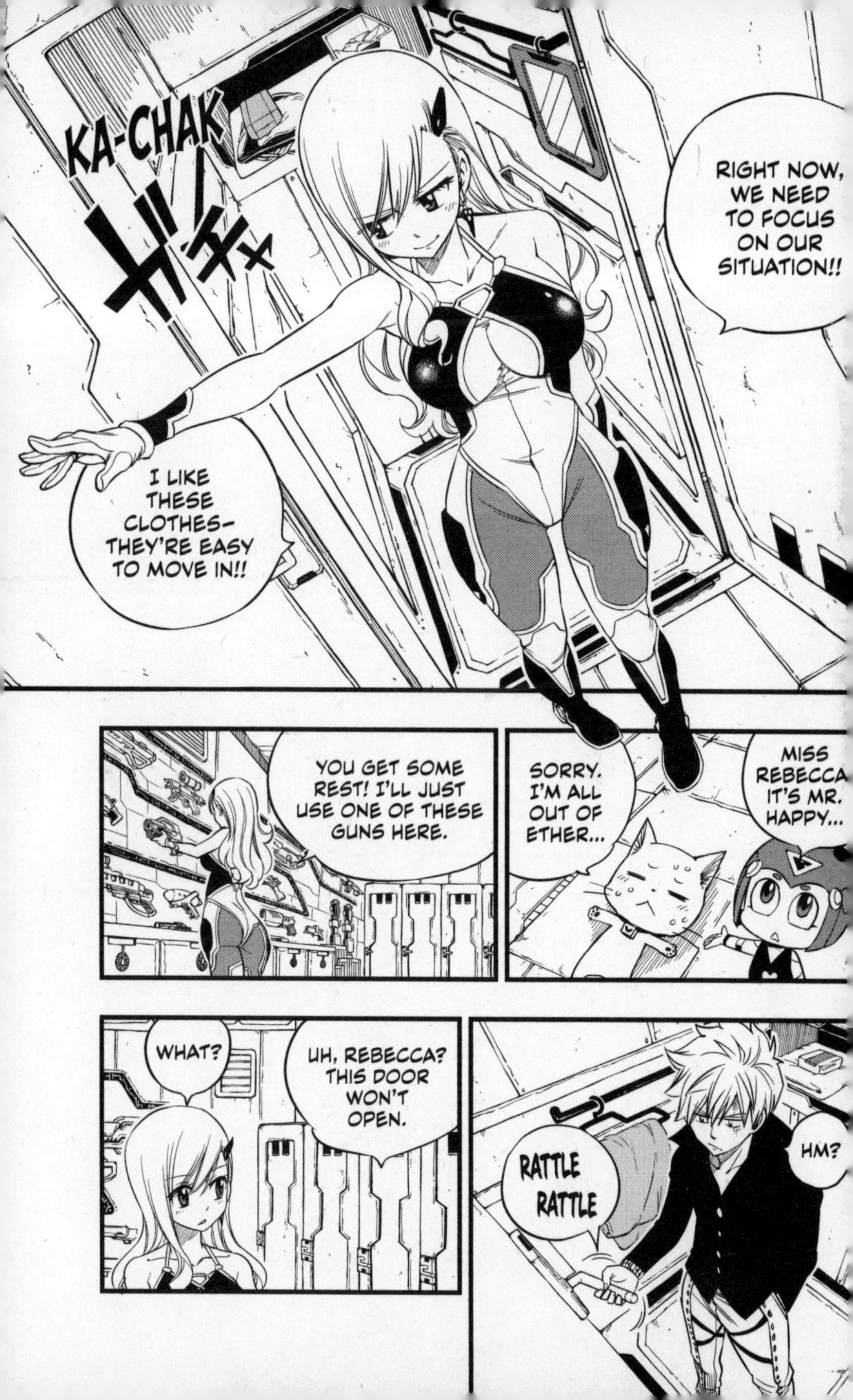

RIGHT NOW, WE NEED TO FOCUS ON OUR SITUATION!!
KA-CHAK
I LIKE THESE CLOTHES—THEY'RE EASY TO MOVE IN!!
MISS REBECCA IT'S MR. HAPPY...
SORRY. I'M ALL OUT OF ETHER...
YOU GET SOME REST! I'LL JUST USE ONE OF THESE GUNS HERE.
HM?
RATTLE RATTLE
UH, REBECCA? THIS DOOR WON'T OPEN.
WHAT?

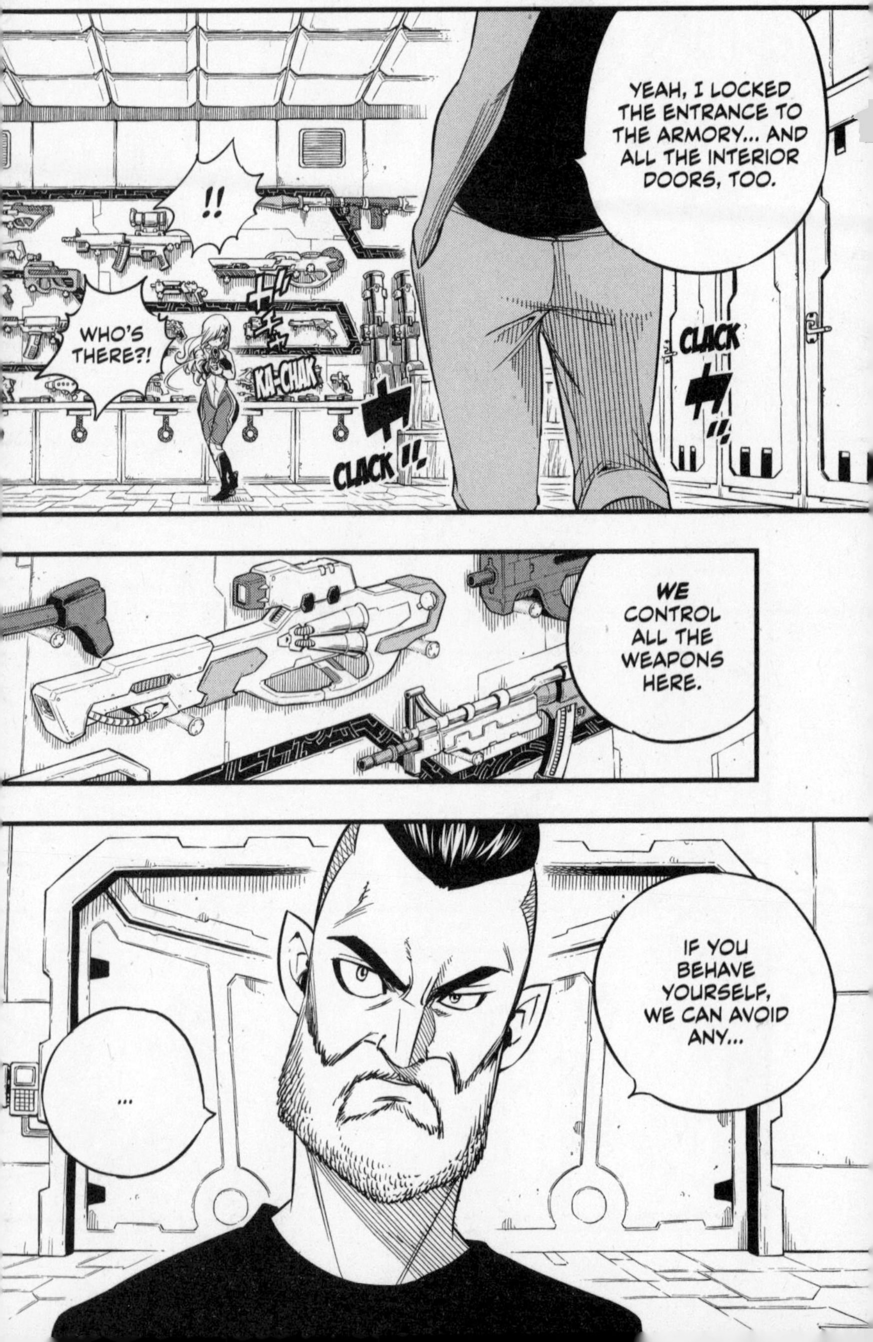
YEAH, I LOCKED THE ENTRANCE TO THE ARMORY... AND ALL THE INTERIOR DOORS, TOO.
CLACK!!
!!
KA-CHAK
CLACK!!
WHO'S THERE?!
WE CONTROL ALL THE WEAPONS HERE.
IF YOU BEHAVE YOURSELF, WE CAN AVOID ANY...
...

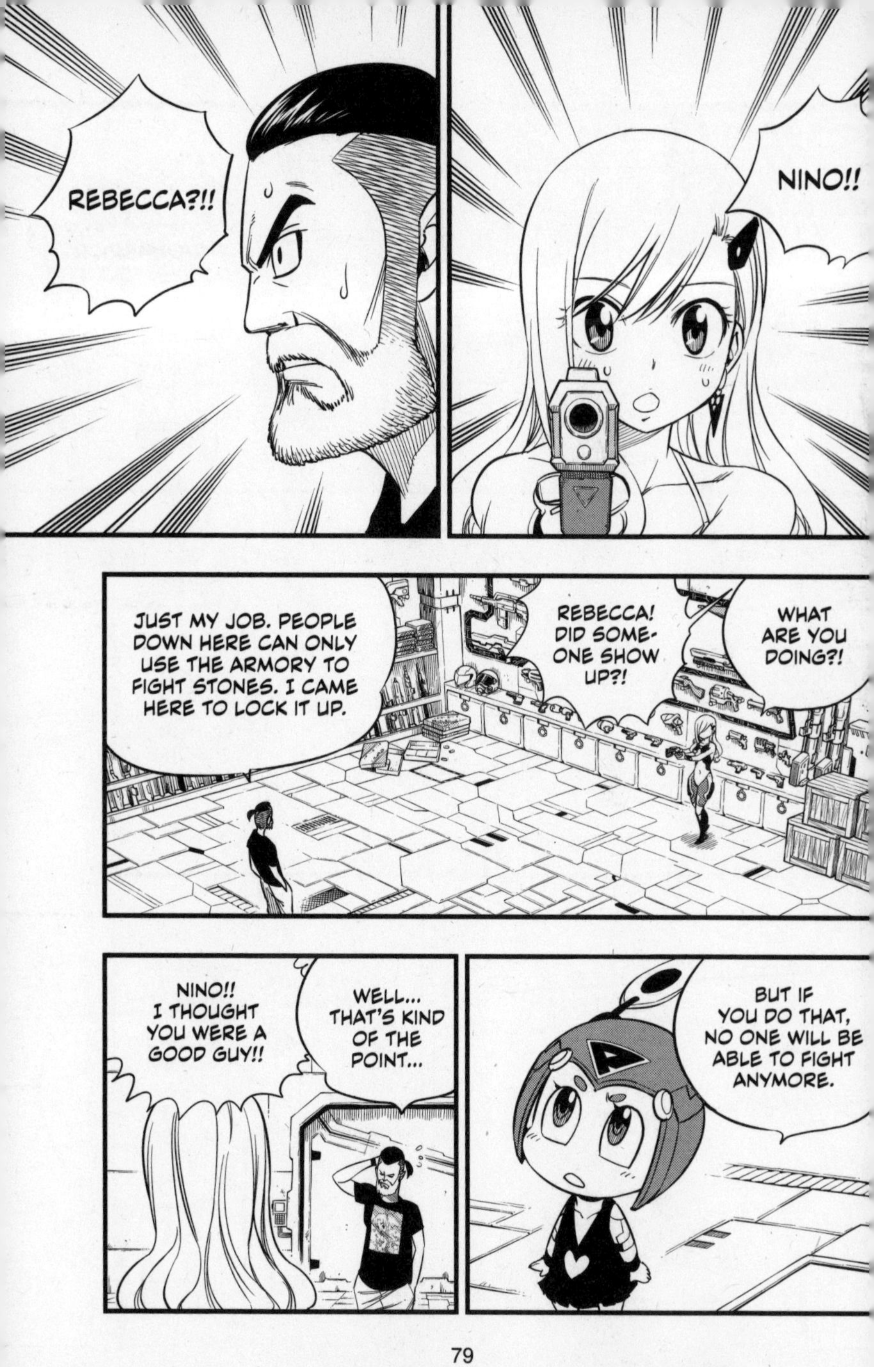
NINO!!
REBECCA?!!
WHAT ARE YOU DOING?!
REBECCA! DID SOME-ONE SHOW UP?!
JUST MY JOB. PEOPLE DOWN HERE CAN ONLY USE THE ARMORY TO FIGHT STONES. I CAME HERE TO LOCK IT UP.
BUT IF YOU DO THAT, NO ONE WILL BE ABLE TO FIGHT ANYMORE.
WELL... THAT'S KIND OF THE POINT...
NINO!! I THOUGHT YOU WERE A GOOD GUY!!

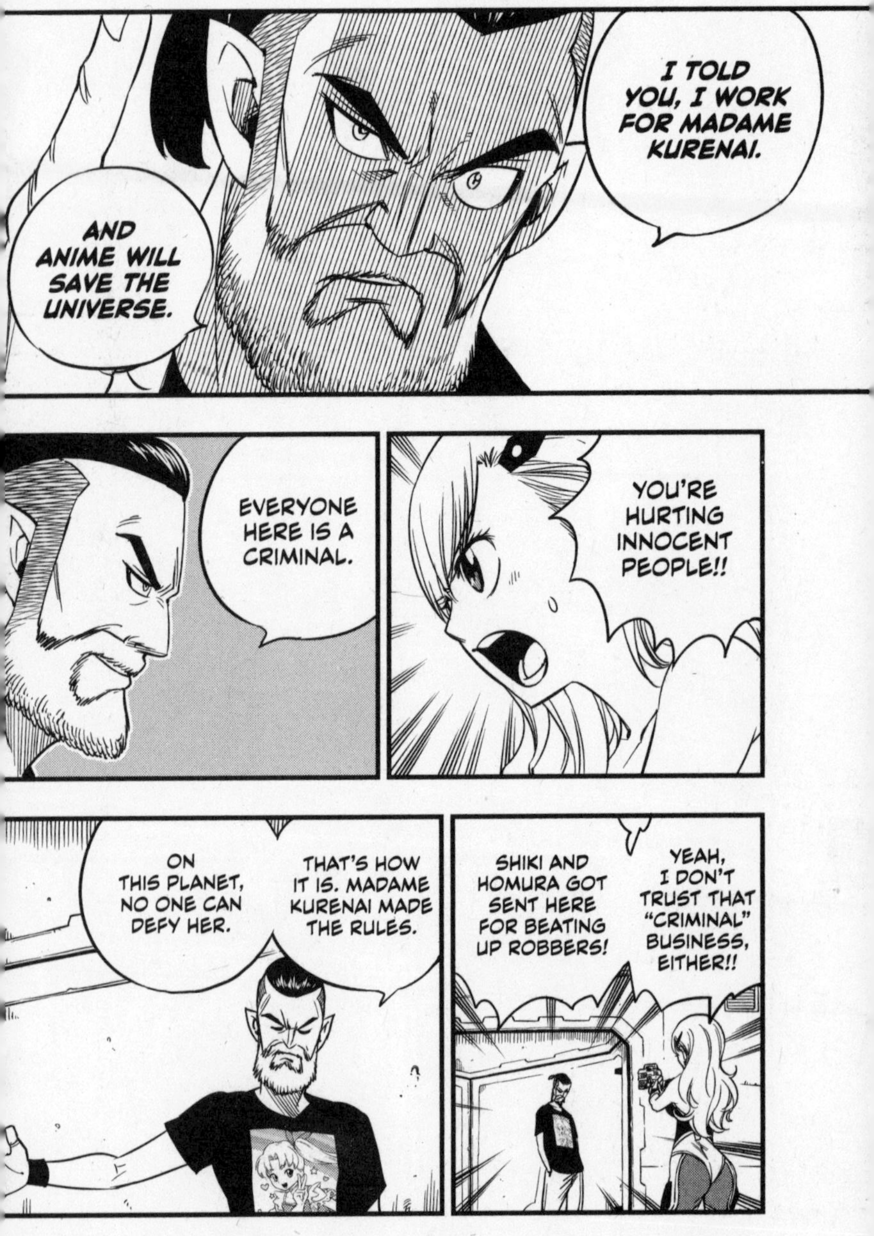
I TOLD YOU, I WORK FOR MADAME KURENAI.
AND ANIME WILL SAVE THE UNIVERSE.
YOU'RE HURTING INNOCENT PEOPLE!!
EVERYONE HERE IS A CRIMINAL.
YEAH, I DON'T TRUST THAT "CRIMINAL" BUSINESS, EITHER!!
SHIKI AND HOMURA GOT SENT HERE FOR BEATING UP ROBBERS!
THAT'S HOW IT IS. MADAME KURENAI MADE THE RULES.
ON THIS PLANET, NO ONE CAN DEFY HER.

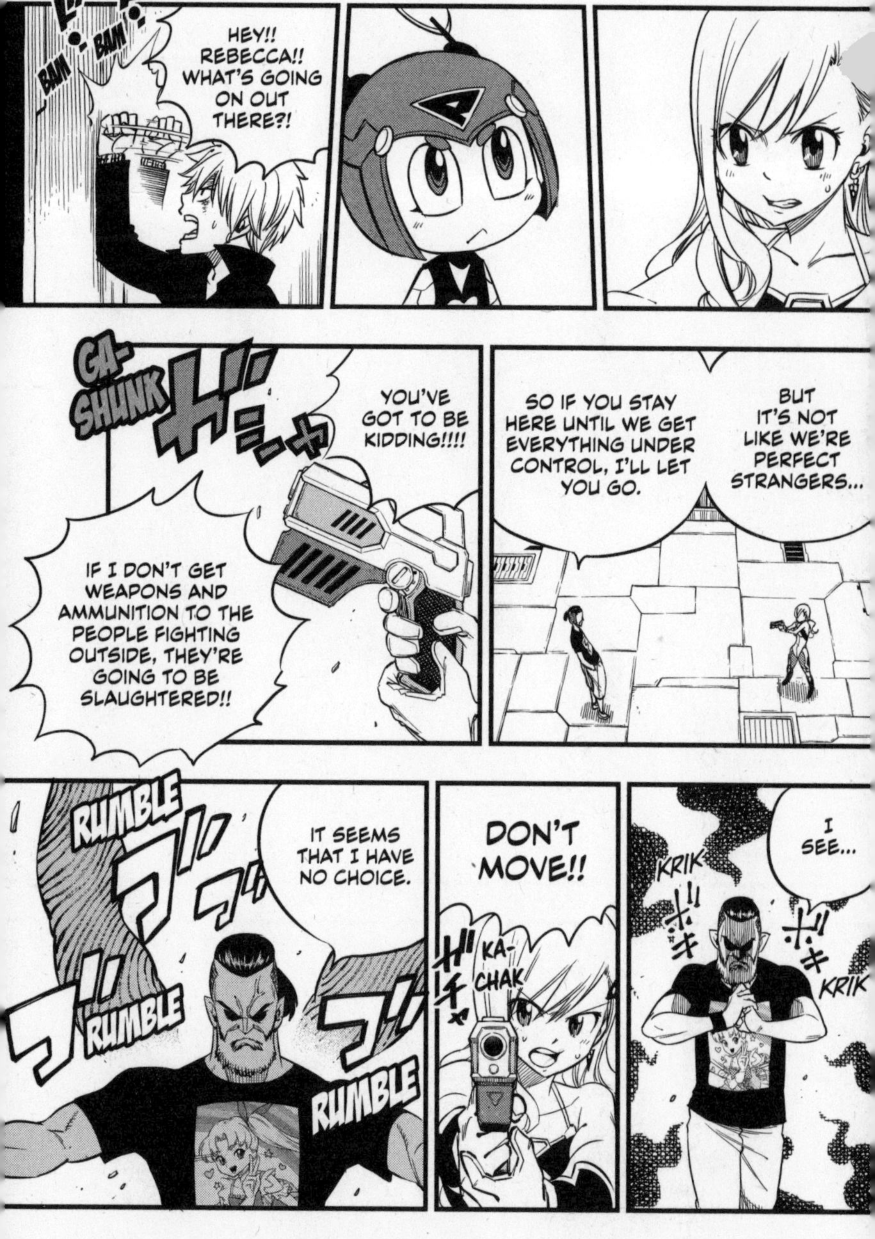
BAM BAM
HEY!! REBECCA!! WHAT'S GOING ON OUT THERE?!
BUT IT'S NOT LIKE WE'RE PERFECT STRANGERS...
SO IF YOU STAY HERE UNTIL WE GET EVERYTHING UNDER CONTROL, I'LL LET YOU GO.
YOU'VE GOT TO BE KIDDING!!!!
GA-SHUNK
IF I DON'T GET WEAPONS AND AMMUNITION TO THE PEOPLE FIGHTING OUTSIDE, THEY'RE GOING TO BE SLAUGHTERED!!
I SEE...
KRIK
KRIK
DON'T MOVE!!
KA-CHAK
IT SEEMS THAT I HAVE NO CHOICE.
RUMBLE
RUMBLE
RUMBLE

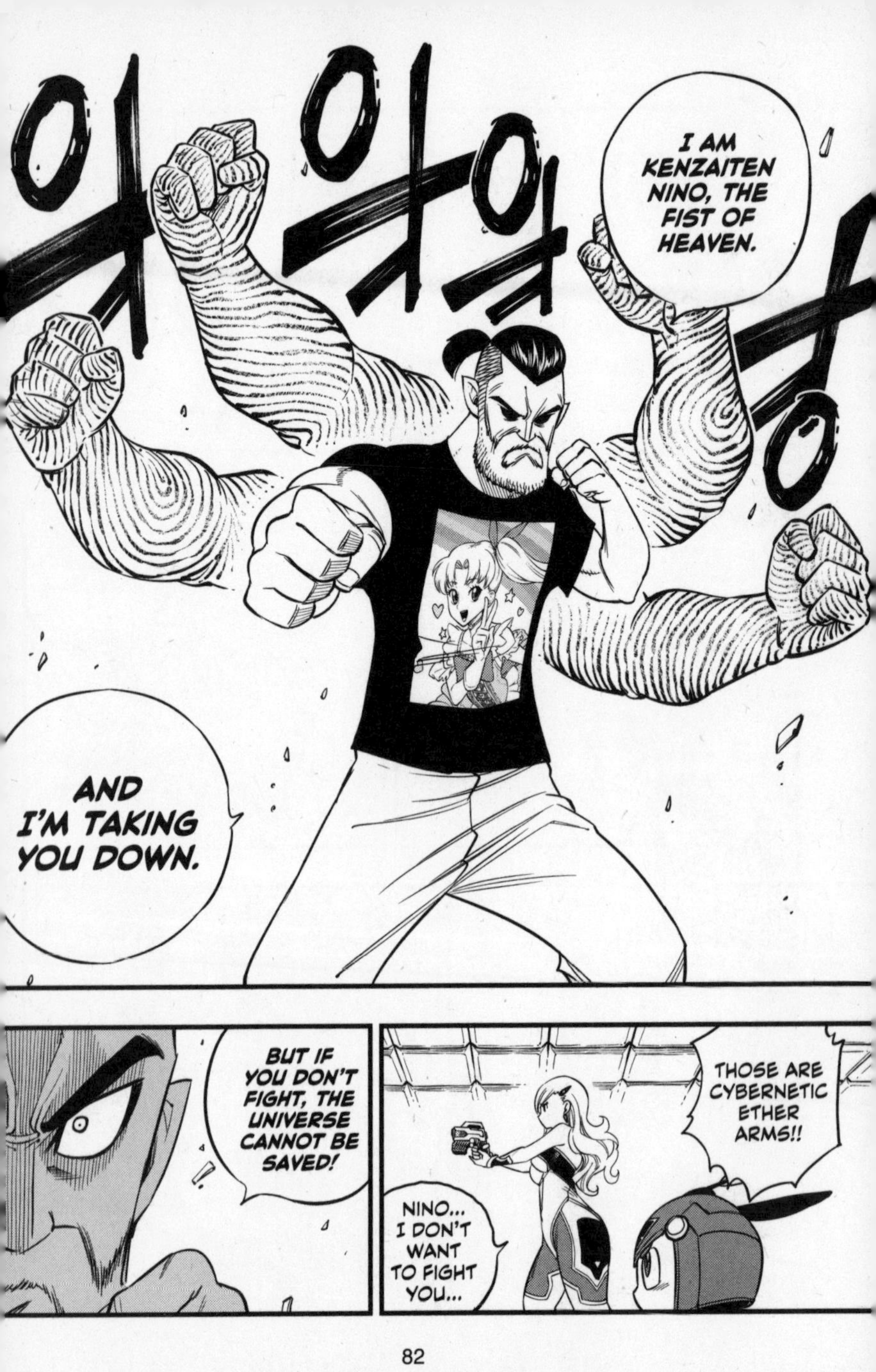
I AM KENZAITEN NINO, THE FIST OF HEAVEN.
AND I'M TAKING YOU DOWN.
THOSE ARE CYBERNETIC ETHER ARMS!!
NINO... I DON'T WANT TO FIGHT YOU...
BUT IF YOU DON'T FIGHT, THE UNIVERSE CANNOT BE SAVED!

EDENS ZERO

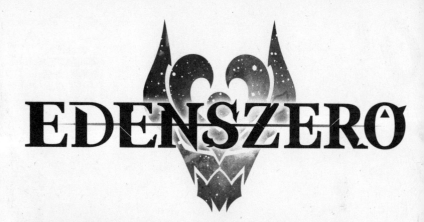

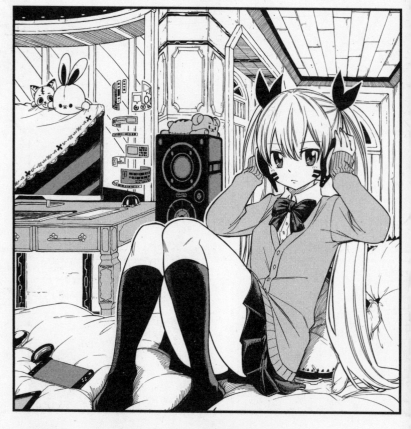

CHAPTER 64: LEAPER

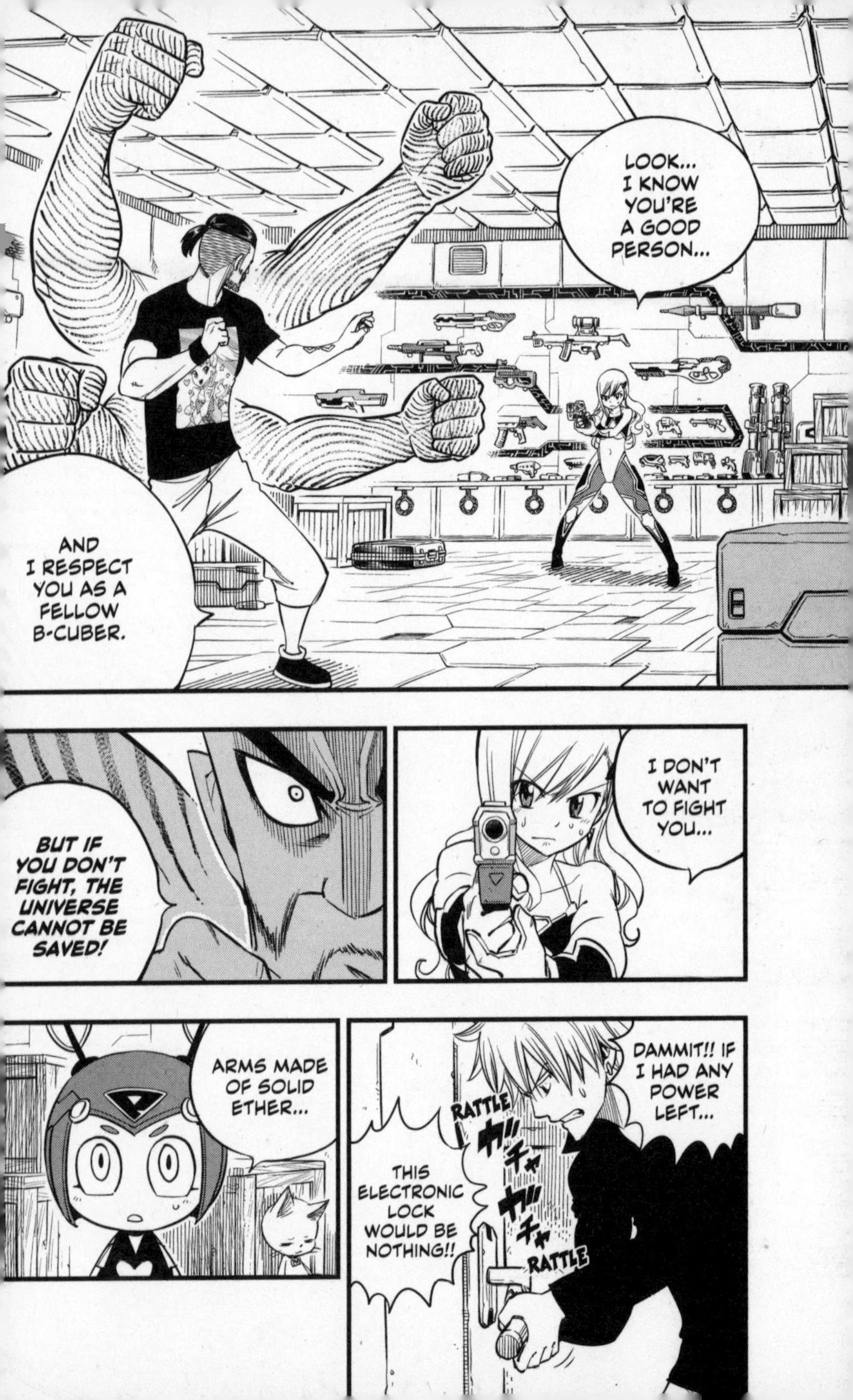
LOOK... I KNOW YOU'RE A GOOD PERSON...
AND I RESPECT YOU AS A FELLOW B-CUBER.
I DON'T WANT TO FIGHT YOU...
BUT IF YOU DON'T FIGHT, THE UNIVERSE CANNOT BE SAVED!
DAMMIT!! IF I HAD ANY POWER LEFT...
RATTLE
ガチャガチャ
RATTLE
THIS ELECTRONIC LOCK WOULD BE NOTHING!!
ARMS MADE OF SOLID ETHER...

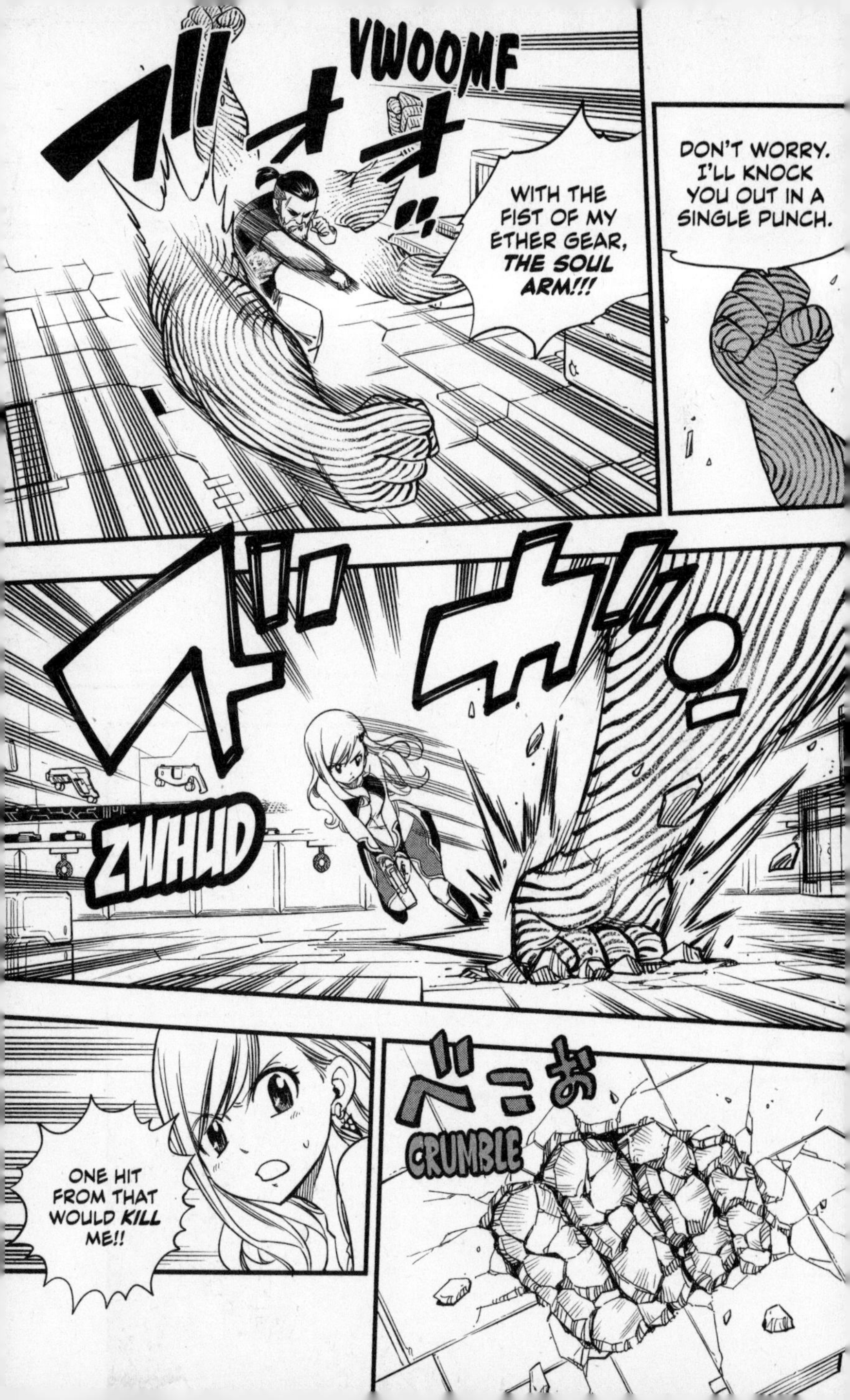
DON'T WORRY. I'LL KNOCK YOU OUT IN A SINGLE PUNCH.
VWOOMF
WITH THE FIST OF MY ETHER GEAR, ***THE SOUL ARM!!!***
ZWHUD
CRUMBLE
ONE HIT FROM THAT WOULD ***KILL*** ME!!

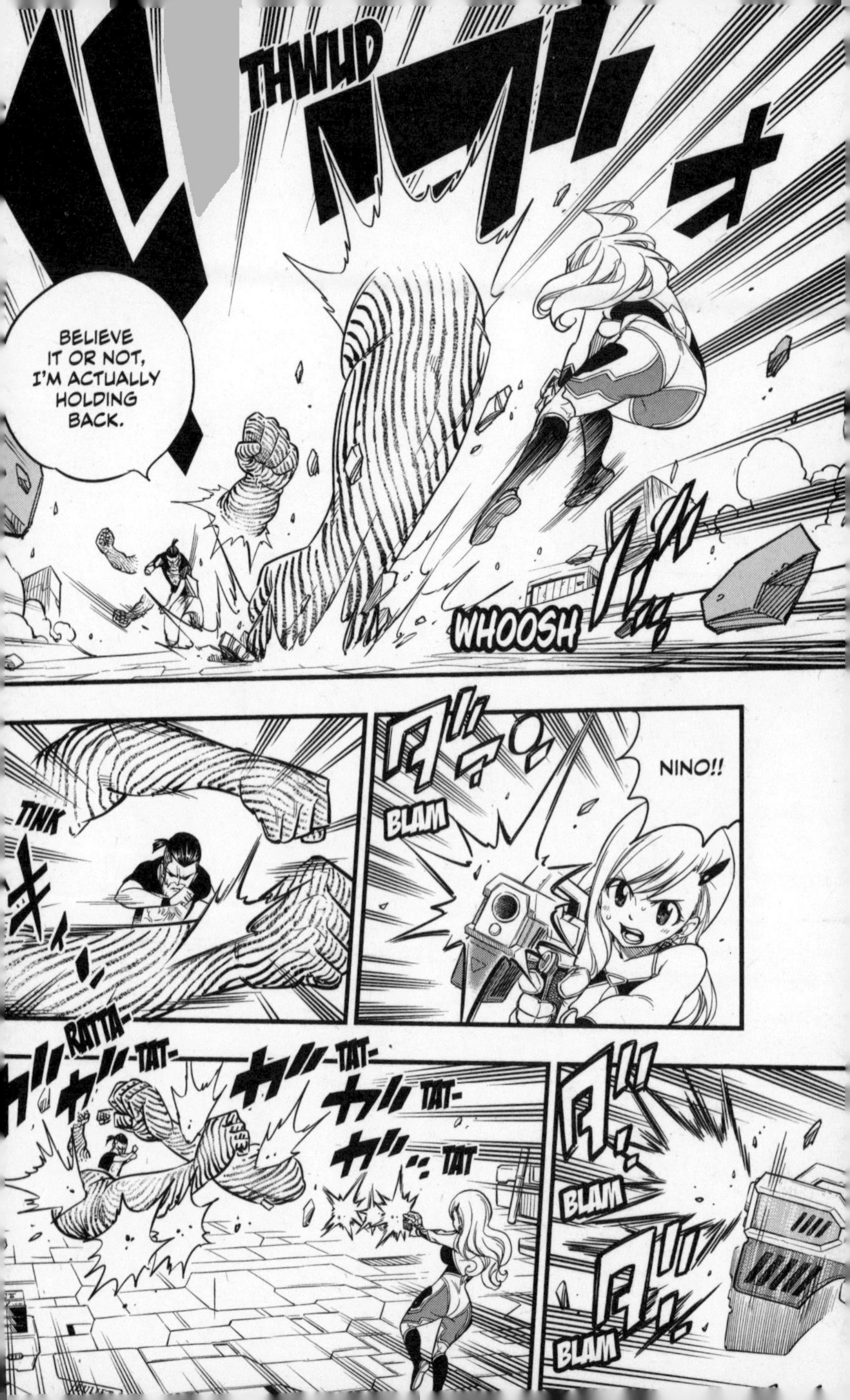
THWUD
BELIEVE IT OR NOT, I'M ACTUALLY HOLDING BACK.
WHOOSH
BLAM
NINO!!
TINK
BLAM
BLAM
RATTA-
-TAT-
-TAT-
TAT-
TAT

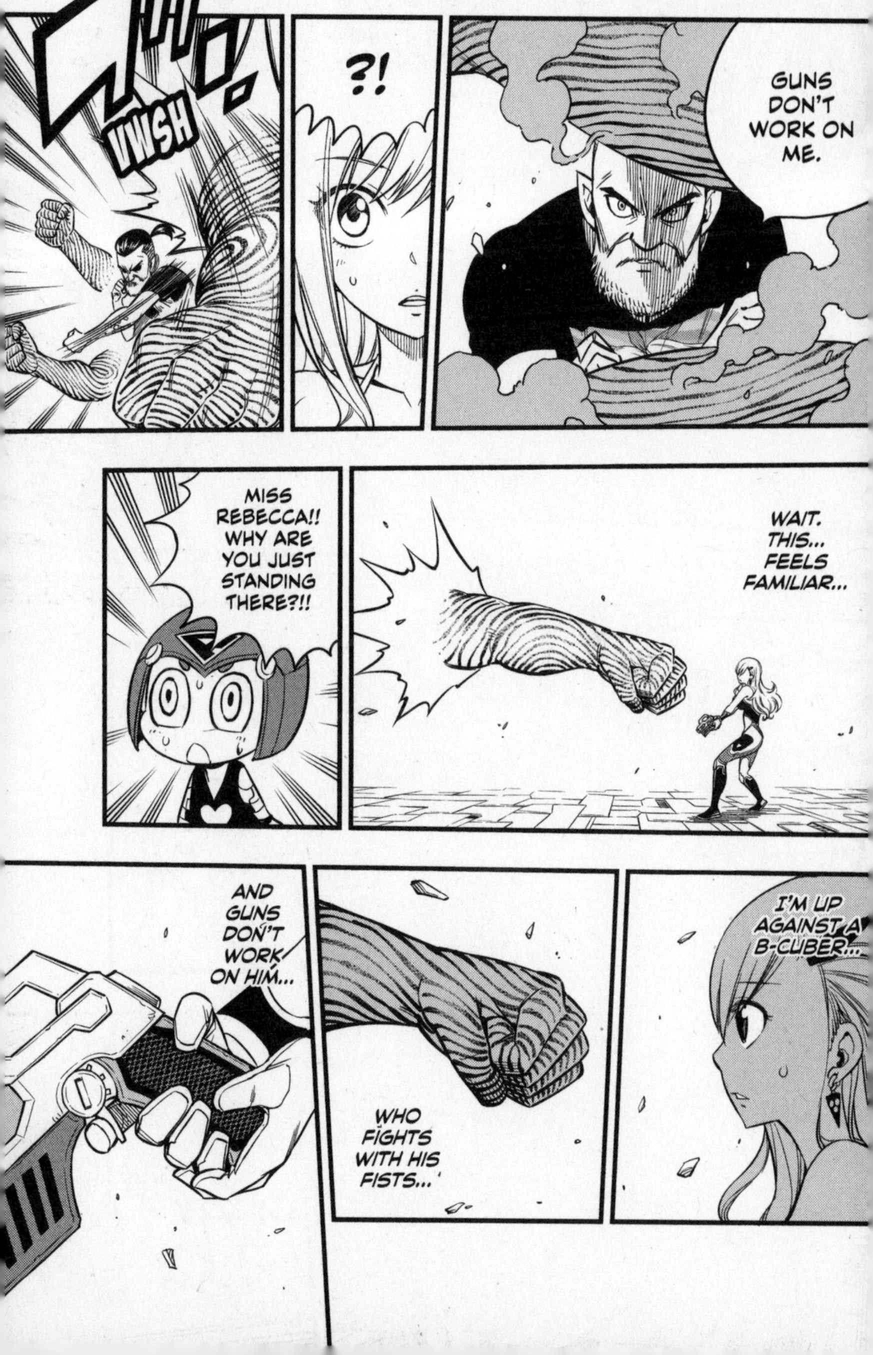
GUNS DON'T WORK ON ME.
?!
VWSH
WAIT. THIS... FEELS FAMILIAR...
MISS REBECCA!! WHY ARE YOU JUST STANDING THERE?!!
I'M UP AGAINST A B-CUBER...
WHO FIGHTS WITH HIS FISTS...
AND GUNS DON'T WORK ON HIM...

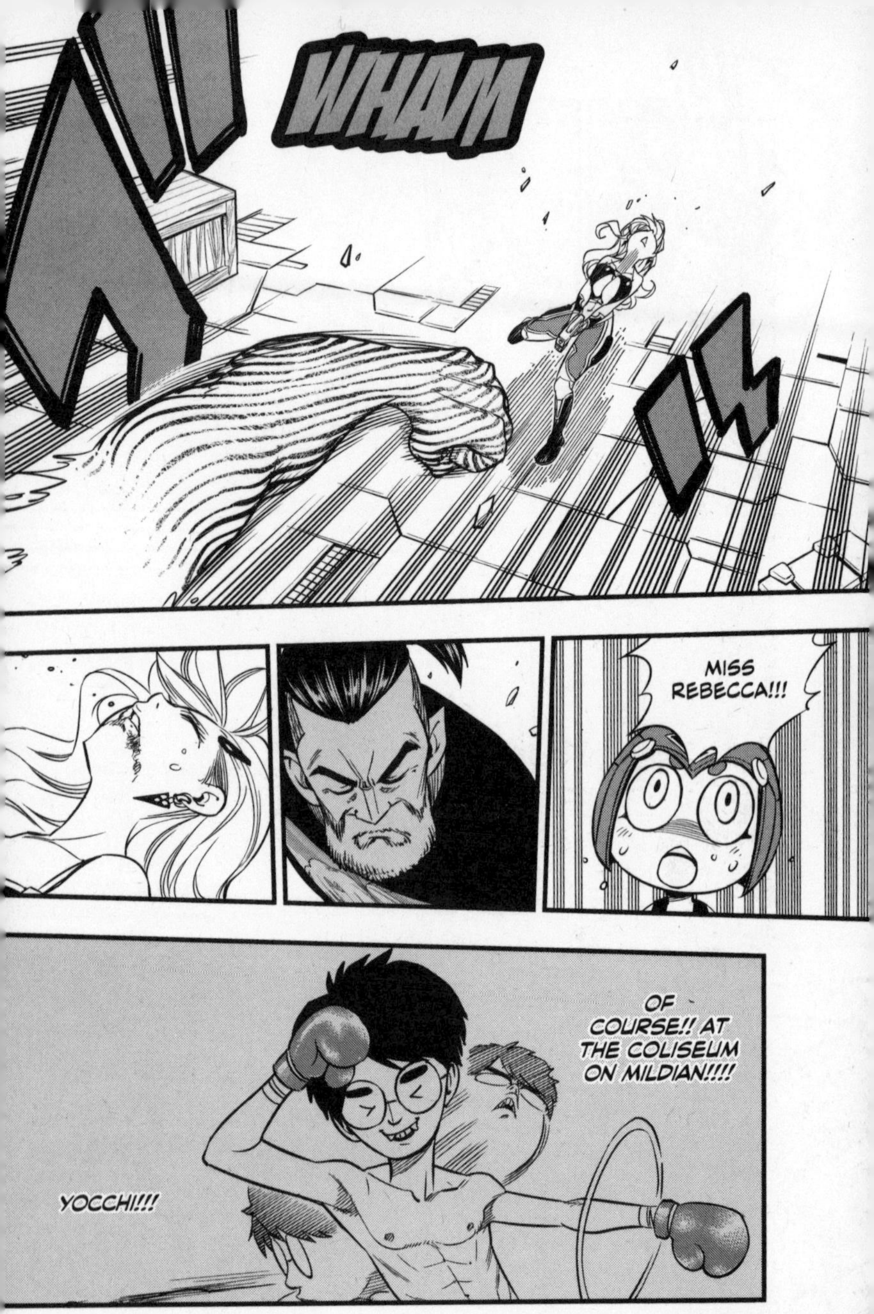
WHAM
MISS REBECCA!!!
OF COURSE!! AT THE COLISEUM ON MILDIAN!!!!
YOCCHI!!!

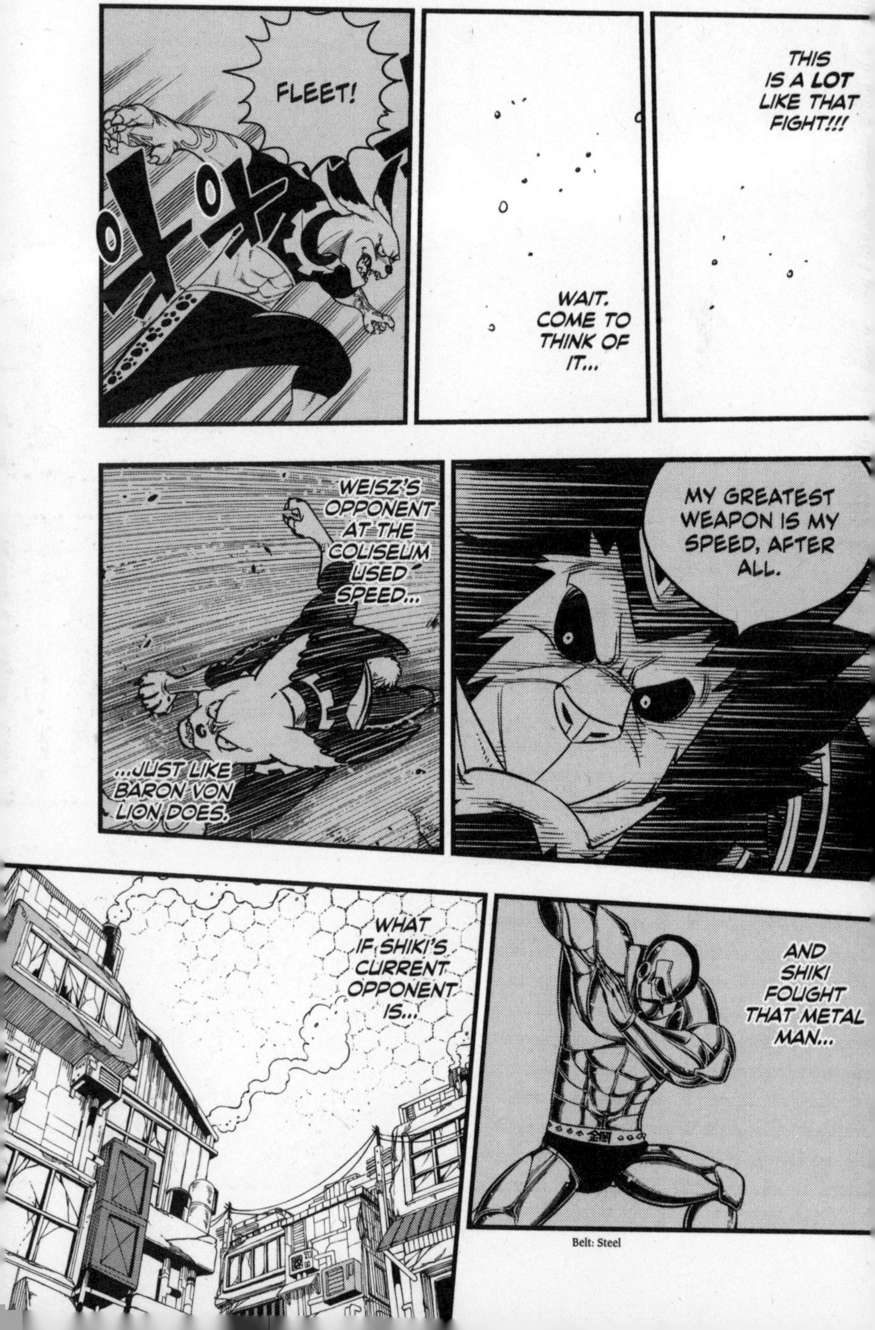
THIS IS A LOT LIKE THAT FIGHT!!!
WAIT. COME TO THINK OF IT...
FLEET!
MY GREATEST WEAPON IS MY SPEED, AFTER ALL.
WEISZ'S OPPONENT AT THE COLISEUM USED SPEED...
...JUST LIKE BARON VON LION DOES.
AND SHIKI FOUGHT THAT METAL MAN...
Belt: Steel
WHAT IF SHIKI'S CURRENT OPPONENT IS...

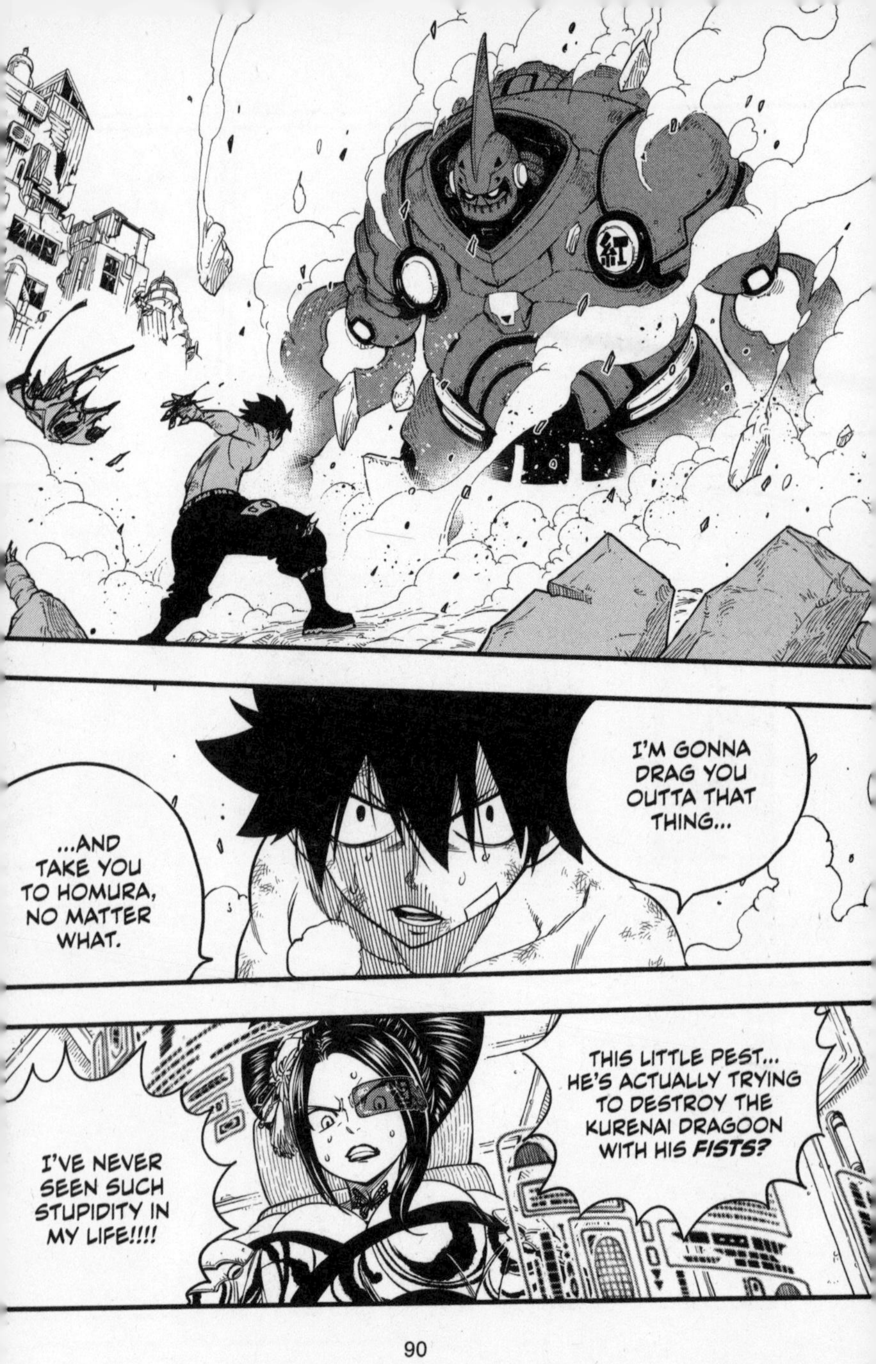
I'M GONNA DRAG YOU OUTTA THAT THING...
...AND TAKE YOU TO HOMURA, NO MATTER WHAT.
THIS LITTLE PEST... HE'S ACTUALLY TRYING TO DESTROY THE KURENAI DRAGOON WITH HIS *FISTS?*
I'VE NEVER SEEN SUCH STUPIDITY IN MY LIFE!!!!

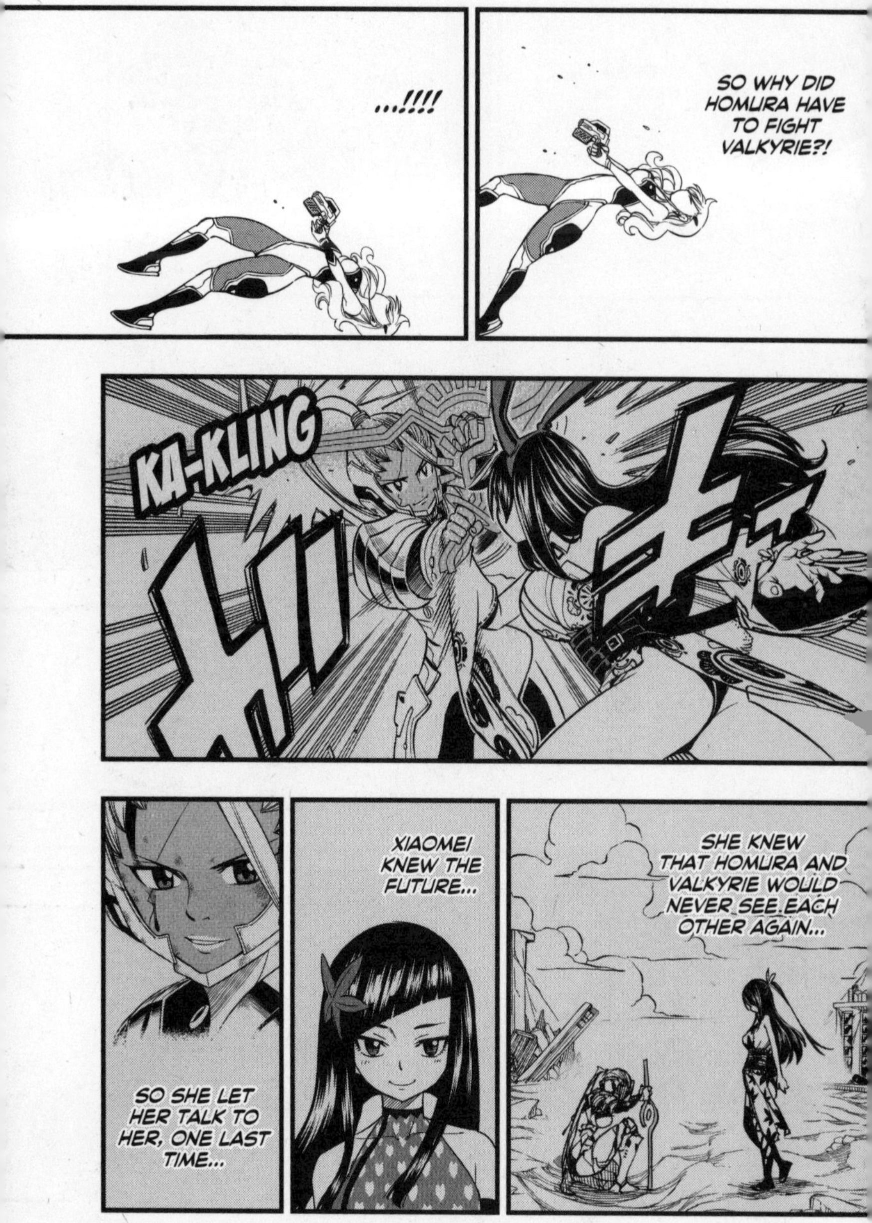
SO WHY DID HOMURA HAVE TO FIGHT VALKYRIE?!
...!!!!
KA-KLING
SHE KNEW THAT HOMURA AND VALKYRIE WOULD NEVER SEE EACH OTHER AGAIN...
XIAOMEI KNEW THE FUTURE...
SO SHE LET HER TALK TO HER, ONE LAST TIME...

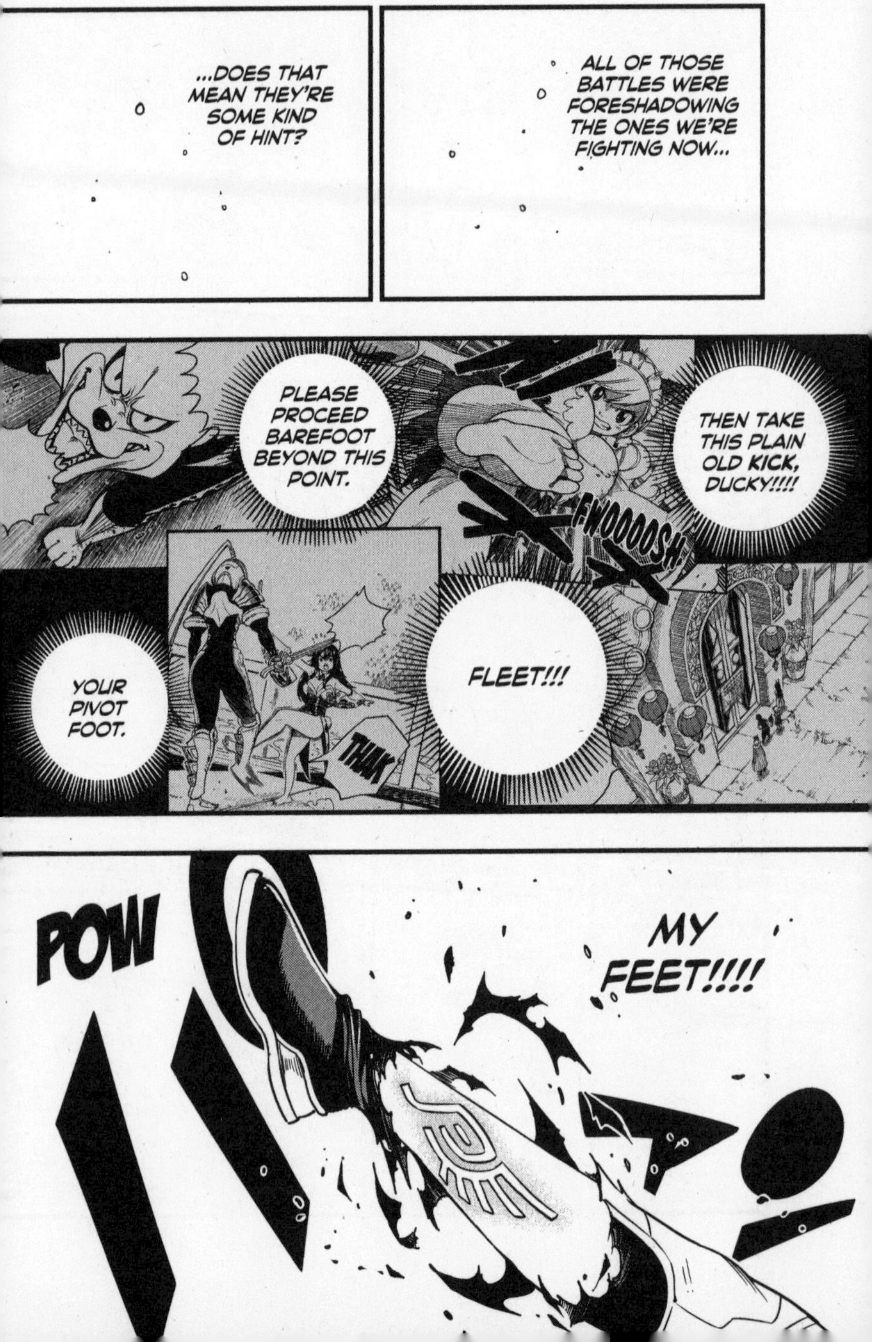
ALL OF THOSE BATTLES WERE FORESHADOWING THE ONES WE'RE FIGHTING NOW...
...DOES THAT MEAN THEY'RE SOME KIND OF HINT?
THEN TAKE THIS PLAIN OLD KICK, DUCKY!!!!
FWOOOOSH
PLEASE PROCEED BAREFOOT BEYOND THIS POINT.
FLEET!!!
THAK
YOUR PIVOT FOOT.
MY FEET!!!!
POW

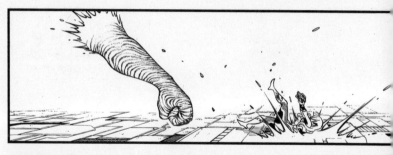

HUH?

SOMEHOW,
I FEEL LIKE
TIME IS GOING
BACKWARDS.

WHAT...

...IS
HAPPENING?

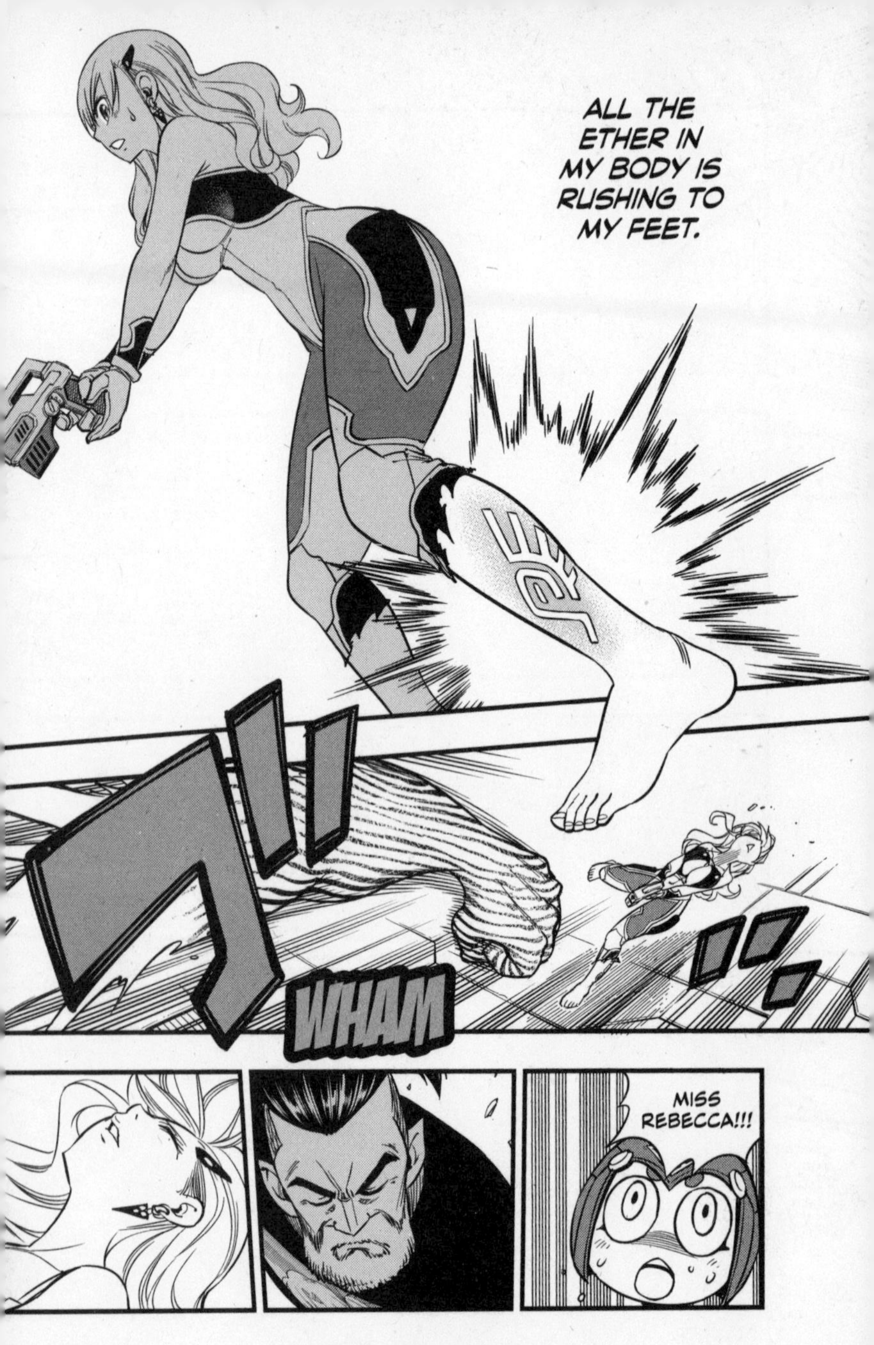
ALL THE ETHER IN MY BODY IS RUSHING TO MY FEET.
WHAM
MISS REBECCA!!!

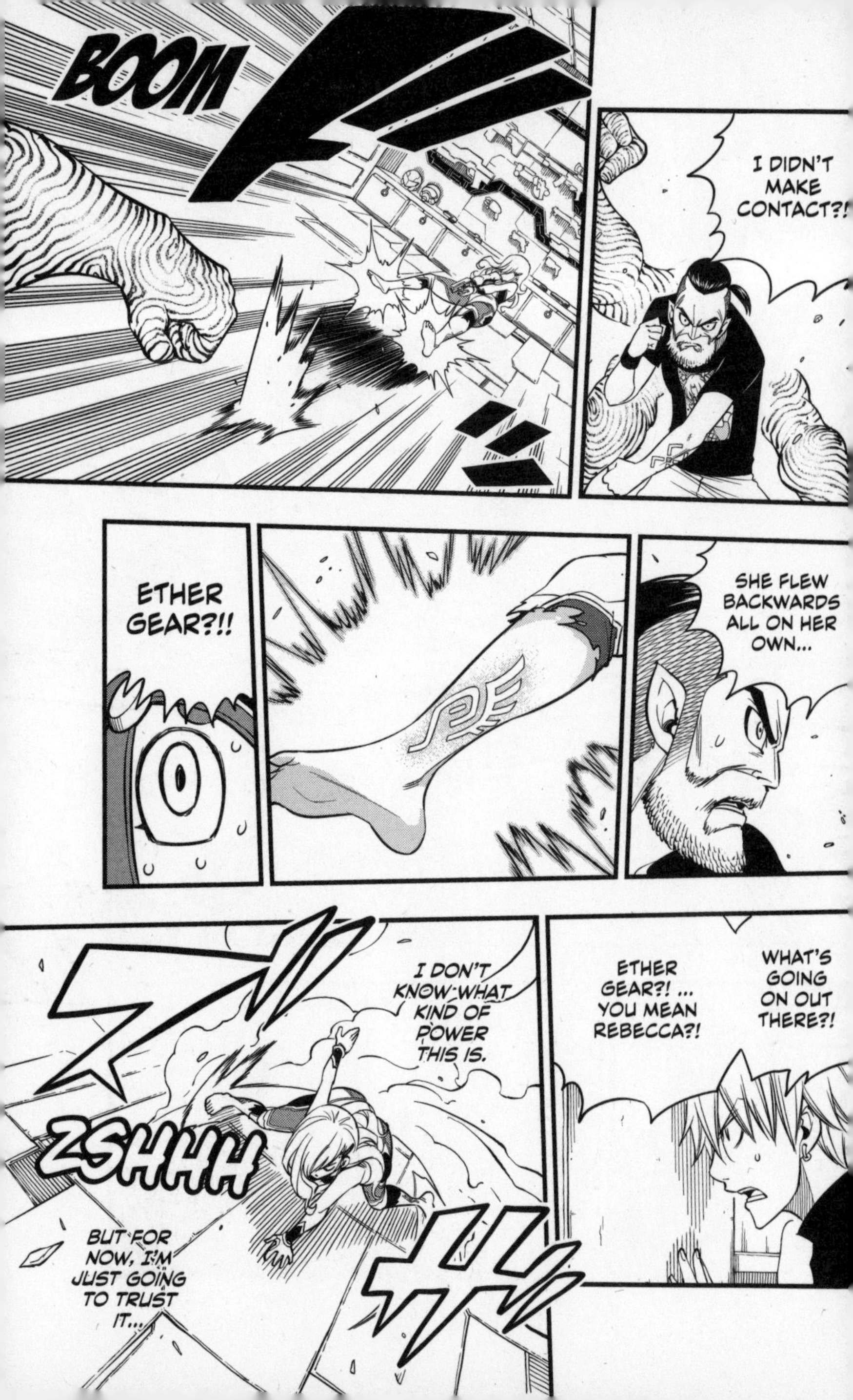

I DIDN'T MAKE CONTACT?!
BOOM
SHE FLEW BACKWARDS ALL ON HER OWN...
ETHER GEAR?!!
WHAT'S GOING ON OUT THERE?!
ETHER GEAR?! ... YOU MEAN REBECCA?!
I DON'T KNOW WHAT KIND OF POWER THIS IS.
ZSHHH
BUT FOR NOW, I'M JUST GOING TO TRUST IT...

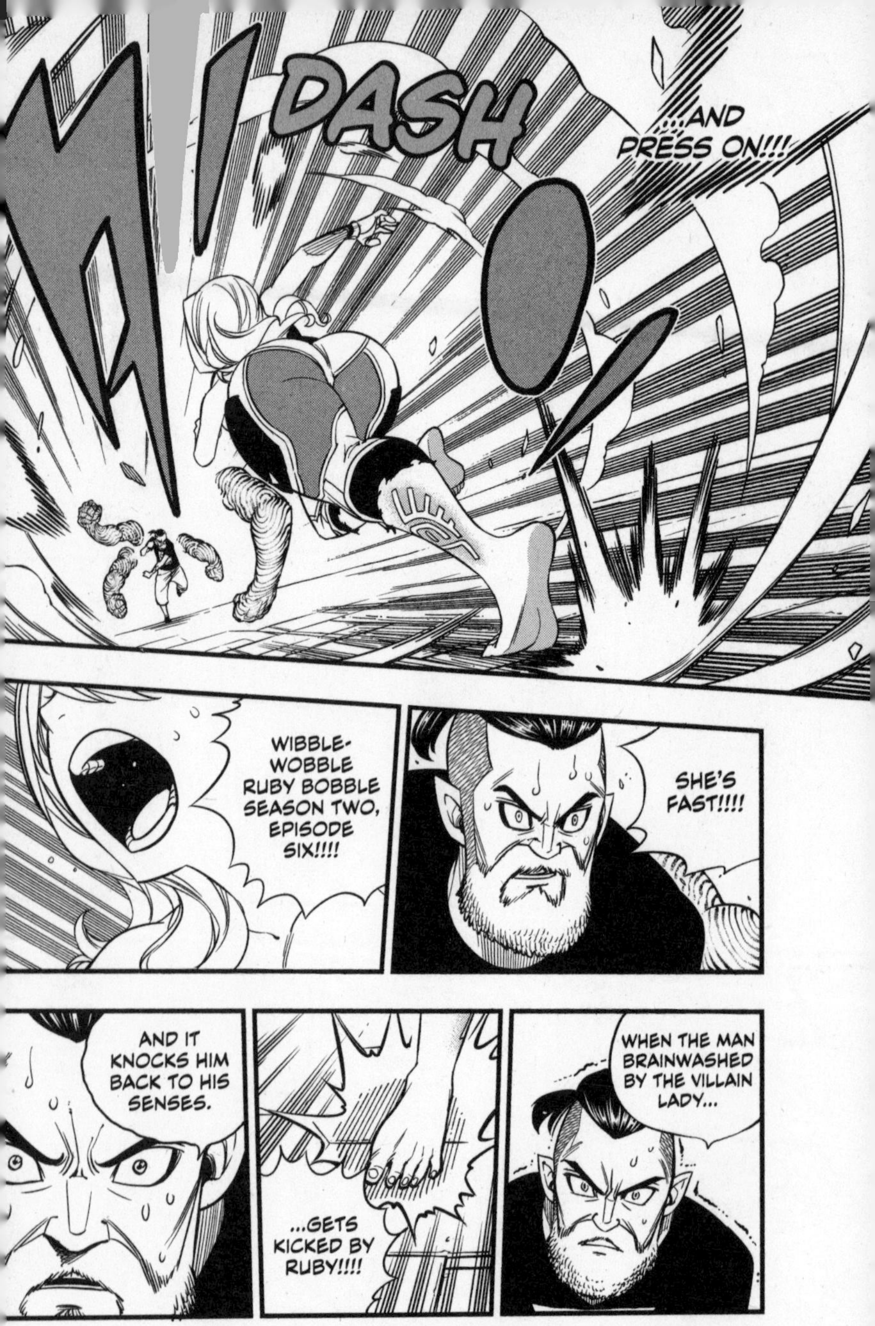
...AND PRESS ON!!!
DASH
SHE'S FAST!!!!
WIBBLE-WOBBLE RUBY BOBBLE SEASON TWO, EPISODE SIX!!!!
WHEN THE MAN BRAINWASHED BY THE VILLAIN LADY...
...GETS KICKED BY RUBY!!!!
AND IT KNOCKS HIM BACK TO HIS SENSES.

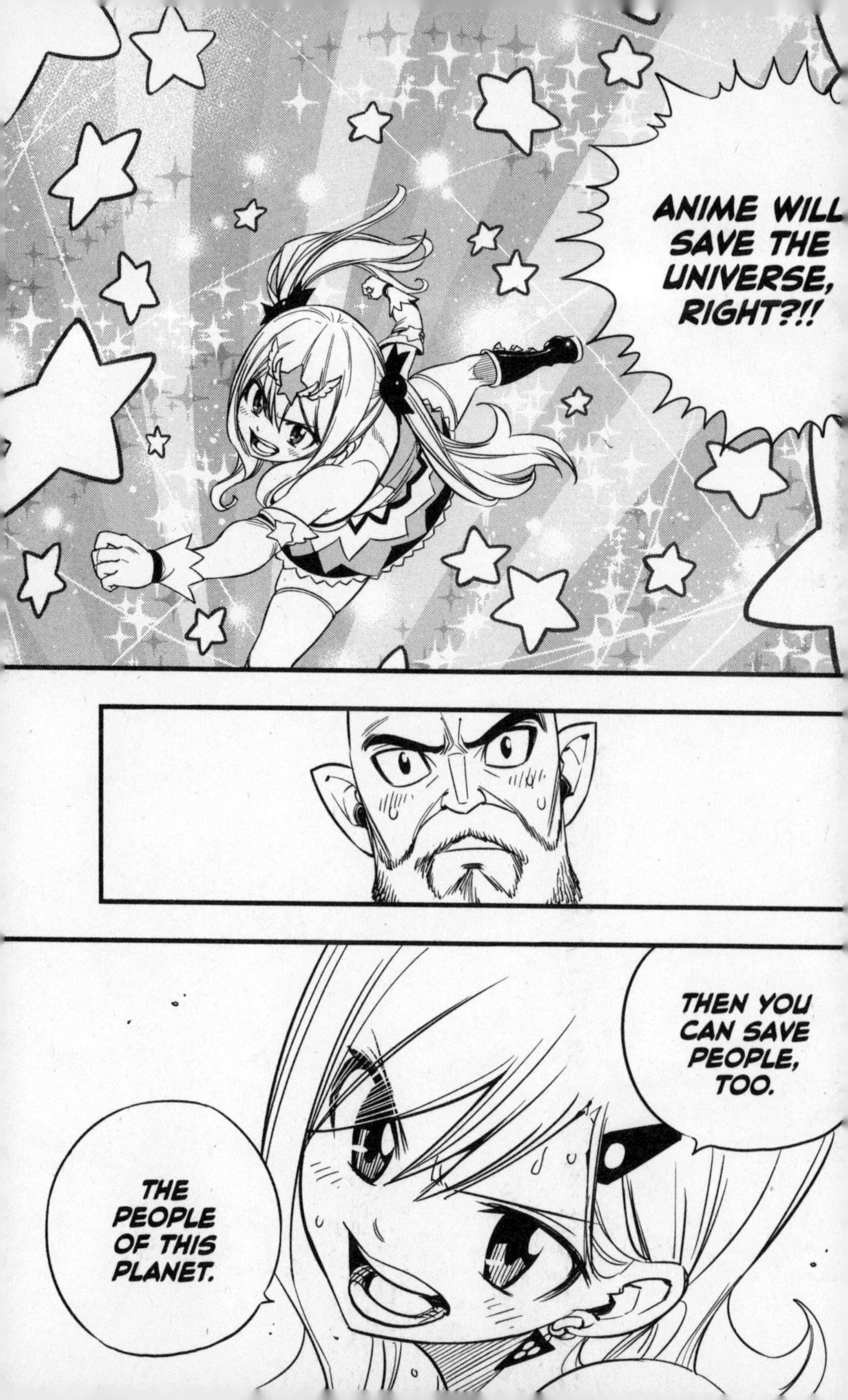
ANIME WILL SAVE THE UNIVERSE, RIGHT?!!
THEN YOU CAN SAVE PEOPLE, TOO.
THE PEOPLE OF THIS PLANET.

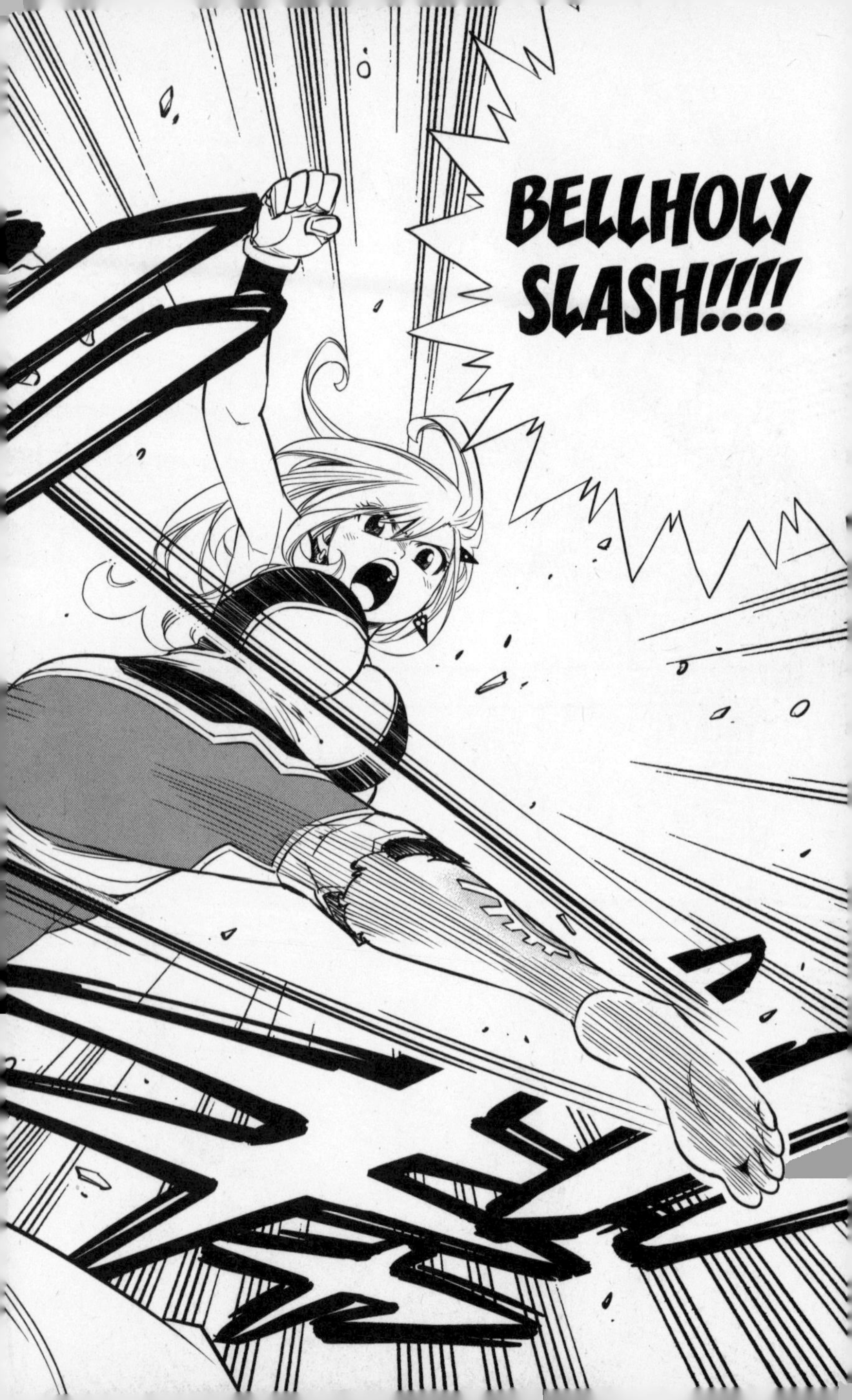
BELLHOLY SLASH!!!!

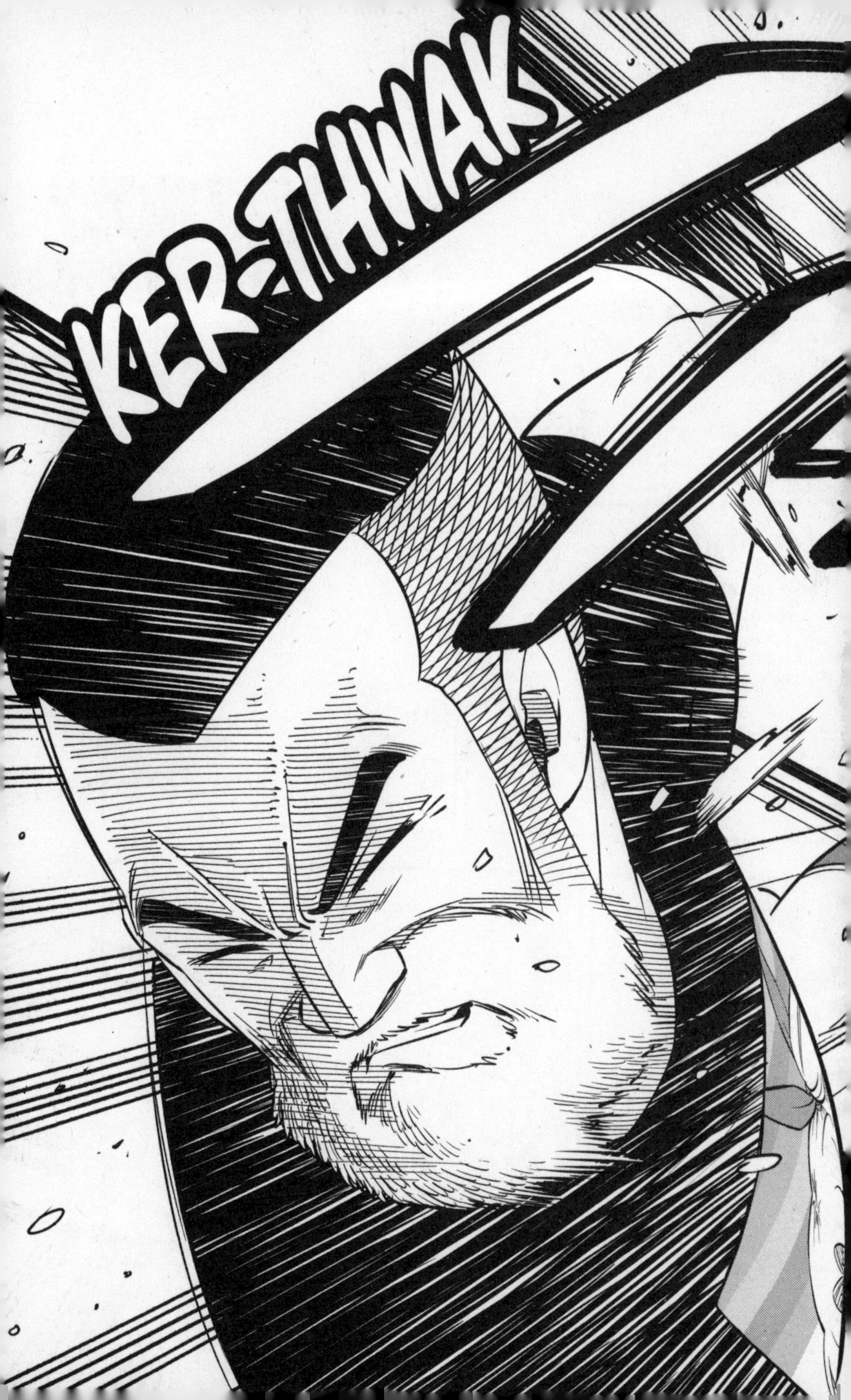
KER-THWAK

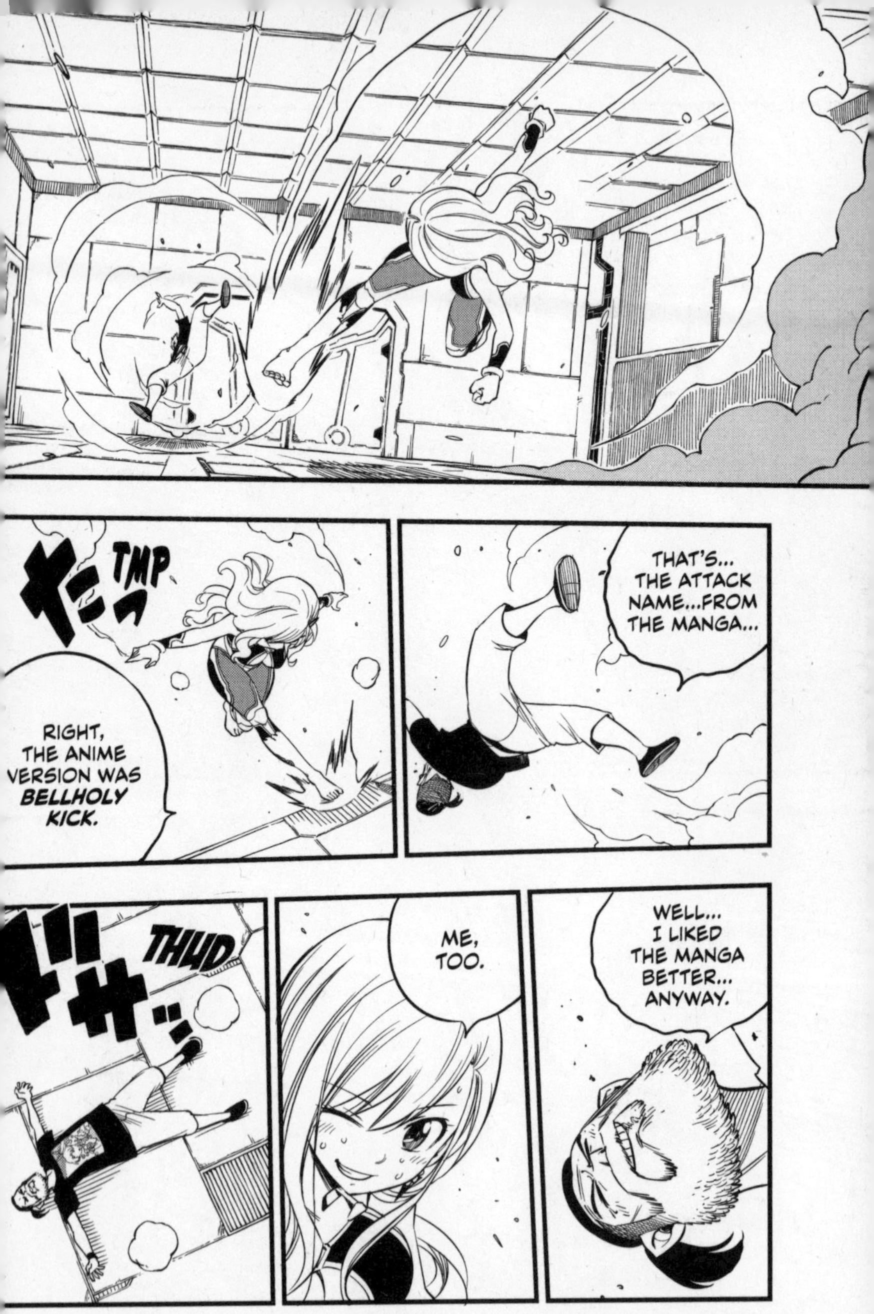
THAT'S... THE ATTACK NAME...FROM THE MANGA...
TMP
RIGHT, THE ANIME VERSION WAS *BELLHOLY KICK.*
WELL... I LIKED THE MANGA BETTER... ANYWAY.
ME, TOO.
THUD

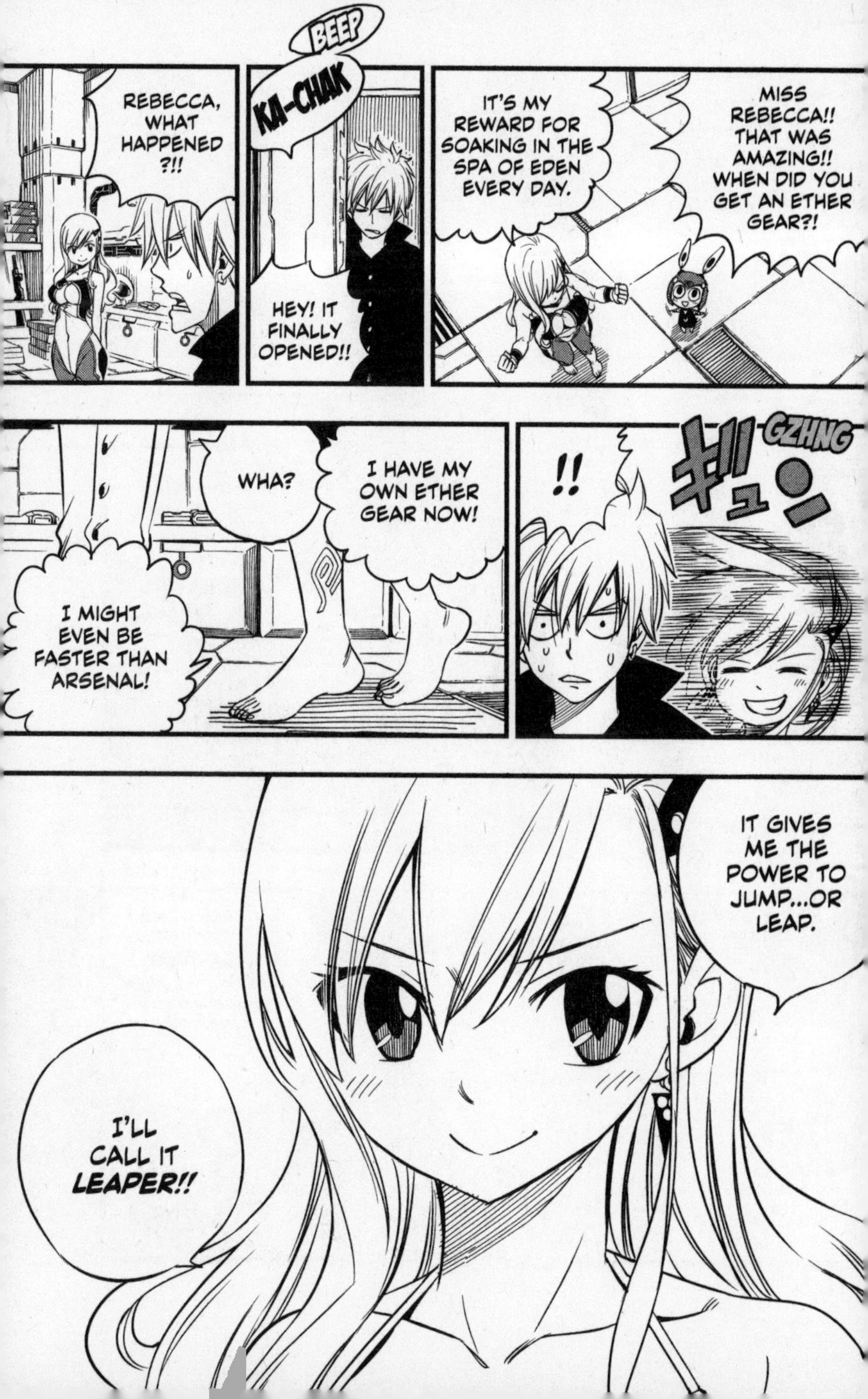
MISS REBECCA!! THAT WAS AMAZING!! WHEN DID YOU GET AN ETHER GEAR?!
IT'S MY REWARD FOR SOAKING IN THE SPA OF EDEN EVERY DAY.
BEEP
KA-CHAK
HEY! IT FINALLY OPENED!!
REBECCA, WHAT HAPPENED?!!
ギュン
GZHNG
!!
I HAVE MY OWN ETHER GEAR NOW!
WHA?
I MIGHT EVEN BE FASTER THAN ARSENAL!
IT GIVES ME THE POWER TO JUMP...OR LEAP.
I'LL CALL IT *LEAPER!!*

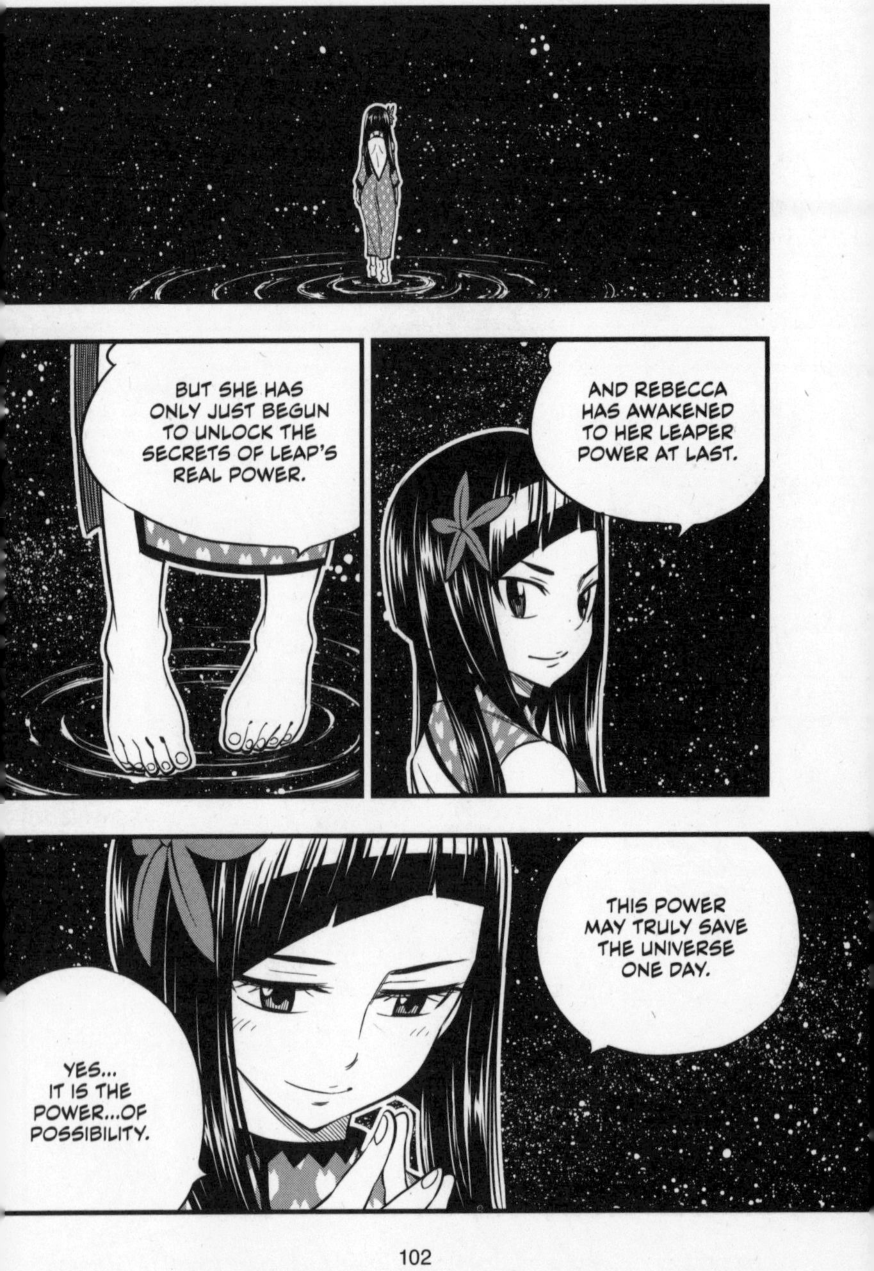
AND REBECCA HAS AWAKENED TO HER LEAPER POWER AT LAST.
BUT SHE HAS ONLY JUST BEGUN TO UNLOCK THE SECRETS OF LEAP'S REAL POWER.
THIS POWER MAY TRULY SAVE THE UNIVERSE ONE DAY.
YES... IT IS THE POWER...OF POSSIBILITY.

EDENS ZERO

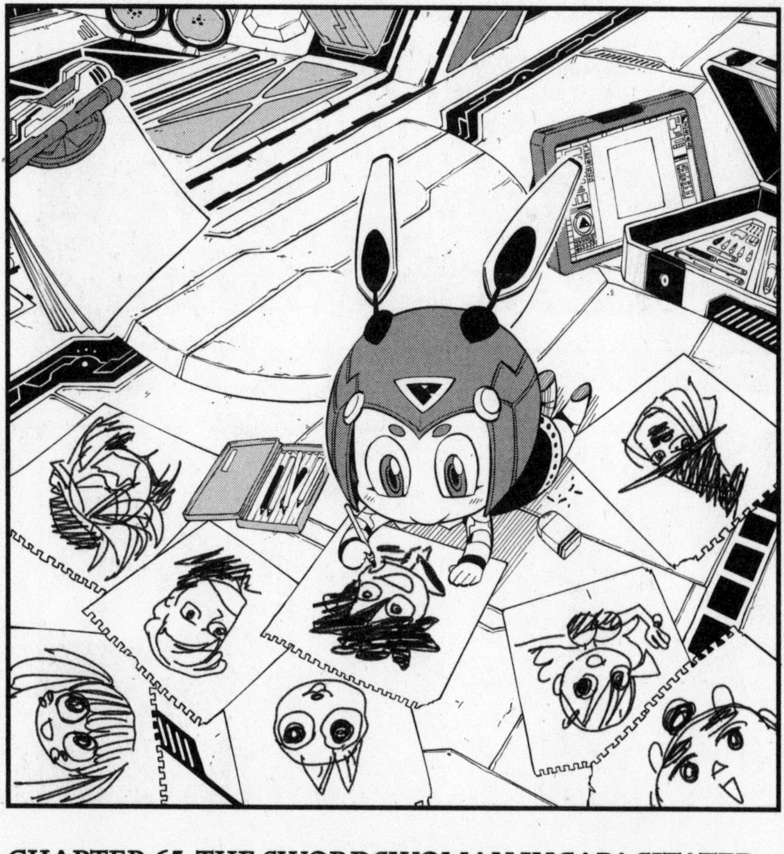

CHAPTER 65: THE SWORDSWOMAN INCAPACITATED

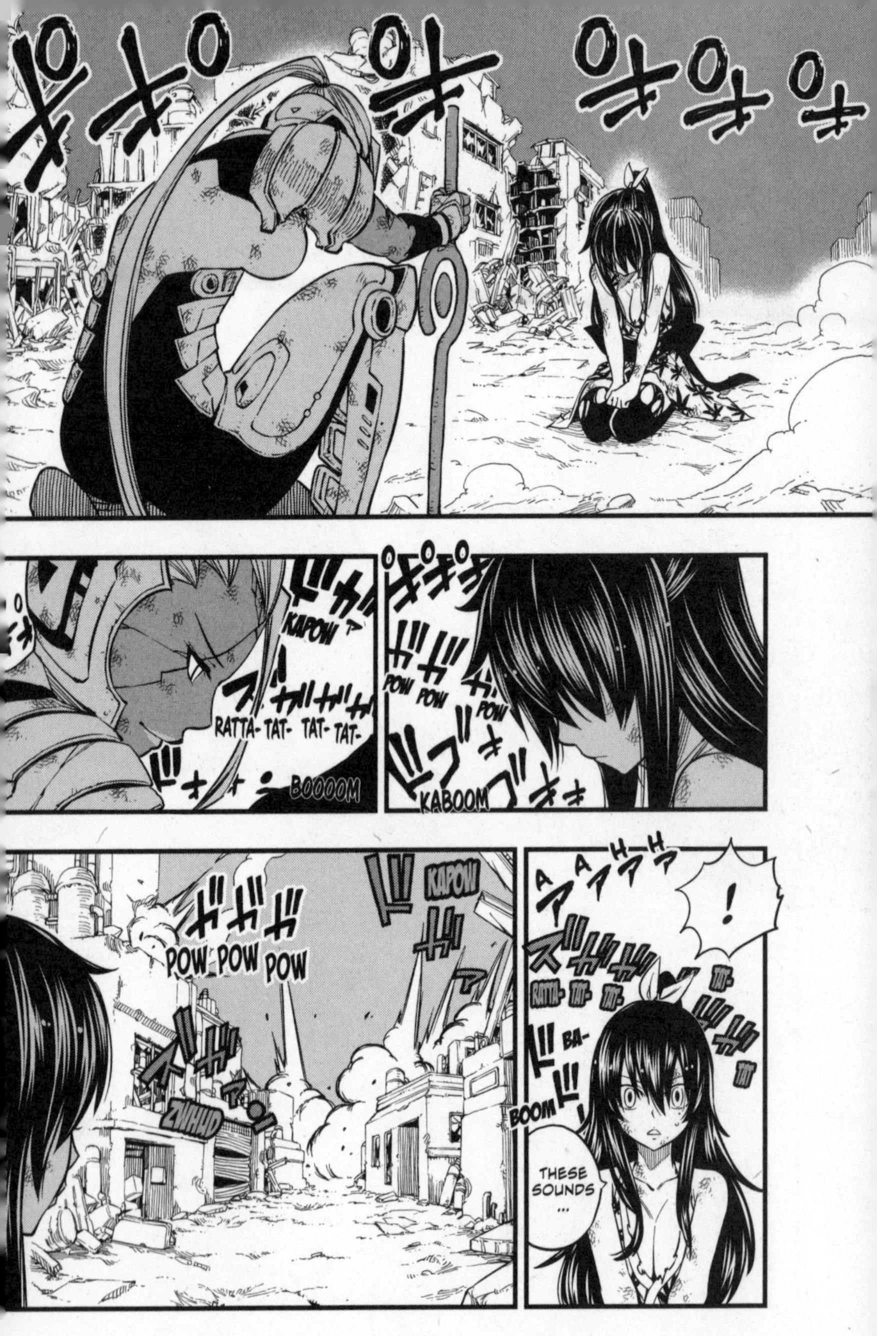
POW POW
POW
KABOOM
KAPOW
RATTA-TAT-TAT-TAT-
BOOOOM
AAHH
!
RATTA-TAT-TAT-TAT-
BA-BOOM
THESE SOUNDS ...
KAPOW
POW POW POW
ZWHUD

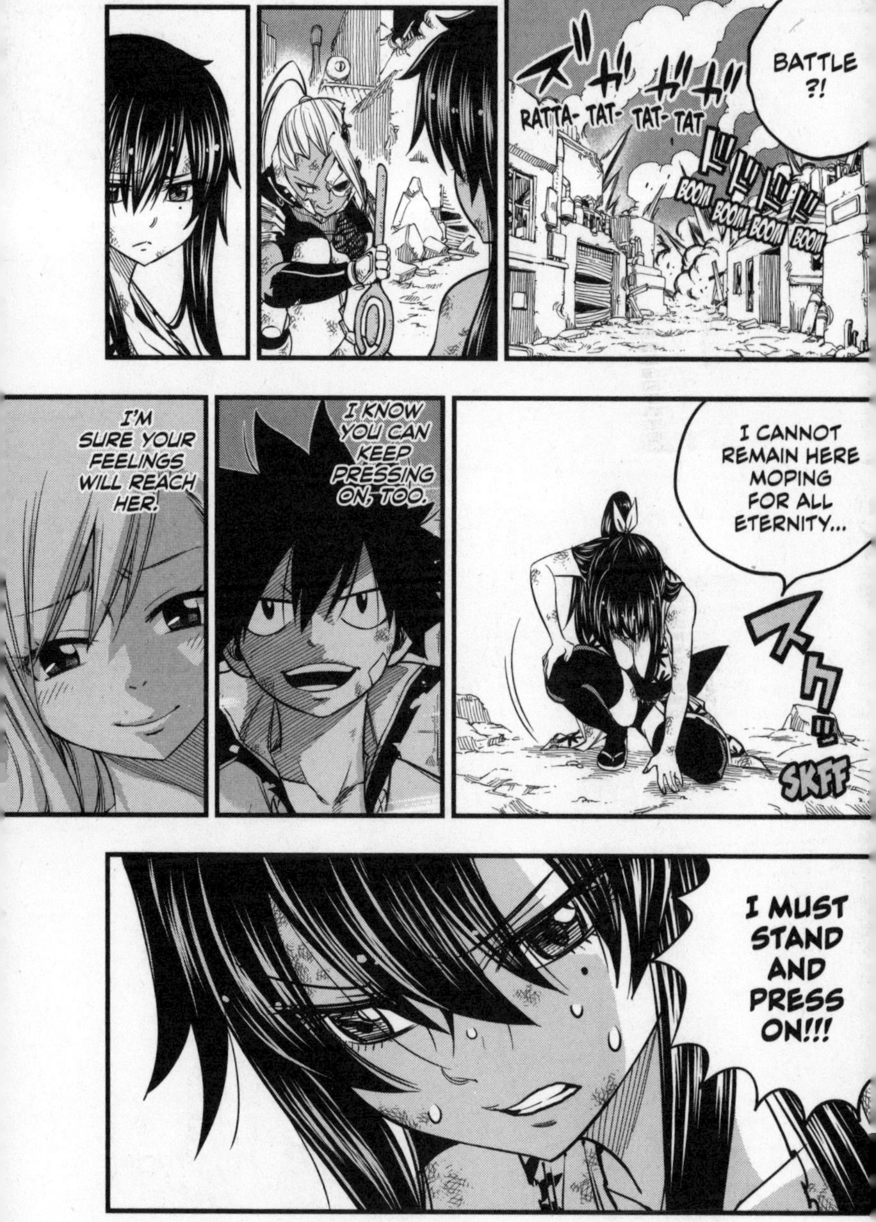
BATTLE ?!
RATTA-TAT-TAT-TAT
BOOM BOOM BOOM BOOM
I CANNOT REMAIN HERE MOPING FOR ALL ETERNITY...
SKFF
I KNOW YOU CAN KEEP PRESSING ON, TOO.
I'M SURE YOUR FEELINGS WILL REACH HER.
I MUST STAND AND PRESS ON!!!

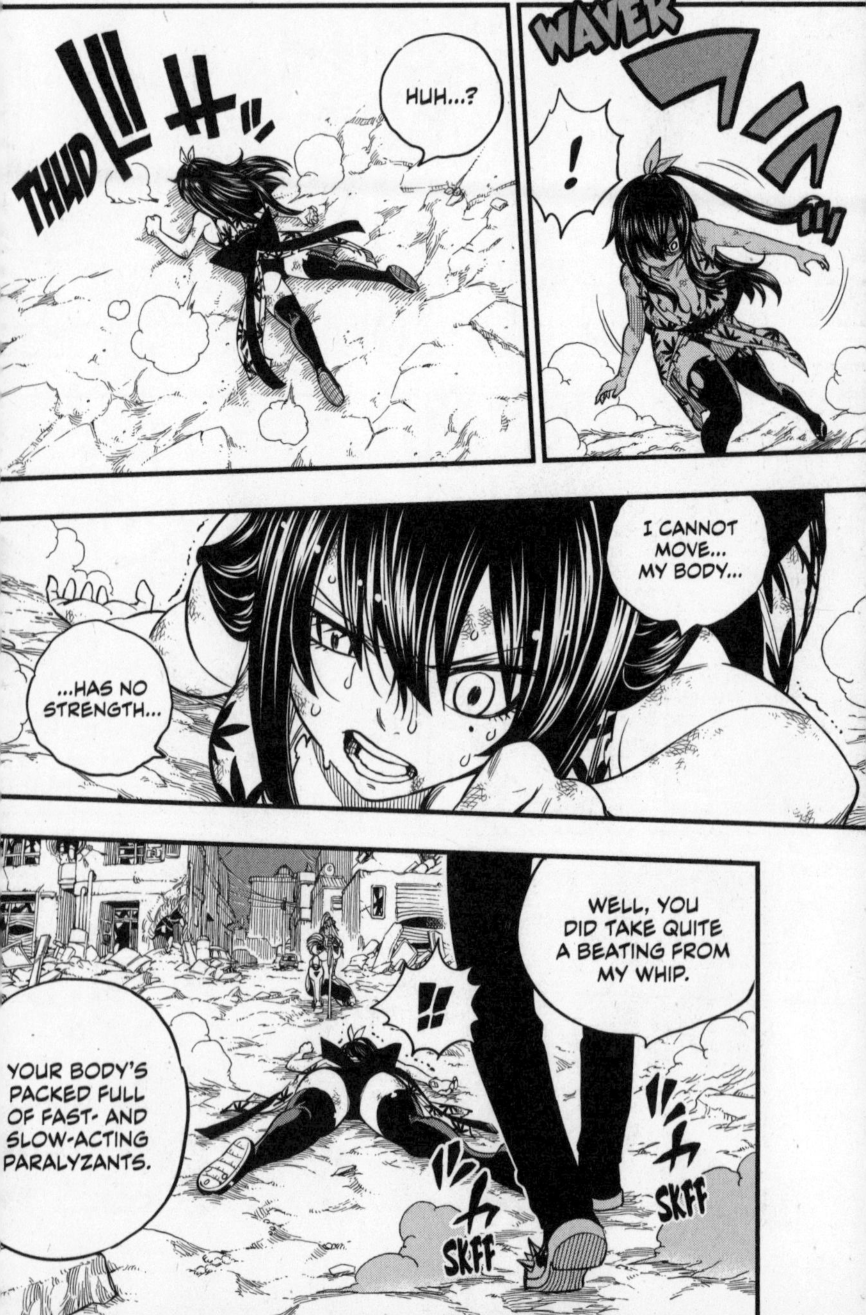
WAVER
!
HUH...?
THUD!!!
I CANNOT MOVE... MY BODY...
...HAS NO STRENGTH...
WELL, YOU DID TAKE QUITE A BEATING FROM MY WHIP.
!!
SKFF
SKFF
YOUR BODY'S PACKED FULL OF FAST- AND SLOW-ACTING PARALYZANTS.

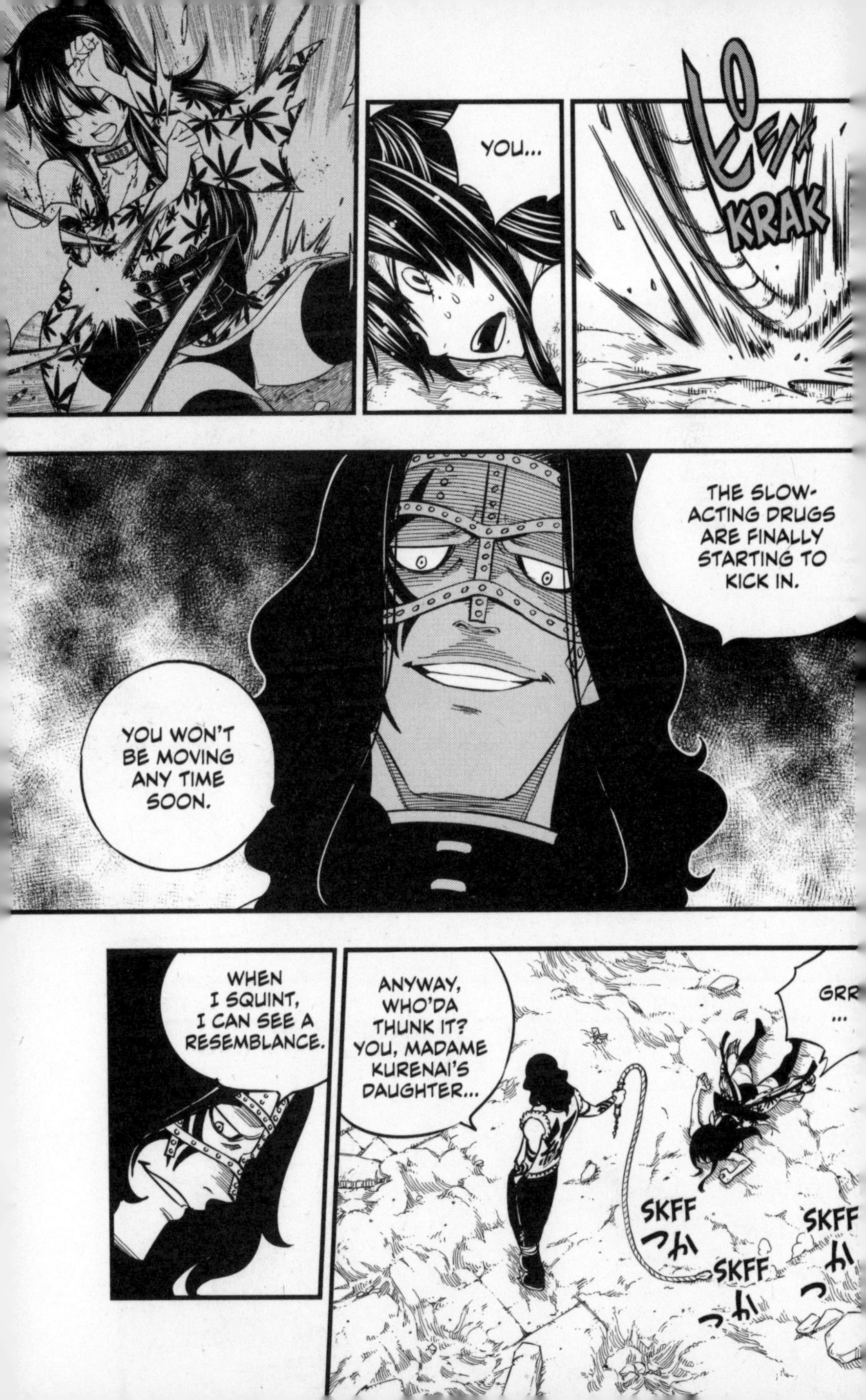
KRAK
YOU...
THE SLOW-ACTING DRUGS ARE FINALLY STARTING TO KICK IN.
YOU WON'T BE MOVING ANY TIME SOON.
GRR...
ANYWAY, WHO'DA THUNK IT? YOU, MADAME KURENAI'S DAUGHTER...
SKFF
SKFF
SKFF
WHEN I SQUINT, I CAN SEE A RESEMBLANCE.

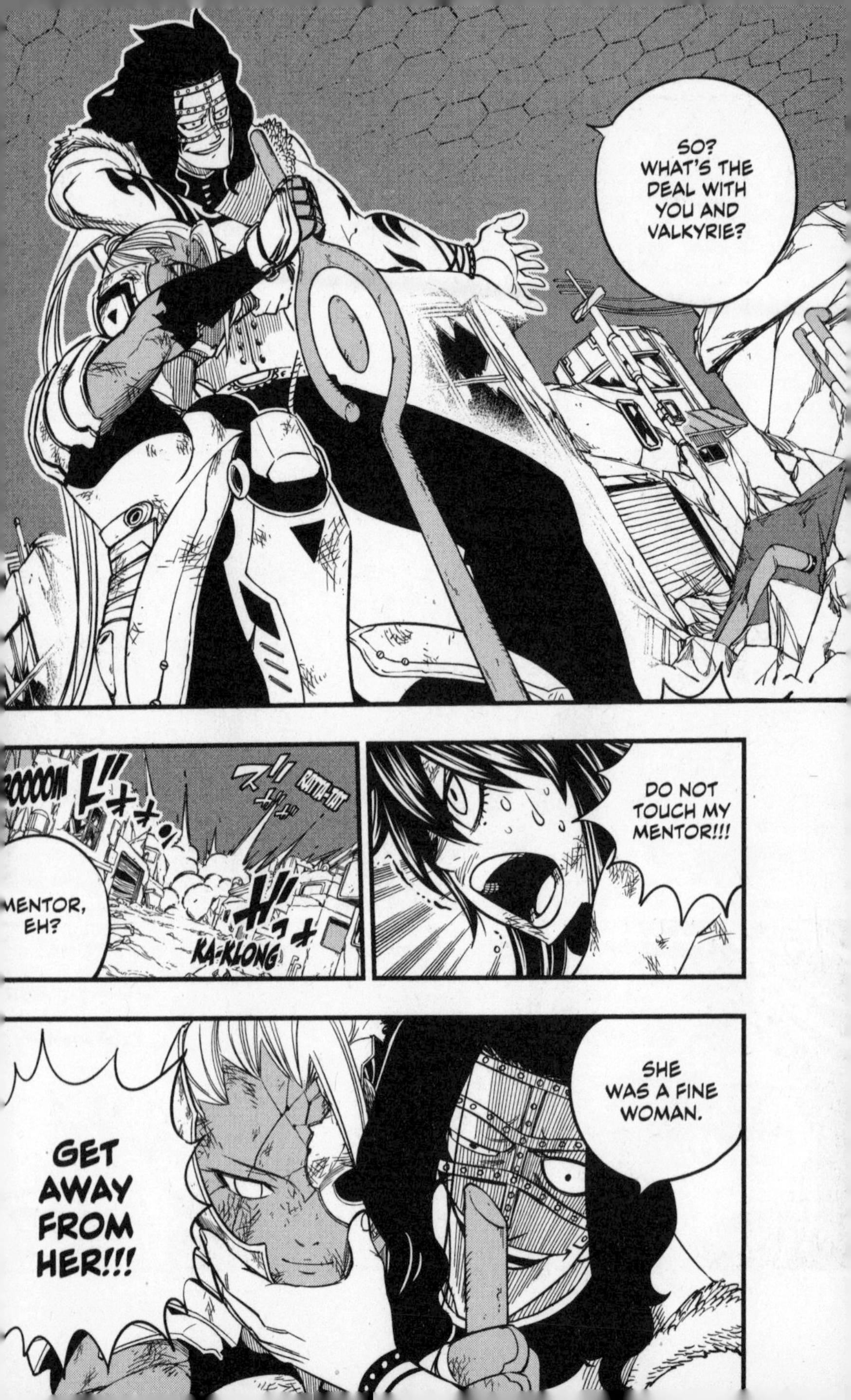
SO? WHAT'S THE DEAL WITH YOU AND VALKYRIE?
DO NOT TOUCH MY MENTOR!!!
RATTA-TAT
ROOOOM
MENTOR, EH?
KA-KLONG
SHE WAS A FINE WOMAN.
GET AWAY FROM HER!!!

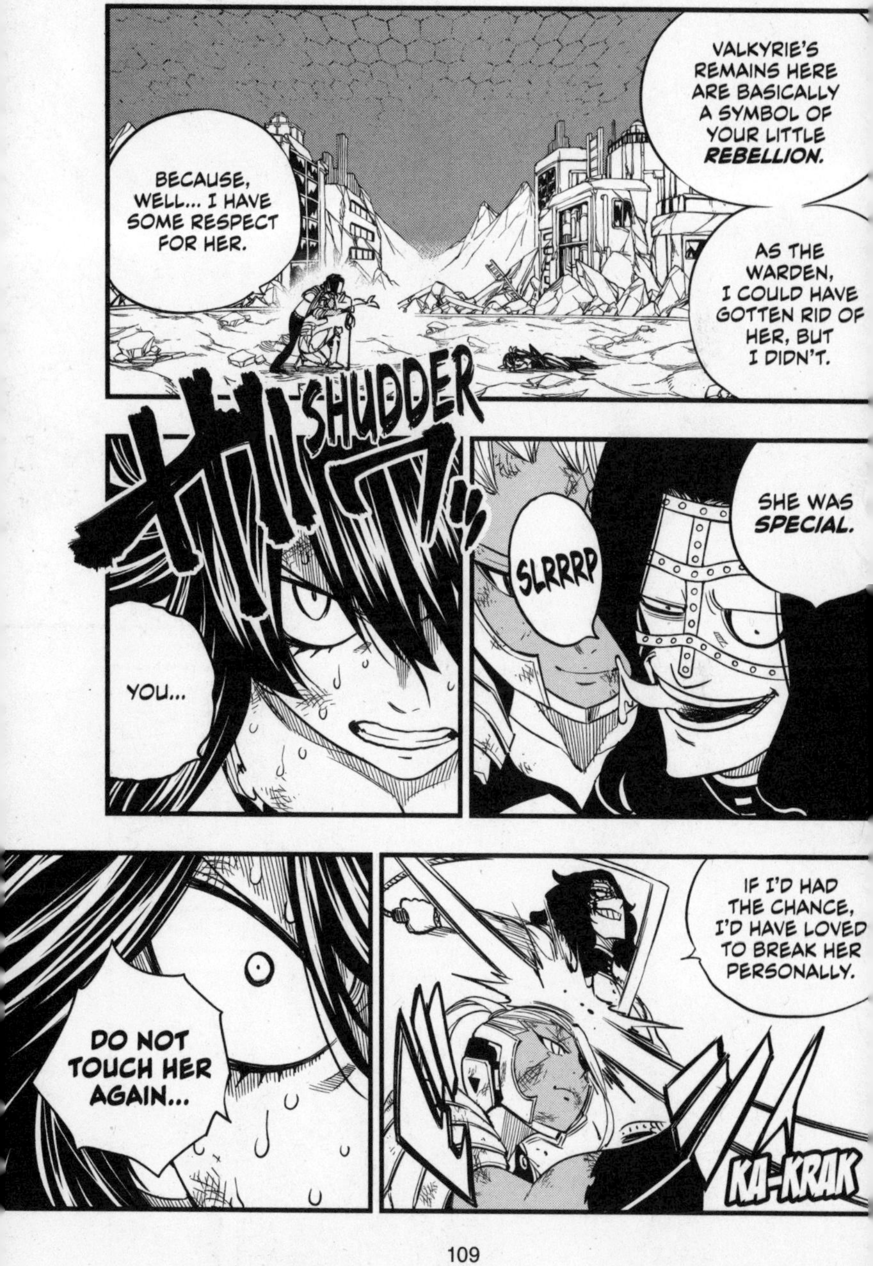

VALKYRIE'S REMAINS HERE ARE BASICALLY A SYMBOL OF YOUR LITTLE ***REBELLION.***
AS THE WARDEN, I COULD HAVE GOTTEN RID OF HER, BUT I DIDN'T.
BECAUSE, WELL... I HAVE SOME RESPECT FOR HER.
SHE WAS ***SPECIAL.***
SLRRRP
SHUDDER
YOU...
IF I'D HAD THE CHANCE, I'D HAVE LOVED TO BREAK HER PERSONALLY.
KA-KRAK
DO NOT TOUCH HER AGAIN...

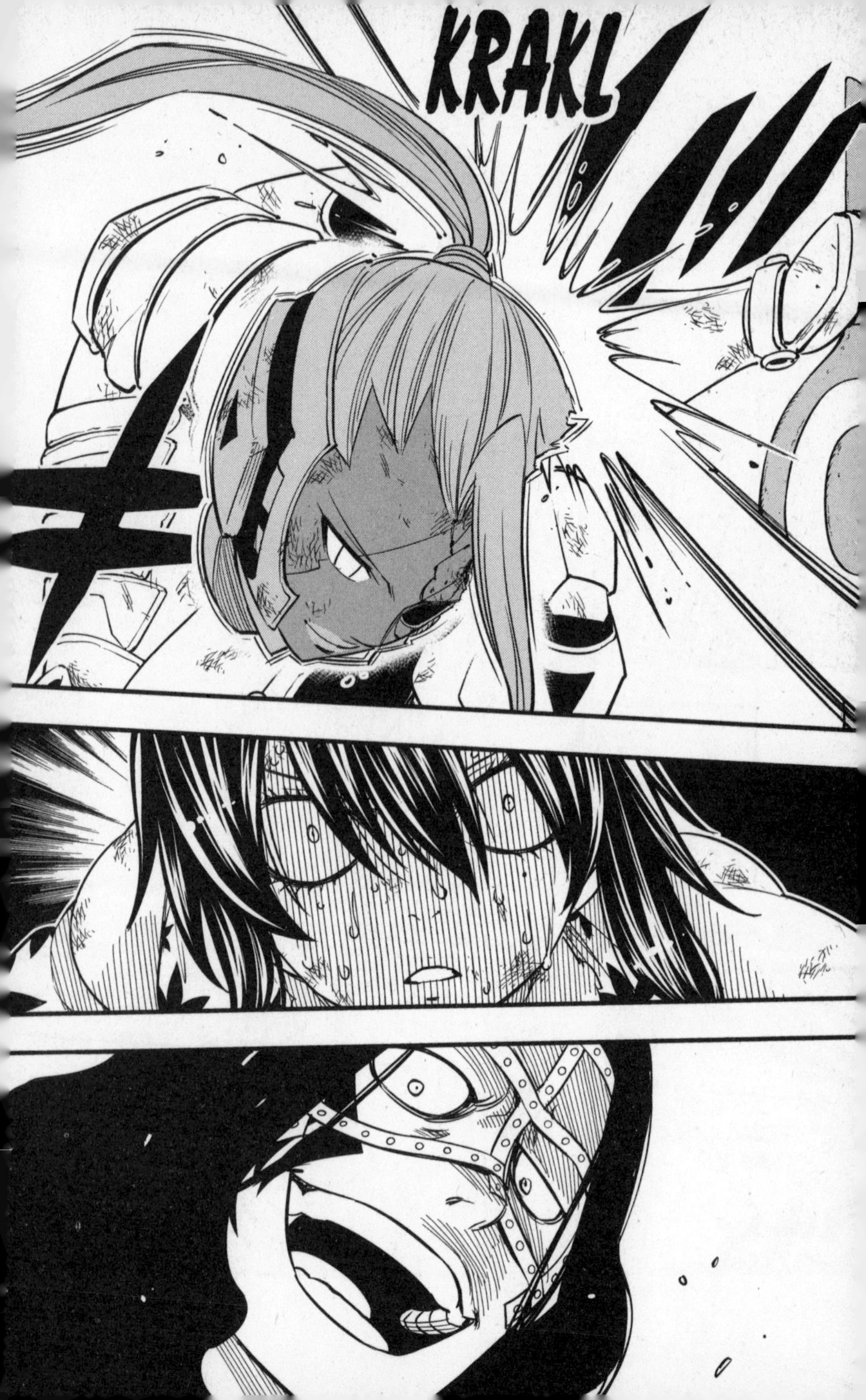
KRAKL

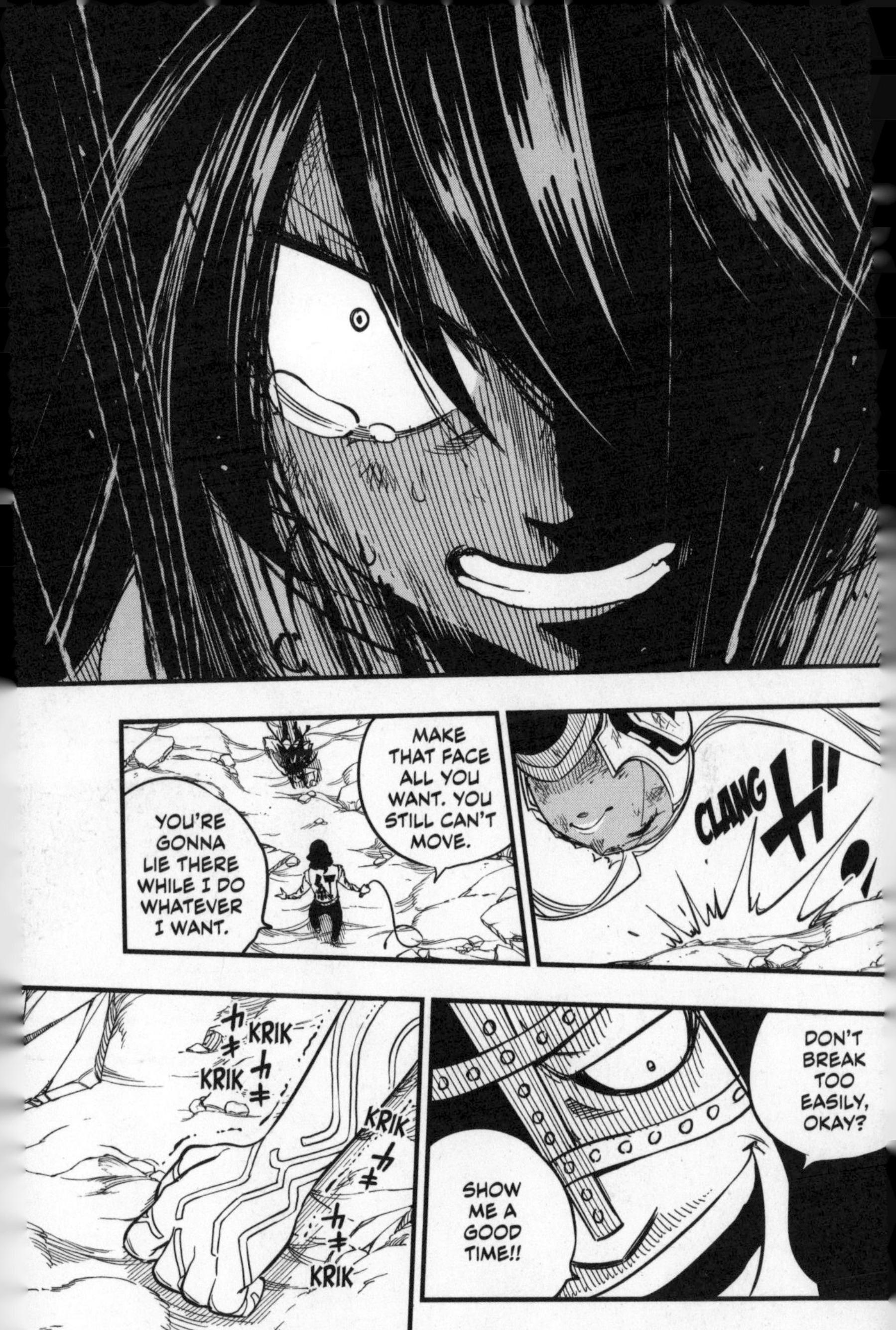
CLANG
MAKE THAT FACE ALL YOU WANT. YOU STILL CAN'T MOVE.
YOU'RE GONNA LIE THERE WHILE I DO WHATEVER I WANT.
DON'T BREAK TOO EASILY, OKAY?
SHOW ME A GOOD TIME!!
KRIK
KRIK
KRIK
KRIK

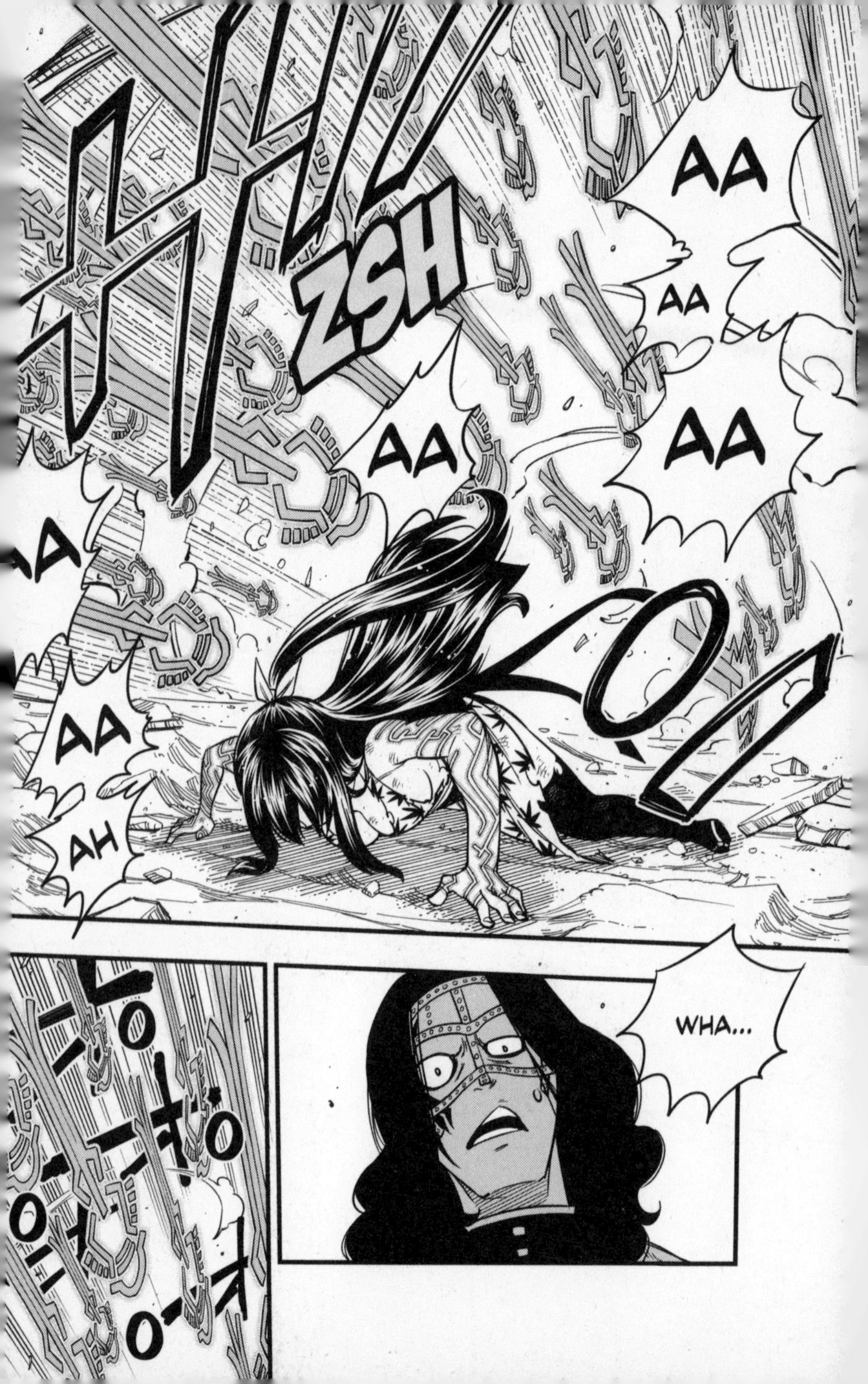
AA
AA
AA
ZSH
AA
AA
AA
AH
WHA...

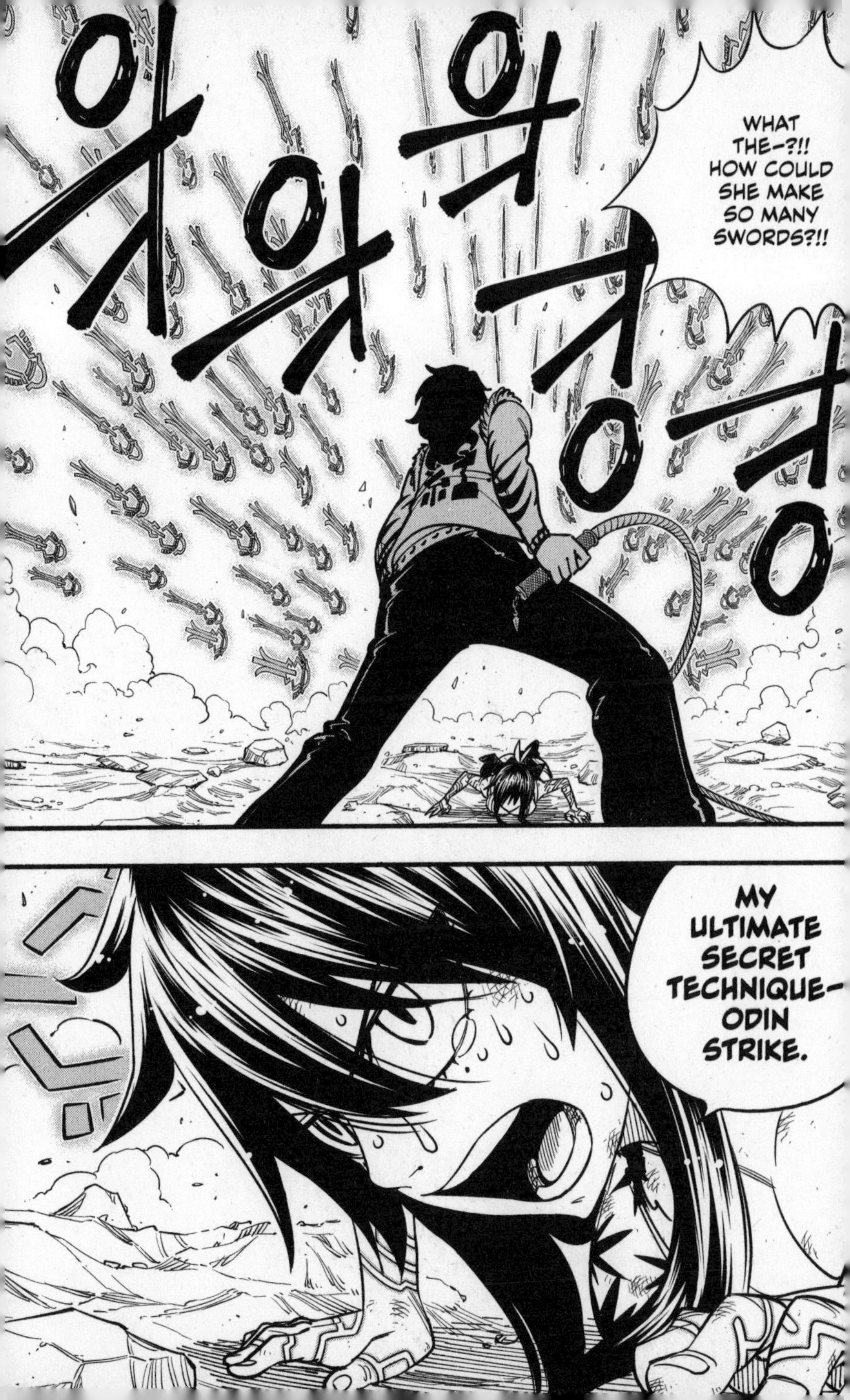
WHAT THE-?!! HOW COULD SHE MAKE SO MANY SWORDS?!!
MY ULTIMATE SECRET TECHNIQUE-ODIN STRIKE.

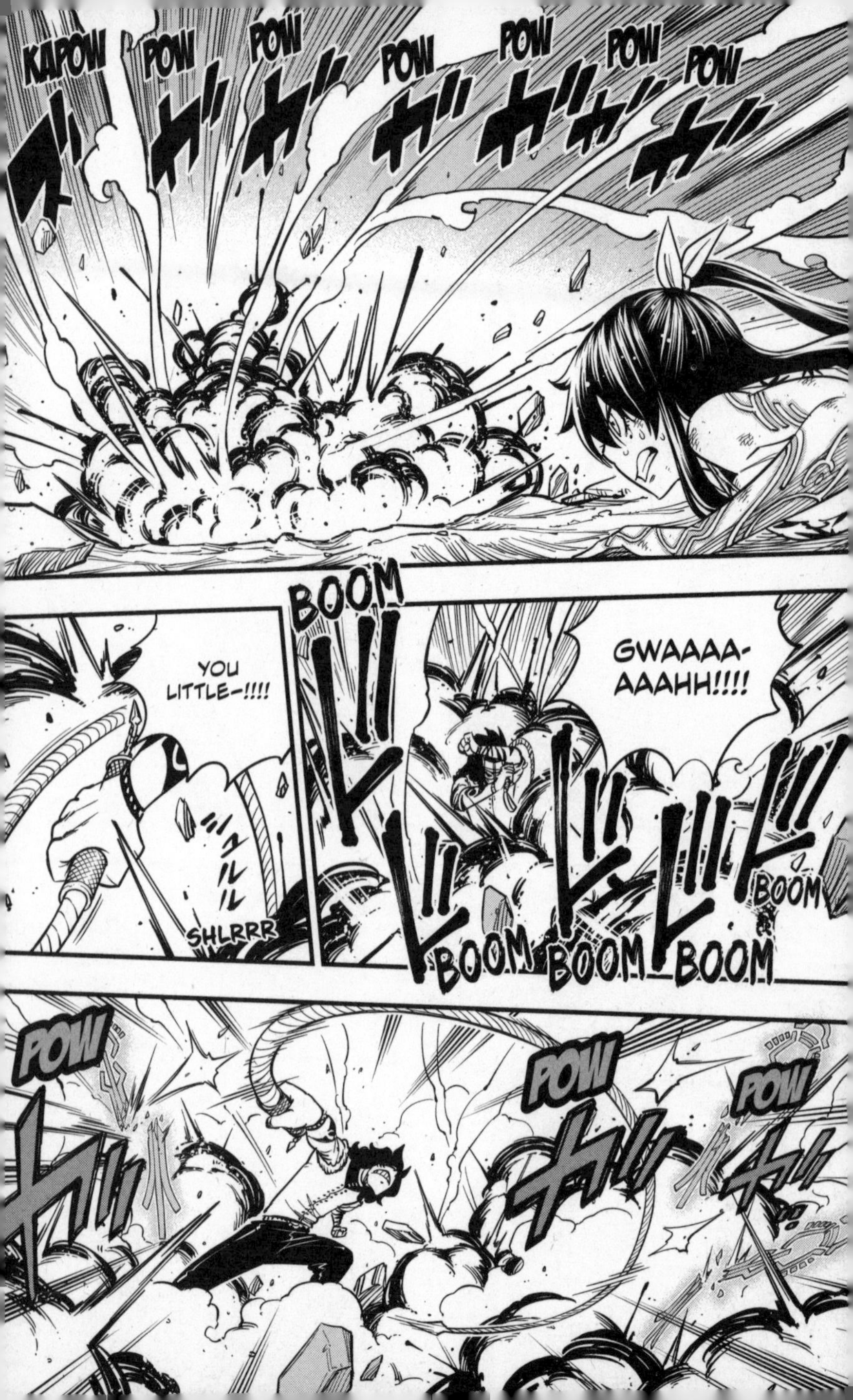
KAPOW POW POW POW POW POW POW
BOOM
GWAAAA-AAAHH!!!!
BOOM BOOM BOOM BOOM
YOU LITTLE-!!!!
SHLRRR
POW POW POW

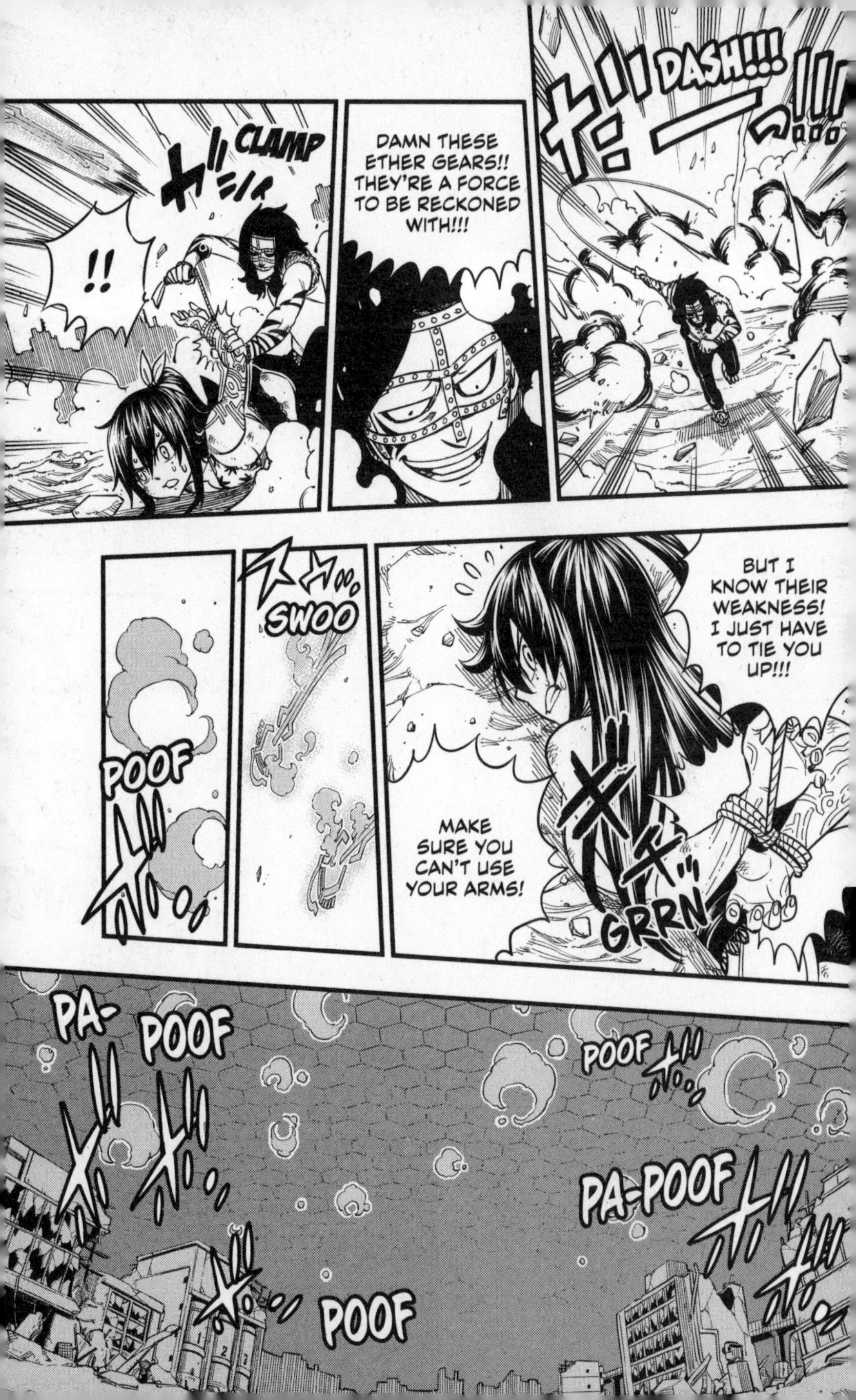
DASH!!!
DAMN THESE ETHER GEARS!! THEY'RE A FORCE TO BE RECKONED WITH!!!
CLAMP
!!
BUT I KNOW THEIR WEAKNESS! I JUST HAVE TO TIE YOU UP!!!
MAKE SURE YOU CAN'T USE YOUR ARMS!
GRRN
SWOO
POOF
POOF
PA-POOF
PA-
POOF
POOF

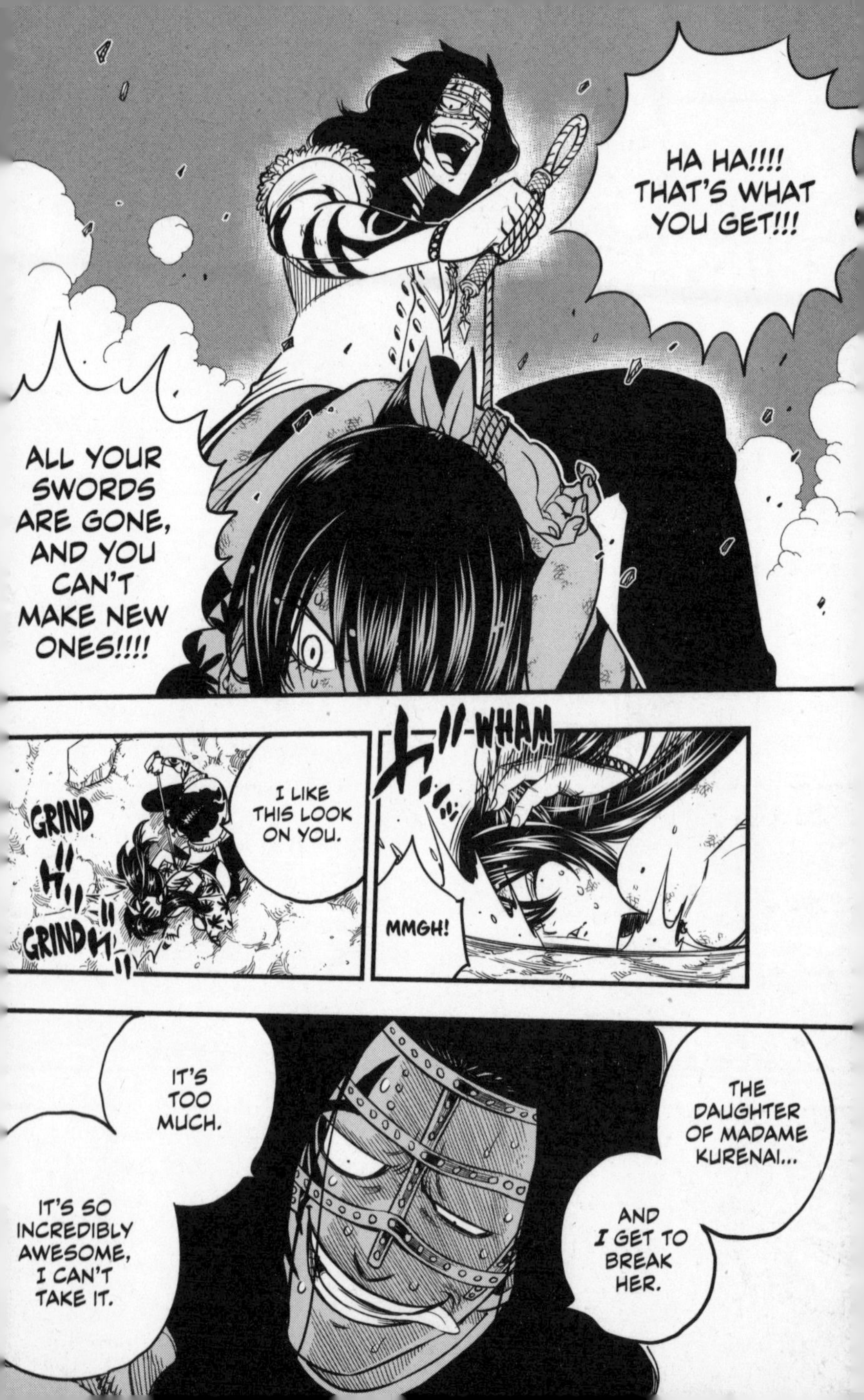
HA HA!!!! THAT'S WHAT YOU GET!!!
ALL YOUR SWORDS ARE GONE, AND YOU CAN'T MAKE NEW ONES!!!!
WHAM
MMGH!
GRIND GRIND
I LIKE THIS LOOK ON YOU.
THE DAUGHTER OF MADAME KURENAI...
AND *I* GET TO BREAK HER.
IT'S TOO MUCH.
IT'S SO INCREDIBLY AWESOME, I CAN'T TAKE IT.

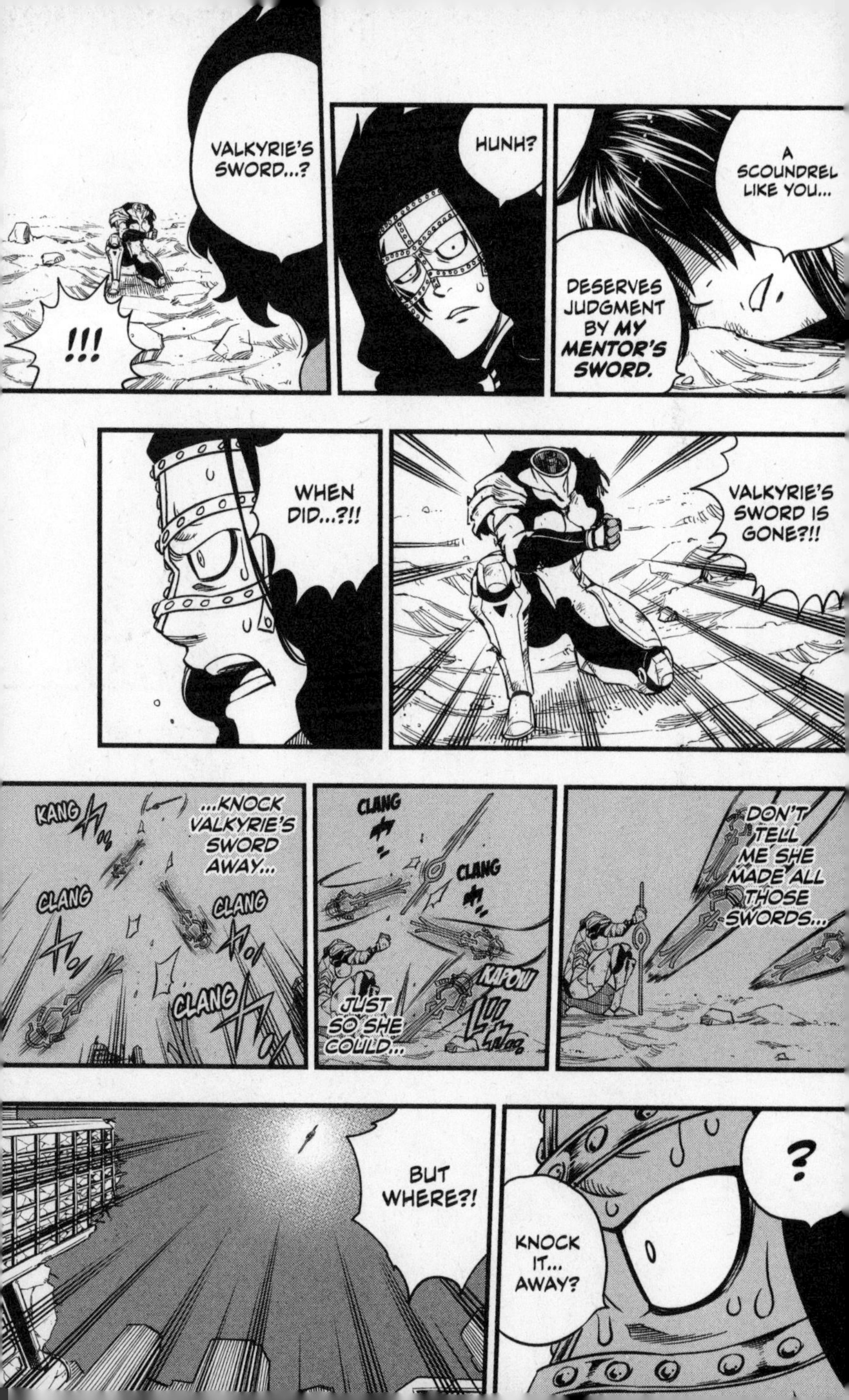
A SCOUNDREL LIKE YOU...
DESERVES JUDGMENT BY MY MENTOR'S SWORD.
HUNH?
VALKYRIE'S SWORD...?
!!!
VALKYRIE'S SWORD IS GONE?!!
WHEN DID...?!!
DON'T TELL ME SHE MADE ALL THOSE SWORDS...
CLANG
CLANG
KAPOW
JUST SO SHE COULD...
KANG
...KNOCK VALKYRIE'S SWORD AWAY...
CLANG
CLANG
CLANG
?
KNOCK IT... AWAY?
BUT WHERE?!

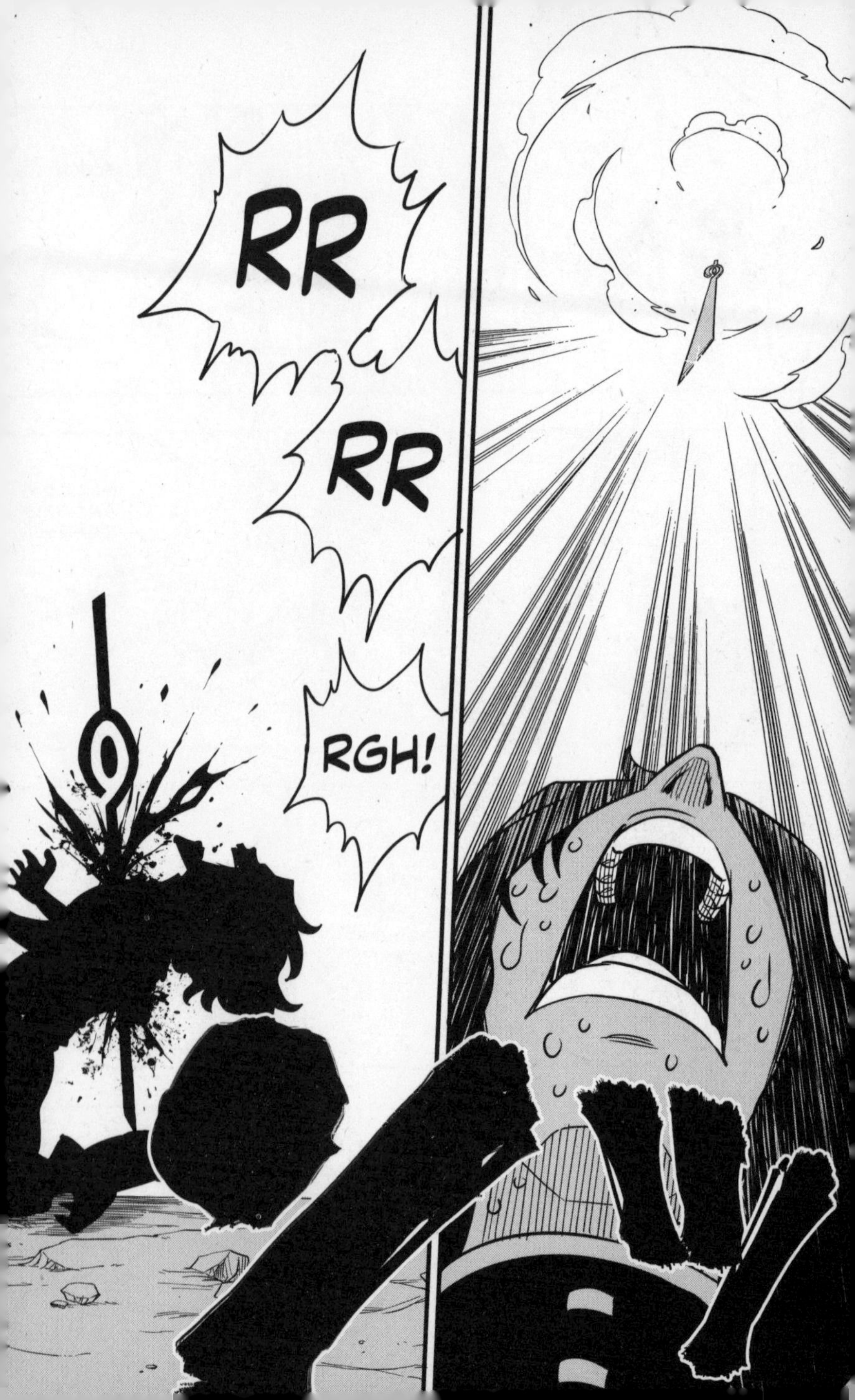
RR
RR
RGH!

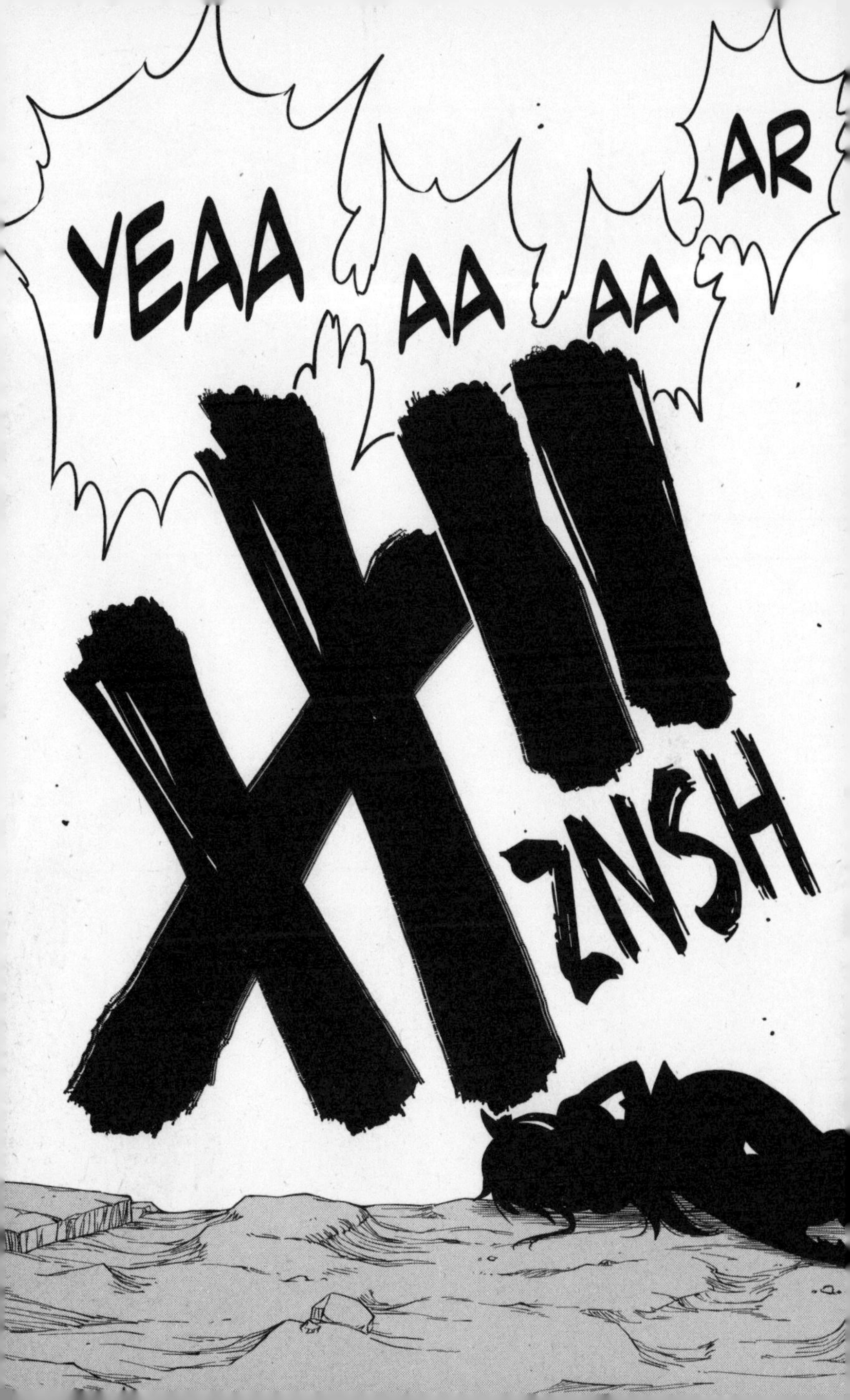
YEAA
AA
AA
AR
ZNSH

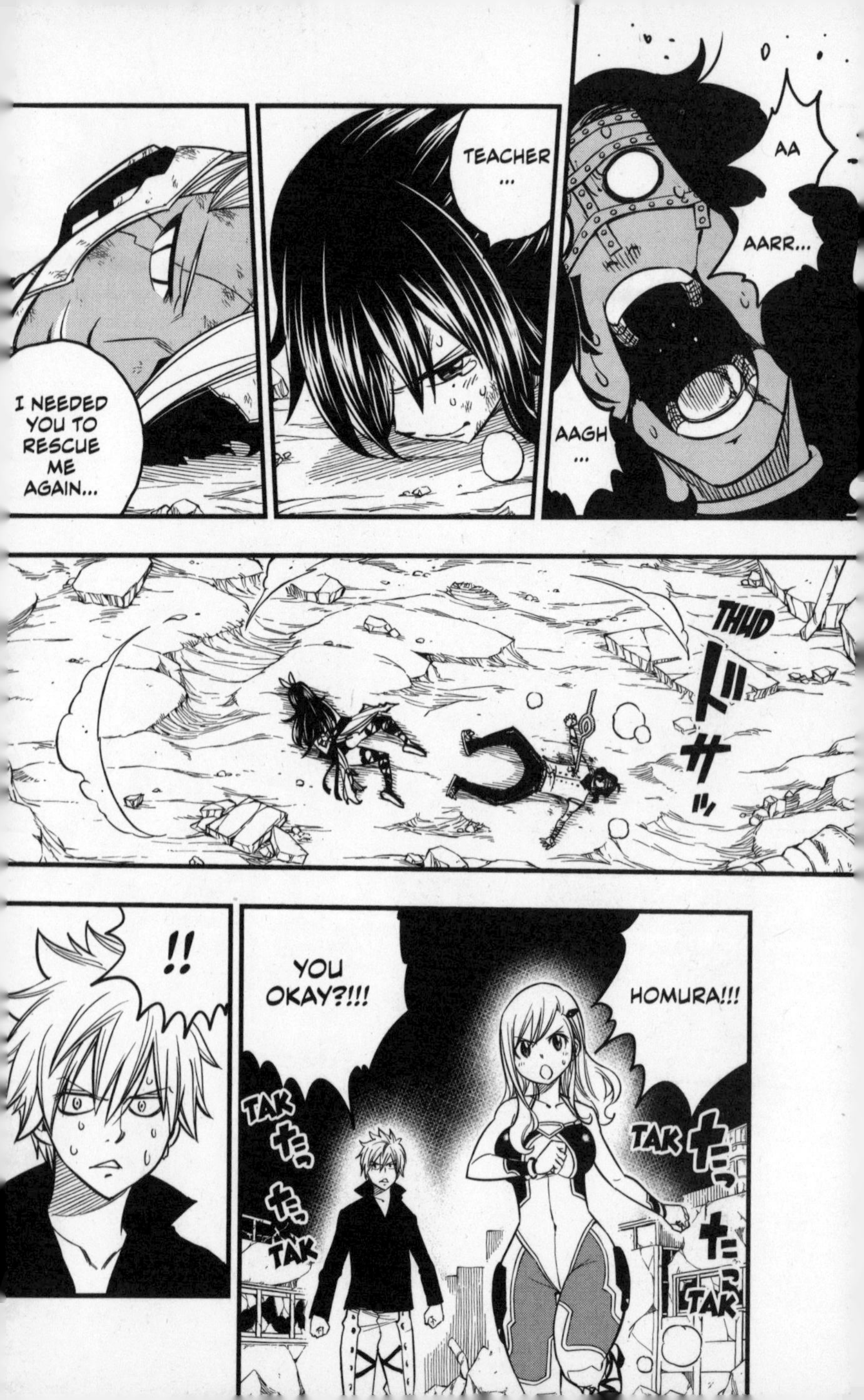
AA
AARR...
AAGH ...
TEACHER ...
I NEEDED YOU TO RESCUE ME AGAIN...
THUD
ドサッ
HOMURA!!!
YOU OKAY?!!!
TAK
TAK
TAK
TAK
!!

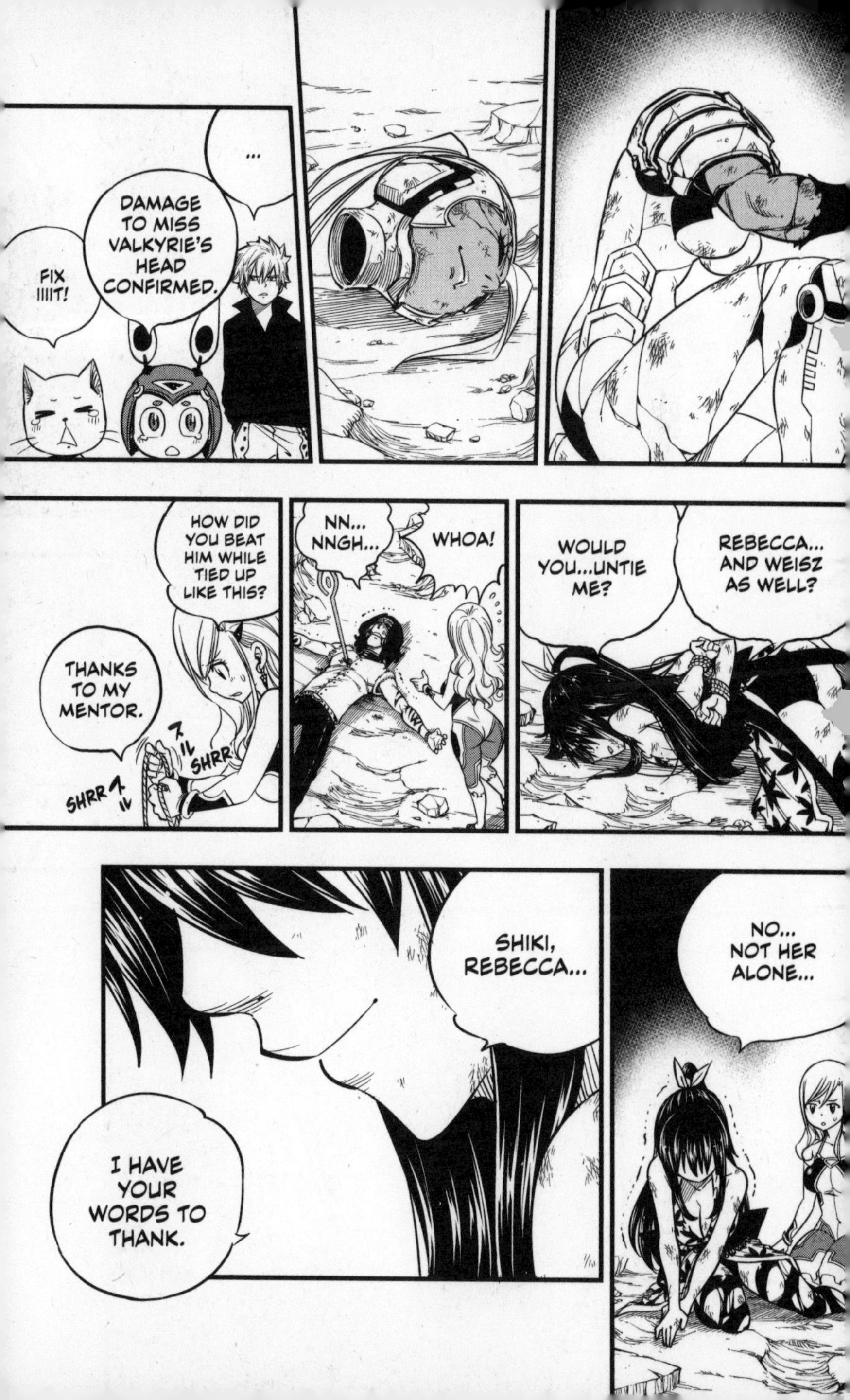
...
DAMAGE TO MISS VALKYRIE'S HEAD CONFIRMED.
FIX IIIIT!
REBECCA... AND WEISZ AS WELL?
WOULD YOU...UNTIE ME?
WHOA!
NN... NNGH...
HOW DID YOU BEAT HIM WHILE TIED UP LIKE THIS?
THANKS TO MY MENTOR.
SHRR
SHRR
NO... NOT HER ALONE...
SHIKI, REBECCA...
I HAVE YOUR WORDS TO THANK.

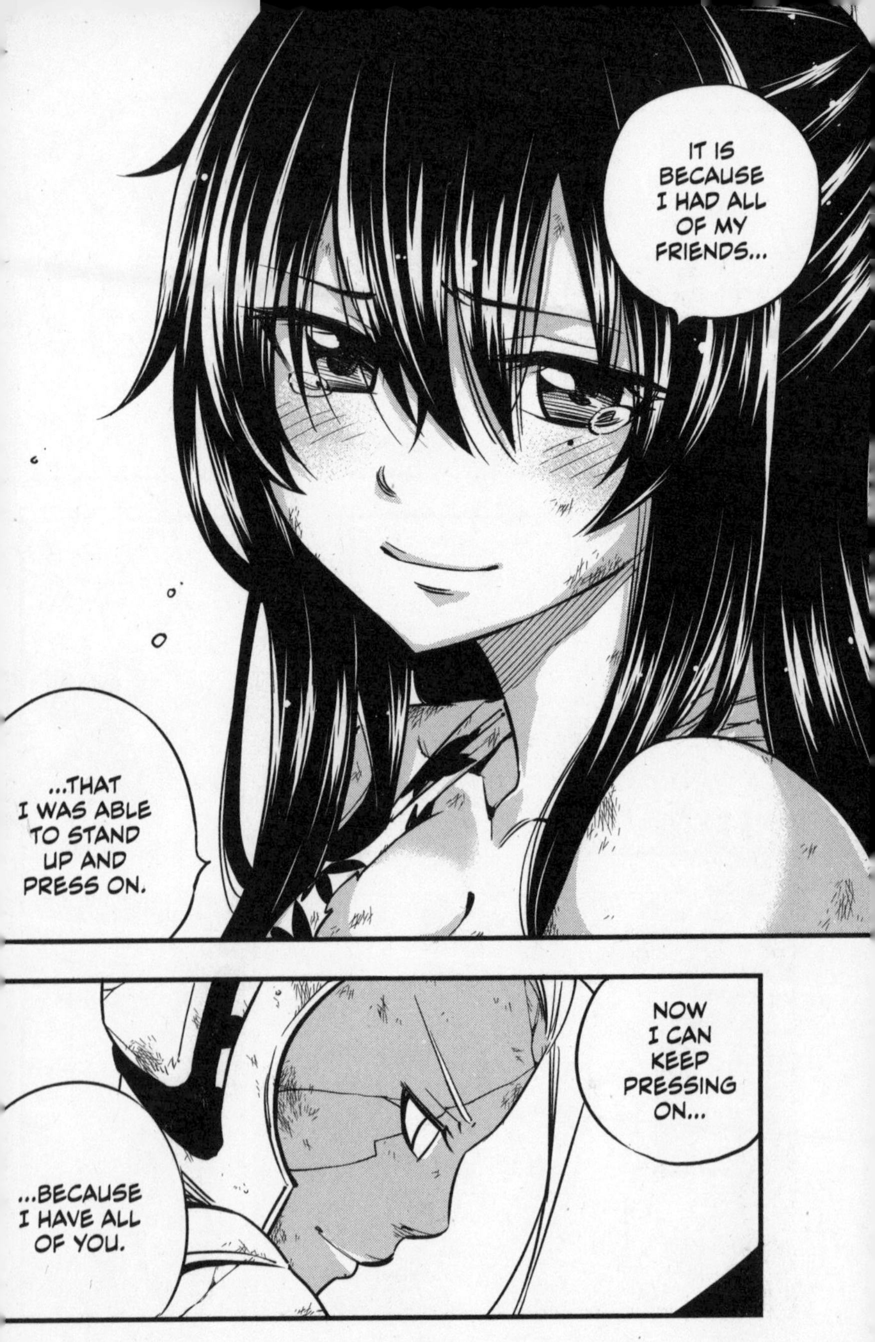
IT IS BECAUSE I HAD ALL OF MY FRIENDS...
...THAT I WAS ABLE TO STAND UP AND PRESS ON.
NOW I CAN KEEP PRESSING ON...
...BECAUSE I HAVE ALL OF YOU.

EDENS ZERO

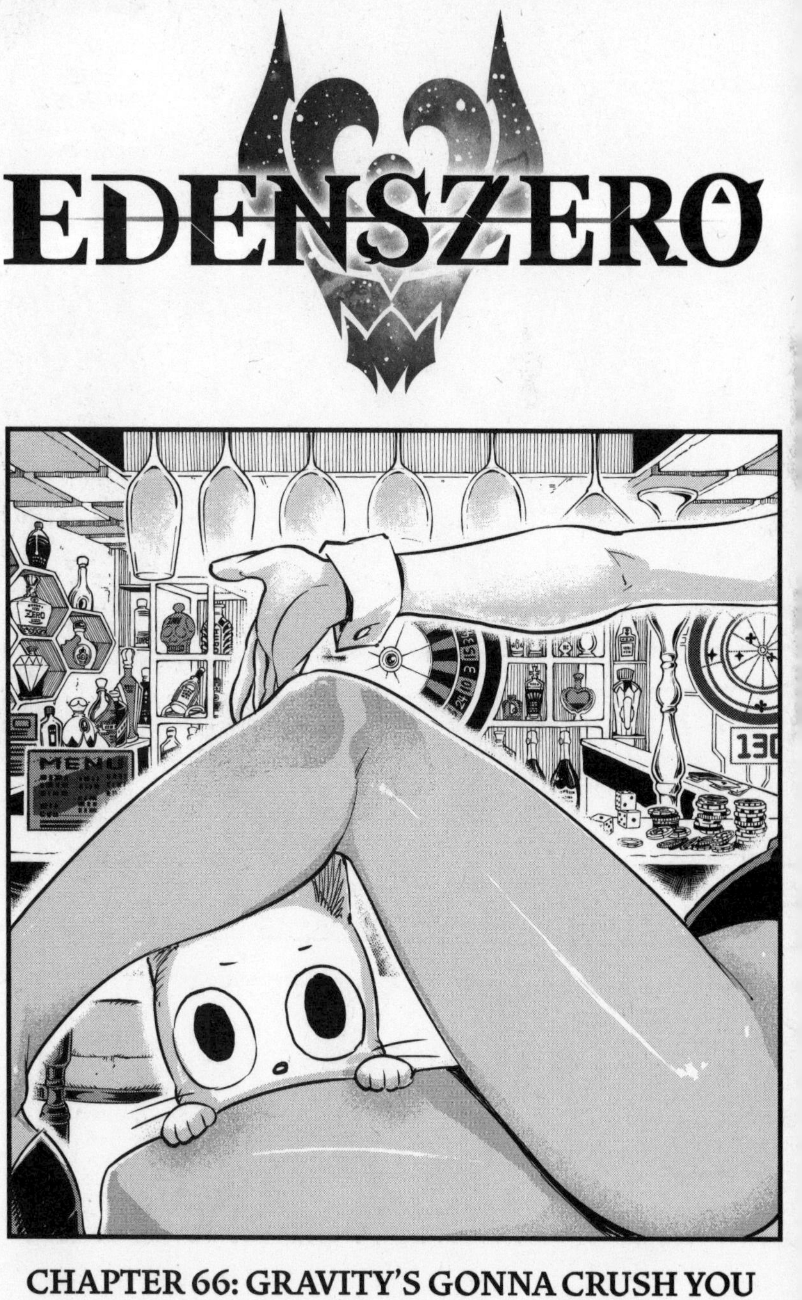
MENU
ZERO
130

CHAPTER 66: GRAVITY'S GONNA CRUSH YOU

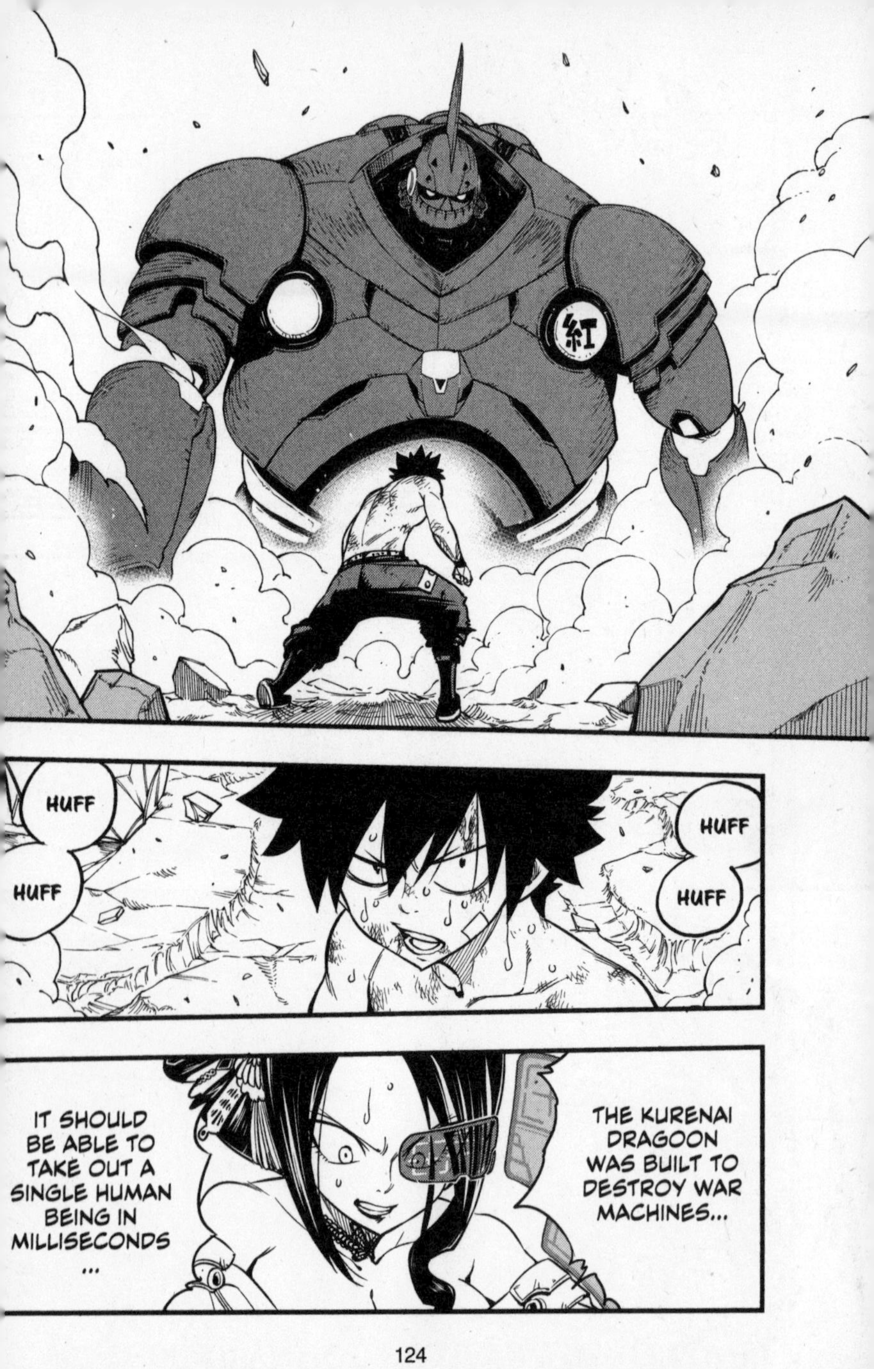
紅
HUFF
HUFF
HUFF
HUFF
THE KURENAI DRAGOON WAS BUILT TO DESTROY WAR MACHINES...
IT SHOULD BE ABLE TO TAKE OUT A SINGLE HUMAN BEING IN MILLISECONDS ...

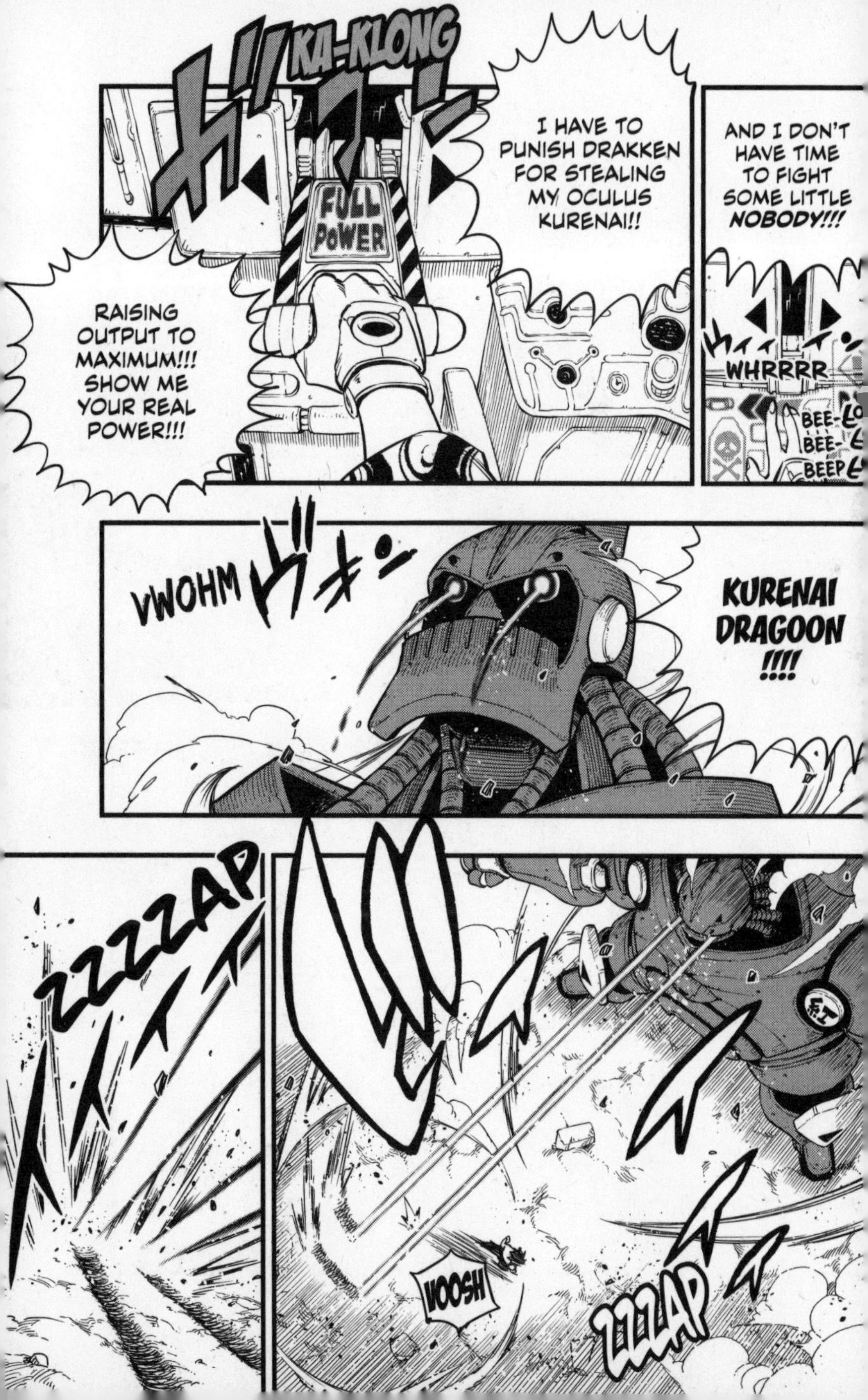
AND I DON'T HAVE TIME TO FIGHT SOME LITTLE *NOBODY!!!*
WHRRRR
BEE-BEE-BEEP
KA-KLONG
FULL POWER
I HAVE TO PUNISH DRAKKEN FOR STEALING MY OCULUS KURENAI!!
RAISING OUTPUT TO MAXIMUM!!! SHOW ME YOUR REAL POWER!!!
KURENAI DRAGOON !!!!
VWOHM
ZZZZAP
VOOSH
ZZZZZAP

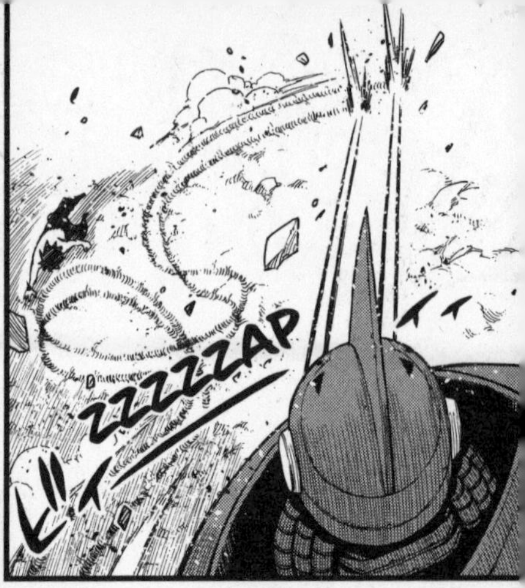
ZZZZZZAP
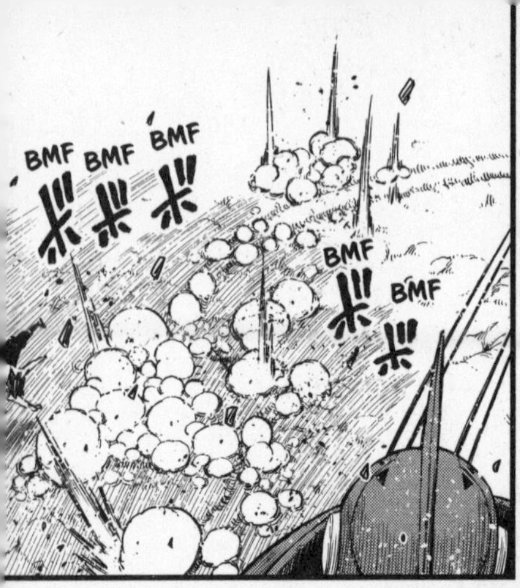
BMF
BMF
BMF
BMF
BMF
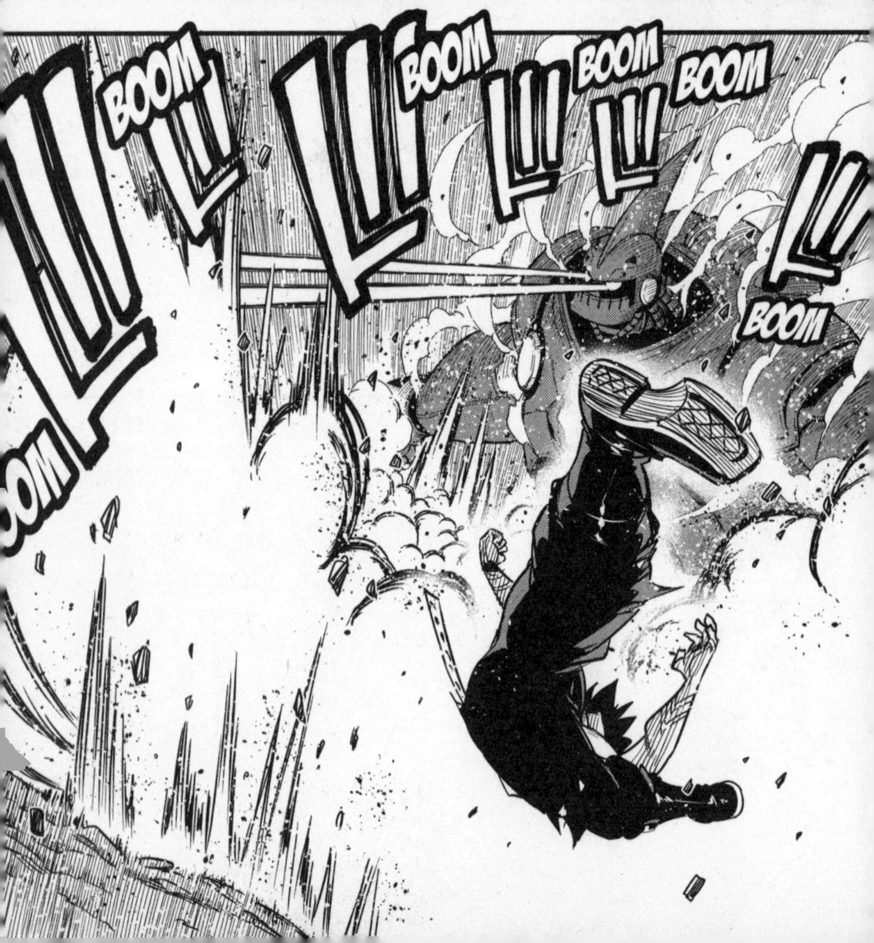
BOOM
BOOM
BOOM
BOOM
BOOM

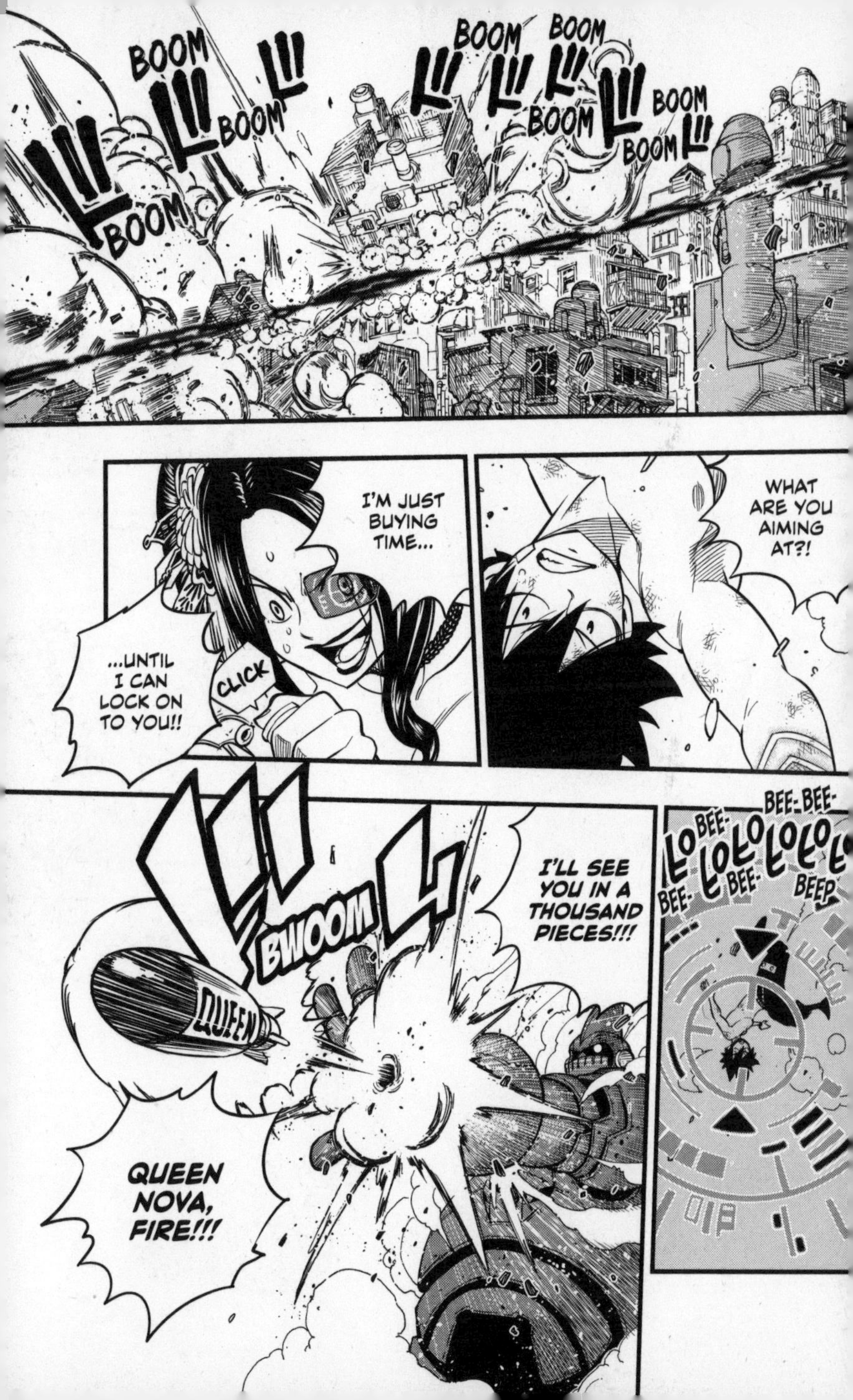
BOOM
BOOM
BOOM
BOOM
BOOM
BOOM
BOOM
BOOM
BOOM
WHAT ARE YOU AIMING AT?!
I'M JUST BUYING TIME...
CLICK
...UNTIL I CAN LOCK ON TO YOU!!
BEE- BEE- BEE- BEE- BEE- BEE- BEEP
I'LL SEE YOU IN A THOUSAND PIECES!!!
BWOOM
QUEEN
QUEEN NOVA, FIRE!!!

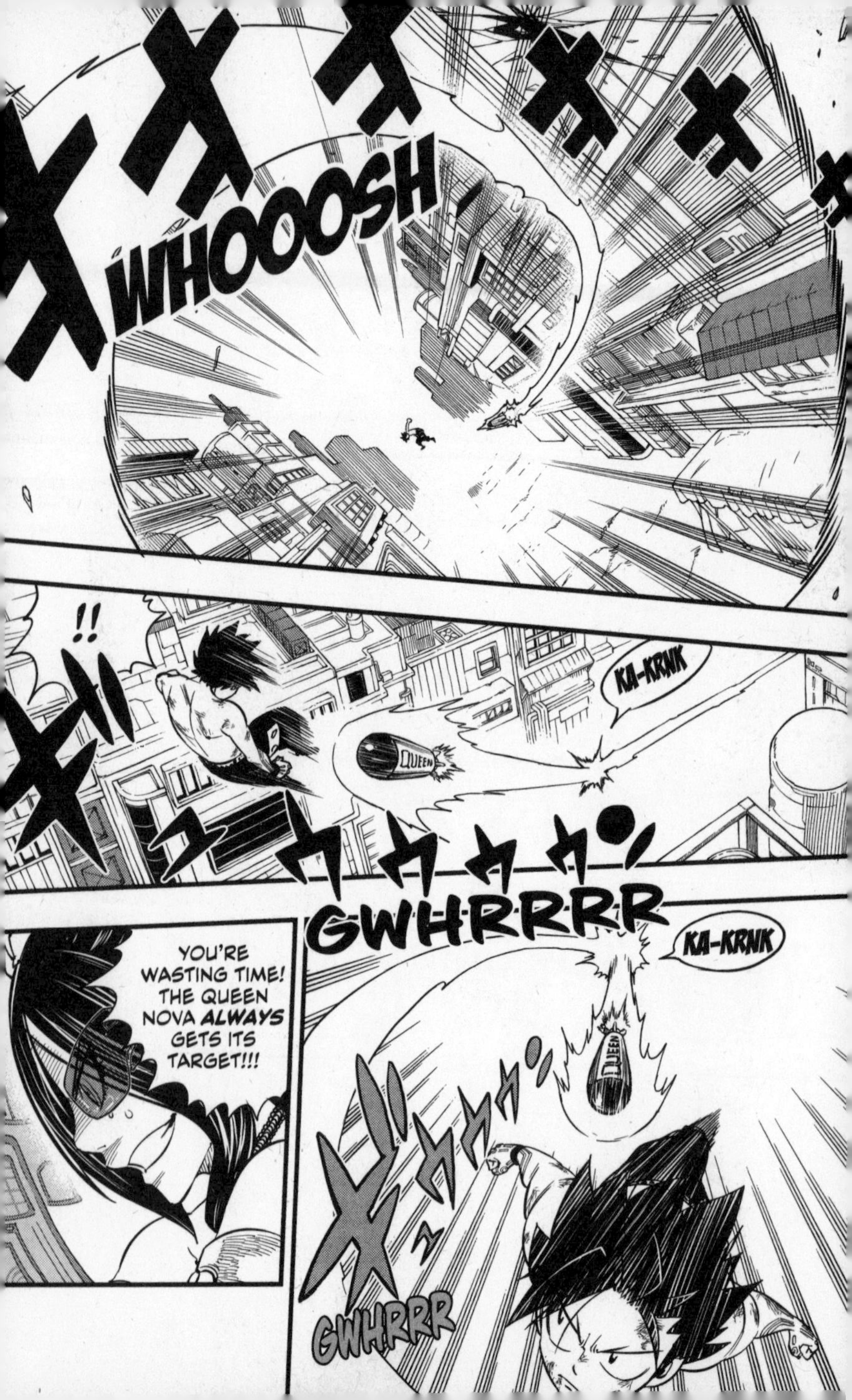
WHOOOSH
KA-KRNK
!!
GWHRRRR
KA-KRNK
GWHRRR
YOU'RE WASTING TIME! THE QUEEN NOVA **ALWAYS** GETS ITS TARGET!!!

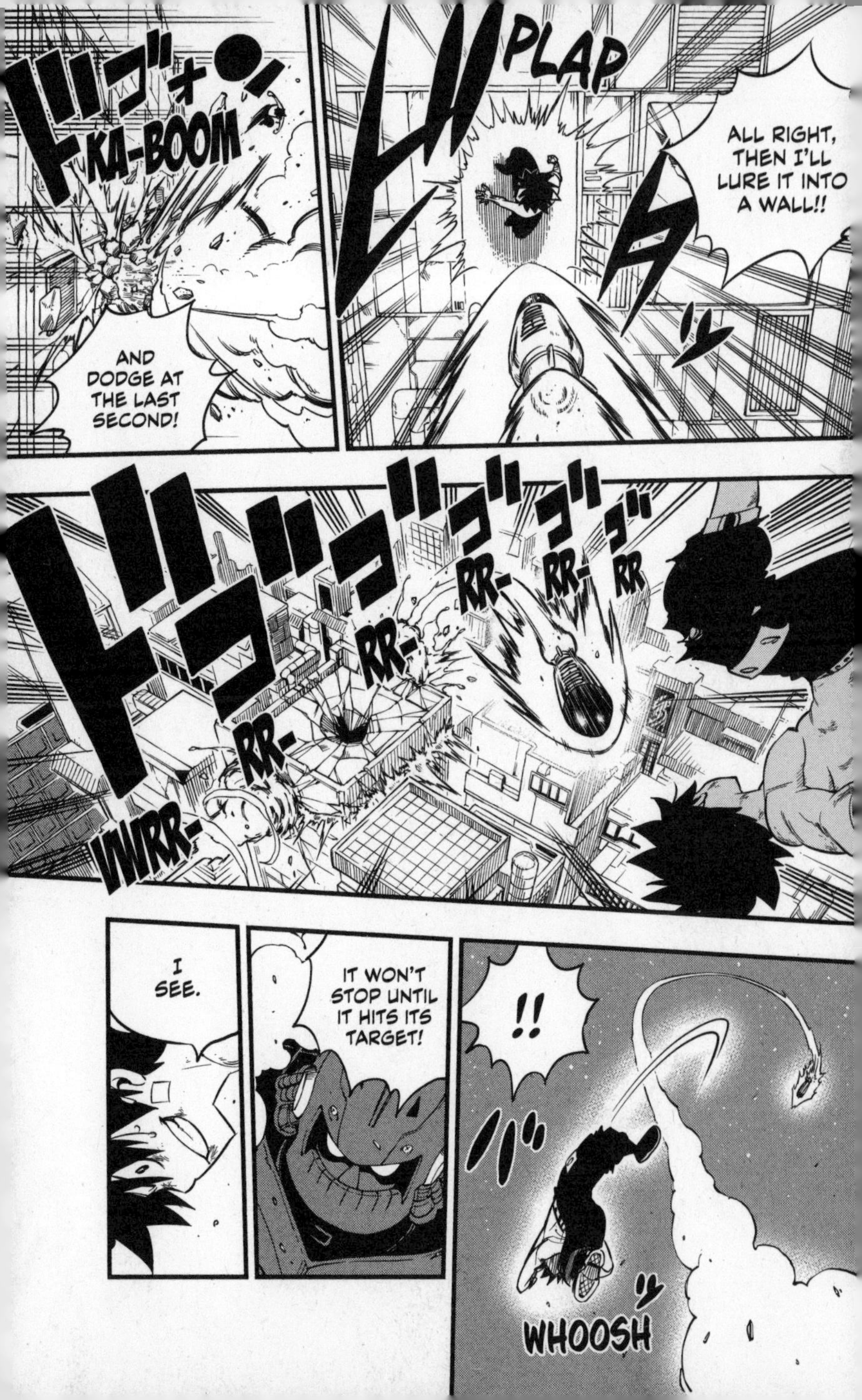
PLAP
ALL RIGHT, THEN I'LL LURE IT INTO A WALL!!
KA-BOOM
AND DODGE AT THE LAST SECOND!
VWRR- RR- RR- RR- RR- RR
!!
WHOOSH
IT WON'T STOP UNTIL IT HITS ITS TARGET!
I SEE.

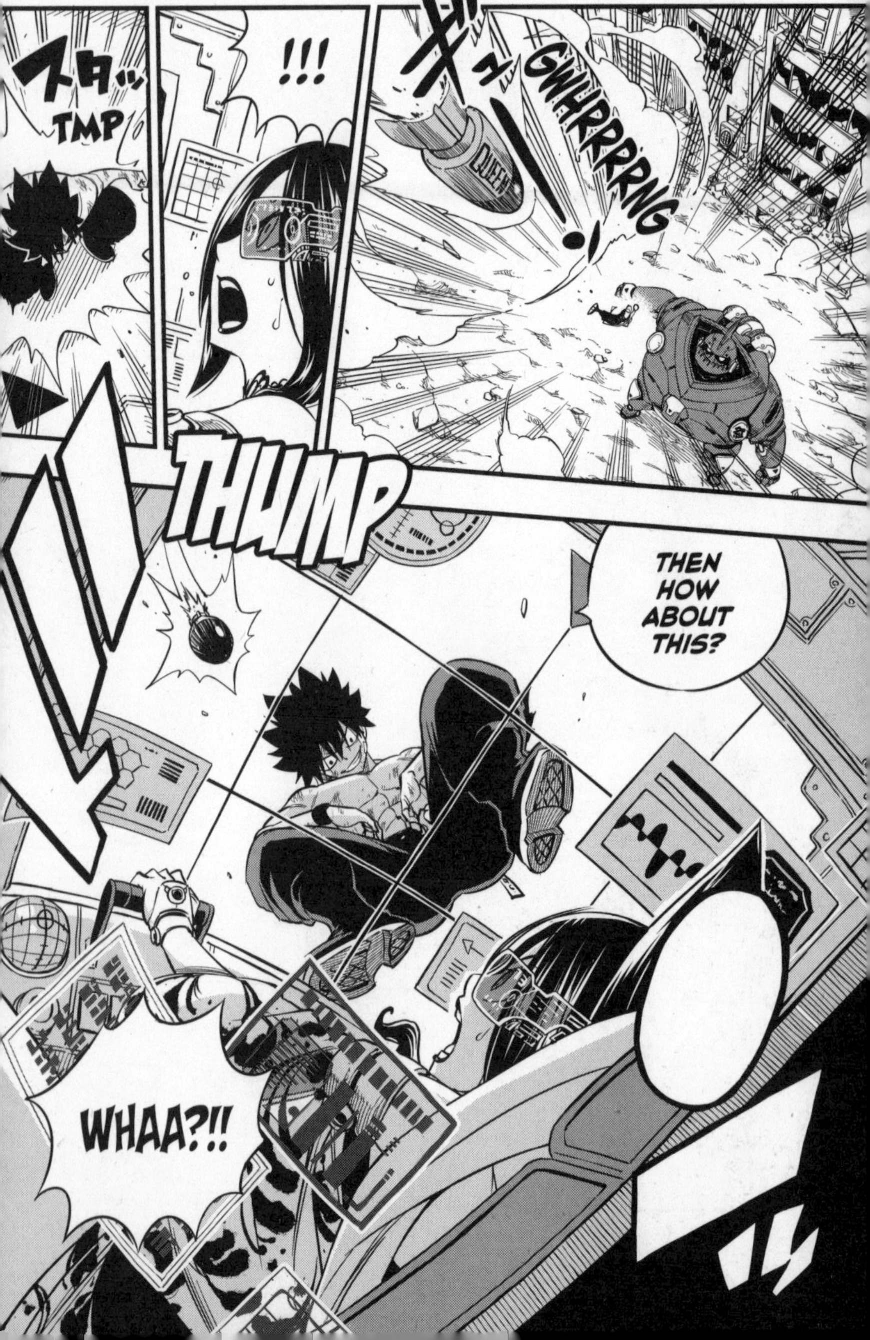
GWHRRRRNG!
QUEEN
!!!
スタッ
TMP
THUMP
THEN HOW ABOUT THIS?
WHAA?!!

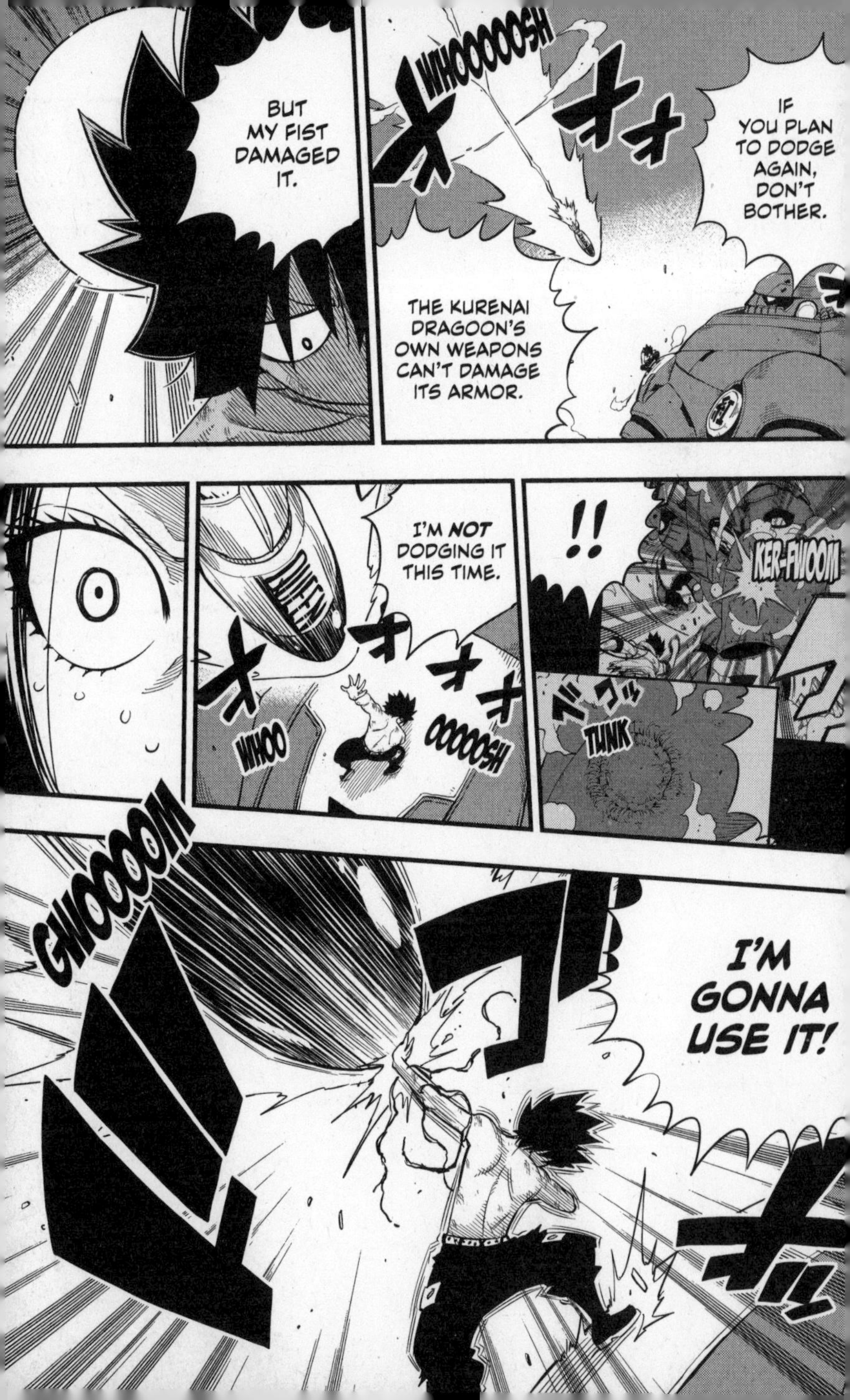
IF YOU PLAN TO DODGE AGAIN, DON'T BOTHER.
WHOOOOOOSH
THE KURENAI DRAGOON'S OWN WEAPONS CAN'T DAMAGE ITS ARMOR.
BUT MY FIST DAMAGED IT.
!!
KER-FWOOM
TUNK
I'M *NOT* DODGING IT THIS TIME.
WHOO
OOOOOSH
I'M GONNA USE IT!
GWOOOOOM

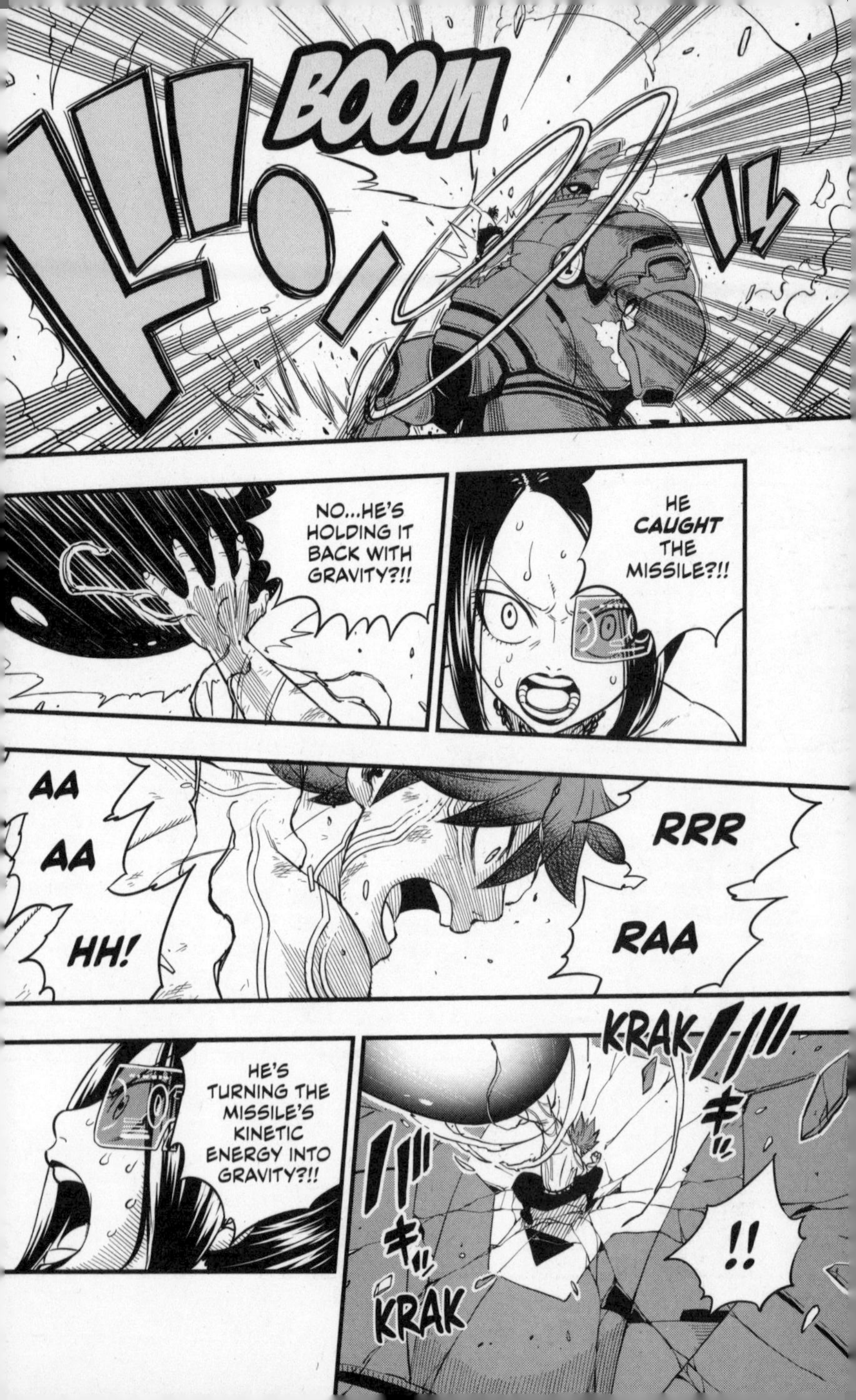
BOOM
HE CAUGHT THE MISSILE?!!
NO...HE'S HOLDING IT BACK WITH GRAVITY?!!
RRR RAA
AA AA HH!
KRAK
!!
KRAK
HE'S TURNING THE MISSILE'S KINETIC ENERGY INTO GRAVITY?!!

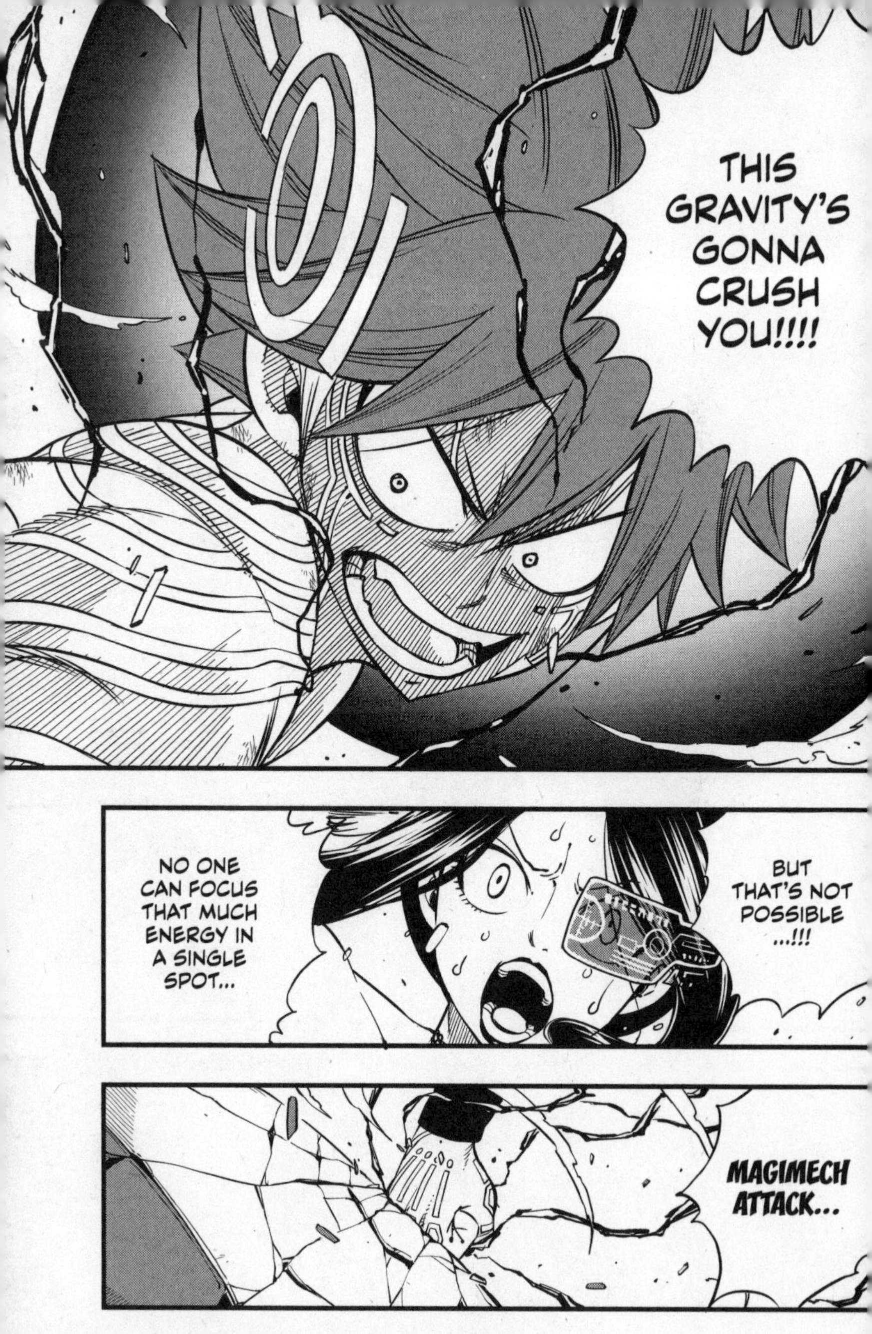
THIS GRAVITY'S GONNA CRUSH YOU!!!!
BUT THAT'S NOT POSSIBLE ...!!!
NO ONE CAN FOCUS THAT MUCH ENERGY IN A SINGLE SPOT...
MAGIMECH ATTACK...

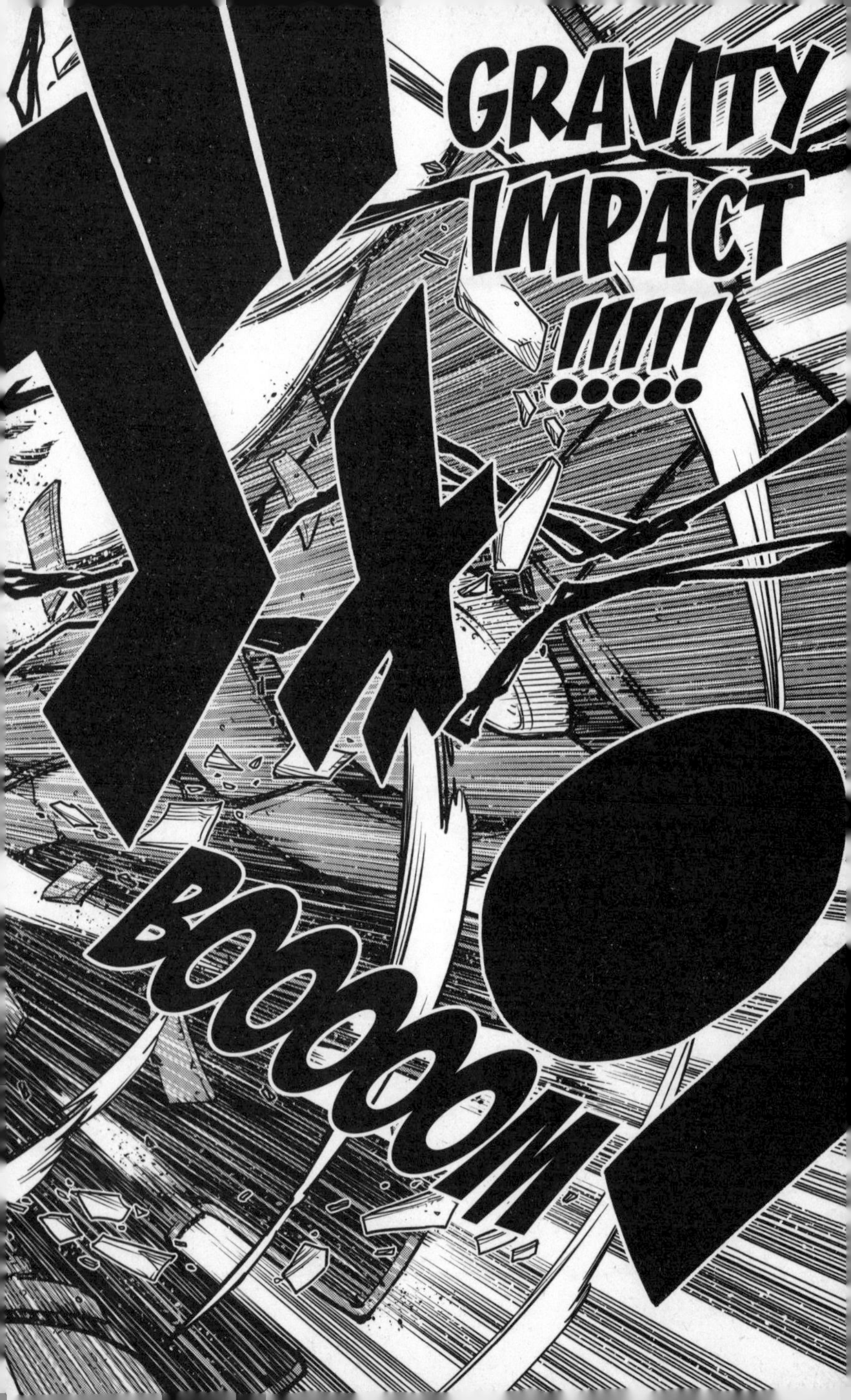
GRAVITY IMPACT !!!!!
BOOOOOM

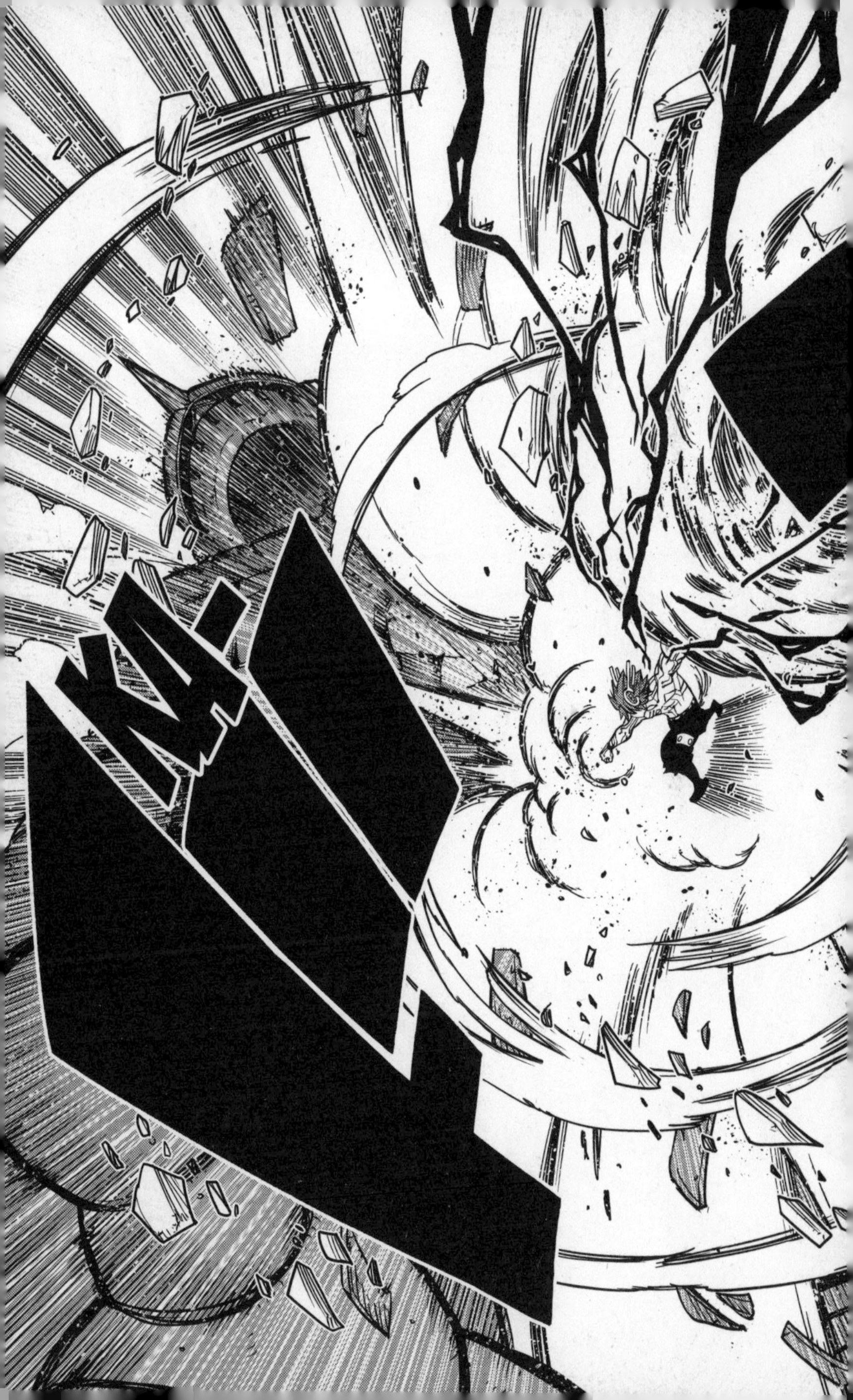

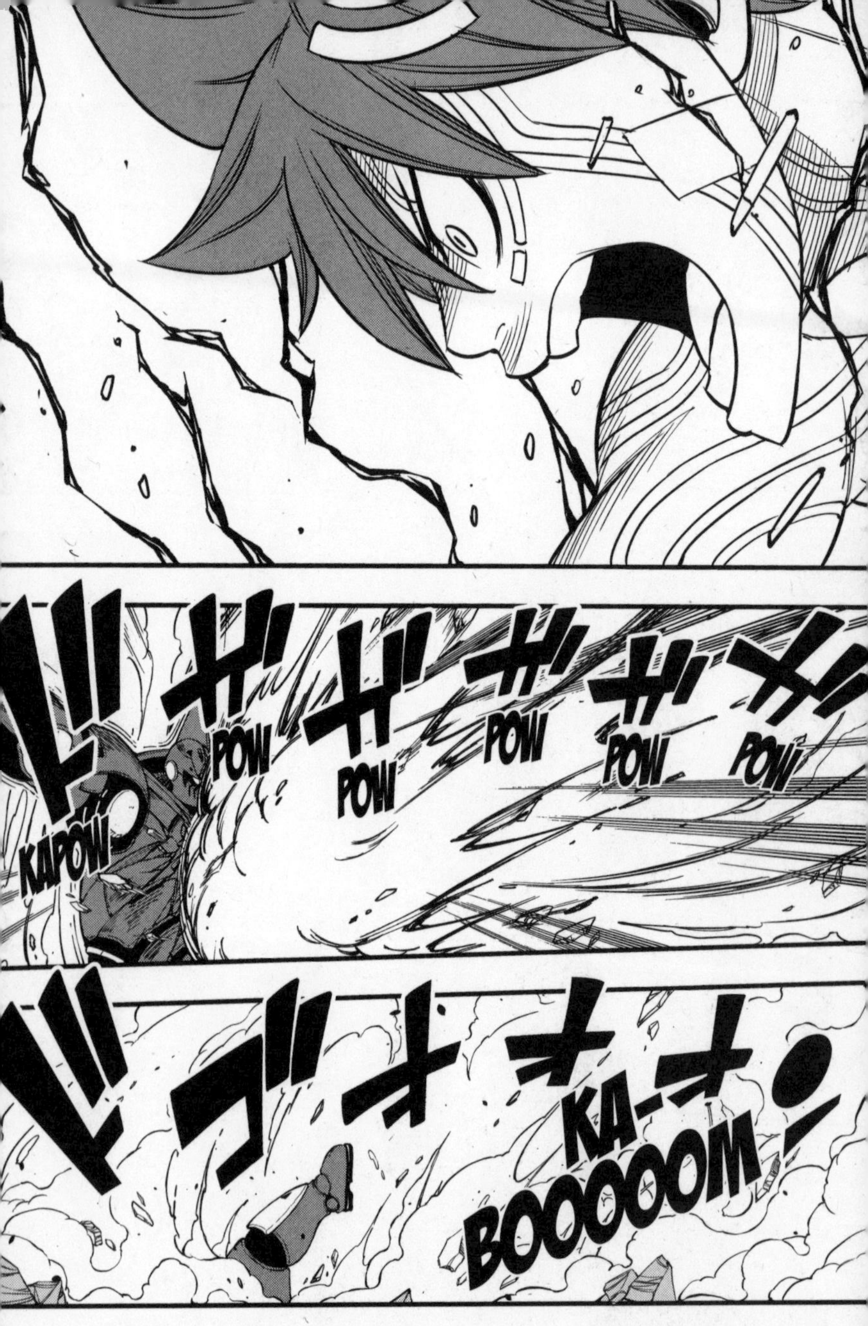
POW
POW
POW
POW
POW
KAPOW
KA-BOOOOOM

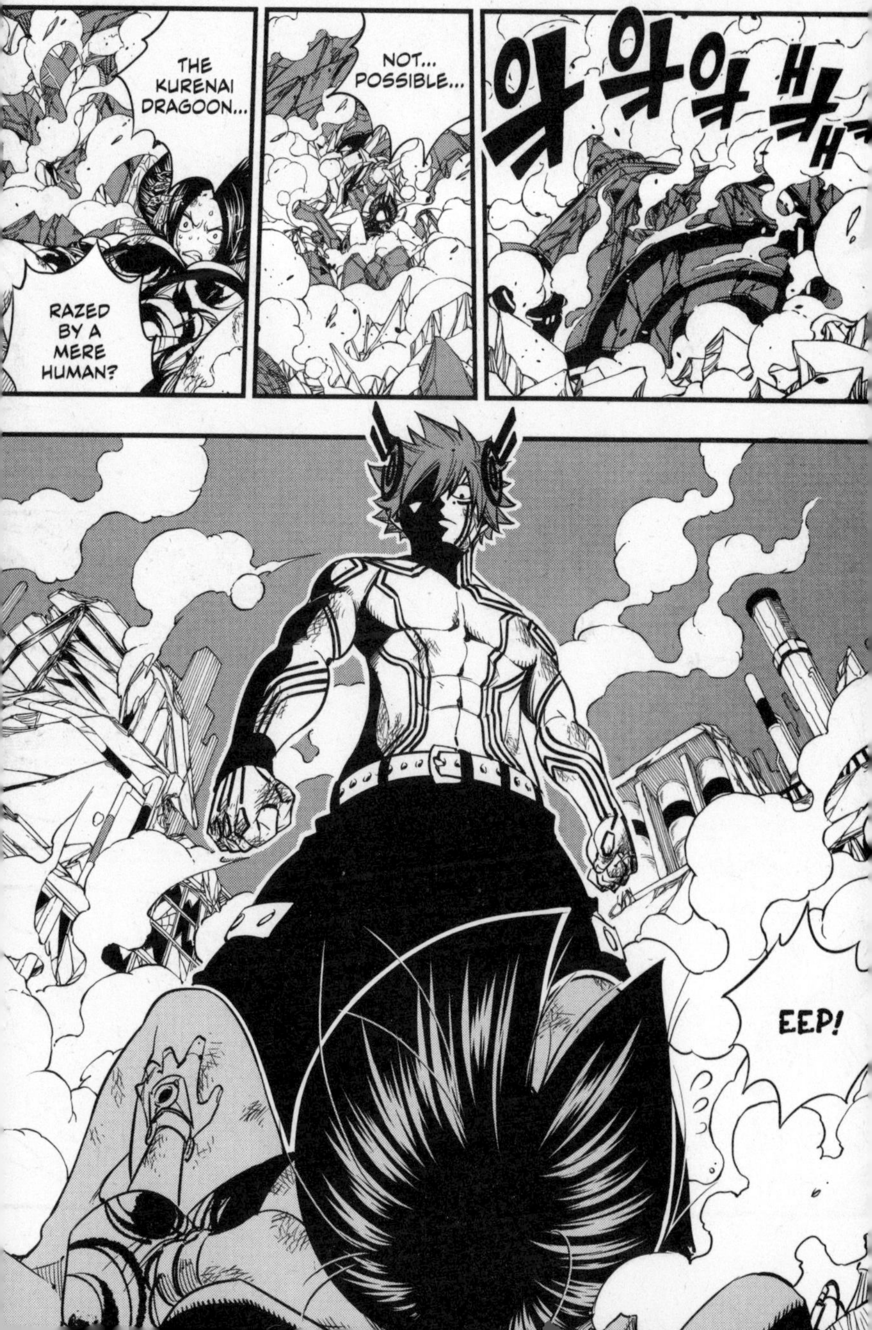
NOT... POSSIBLE...
THE KURENAI DRAGOON...
RAZED BY A MERE HUMAN?
EEP!

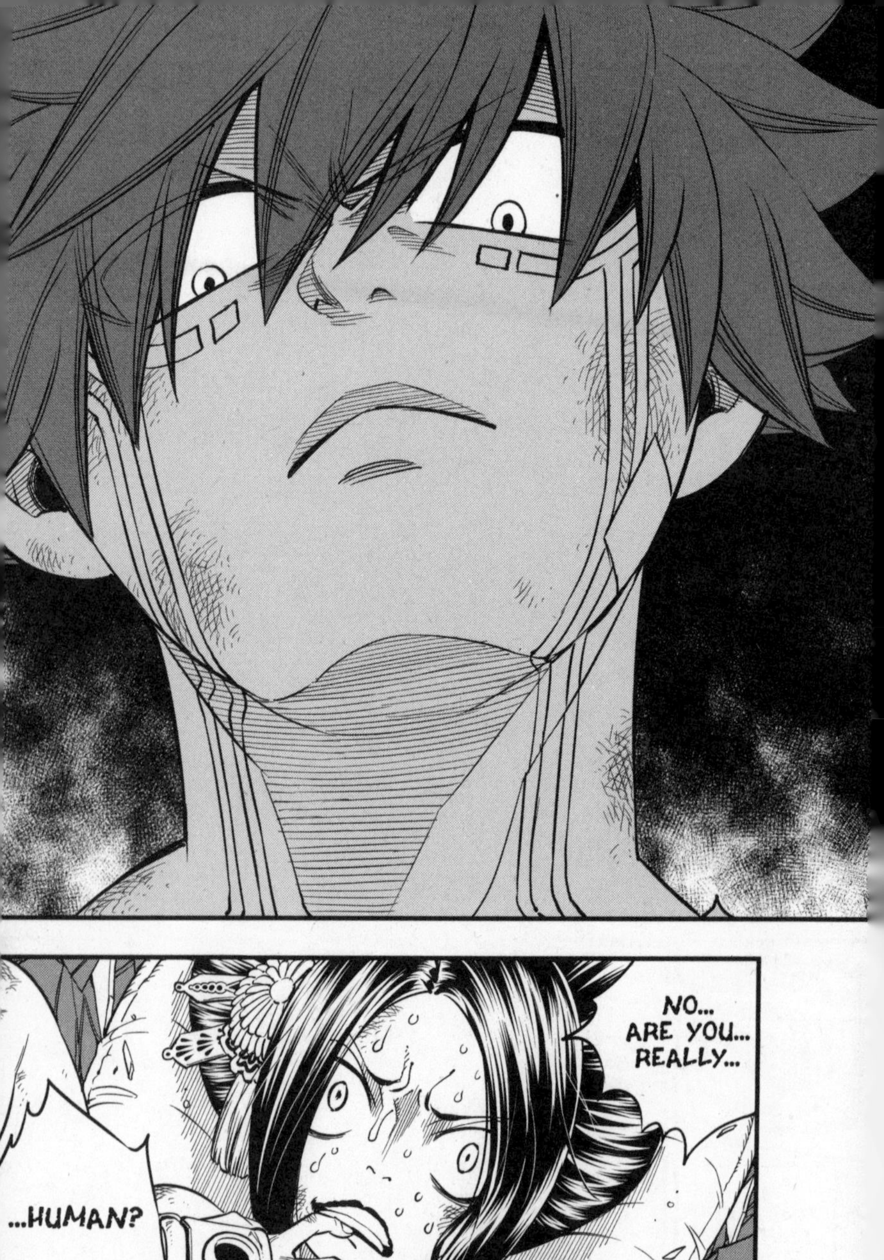
NO...
ARE YOU...
REALLY...
...HUMAN?

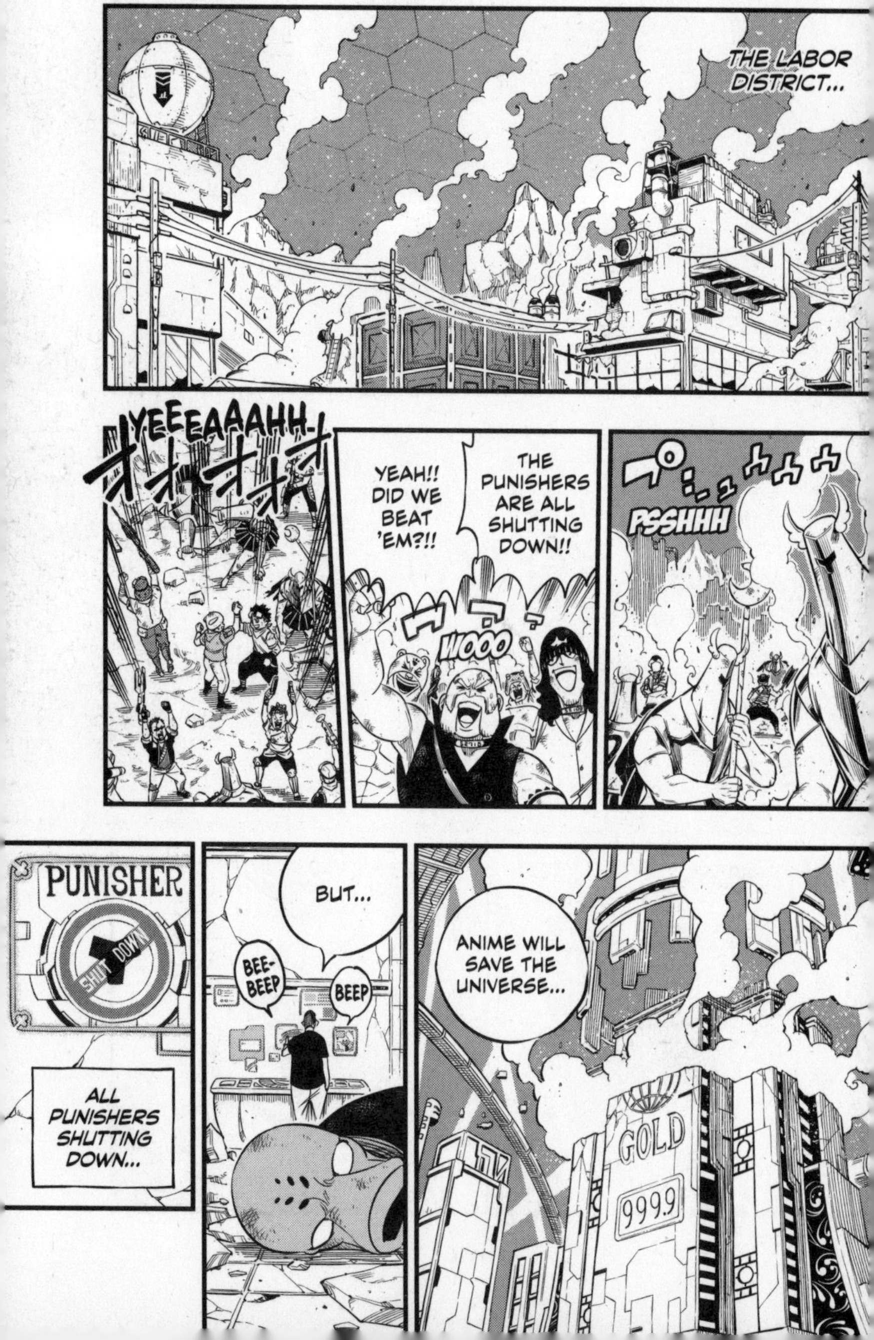
THE LABOR DISTRICT...
PSSHHH
THE PUNISHERS ARE ALL SHUTTING DOWN!!
YEAH!! DID WE BEAT 'EM?!!
WOOO
YEEEAAAHH
ANIME WILL SAVE THE UNIVERSE...
GOLD
9999
BUT...
BEEP
BEE-BEEP
PUNISHER
SHUT DOWN
ALL PUNISHERS SHUTTING DOWN...

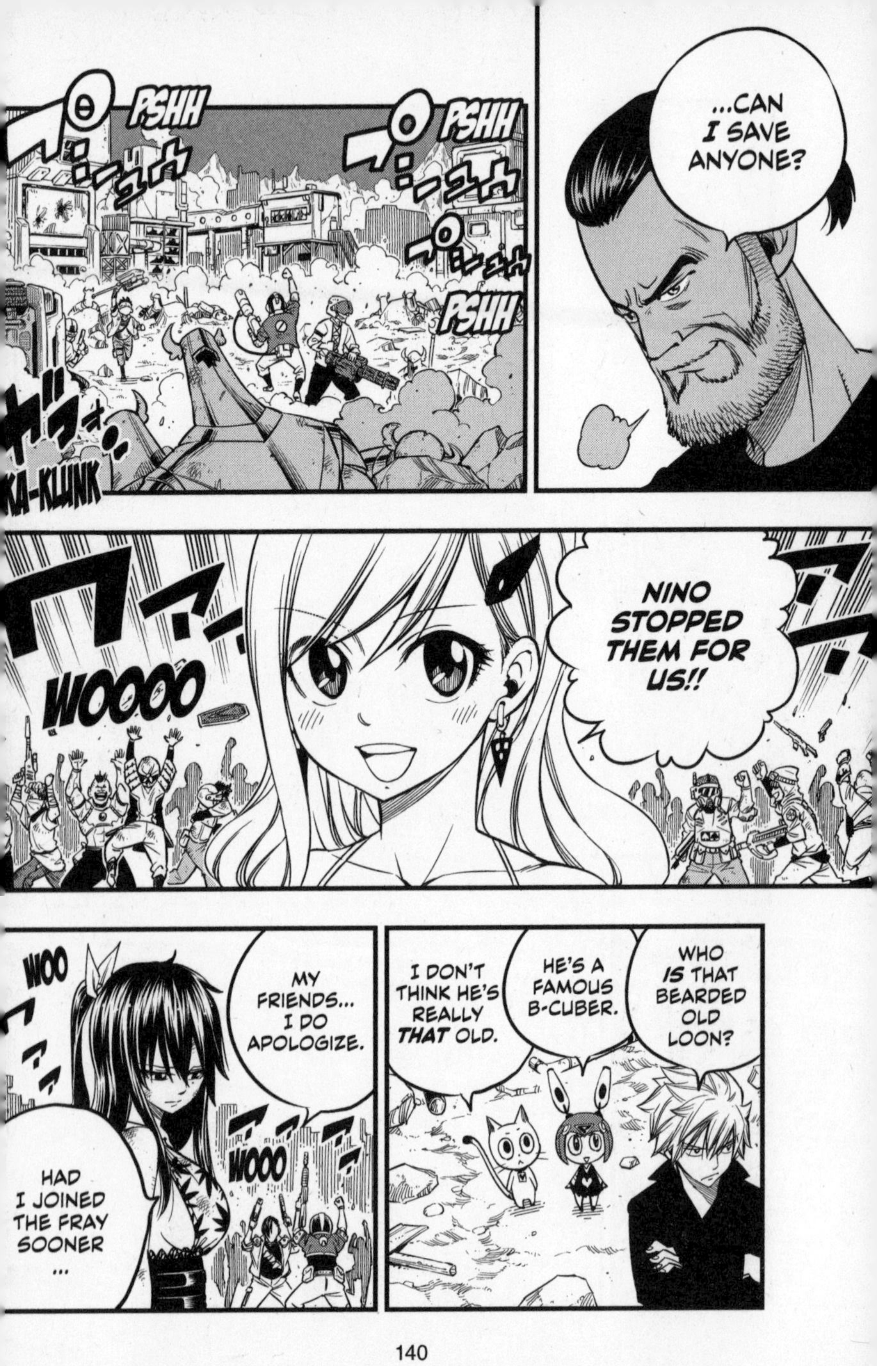
...CAN I SAVE ANYONE?
PSHH
PSHH
PSHH
KA-KLUNK
NINO STOPPED THEM FOR US!!
WOOOO
WHO IS THAT BEARDED OLD LOON?
HE'S A FAMOUS B-CUBER.
I DON'T THINK HE'S REALLY THAT OLD.
MY FRIENDS... I DO APOLOGIZE.
WOO
WOOO
HAD I JOINED THE FRAY SOONER ...

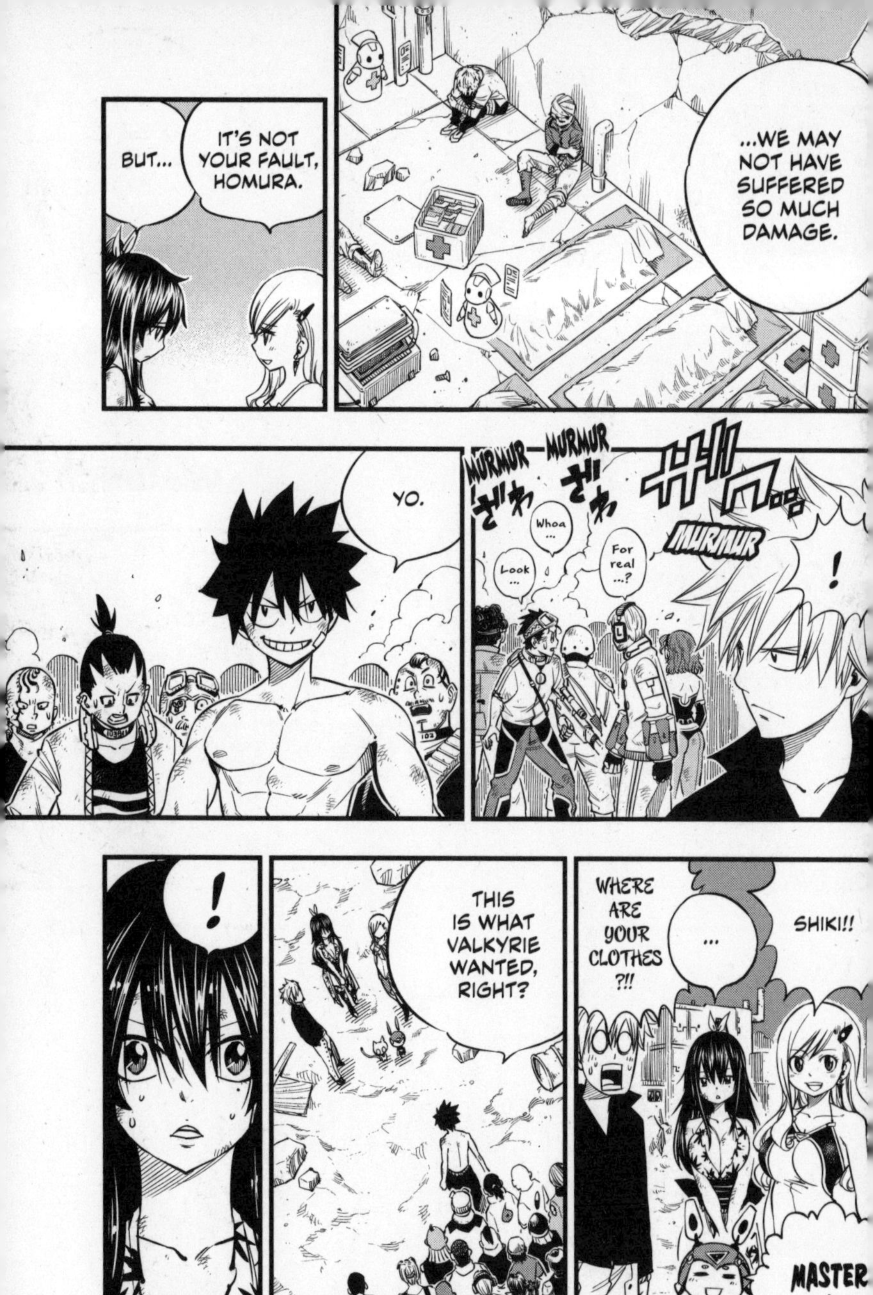
...WE MAY NOT HAVE SUFFERED SO MUCH DAMAGE.
IT'S NOT YOUR FAULT, HOMURA.
BUT...
MURMUR
MURMUR
MURMUR
ざわ
ざわ
For real ...?
Whoa ...
Look ...
!
YO.
SHIKI!!
...
WHERE ARE YOUR CLOTHES ?!!
MASTER !
THIS IS WHAT VALKYRIE WANTED, RIGHT?
!

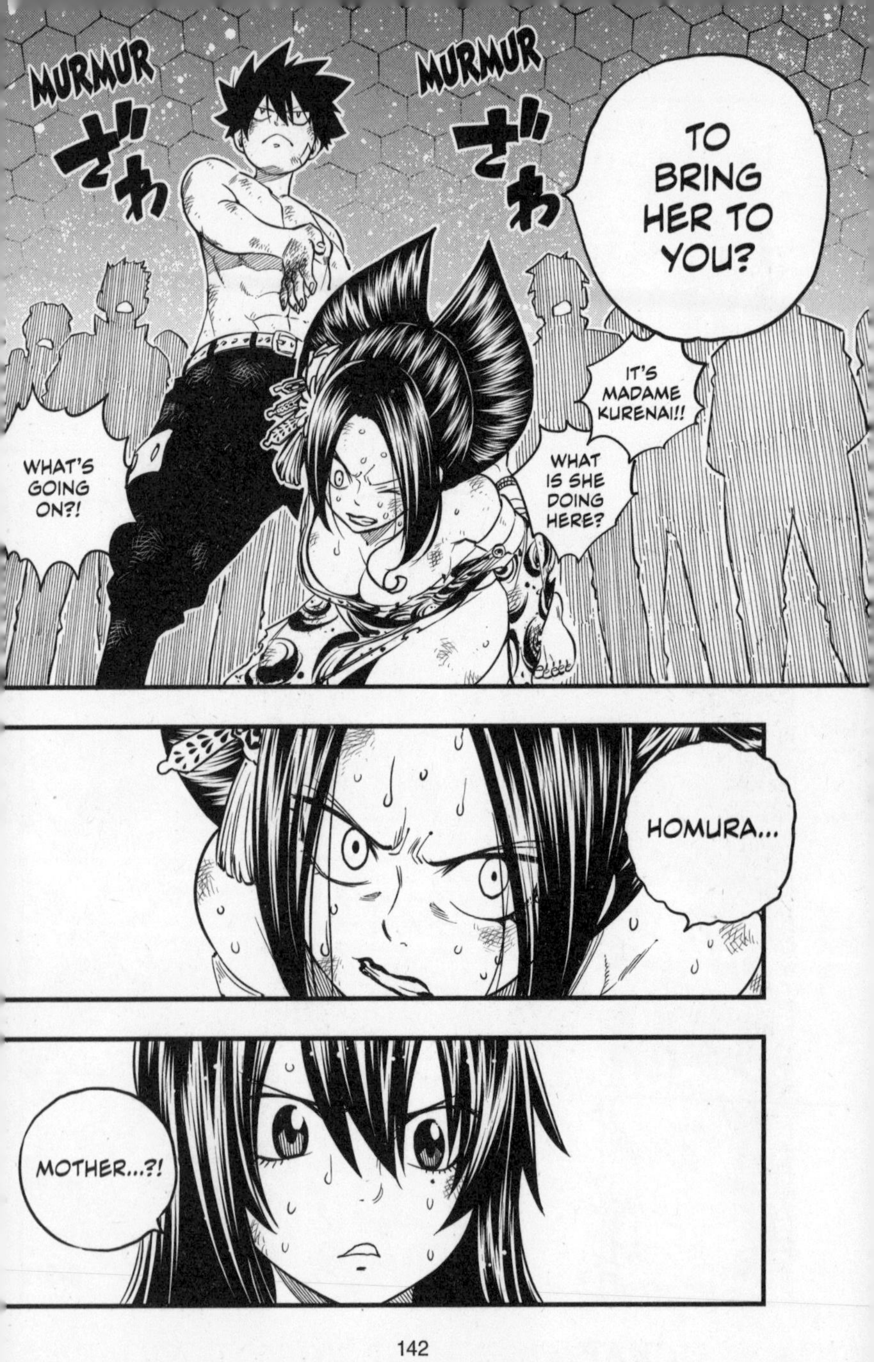
TO BRING HER TO YOU?
MURMUR
ざわ
MURMUR
ざわ
IT'S MADAME KURENAI!!
WHAT IS SHE DOING HERE?
WHAT'S GOING ON?!
HOMURA...
MOTHER...?!

EDENS ZERO

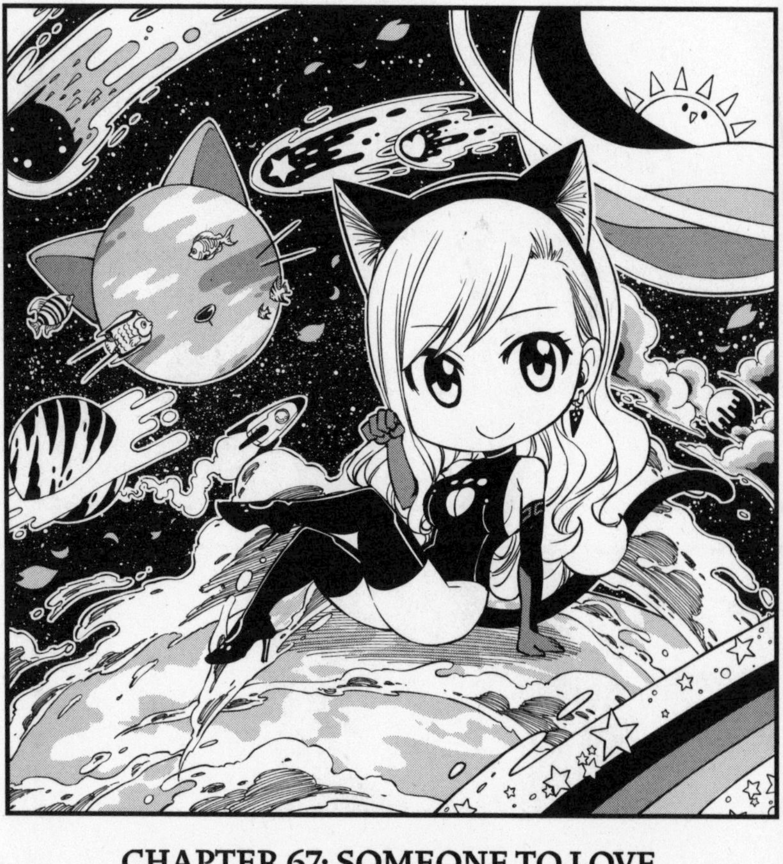

CHAPTER 67: SOMEONE TO LOVE

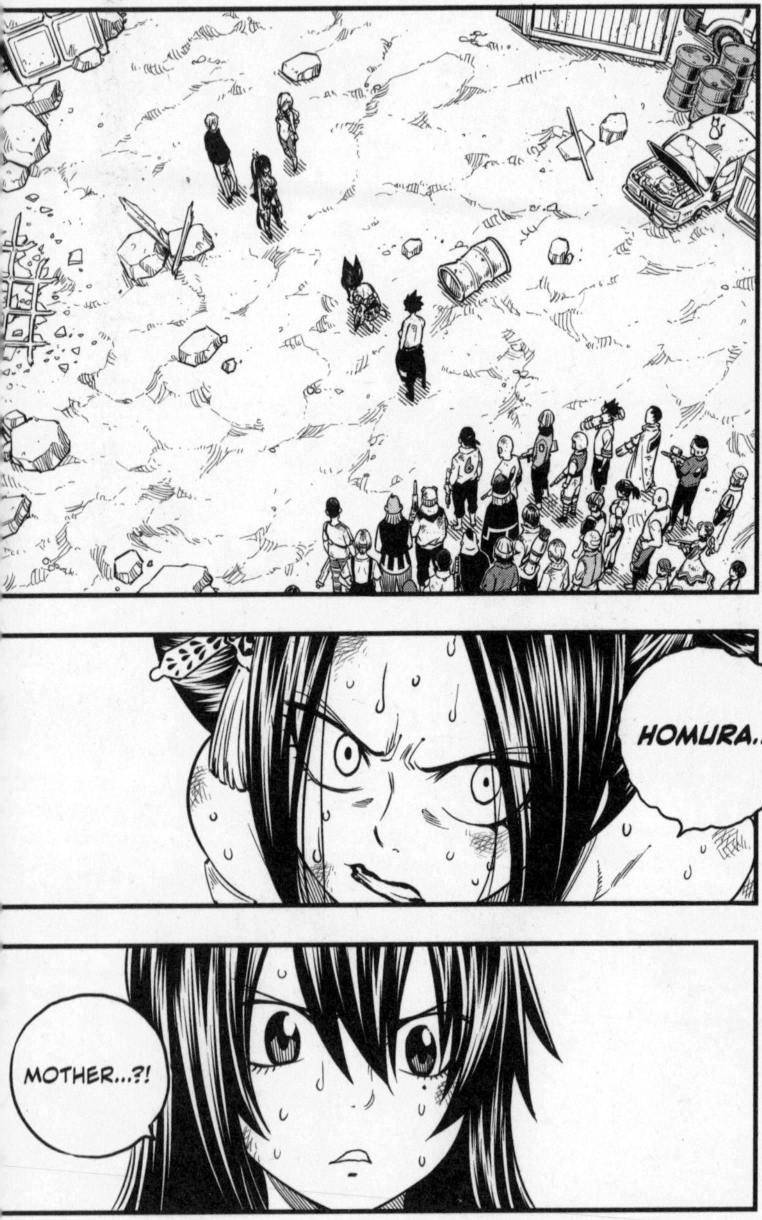
HOMURA...
MOTHER...?!

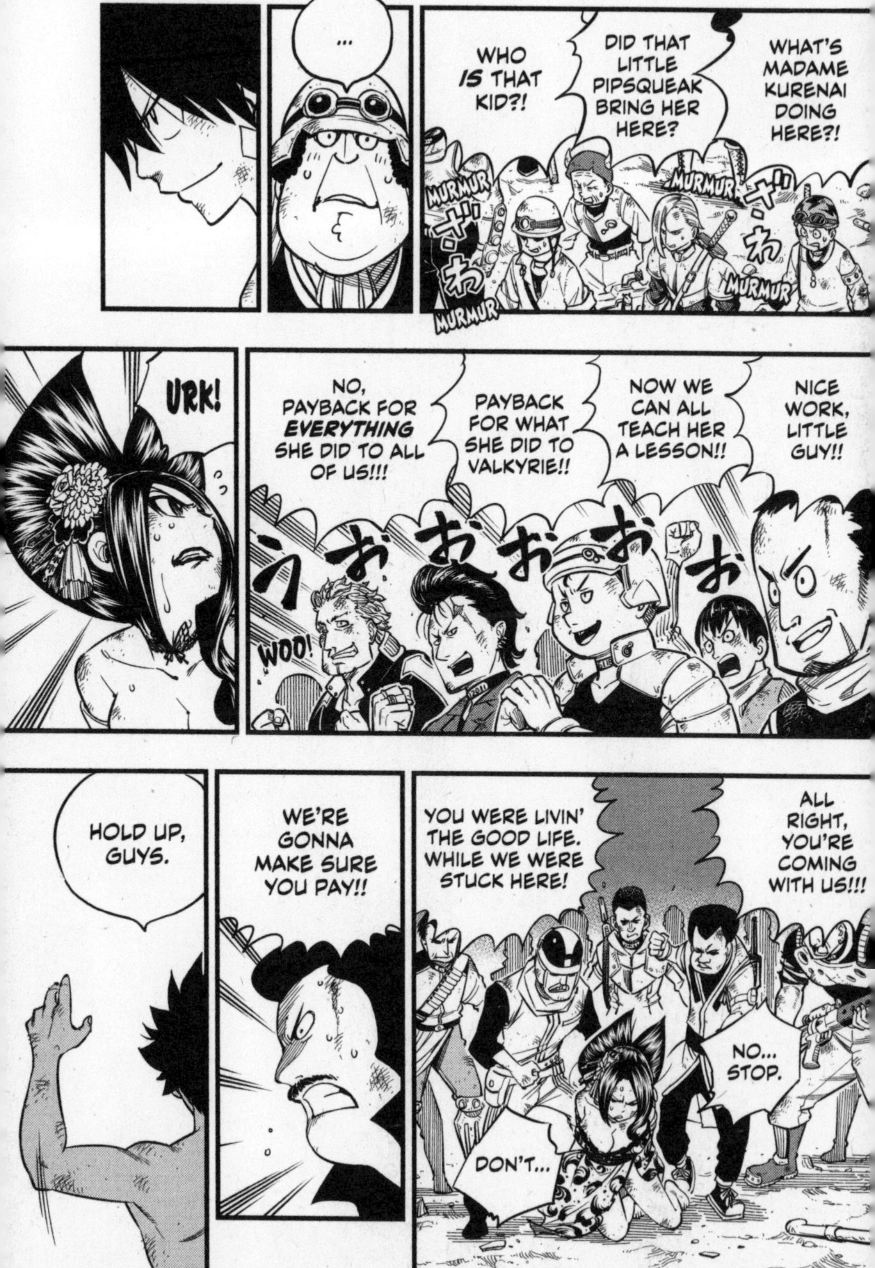
WHAT'S MADAME KURENAI DOING HERE?!
DID THAT LITTLE PIPSQUEAK BRING HER HERE?
WHO *IS* THAT KID?!
MURMUR
ざわ
MURMUR
ざわ
MURMUR
MURMUR
...
NICE WORK, LITTLE GUY!!
NOW WE CAN ALL TEACH HER A LESSON!!
PAYBACK FOR WHAT SHE DID TO VALKYRIE!!
NO, PAYBACK FOR ***EVERYTHING*** SHE DID TO ALL OF US!!!
うおおおお
WOO!
URK!
ALL RIGHT, YOU'RE COMING WITH US!!!
YOU WERE LIVIN' THE GOOD LIFE. WHILE WE WERE STUCK HERE!
NO... STOP.
DON'T...
WE'RE GONNA MAKE SURE YOU PAY!!
HOLD UP, GUYS.

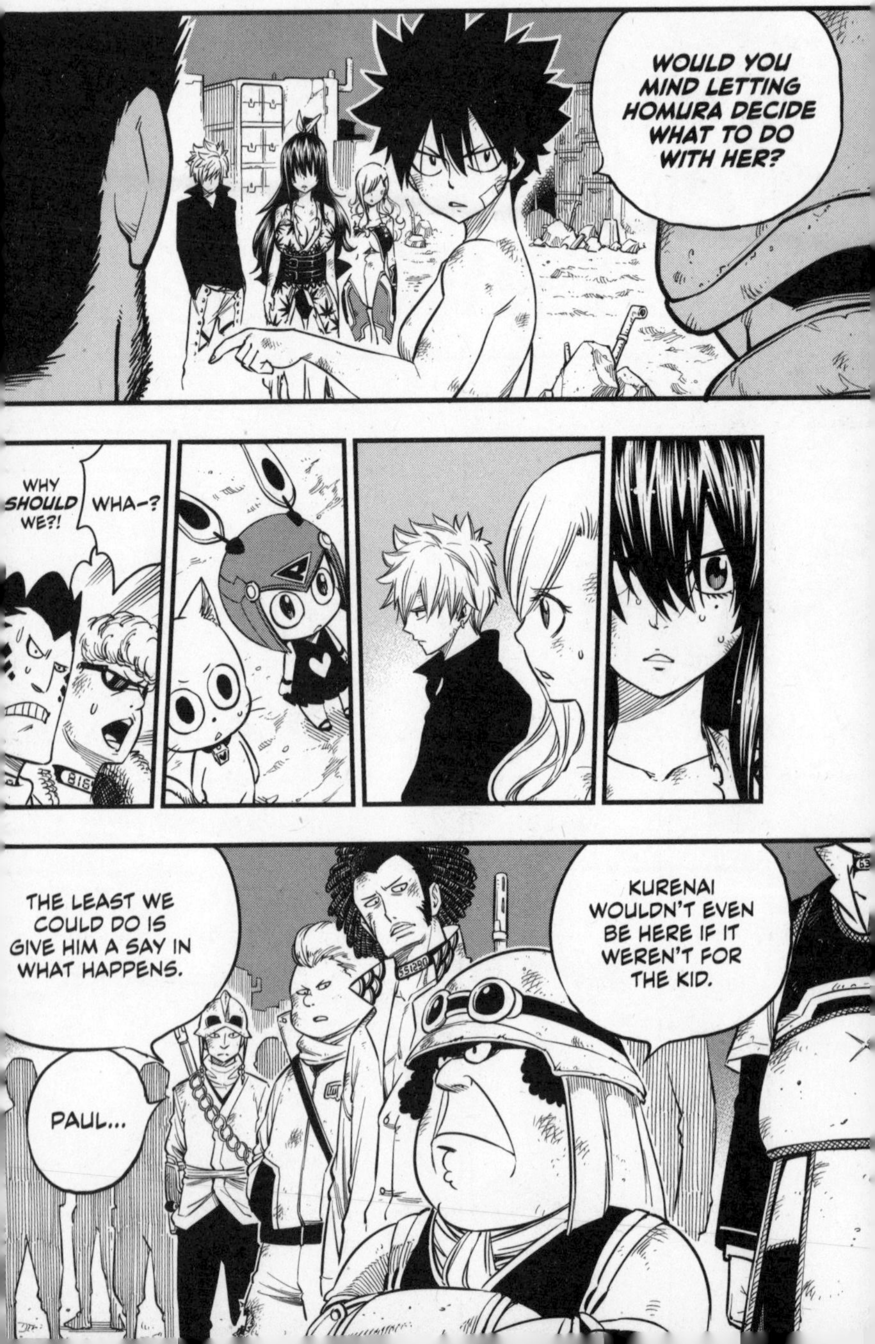
WOULD YOU MIND LETTING HOMURA DECIDE WHAT TO DO WITH HER?
WHA-?
WHY SHOULD WE?!
KURENAI WOULDN'T EVEN BE HERE IF IT WEREN'T FOR THE KID.
THE LEAST WE COULD DO IS GIVE HIM A SAY IN WHAT HAPPENS.
PAUL...

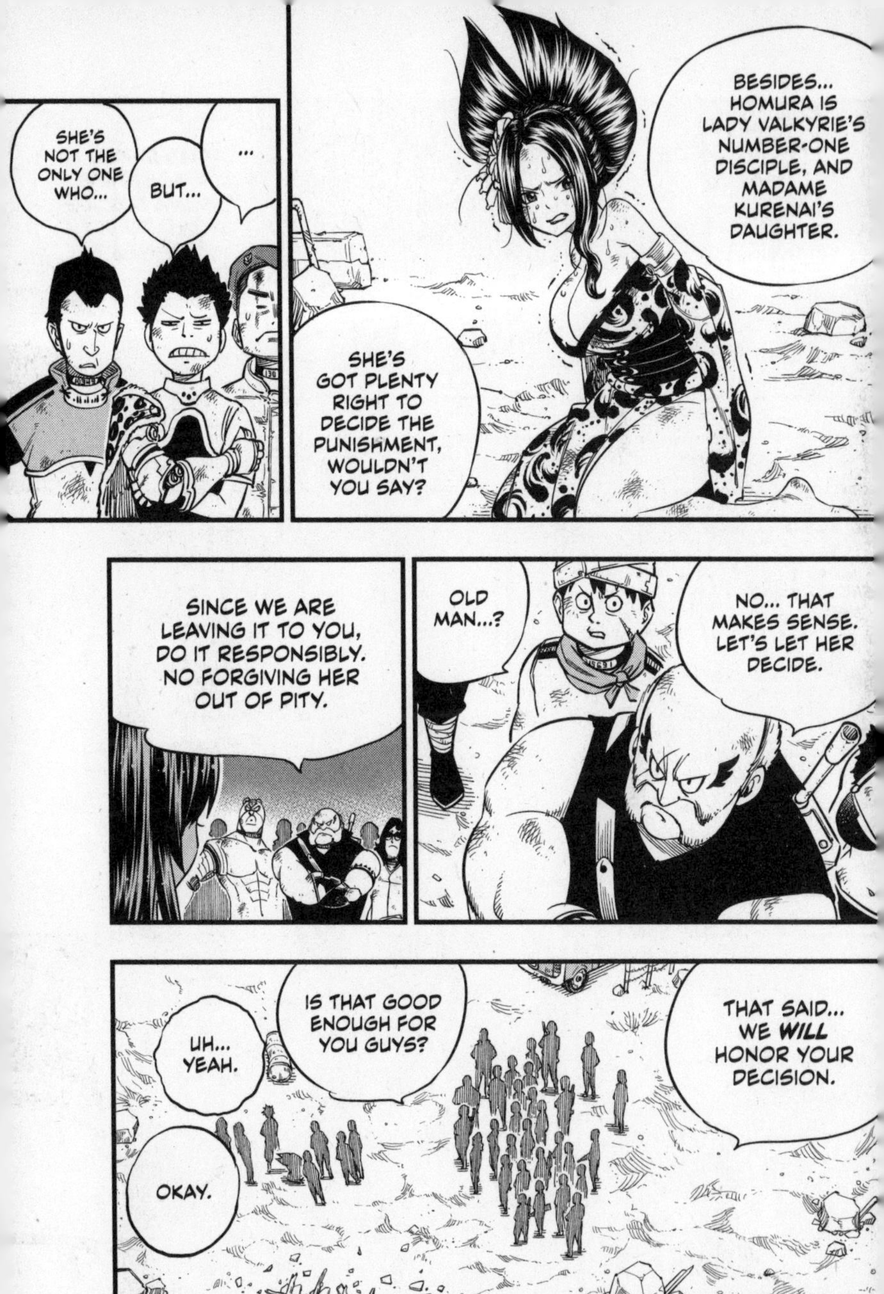
BESIDES... HOMURA IS LADY VALKYRIE'S NUMBER-ONE DISCIPLE, AND MADAME KURENAI'S DAUGHTER.
SHE'S GOT PLENTY RIGHT TO DECIDE THE PUNISHMENT, WOULDN'T YOU SAY?
...
BUT...
SHE'S NOT THE ONLY ONE WHO...
NO... THAT MAKES SENSE. LET'S LET HER DECIDE.
OLD MAN...?
SINCE WE ARE LEAVING IT TO YOU, DO IT RESPONSIBLY. NO FORGIVING HER OUT OF PITY.
THAT SAID... WE *WILL* HONOR YOUR DECISION.
IS THAT GOOD ENOUGH FOR YOU GUYS?
UH... YEAH.
OKAY.

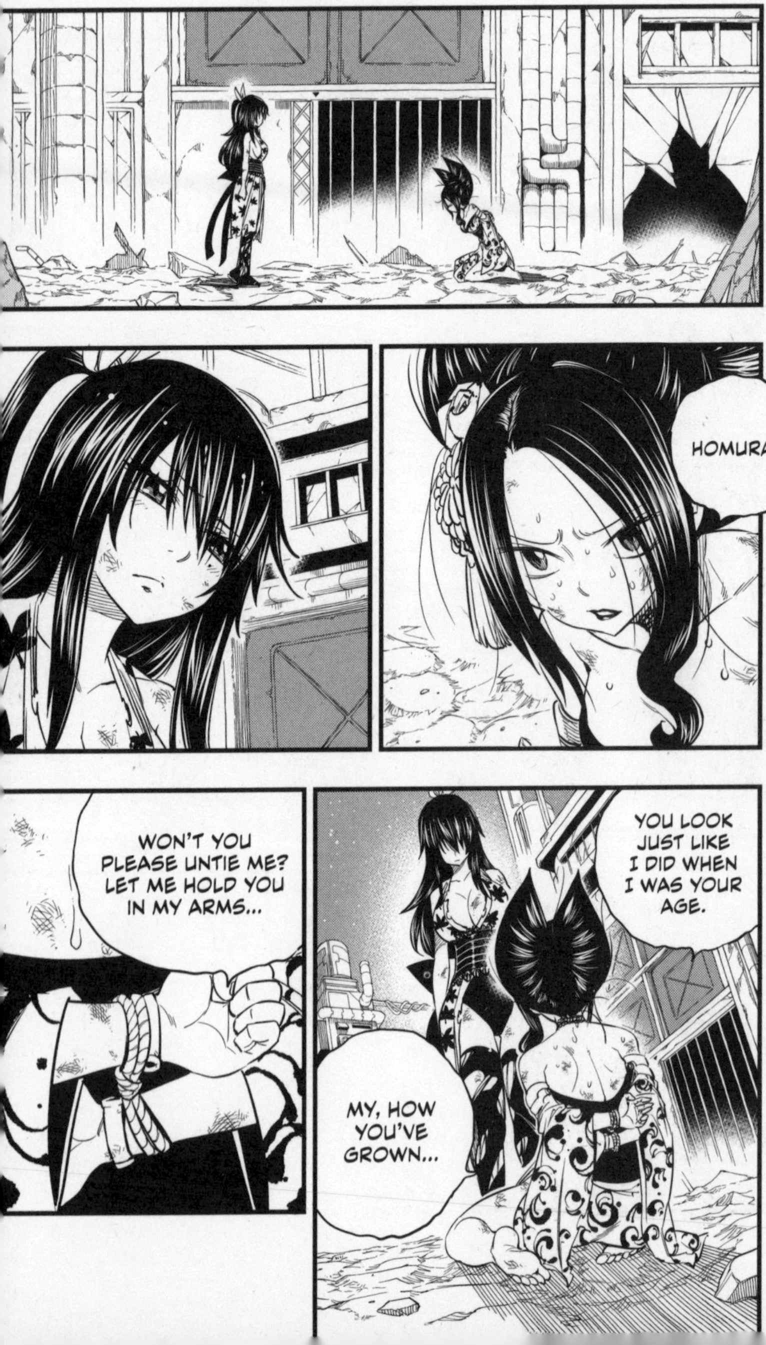
HOMURA...
YOU LOOK JUST LIKE I DID WHEN I WAS YOUR AGE.
MY, HOW YOU'VE GROWN...
WON'T YOU PLEASE UNTIE ME? LET ME HOLD YOU IN MY ARMS...

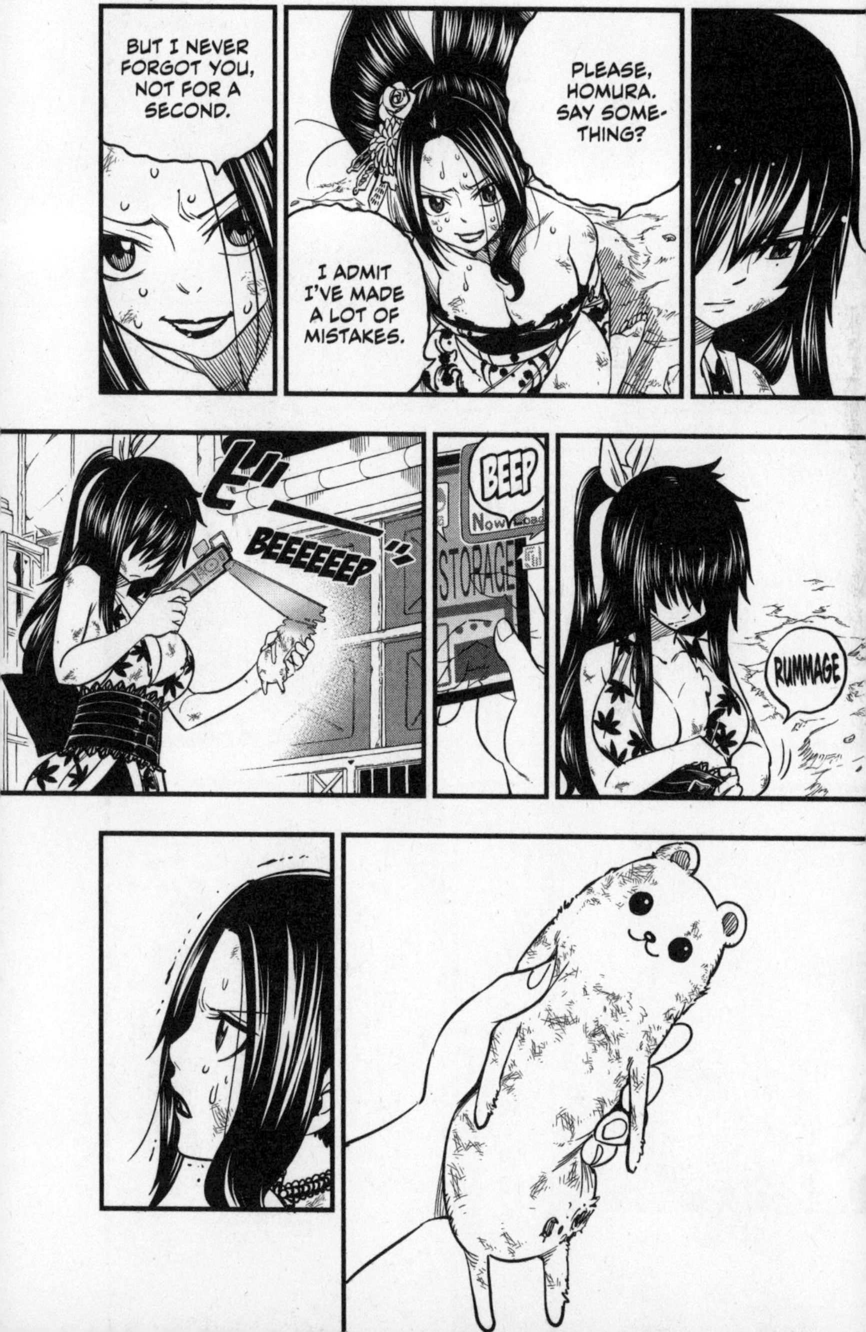
PLEASE, HOMURA. SAY SOME-THING?
I ADMIT I'VE MADE A LOT OF MISTAKES.
BUT I NEVER FORGOT YOU, NOT FOR A SECOND.
RUMMAGE
BEEP
STORAGE
BEEEEEEEP

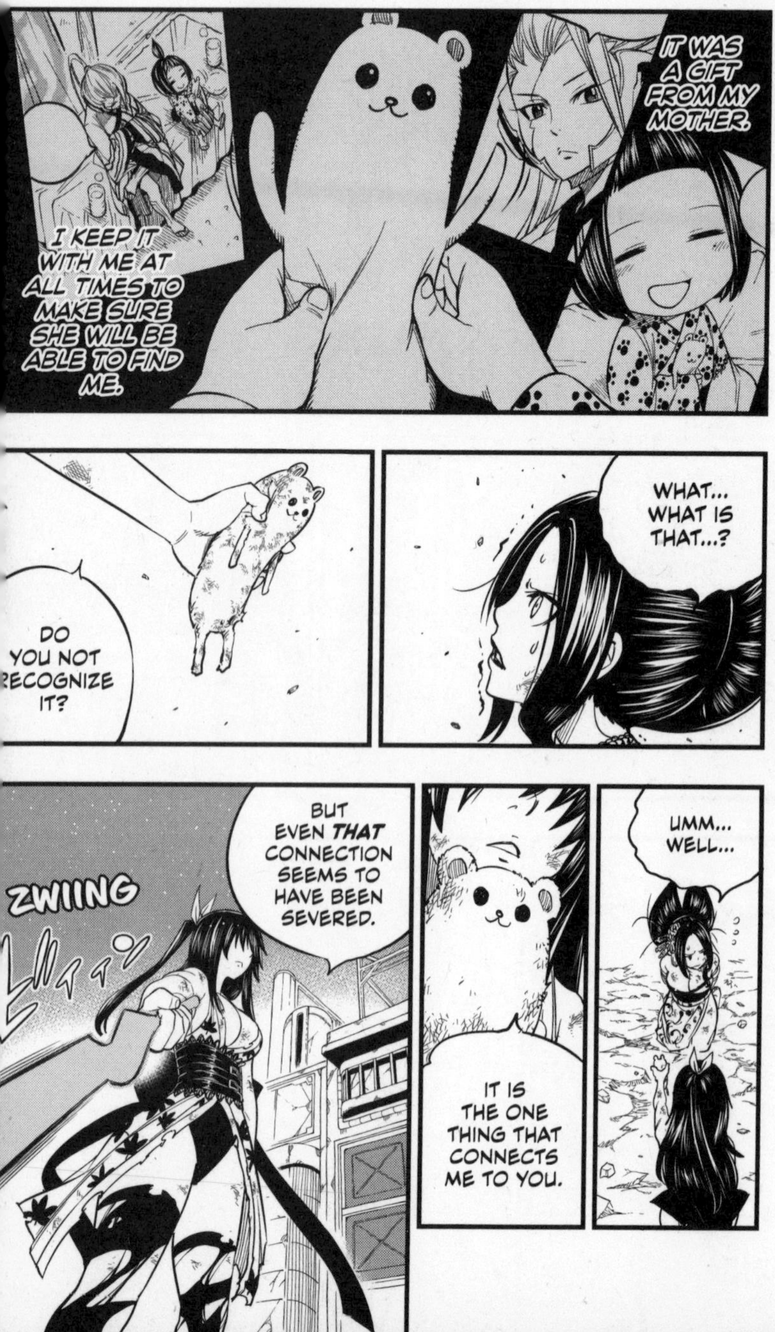
IT WAS A GIFT FROM MY MOTHER.
I KEEP IT WITH ME AT ALL TIMES TO MAKE SURE SHE WILL BE ABLE TO FIND ME.
WHAT... WHAT IS THAT...?
DO YOU NOT RECOGNIZE IT?
UMM... WELL...
IT IS THE ONE THING THAT CONNECTS ME TO YOU.
BUT EVEN *THAT* CONNECTION SEEMS TO HAVE BEEN SEVERED.
ZWIING

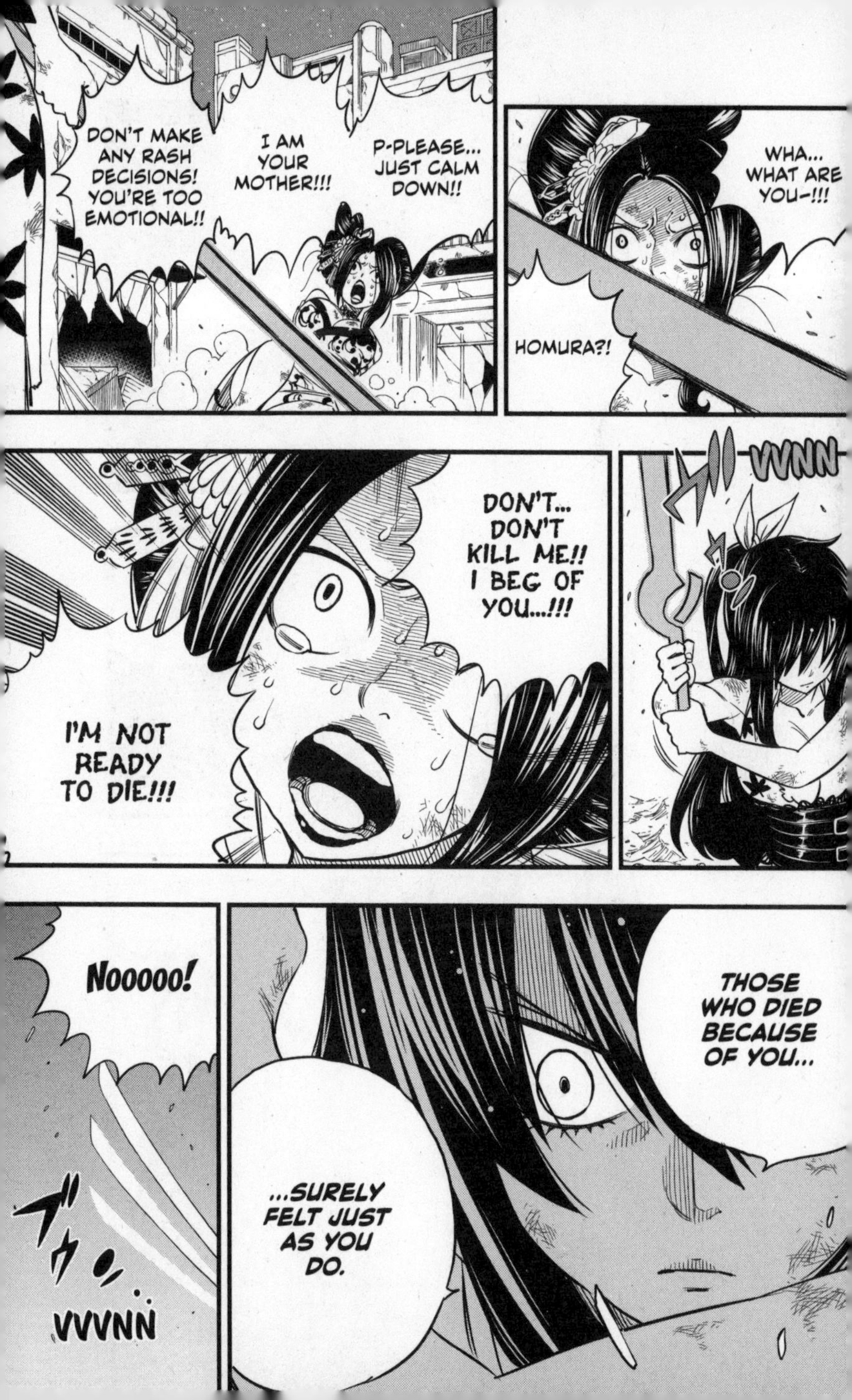
WHA... WHAT ARE YOU-!!!
HOMURA?!
P-PLEASE... JUST CALM DOWN!!
I AM YOUR MOTHER!!!
DON'T MAKE ANY RASH DECISIONS! YOU'RE TOO EMOTIONAL!!
VVNN
DON'T... DON'T KILL ME!! I BEG OF YOU...!!!
I'M NOT READY TO DIE!!!
THOSE WHO DIED BECAUSE OF YOU...
...SURELY FELT JUST AS YOU DO.
Nooooo!
VVVNN

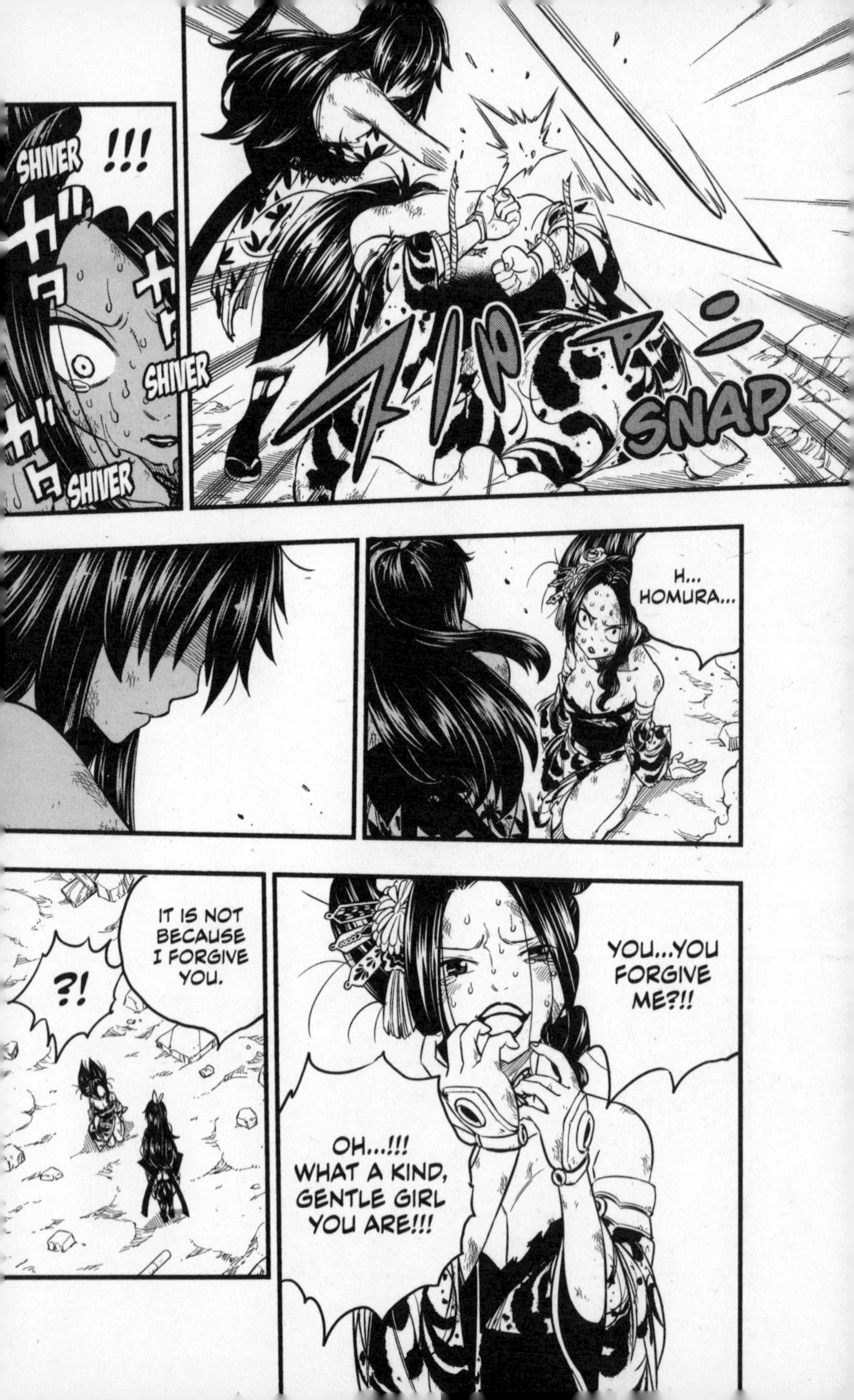
SNAP
!!!
SHIVER
SHIVER
SHIVER
H... HOMURA...
YOU...YOU FORGIVE ME?!!
OH...!!! WHAT A KIND, GENTLE GIRL YOU ARE!!!
IT IS NOT BECAUSE I FORGIVE YOU.
?!

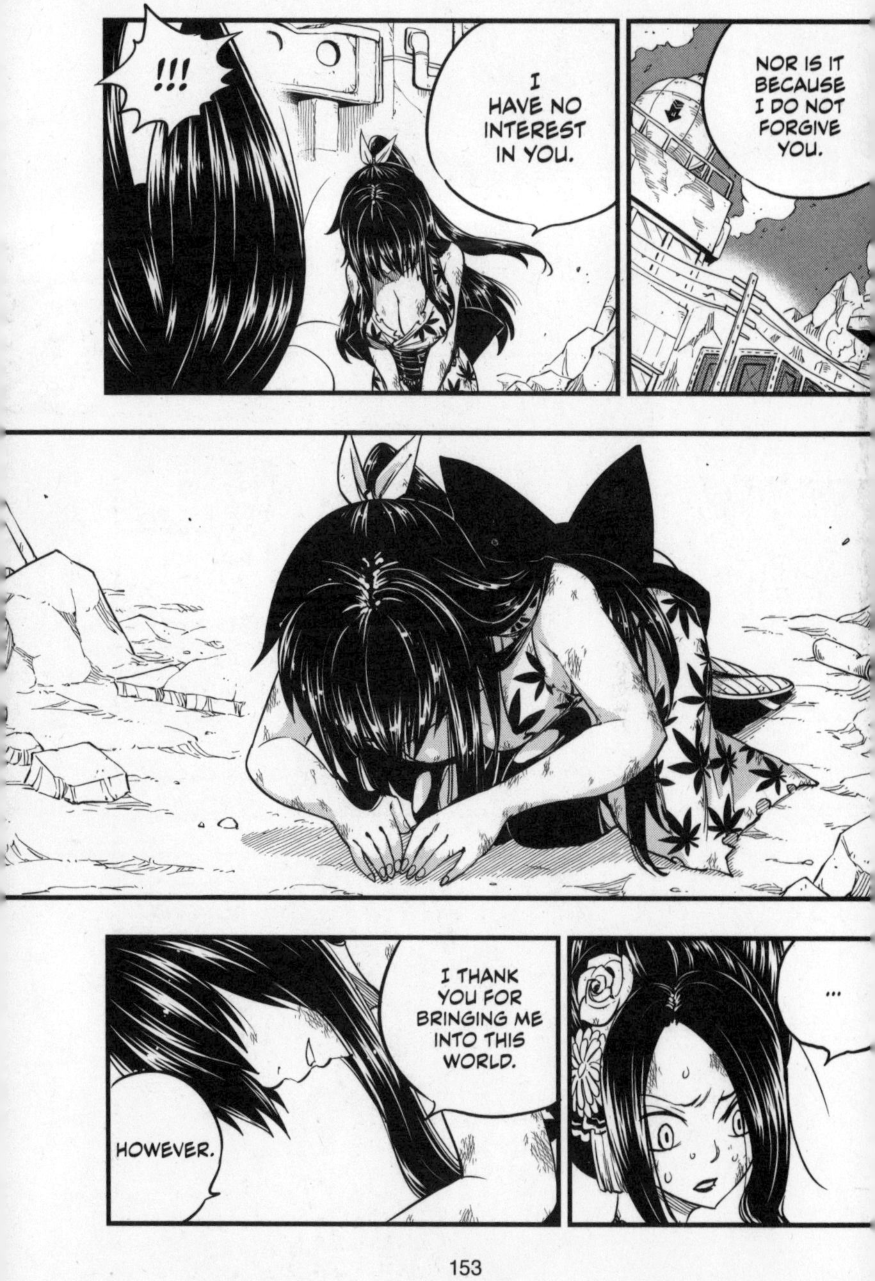
!!!
I HAVE NO INTEREST IN YOU.
NOR IS IT BECAUSE I DO NOT FORGIVE YOU.
I THANK YOU FOR BRINGING ME INTO THIS WORLD.
HOWEVER.
...

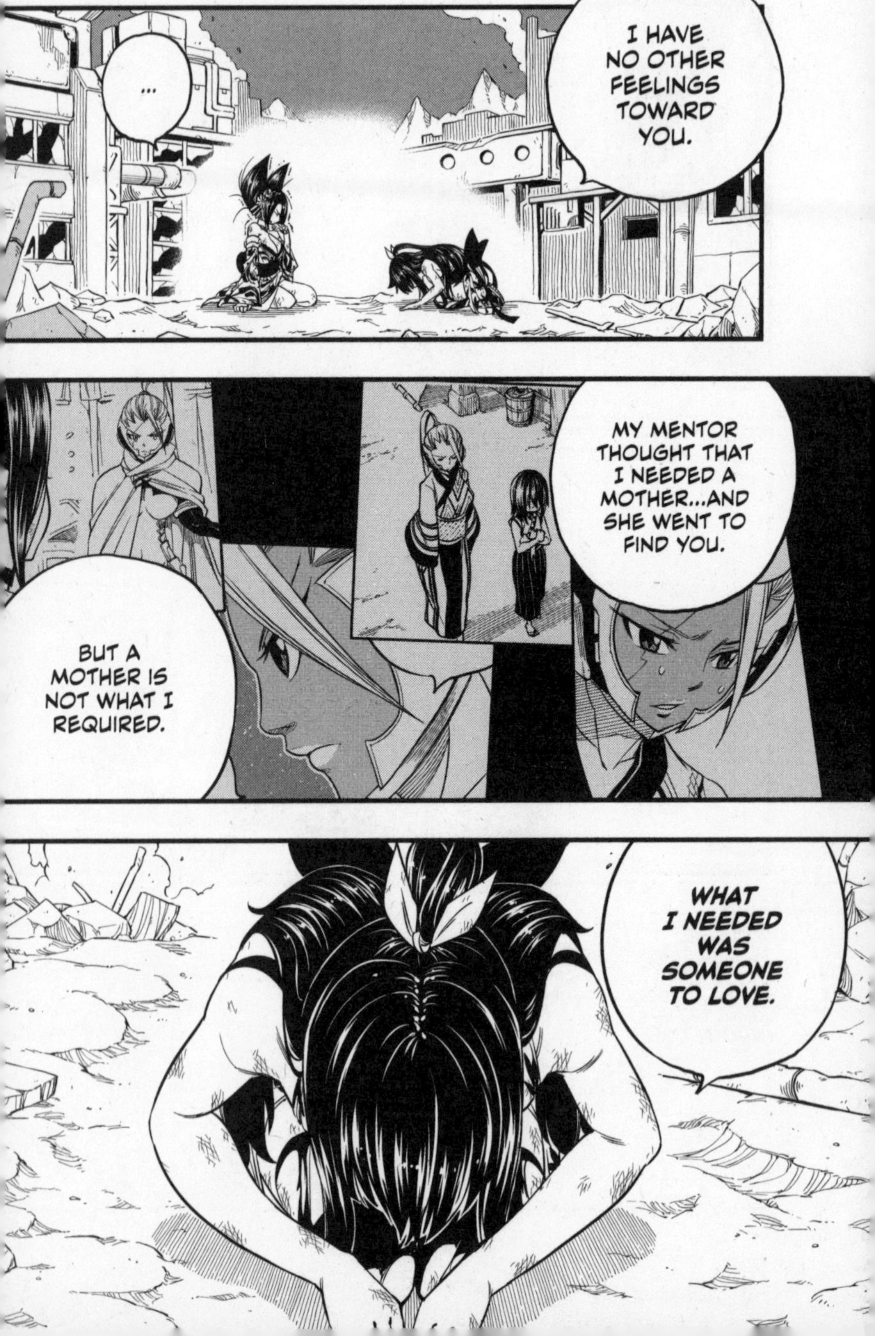
I HAVE NO OTHER FEELINGS TOWARD YOU.
...
MY MENTOR THOUGHT THAT I NEEDED A MOTHER...AND SHE WENT TO FIND YOU.
BUT A MOTHER IS NOT WHAT I REQUIRED.
WHAT I NEEDED WAS SOMEONE TO LOVE.

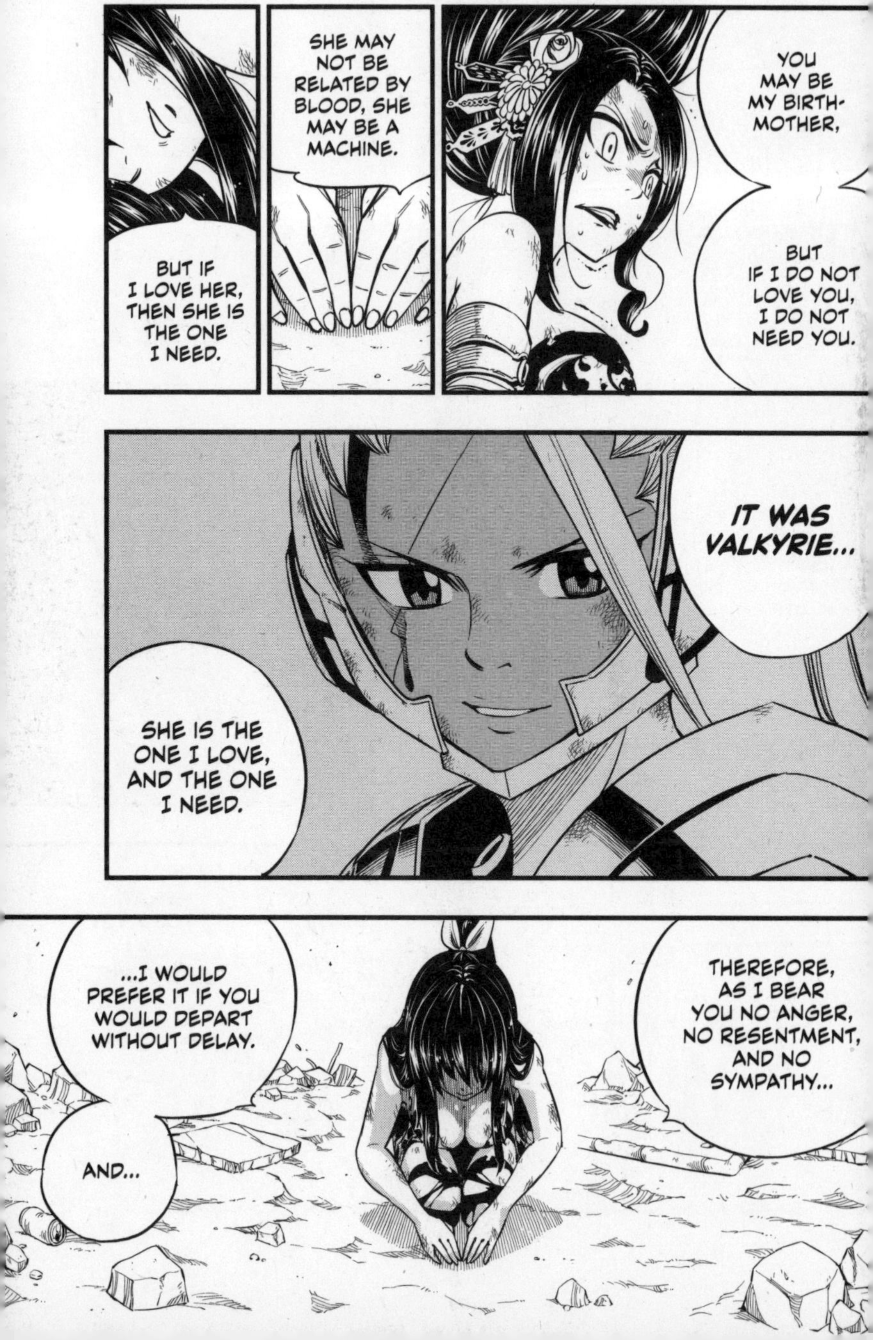
YOU MAY BE MY BIRTH-MOTHER,
BUT IF I DO NOT LOVE YOU, I DO NOT NEED YOU.
SHE MAY NOT BE RELATED BY BLOOD, SHE MAY BE A MACHINE.
BUT IF I LOVE HER, THEN SHE IS THE ONE I NEED.
IT WAS VALKYRIE...
SHE IS THE ONE I LOVE, AND THE ONE I NEED.
THEREFORE, AS I BEAR YOU NO ANGER, NO RESENTMENT, AND NO SYMPATHY...
...I WOULD PREFER IT IF YOU WOULD DEPART WITHOUT DELAY.
AND...

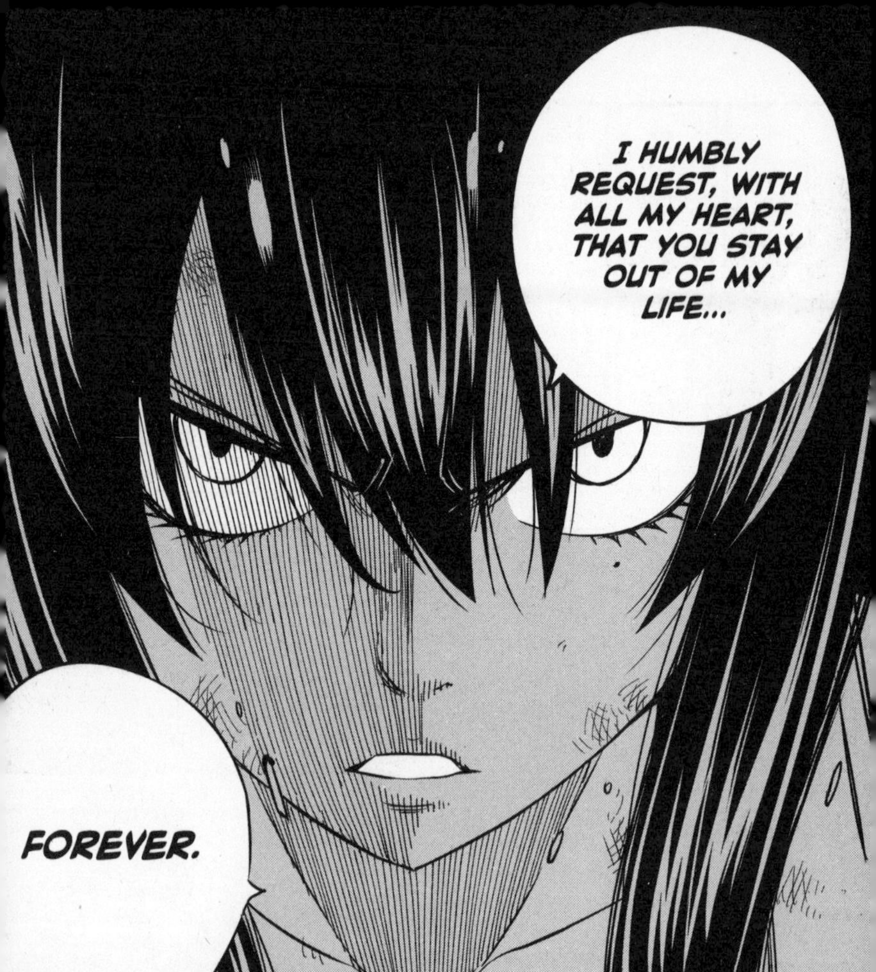
I HUMBLY REQUEST, WITH ALL MY HEART, THAT YOU STAY OUT OF MY LIFE...
FOREVER.
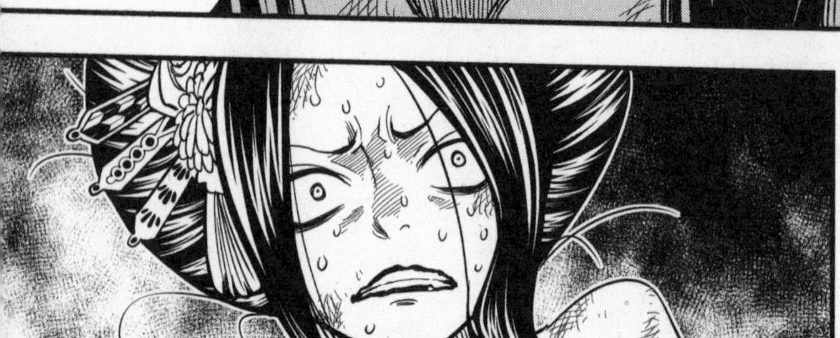

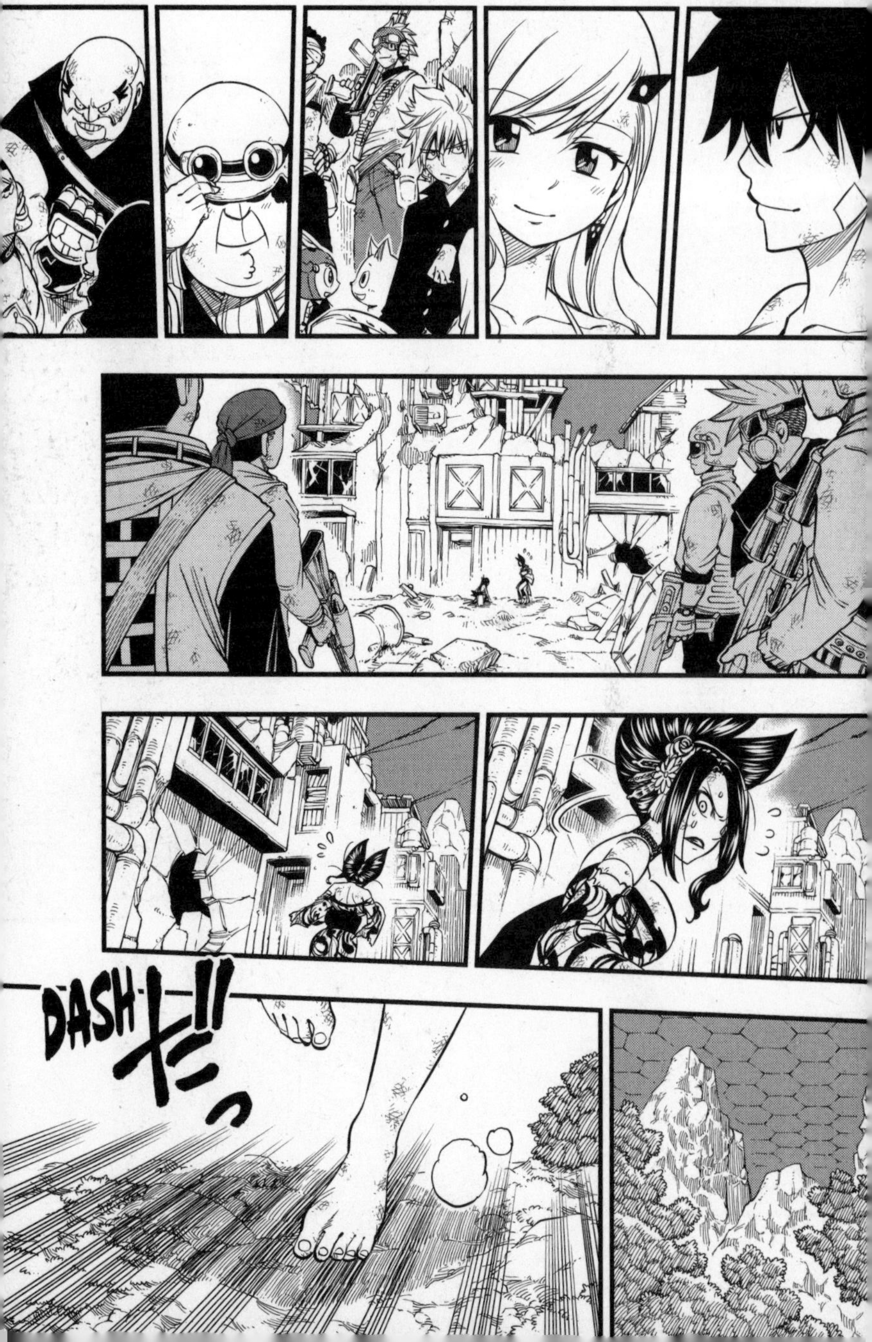
DASH

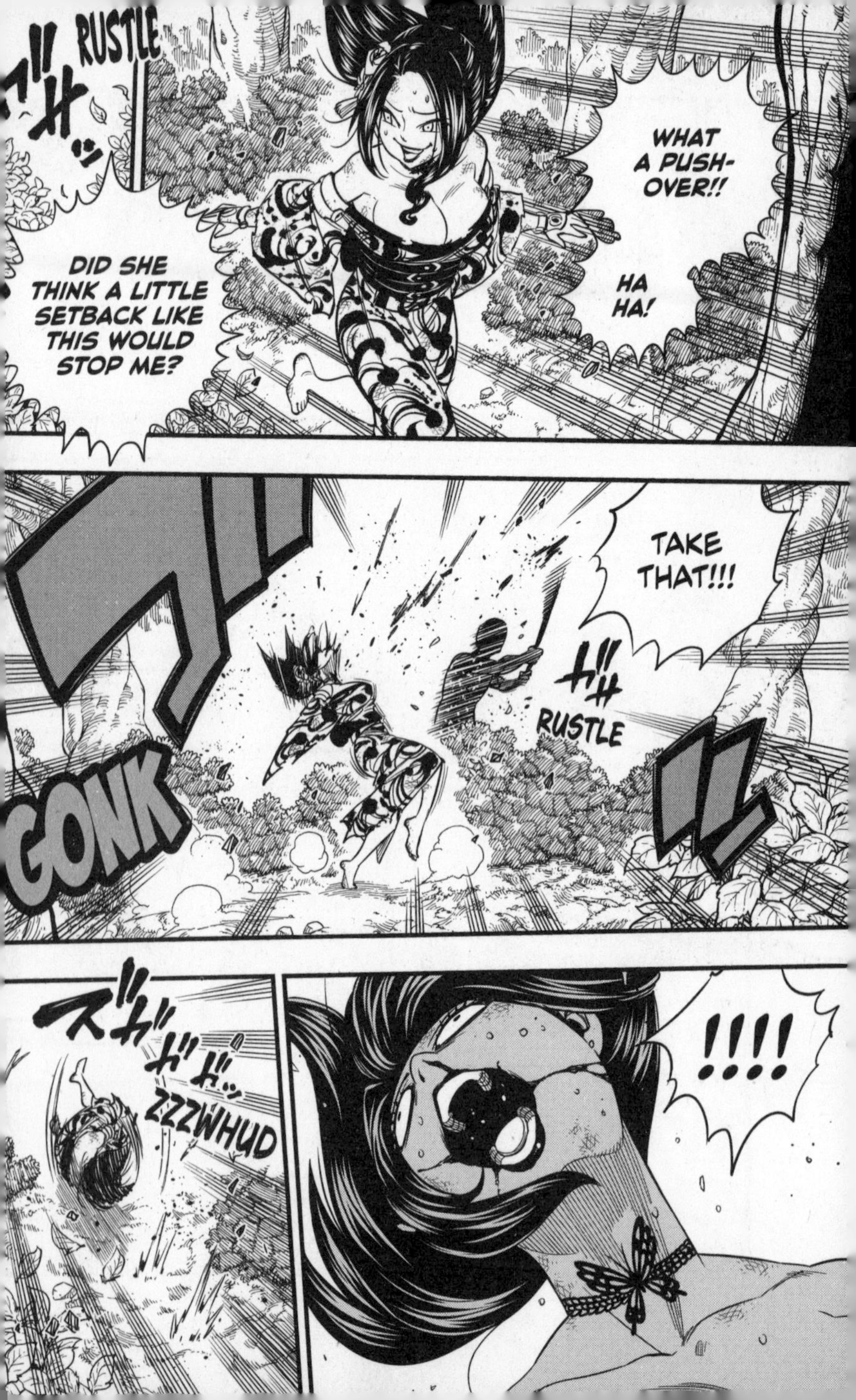
WHAT A PUSH-OVER!!
HA HA!
RUSTLE
DID SHE THINK A LITTLE SETBACK LIKE THIS WOULD STOP ME?
TAKE THAT!!!
RUSTLE
GONK
!!!!
ZZZWHUD

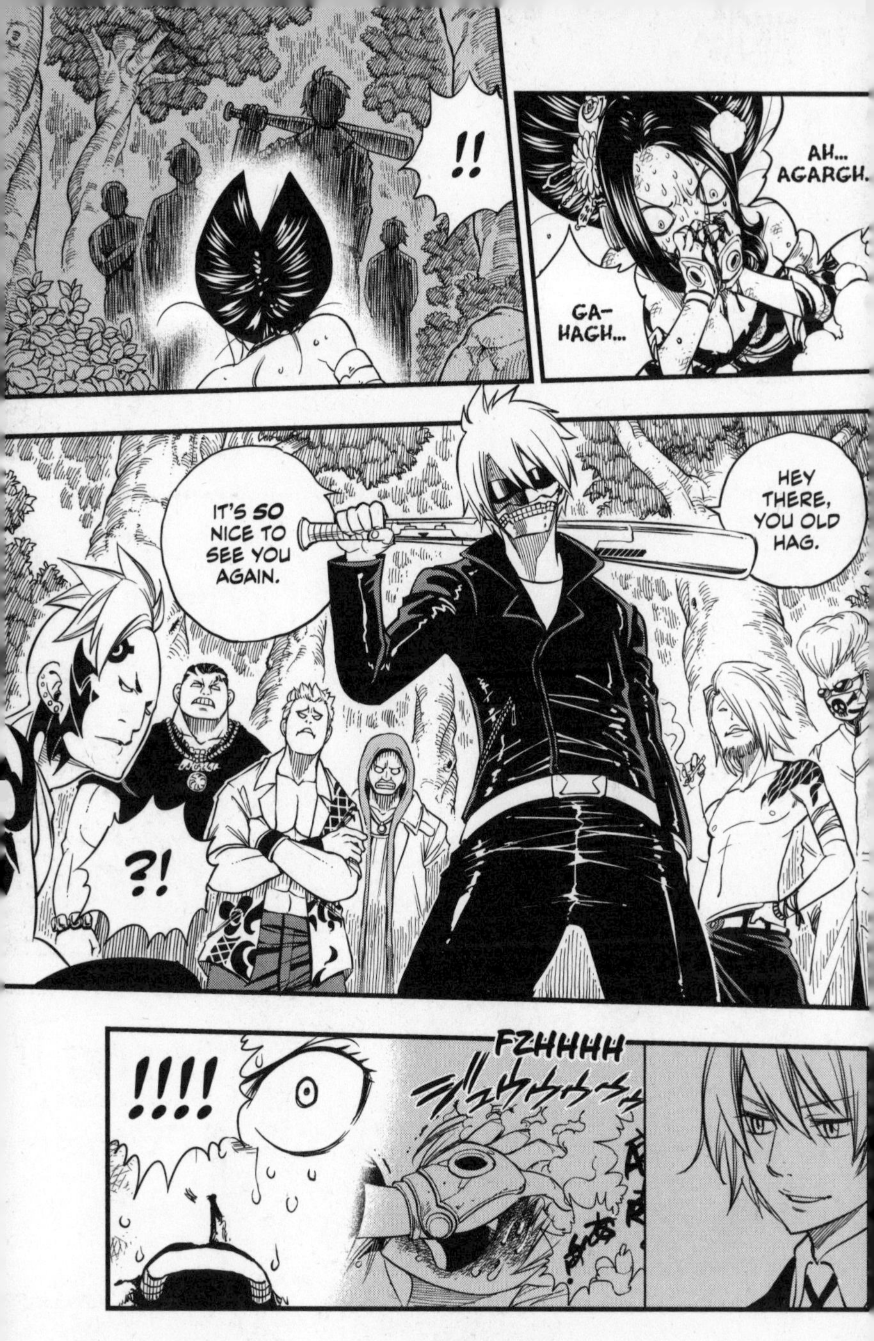
AH... AGARGH.
GA-HAGH...
!!
HEY THERE, YOU OLD HAG.
IT'S SO NICE TO SEE YOU AGAIN.
?!
FZHHHH
!!!!

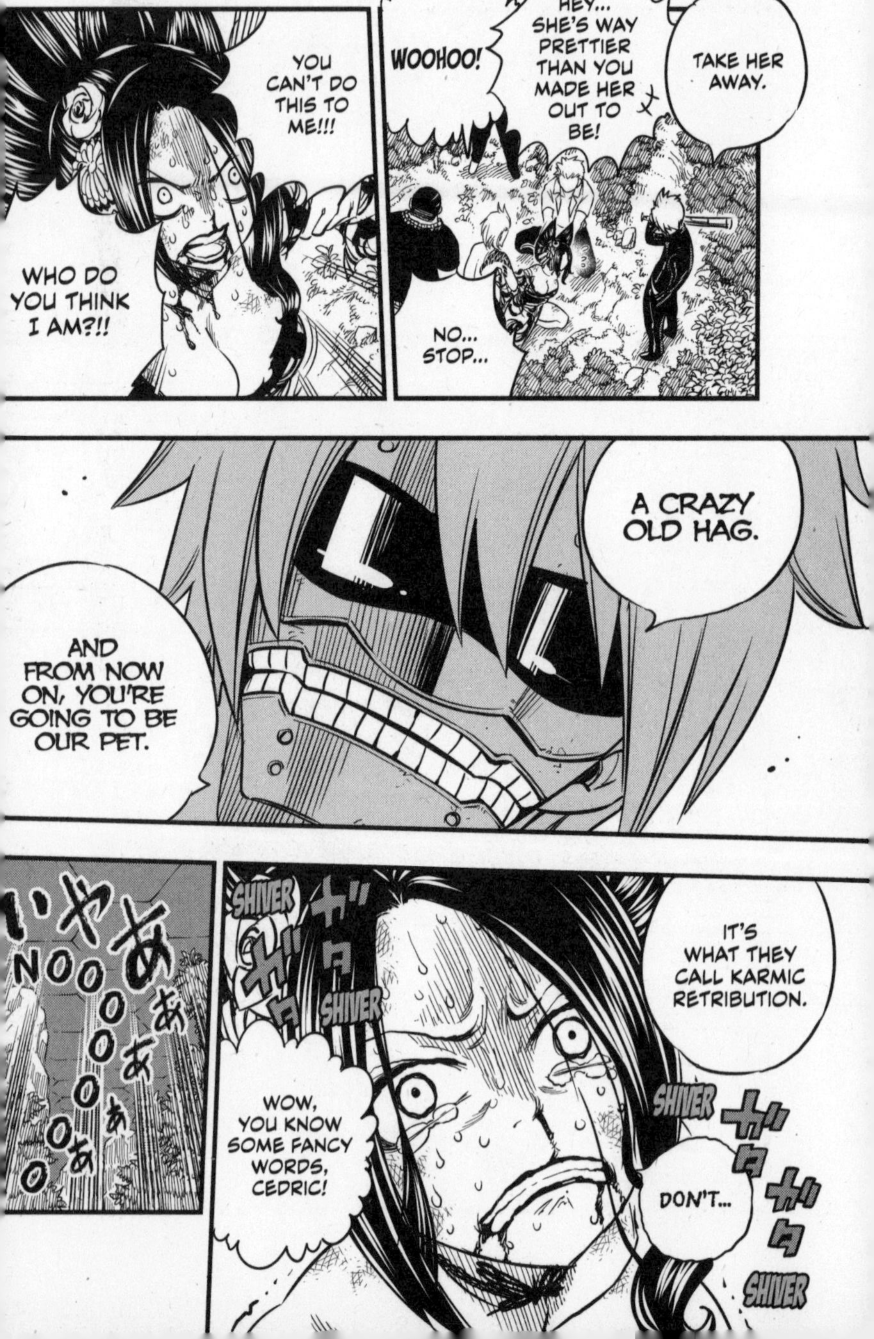
TAKE HER AWAY.
HEY... SHE'S WAY PRETTIER THAN YOU MADE HER OUT TO BE!
WOOHOO!
NO... STOP...
YOU CAN'T DO THIS TO ME!!!
WHO DO YOU THINK I AM?!!
A CRAZY OLD HAG.
AND FROM NOW ON, YOU'RE GOING TO BE OUR PET.
IT'S WHAT THEY CALL KARMIC RETRIBUTION.
SHIVER
DON'T...
SHIVER
SHIVER
SHIVER
WOW, YOU KNOW SOME FANCY WORDS, CEDRIC!
いやあああ
NOOOOOOOOO

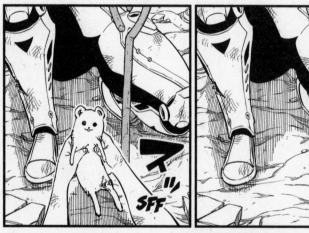

IF THIS DOLL REPRESENTS MY CONNECTION TO MY MOTHER...

THEN I WISH FOR YOU TO HAVE IT.

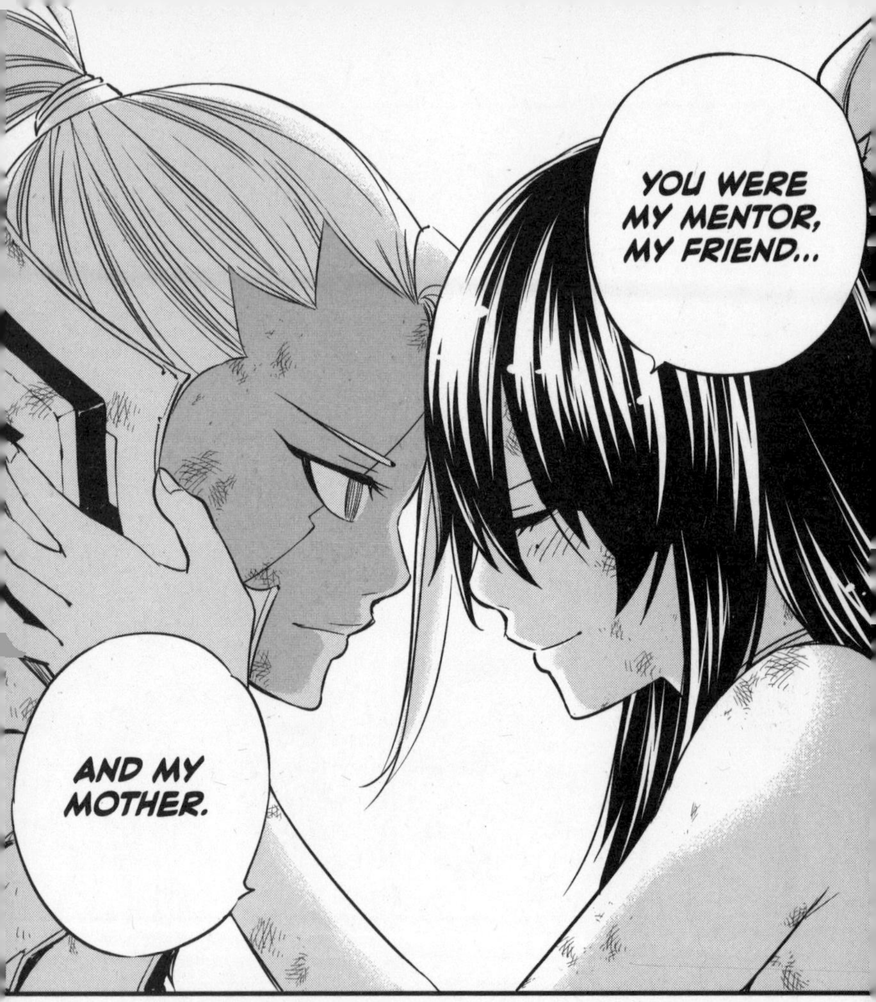
YOU WERE MY MENTOR, MY FRIEND...
AND MY MOTHER.

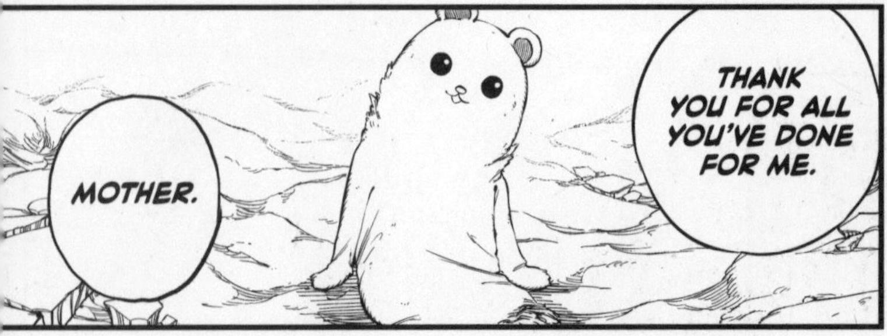
THANK YOU FOR ALL YOU'VE DONE FOR ME.
MOTHER.

EDENS ZERO

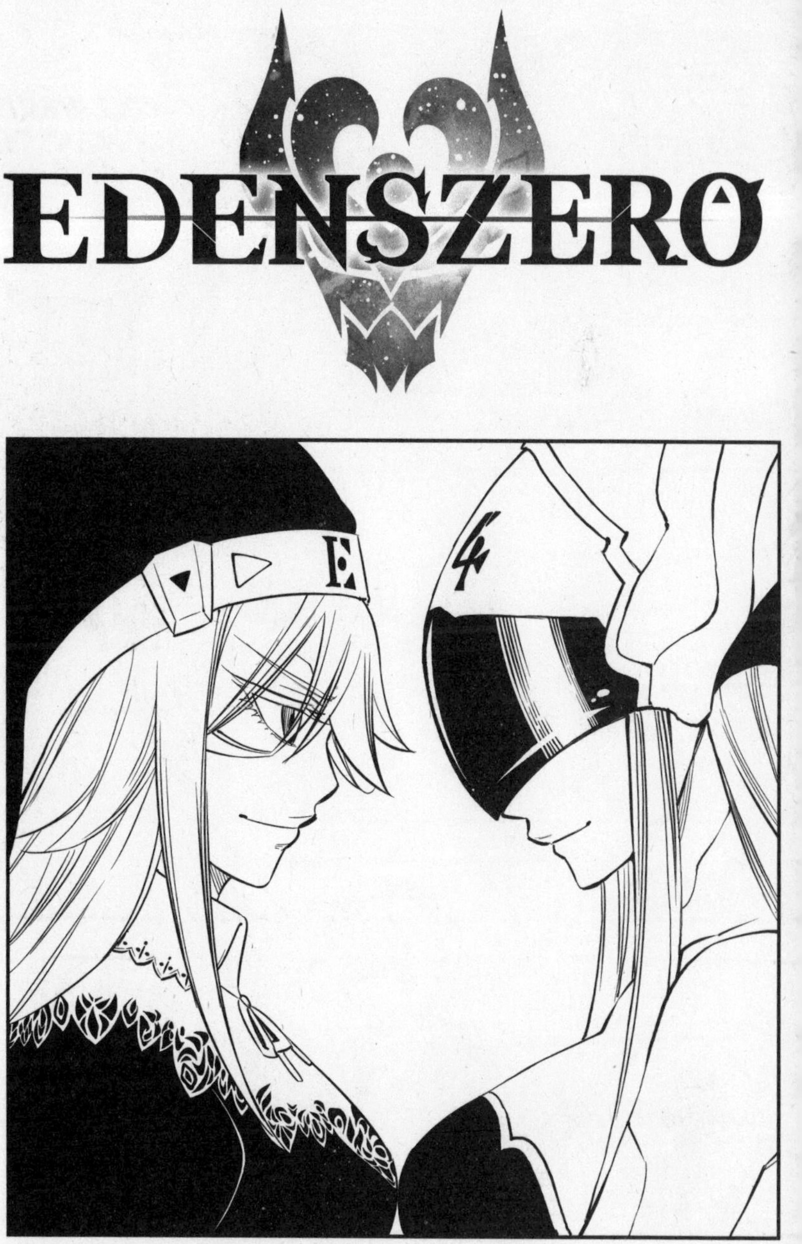

CHAPTER 68: VALKYRIE

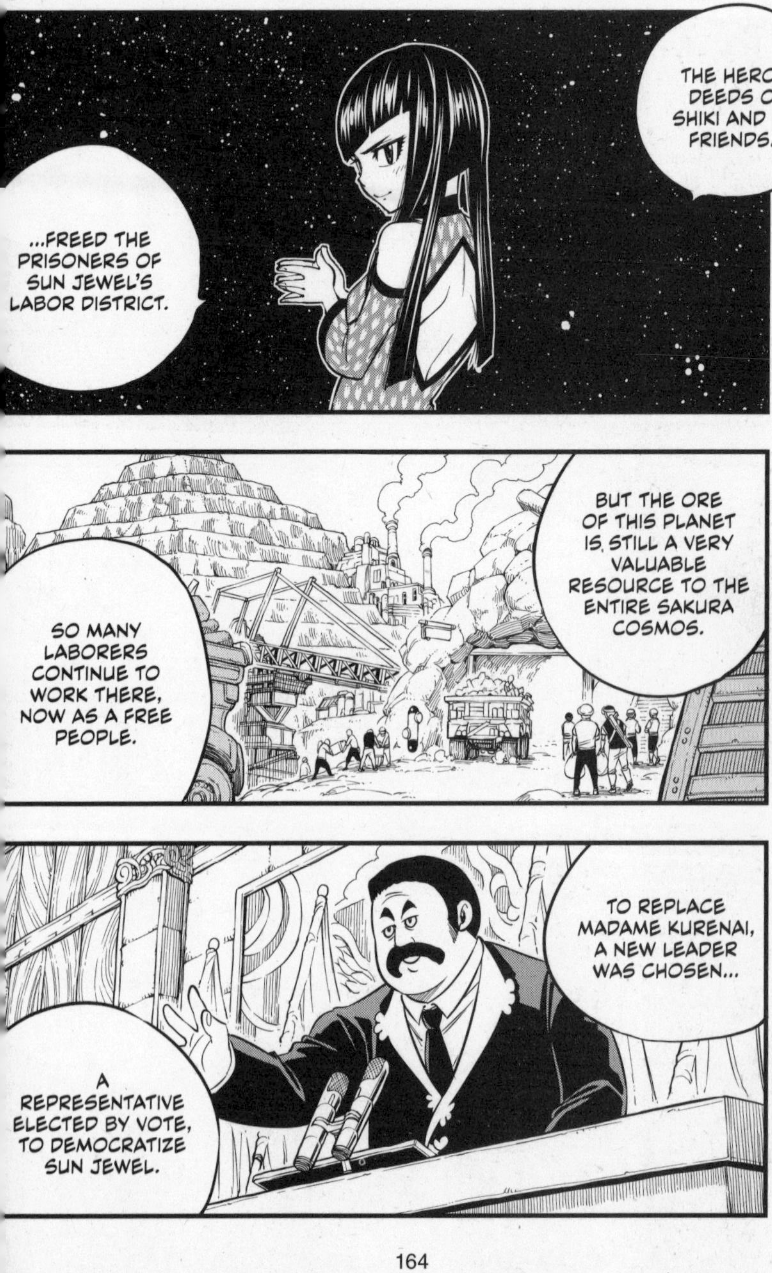
THE HEROIC DEEDS OF SHIKI AND HIS FRIENDS...
...FREED THE PRISONERS OF SUN JEWEL'S LABOR DISTRICT.
BUT THE ORE OF THIS PLANET IS STILL A VERY VALUABLE RESOURCE TO THE ENTIRE SAKURA COSMOS.
SO MANY LABORERS CONTINUE TO WORK THERE, NOW AS A FREE PEOPLE.
TO REPLACE MADAME KURENAI, A NEW LEADER WAS CHOSEN...
A REPRESENTATIVE ELECTED BY VOTE, TO DEMOCRATIZE SUN JEWEL.

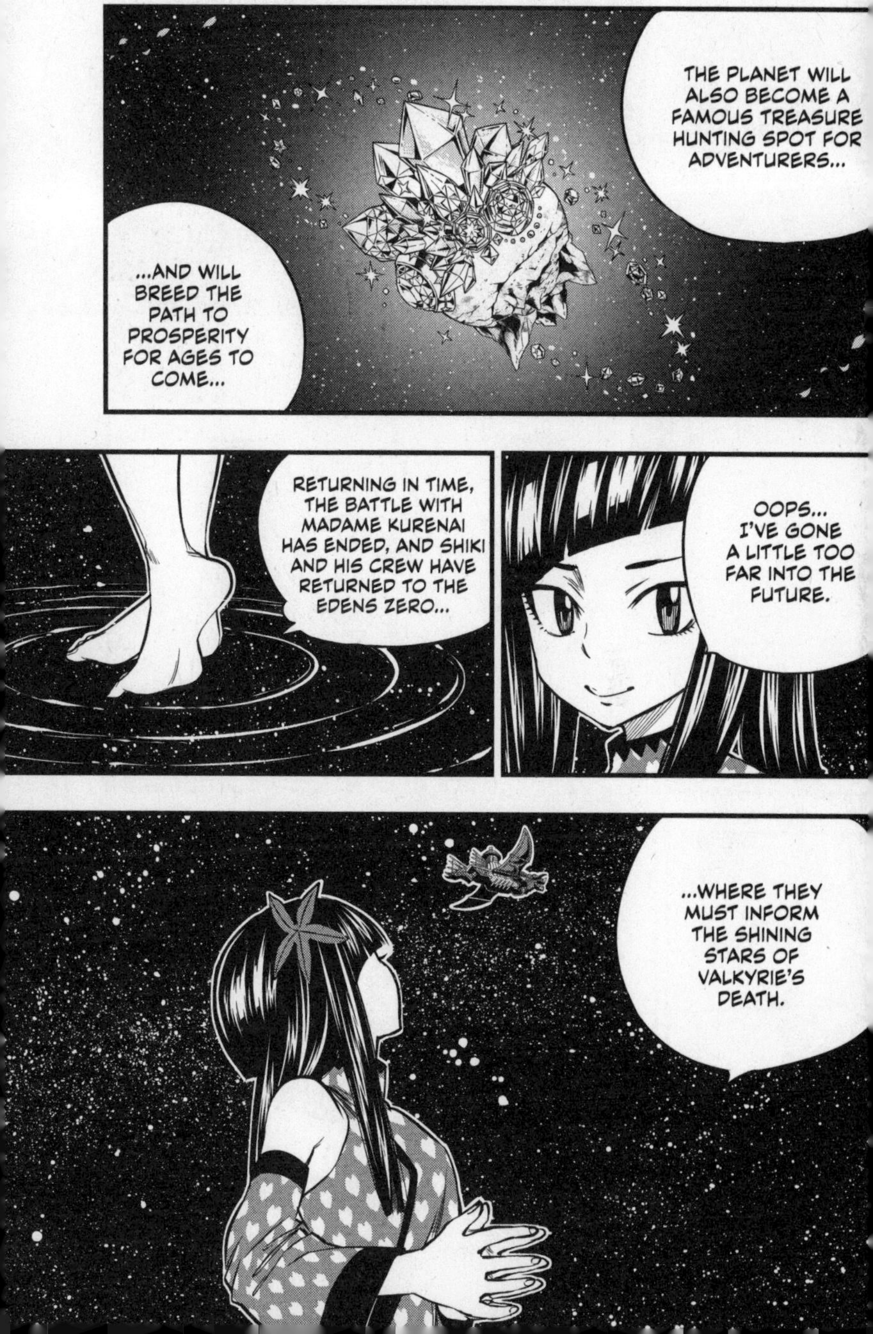
THE PLANET WILL ALSO BECOME A FAMOUS TREASURE HUNTING SPOT FOR ADVENTURERS...
...AND WILL BREED THE PATH TO PROSPERITY FOR AGES TO COME...
OOPS... I'VE GONE A LITTLE TOO FAR INTO THE FUTURE.
RETURNING IN TIME, THE BATTLE WITH MADAME KURENAI HAS ENDED, AND SHIKI AND HIS CREW HAVE RETURNED TO THE EDENS ZERO...
...WHERE THEY MUST INFORM THE SHINING STARS OF VALKYRIE'S DEATH.

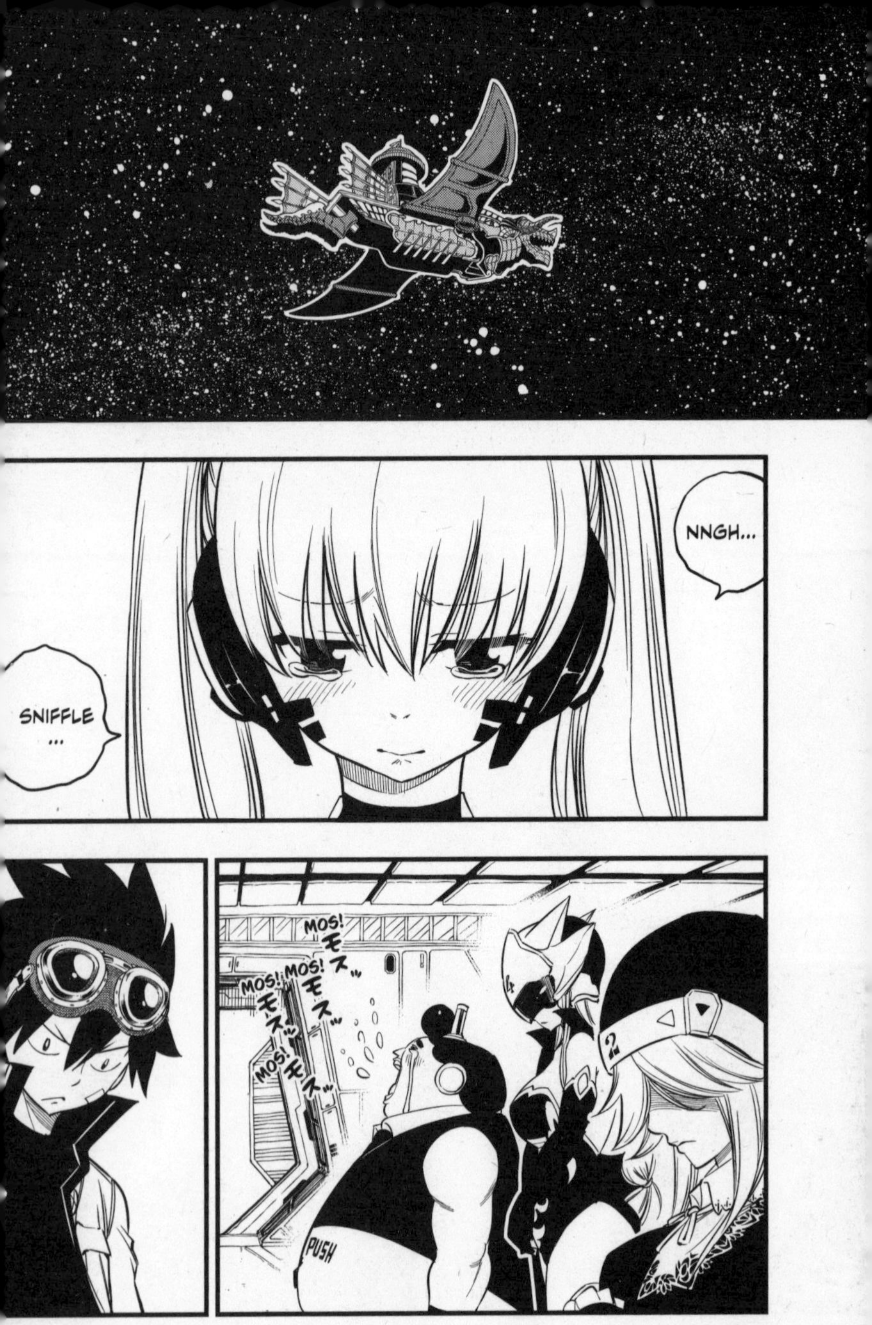
NNGH...
SNIFFLE ...
MOS! モスッ
MOS! モスッ
MOS! モスッ
MOS! モスッ
PUSH

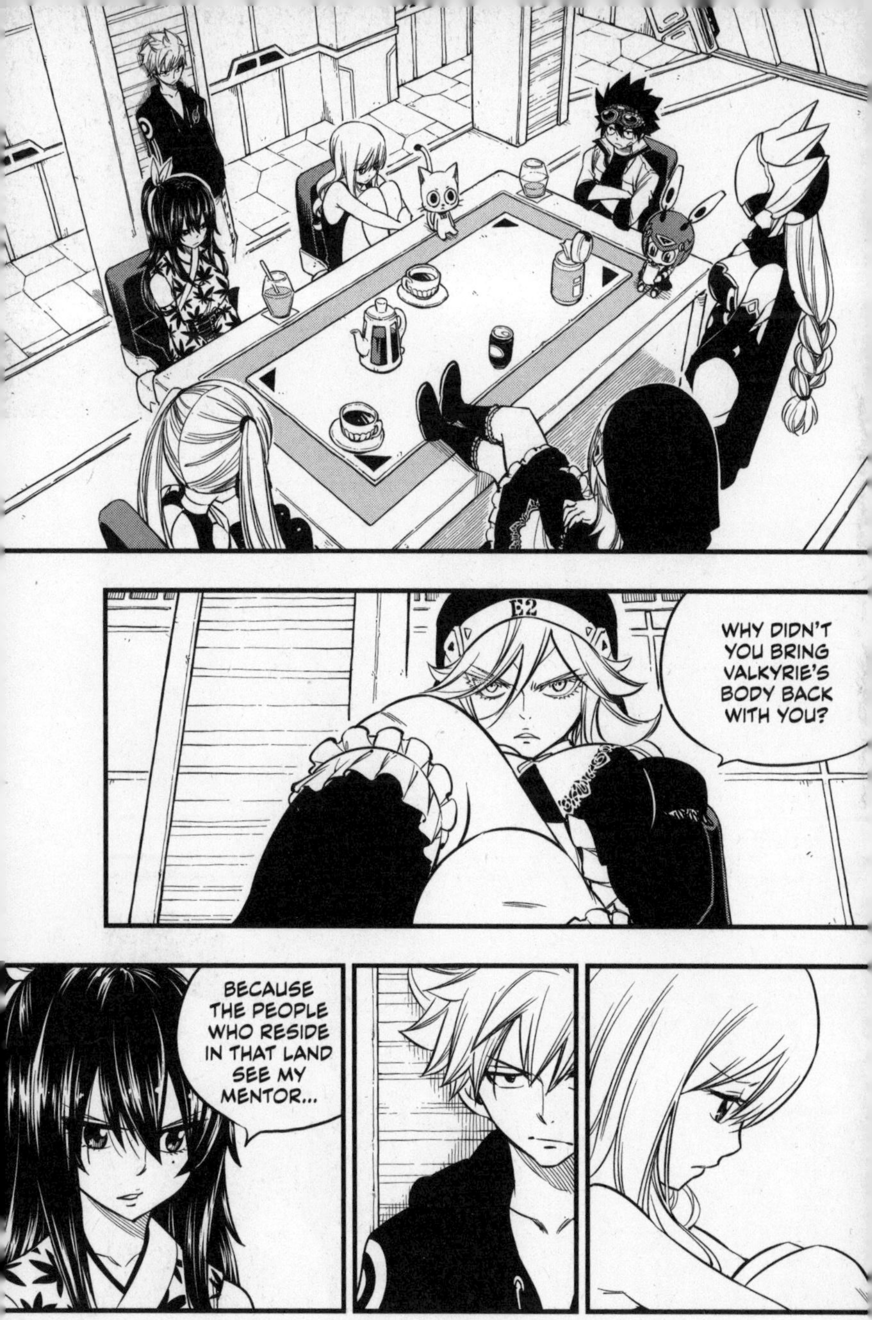

WHY DIDN'T YOU BRING VALKYRIE'S BODY BACK WITH YOU?
BECAUSE THE PEOPLE WHO RESIDE IN THAT LAND SEE MY MENTOR...

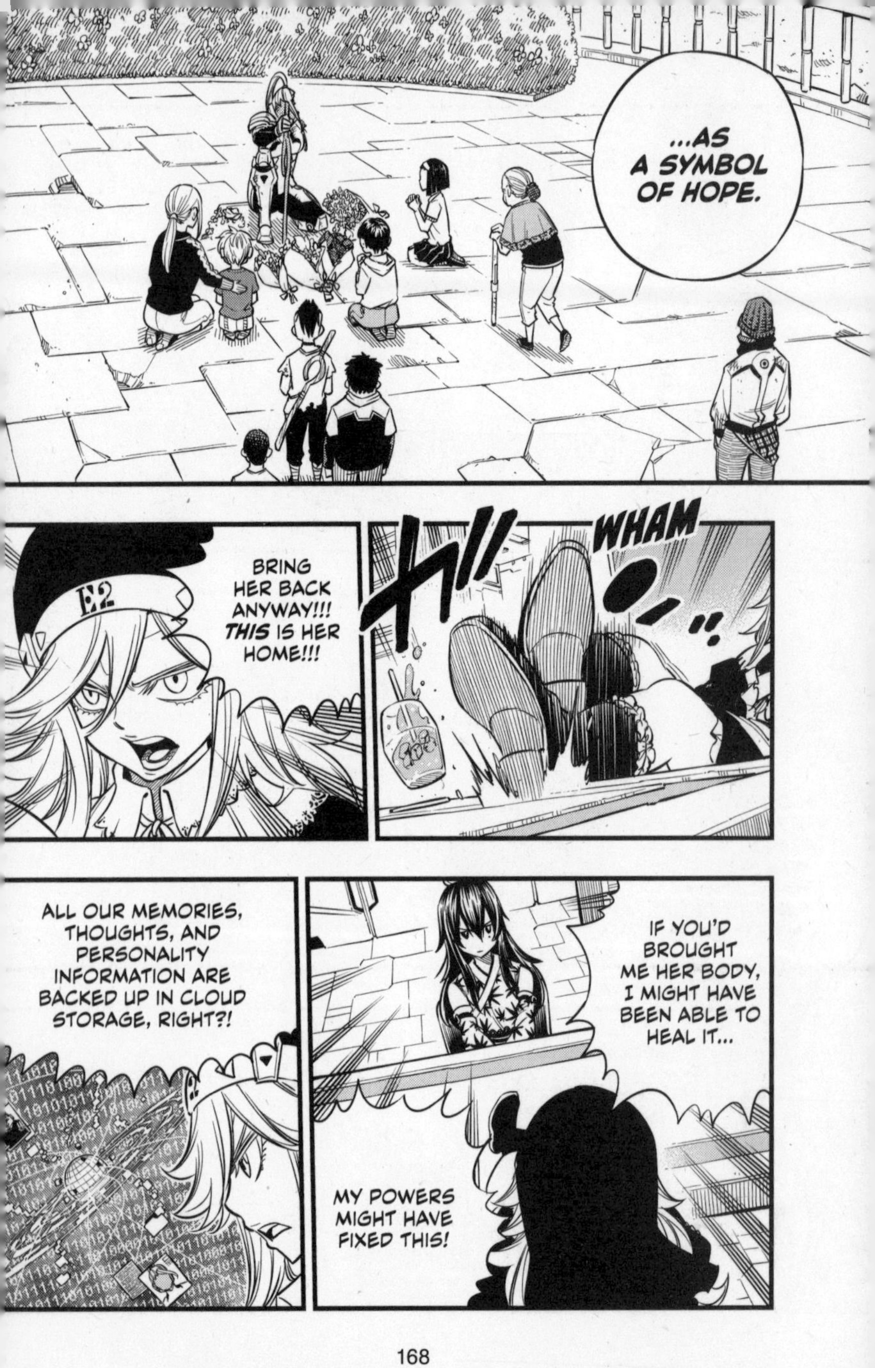
...AS A SYMBOL OF HOPE.
WHAM
BRING HER BACK ANYWAY!!! *THIS* IS HER HOME!!!
IF YOU'D BROUGHT ME HER BODY, I MIGHT HAVE BEEN ABLE TO HEAL IT...
MY POWERS MIGHT HAVE FIXED THIS!
ALL OUR MEMORIES, THOUGHTS, AND PERSONALITY INFORMATION ARE BACKED UP IN CLOUD STORAGE, RIGHT?!

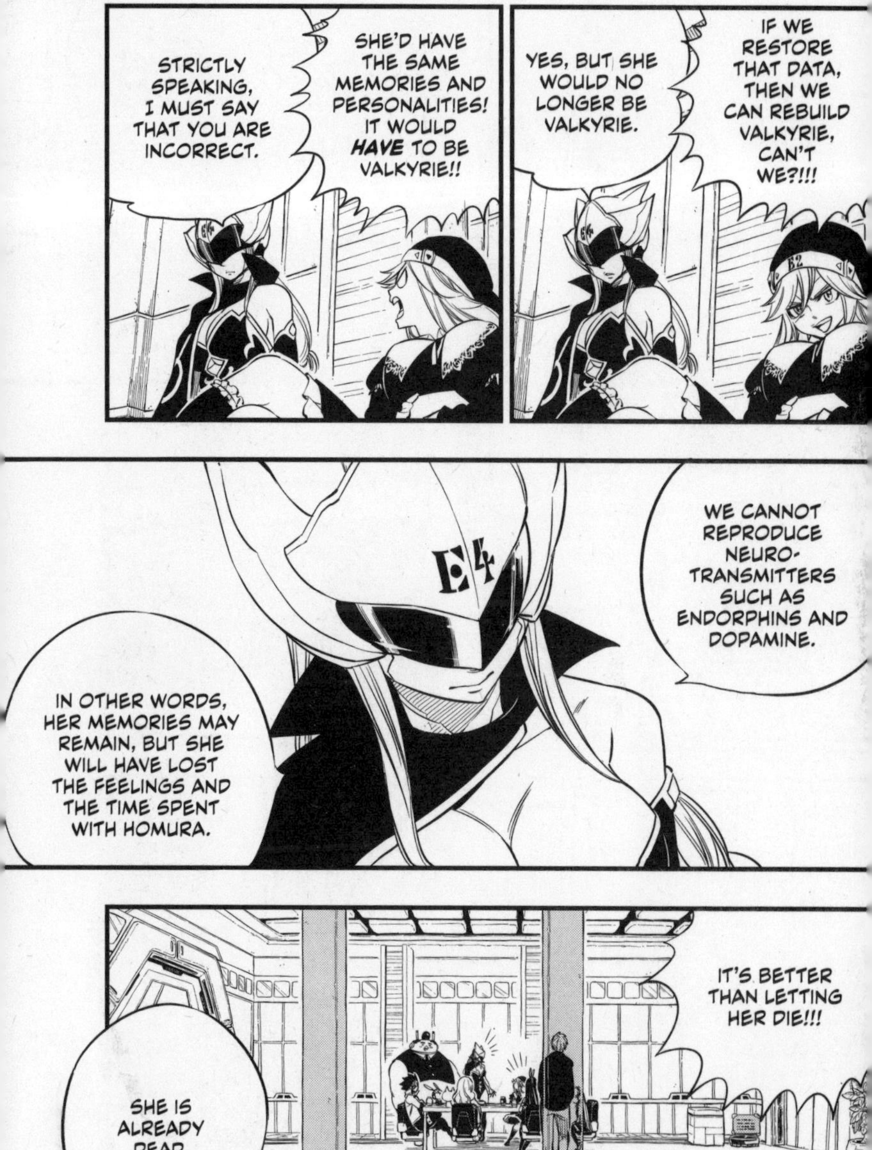
IF WE RESTORE THAT DATA, THEN WE CAN REBUILD VALKYRIE, CAN'T WE?!!!
YES, BUT SHE WOULD NO LONGER BE VALKYRIE.
SHE'D HAVE THE SAME MEMORIES AND PERSONALITIES! IT WOULD **HAVE** TO BE VALKYRIE!!
STRICTLY SPEAKING, I MUST SAY THAT YOU ARE INCORRECT.
WE CANNOT REPRODUCE NEURO-TRANSMITTERS SUCH AS ENDORPHINS AND DOPAMINE.
IN OTHER WORDS, HER MEMORIES MAY REMAIN, BUT SHE WILL HAVE LOST THE FEELINGS AND THE TIME SPENT WITH HOMURA.
IT'S BETTER THAN LETTING HER DIE!!!
SHE IS ALREADY DEAD.

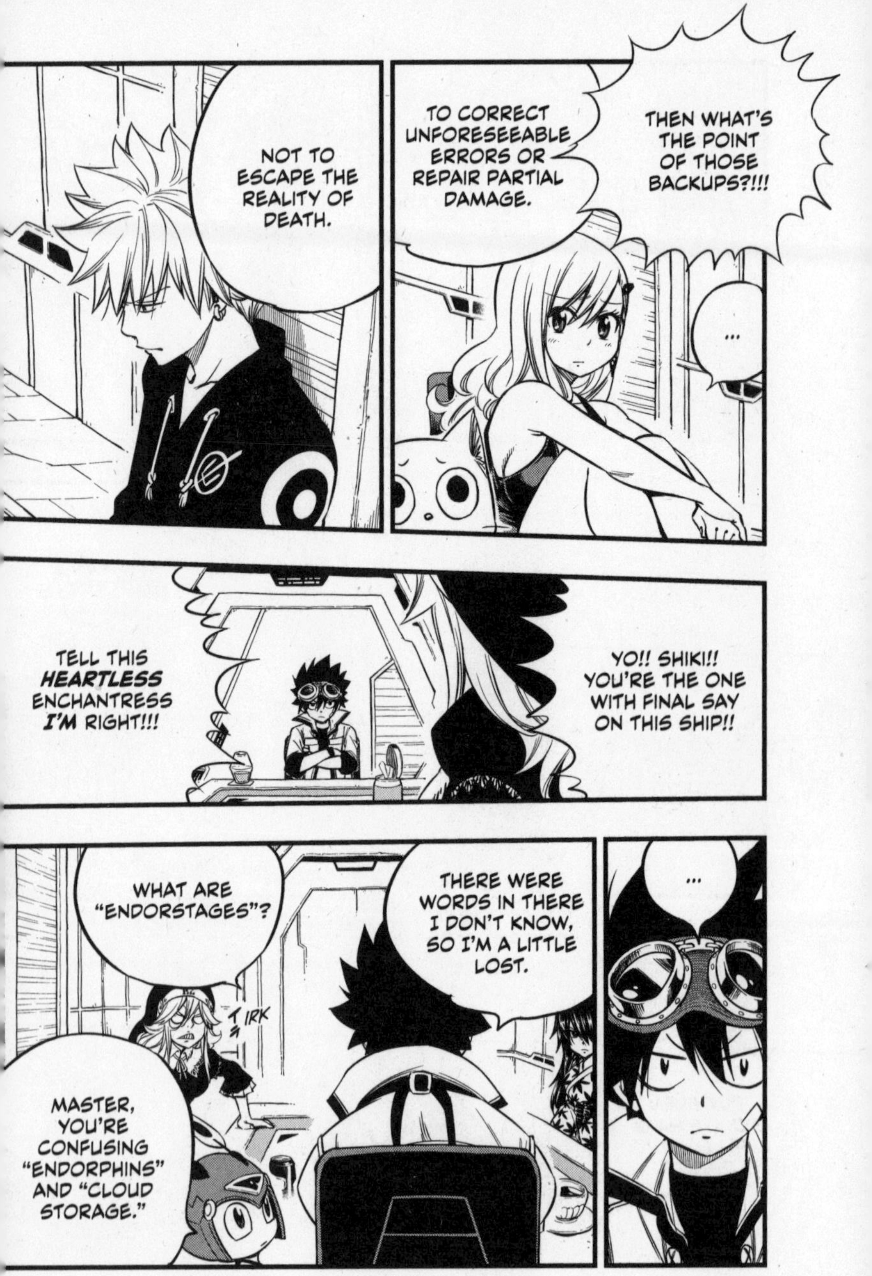
THEN WHAT'S THE POINT OF THOSE BACKUPS?!!!
TO CORRECT UNFORESEEABLE ERRORS OR REPAIR PARTIAL DAMAGE.
...
NOT TO ESCAPE THE REALITY OF DEATH.
YO!! SHIKI!! YOU'RE THE ONE WITH FINAL SAY ON THIS SHIP!!
TELL THIS ***HEARTLESS*** ENCHANTRESS ***I'M*** RIGHT!!!
...
THERE WERE WORDS IN THERE I DON'T KNOW, SO I'M A LITTLE LOST.
WHAT ARE "ENDORSTAGES"?
IRK
MASTER, YOU'RE CONFUSING "ENDORPHINS" AND "CLOUD STORAGE."

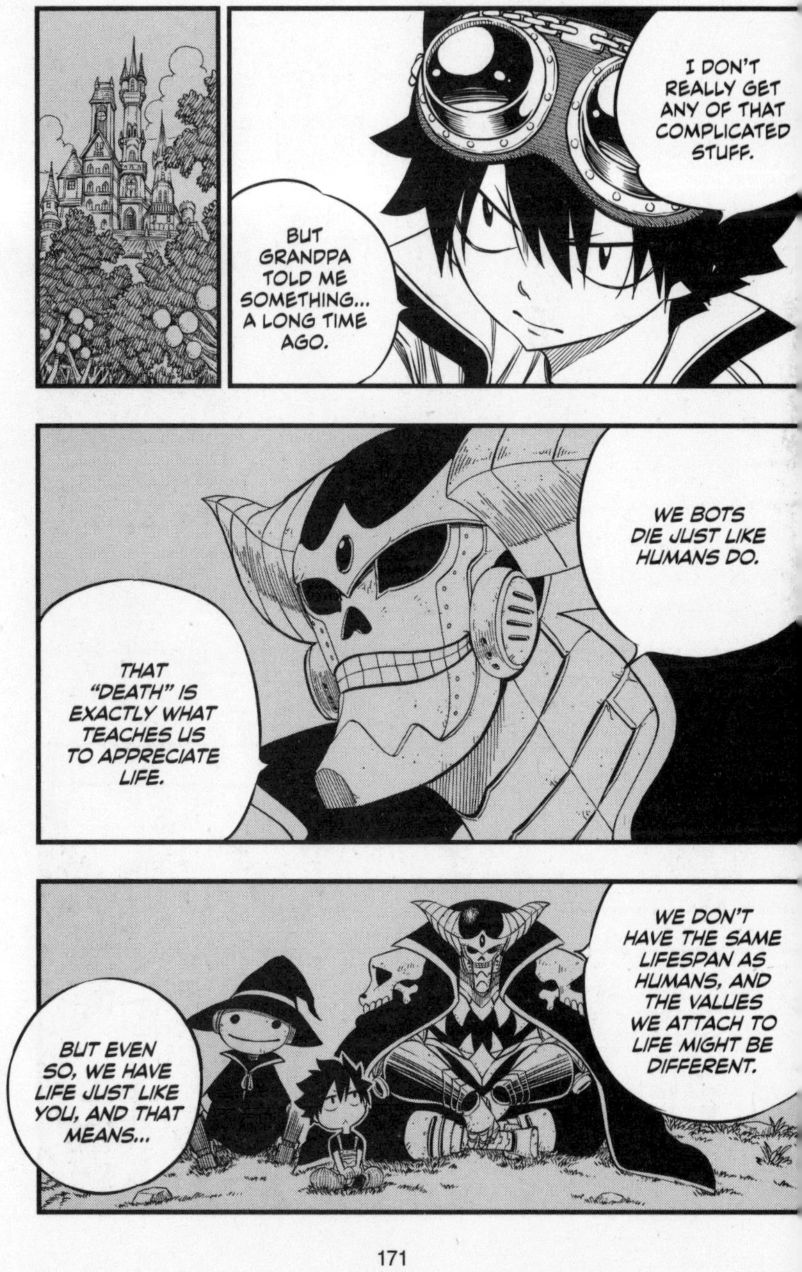
I DON'T REALLY GET ANY OF THAT COMPLICATED STUFF.
BUT GRANDPA TOLD ME SOMETHING... A LONG TIME AGO.
WE BOTS DIE JUST LIKE HUMANS DO.
THAT "DEATH" IS EXACTLY WHAT TEACHES US TO APPRECIATE LIFE.
WE DON'T HAVE THE SAME LIFESPAN AS HUMANS, AND THE VALUES WE ATTACH TO LIFE MIGHT BE DIFFERENT.
BUT EVEN SO, WE HAVE LIFE JUST LIKE YOU, AND THAT MEANS...

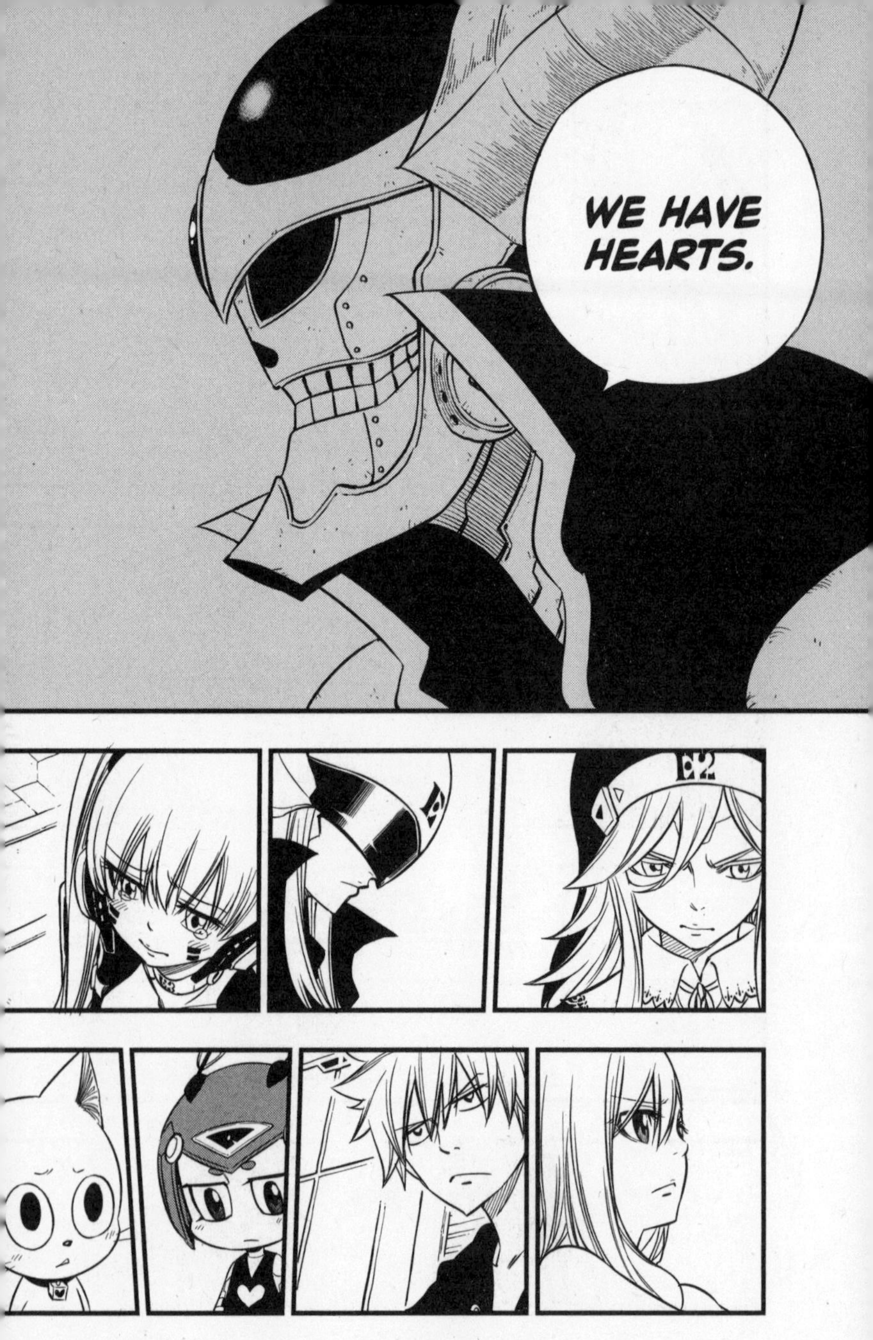
WE HAVE HEARTS.

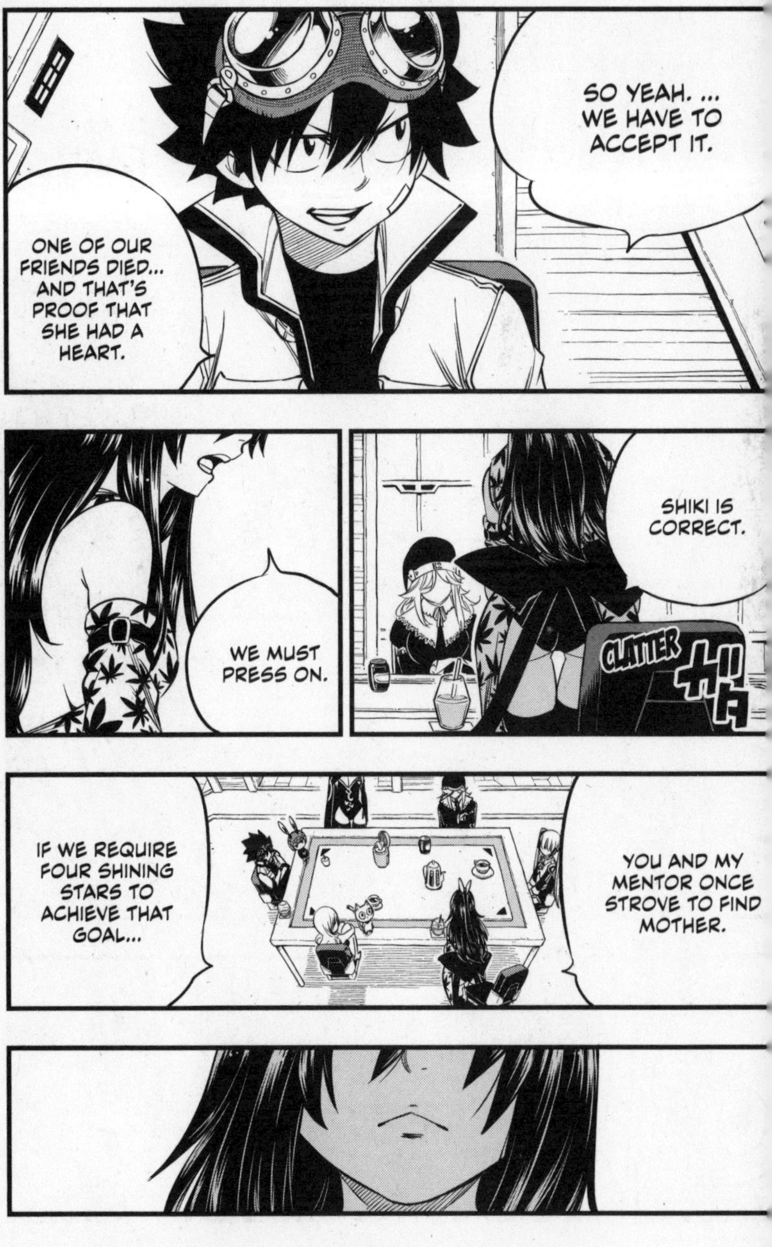
SO YEAH. ... WE HAVE TO ACCEPT IT.
ONE OF OUR FRIENDS DIED... AND THAT'S PROOF THAT SHE HAD A HEART.
SHIKI IS CORRECT.
CLATTER
ガタ
WE MUST PRESS ON.
YOU AND MY MENTOR ONCE STROVE TO FIND MOTHER.
IF WE REQUIRE FOUR SHINING STARS TO ACHIEVE THAT GOAL...

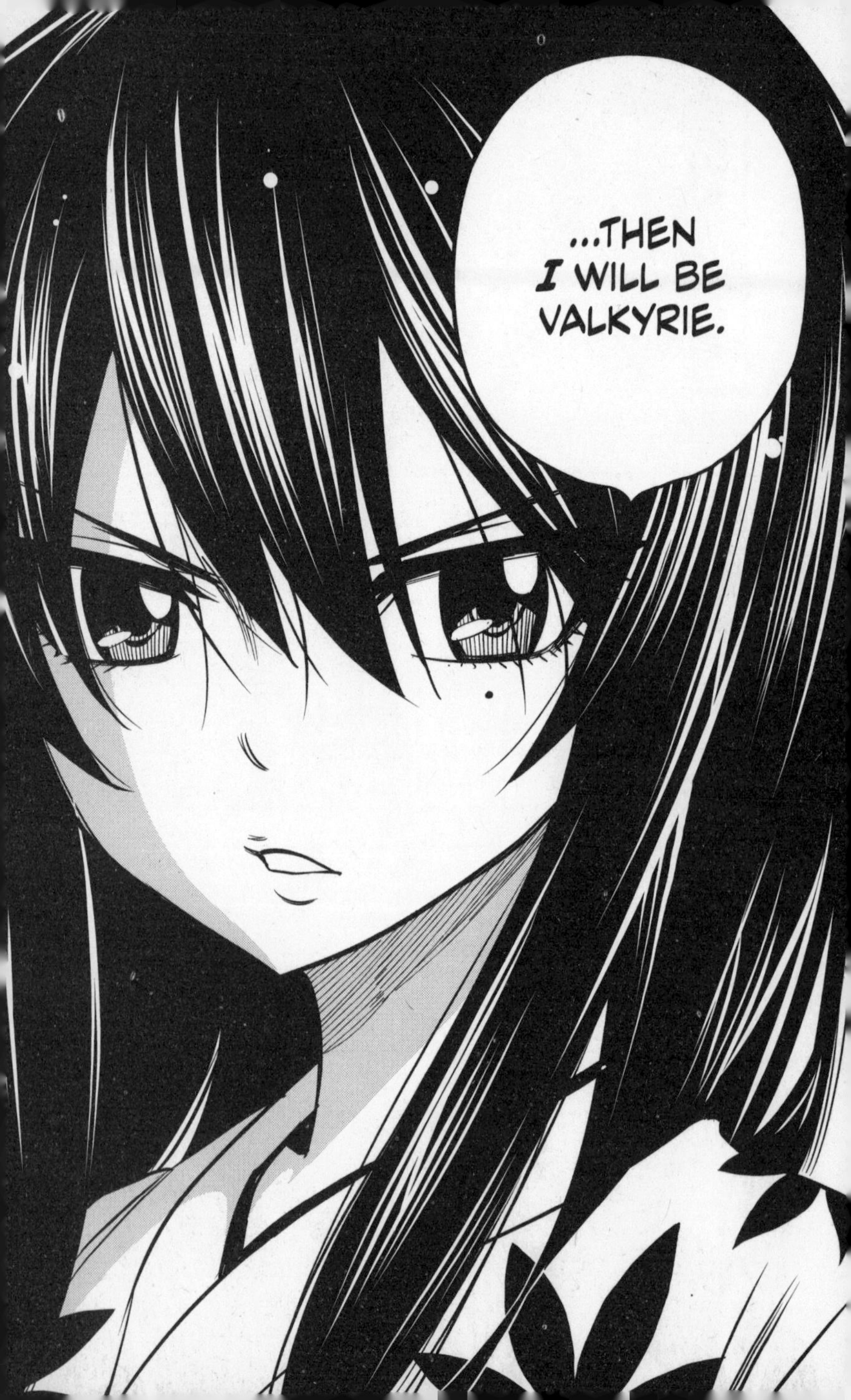
...THEN I WILL BE VALKYRIE.

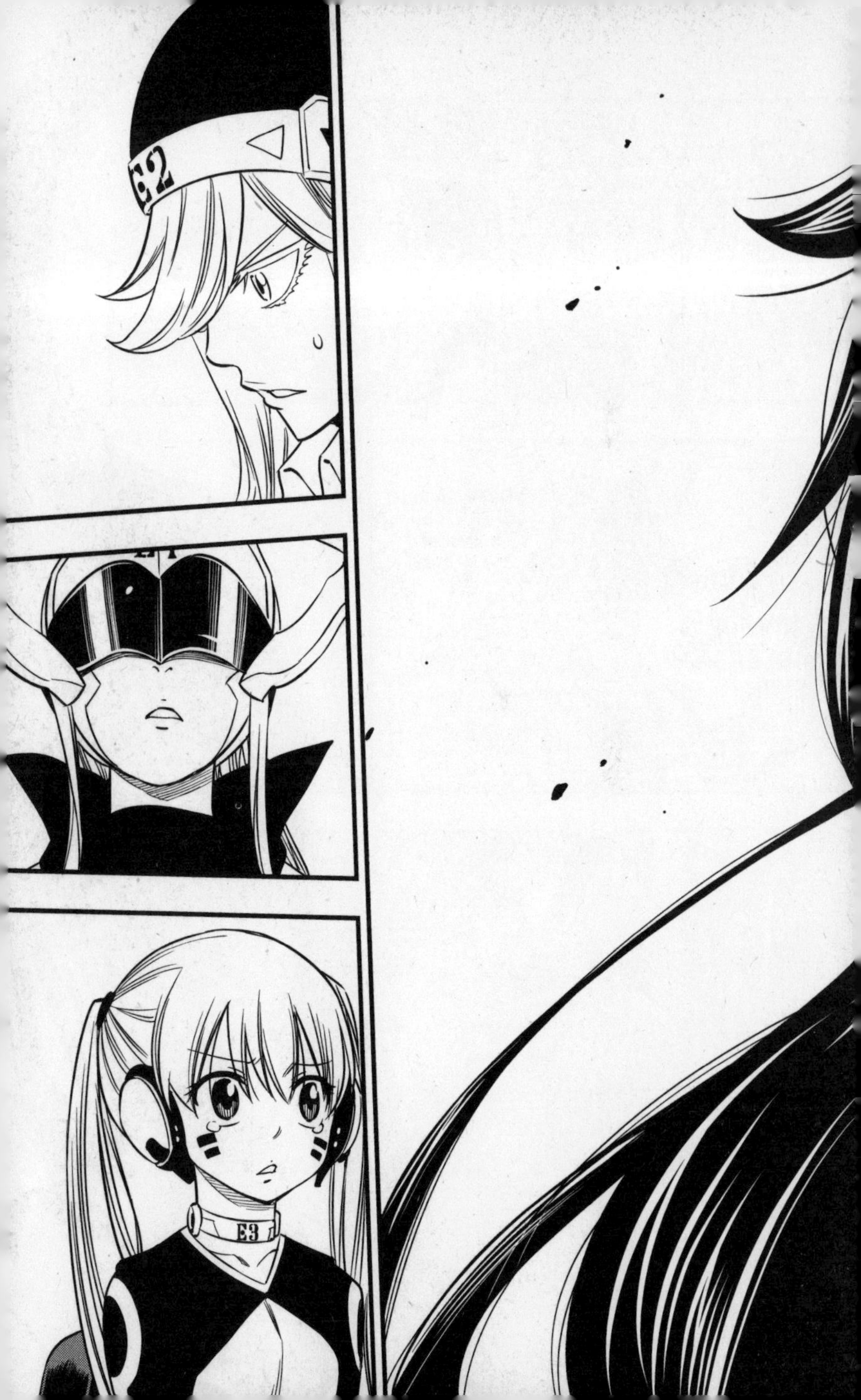
E2
E3

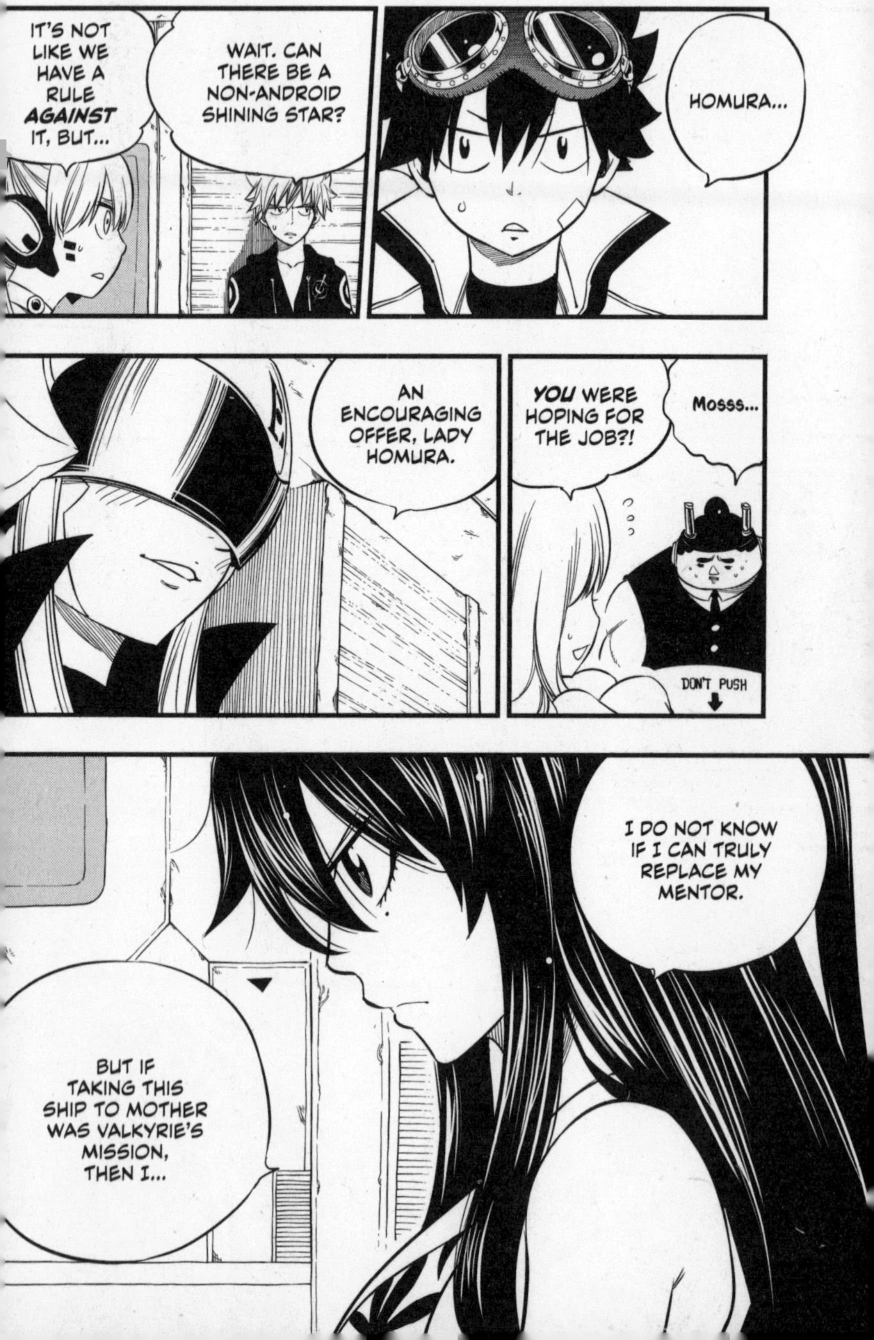
HOMURA...
WAIT. CAN THERE BE A NON-ANDROID SHINING STAR?
IT'S NOT LIKE WE HAVE A RULE AGAINST IT, BUT...
Mosss...
YOU WERE HOPING FOR THE JOB?!
DON'T PUSH
AN ENCOURAGING OFFER, LADY HOMURA.
I DO NOT KNOW IF I CAN TRULY REPLACE MY MENTOR.
BUT IF TAKING THIS SHIP TO MOTHER WAS VALKYRIE'S MISSION, THEN I...

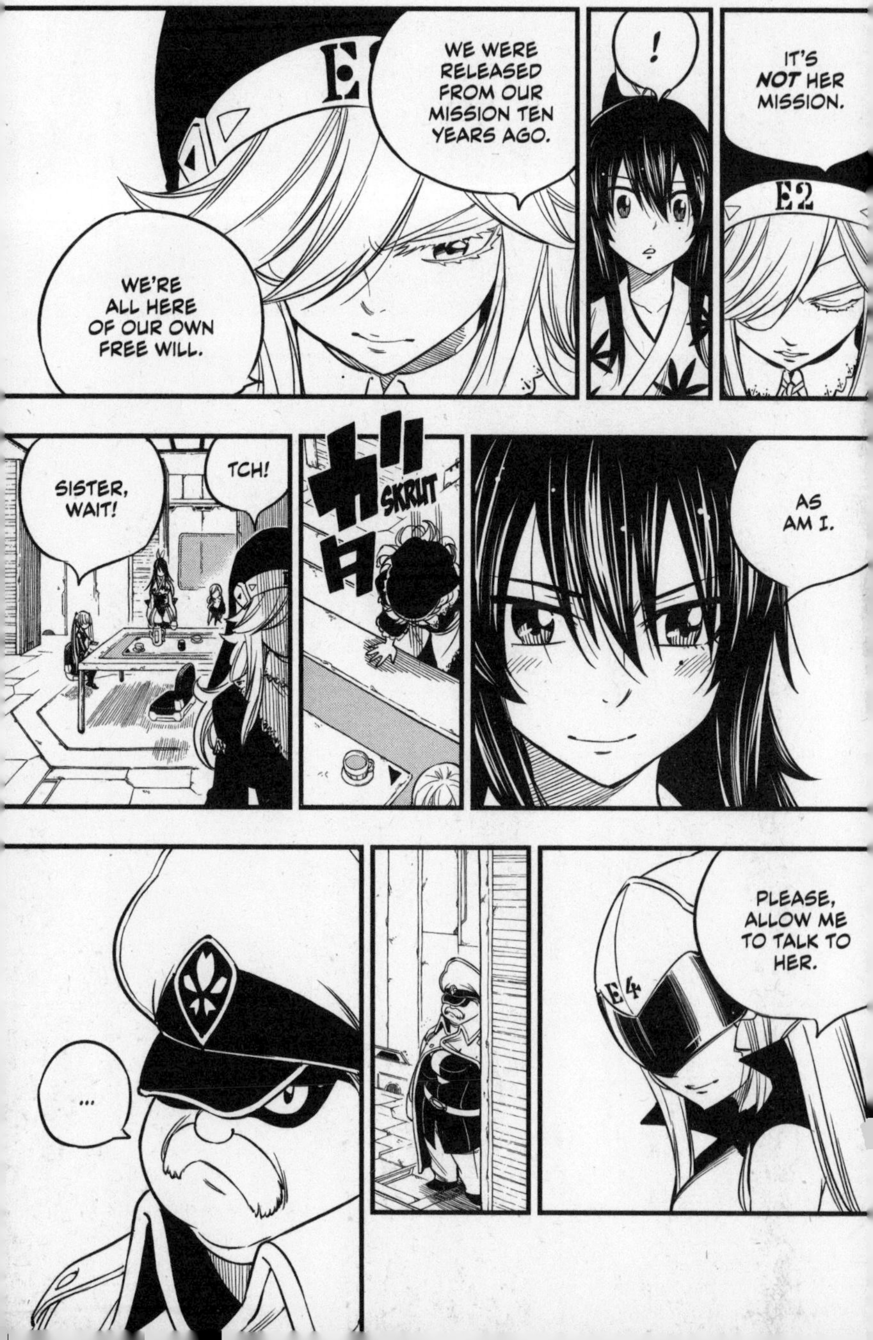
IT'S *NOT* HER MISSION.
!
WE WERE RELEASED FROM OUR MISSION TEN YEARS AGO.
WE'RE ALL HERE OF OUR OWN FREE WILL.
AS AM I.
SKRUT
TCH!
SISTER, WAIT!
PLEASE, ALLOW ME TO TALK TO HER.
...

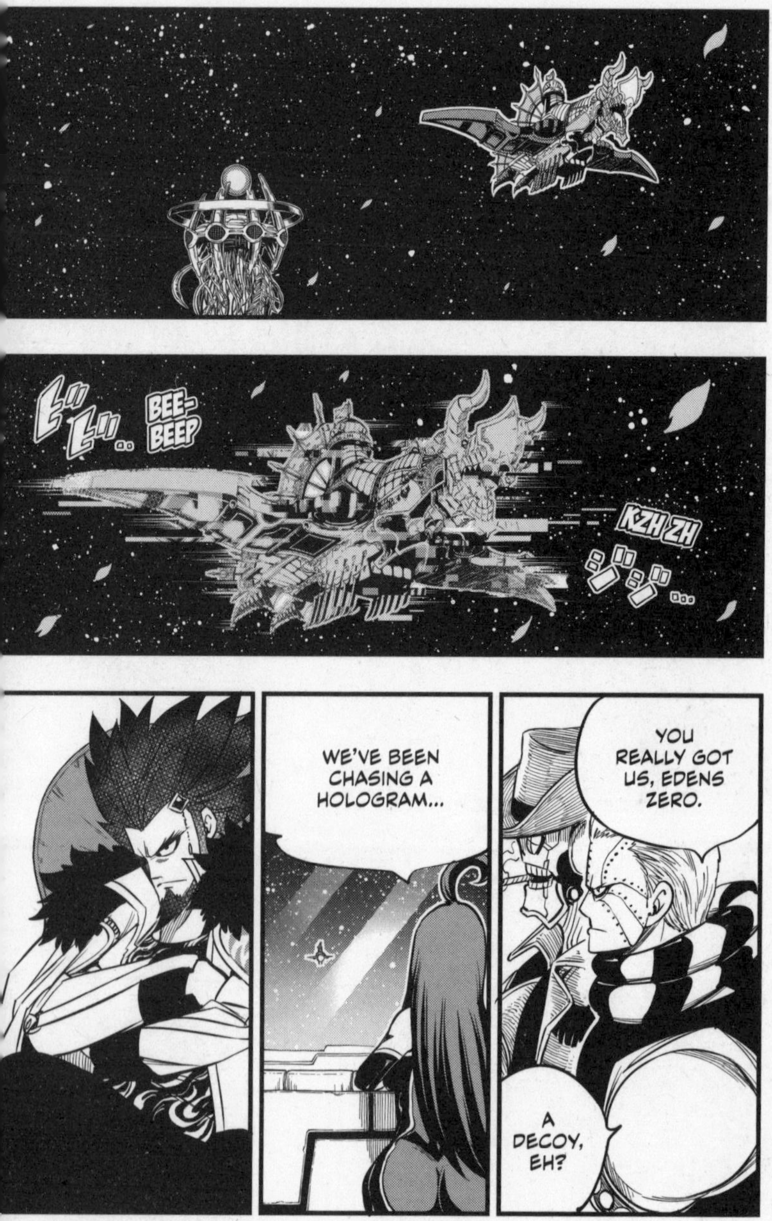
BEE-BEEP
KZH ZH
YOU REALLY GOT US, EDENS ZERO.
A DECOY, EH?
WE'VE BEEN CHASING A HOLOGRAM...

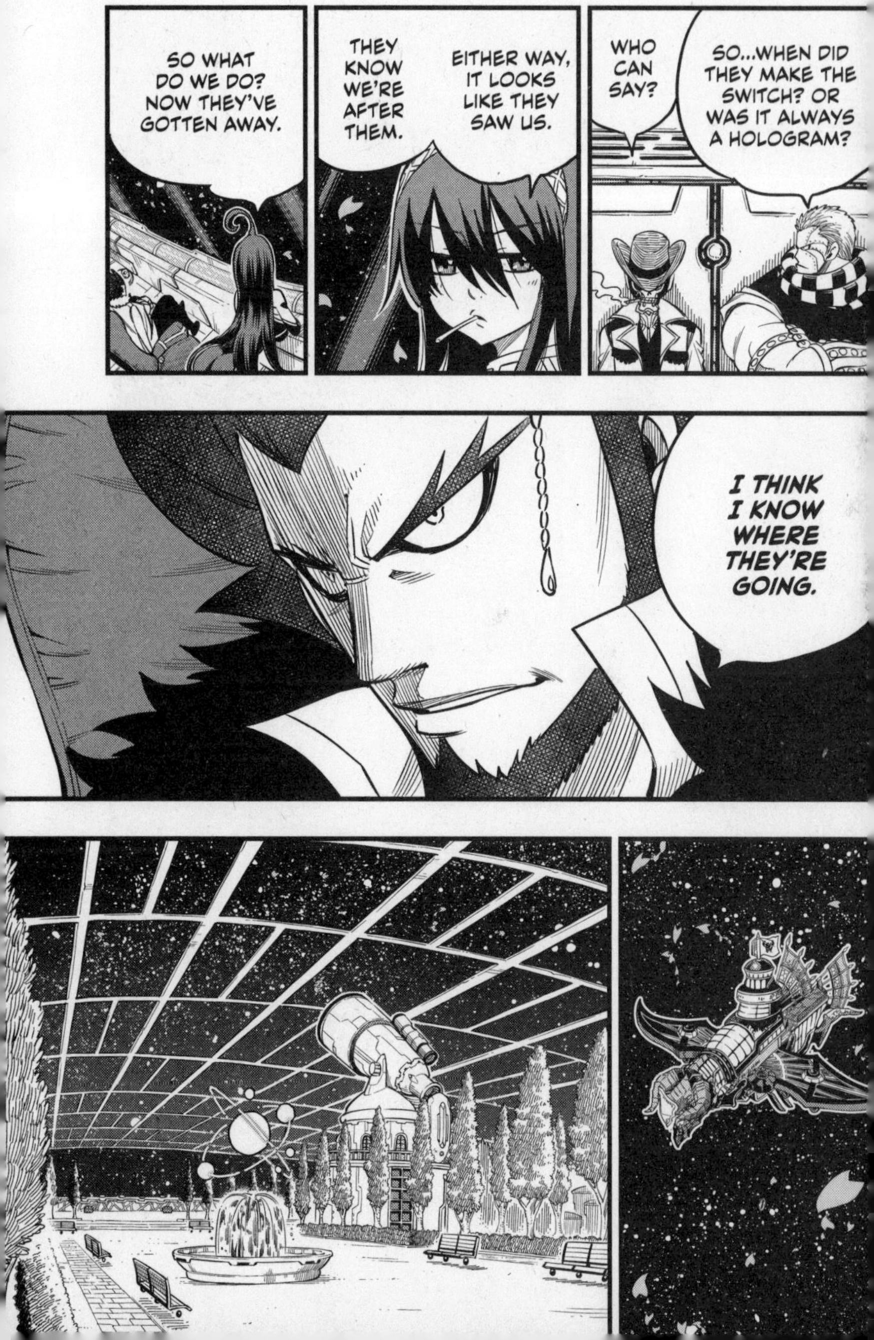
SO...WHEN DID THEY MAKE THE SWITCH? OR WAS IT ALWAYS A HOLOGRAM?
WHO CAN SAY?
EITHER WAY, IT LOOKS LIKE THEY SAW US.
THEY KNOW WE'RE AFTER THEM.
SO WHAT DO WE DO? NOW THEY'VE GOTTEN AWAY.
I THINK I KNOW WHERE THEY'RE GOING.

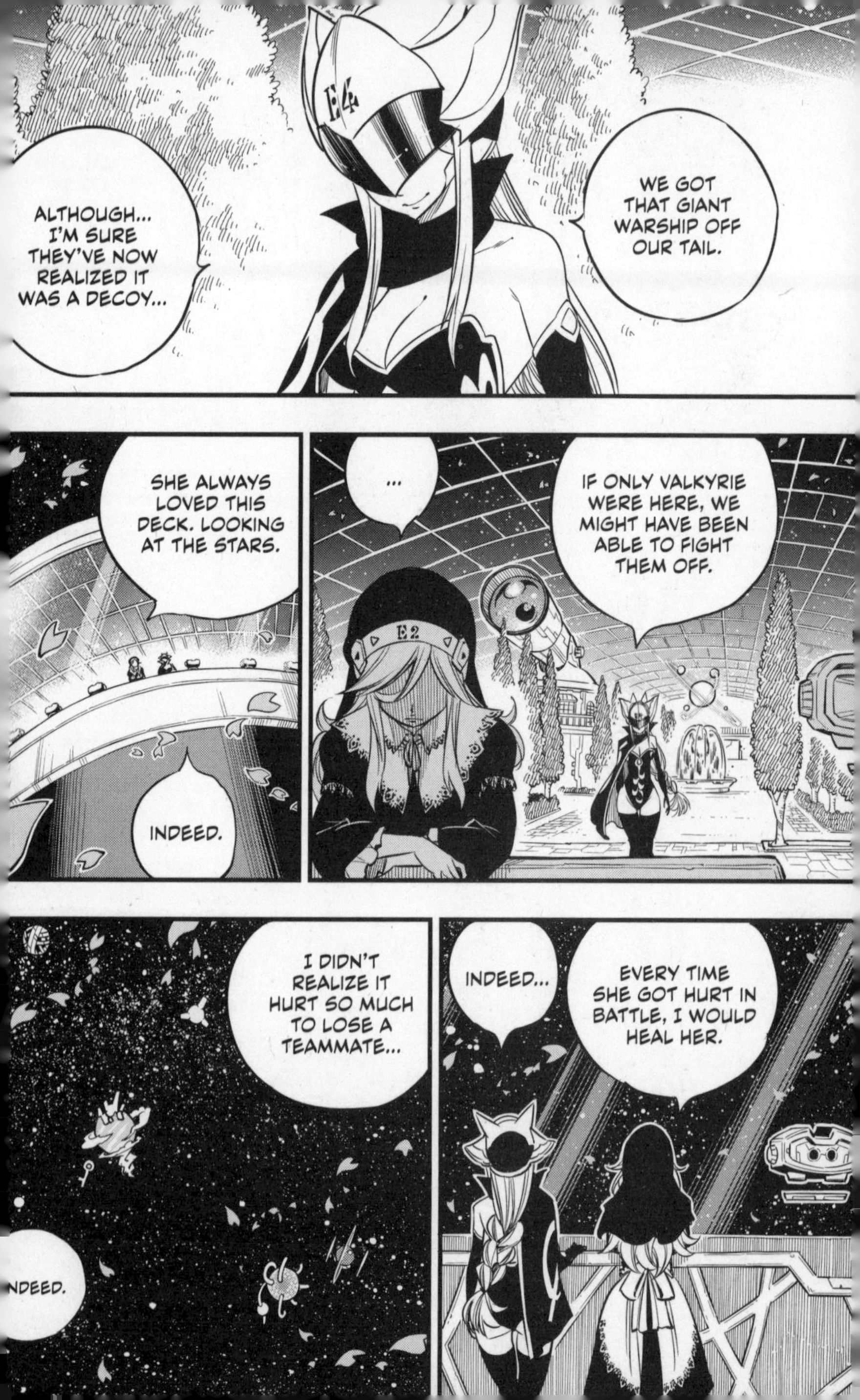
WE GOT THAT GIANT WARSHIP OFF OUR TAIL.
ALTHOUGH... I'M SURE THEY'VE NOW REALIZED IT WAS A DECOY...
IF ONLY VALKYRIE WERE HERE, WE MIGHT HAVE BEEN ABLE TO FIGHT THEM OFF.
...
SHE ALWAYS LOVED THIS DECK. LOOKING AT THE STARS.
INDEED.
EVERY TIME SHE GOT HURT IN BATTLE, I WOULD HEAL HER.
INDEED...
I DIDN'T REALIZE IT HURT SO MUCH TO LOSE A TEAMMATE...
NDEED.

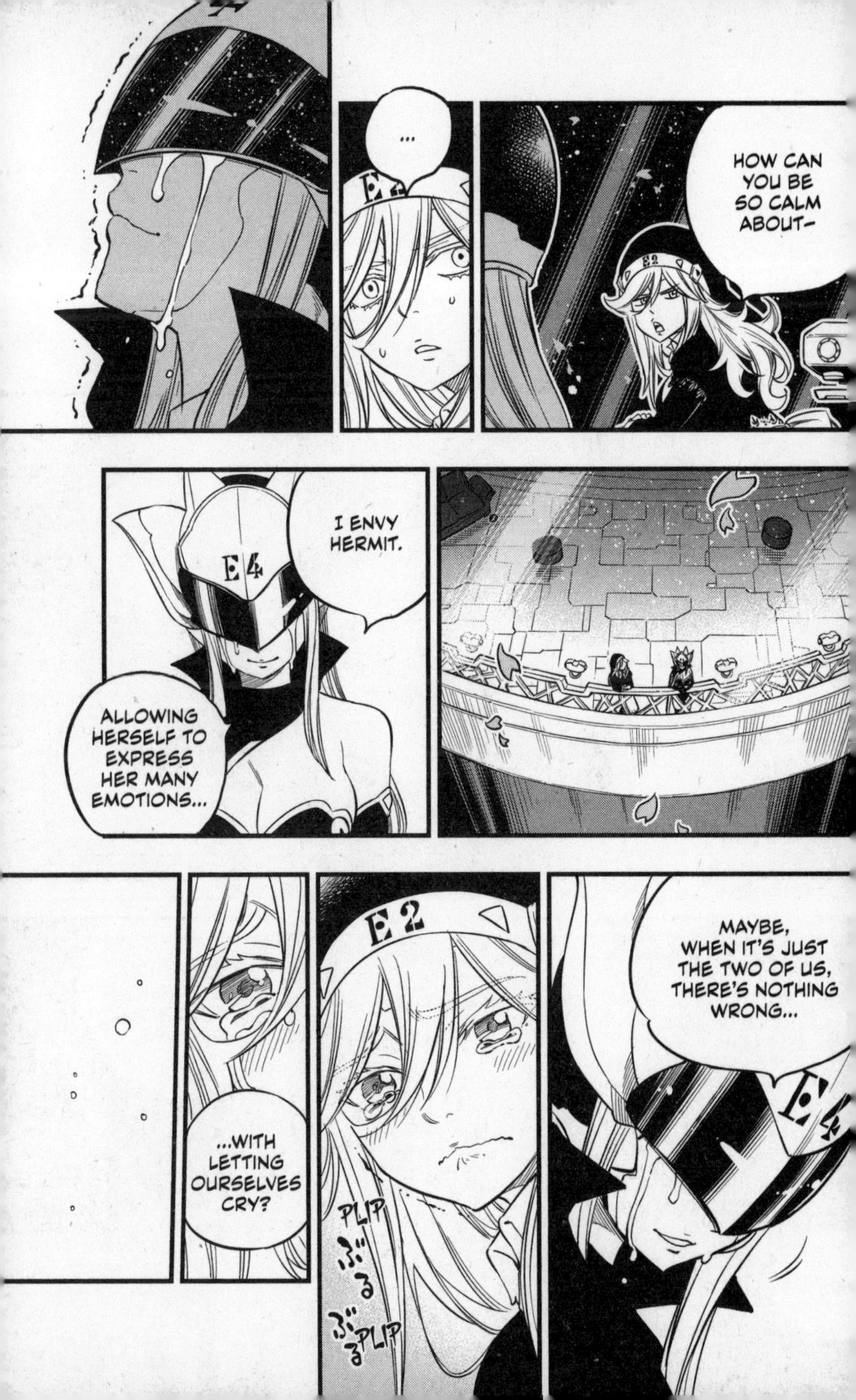
HOW CAN YOU BE SO CALM ABOUT-
...
I ENVY HERMIT.
ALLOWING HERSELF TO EXPRESS HER MANY EMOTIONS...
MAYBE, WHEN IT'S JUST THE TWO OF US, THERE'S NOTHING WRONG...
PLIP
ぶる
ぶる
PLIP
...WITH LETTING OURSELVES CRY?

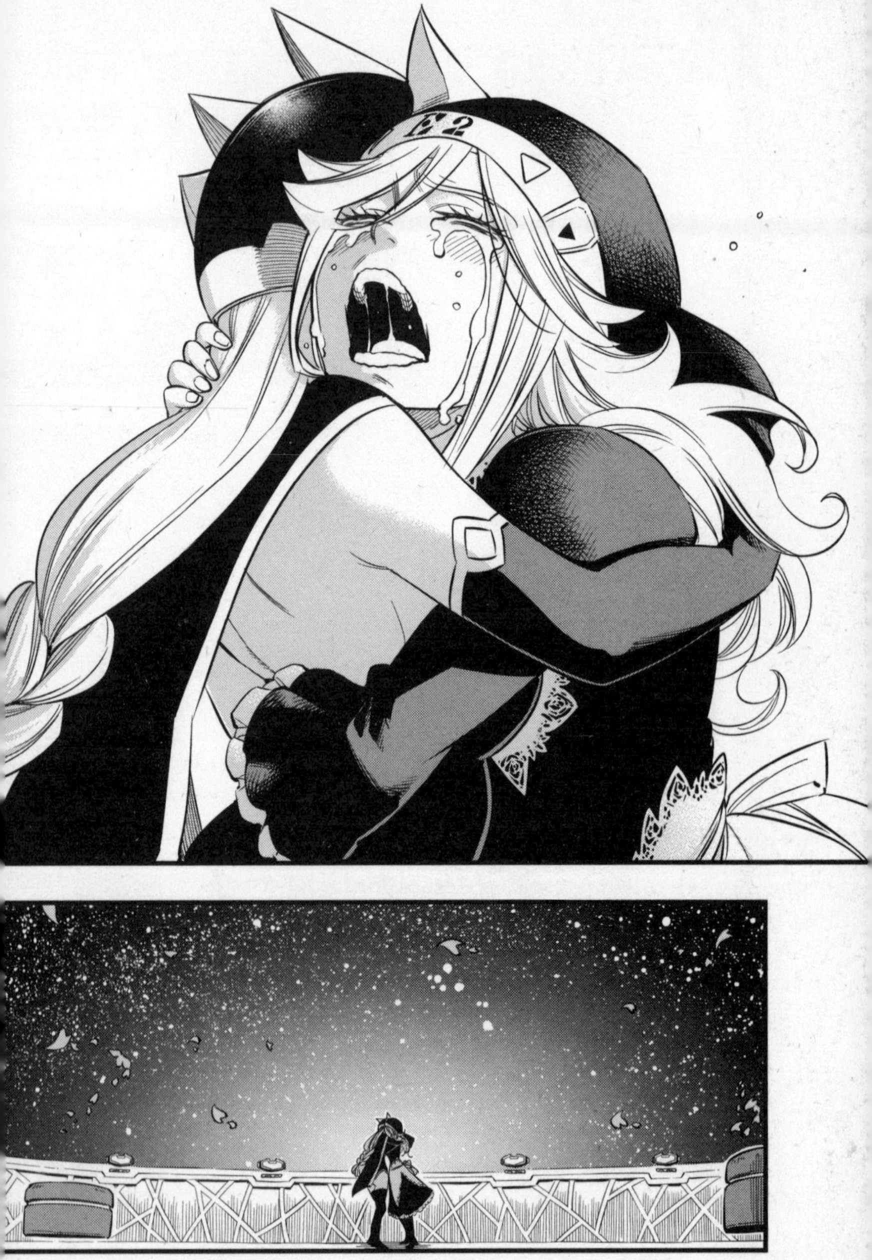

TO BE CONTINUED...

AFTERWORD

The way I work has changed a lot! It was true when I switched from analogue to digital, too, but the way I work in general has changed a lot with the changing times.

I'm worried about how people these days will react to me writing stuff like this, but in the past, I had a pretty harsh working environment. It was rough on me and my staff.

My staff would stay over from Wednesday to Saturday and work. And when we didn't finish on Saturday, sometimes we would work all night with no sleep. That was the general style of work for manga in those days, so we just kept at it without ever questioning it.

A major factor in changing that, is the changing times. In these days, the mind-over-matter attitude of, "Just work!" doesn't really fly anymore, and people are expected to have appropriate work hours. From the perspective of a manager who keeps his staff attached to their desks for long hours, this is a very difficult problem. I want them to do the job like they should. But it takes time to finish 20 pages of manga. The "We'll get through it with sheer force of will!" attitude that worked in the past doesn't work anymore.

So, through a lot of trial and error, we've arrived at using digital art. There are a lot of advantages to working digitally. The first of which, is that our speed has gone way up. Of course, when you're not used to it, you feel like, "Analogue was way faster!", but once you get the hang of it, it's much faster than analogue. From my experience, it goes about twice as fast. To get technical, I don't need to do a draft, I don't need to erase pencil lines, I can paint over large areas instantaneously, etc. etc. And it's just faster than analogue. I guess the one drawback is that sometimes work gets slowed down because of computer problems.

And by switching to digital, my staff can now work from home. We get together twice a week so I can give instructions and do a final check of the finished chapter, but other than that, they can work at their own pace from their own homes. Then we finish it and get three days off a week! I think the work environment has gotten a lot better.

Now, as for why I'm talking about this, until just the other day, I was working at the ridiculous pace of two series a week (and if you include storyboarding, it was three a week), but even in the midst of this almost stupid amount of work, my staff never had to pull all-nighters, they went home on time, and we still had four-day work weeks. Of course it goes without saying that it was harder than usual, but I'm very proud of it, and it was a new reminder of just how excellent my staff really is.

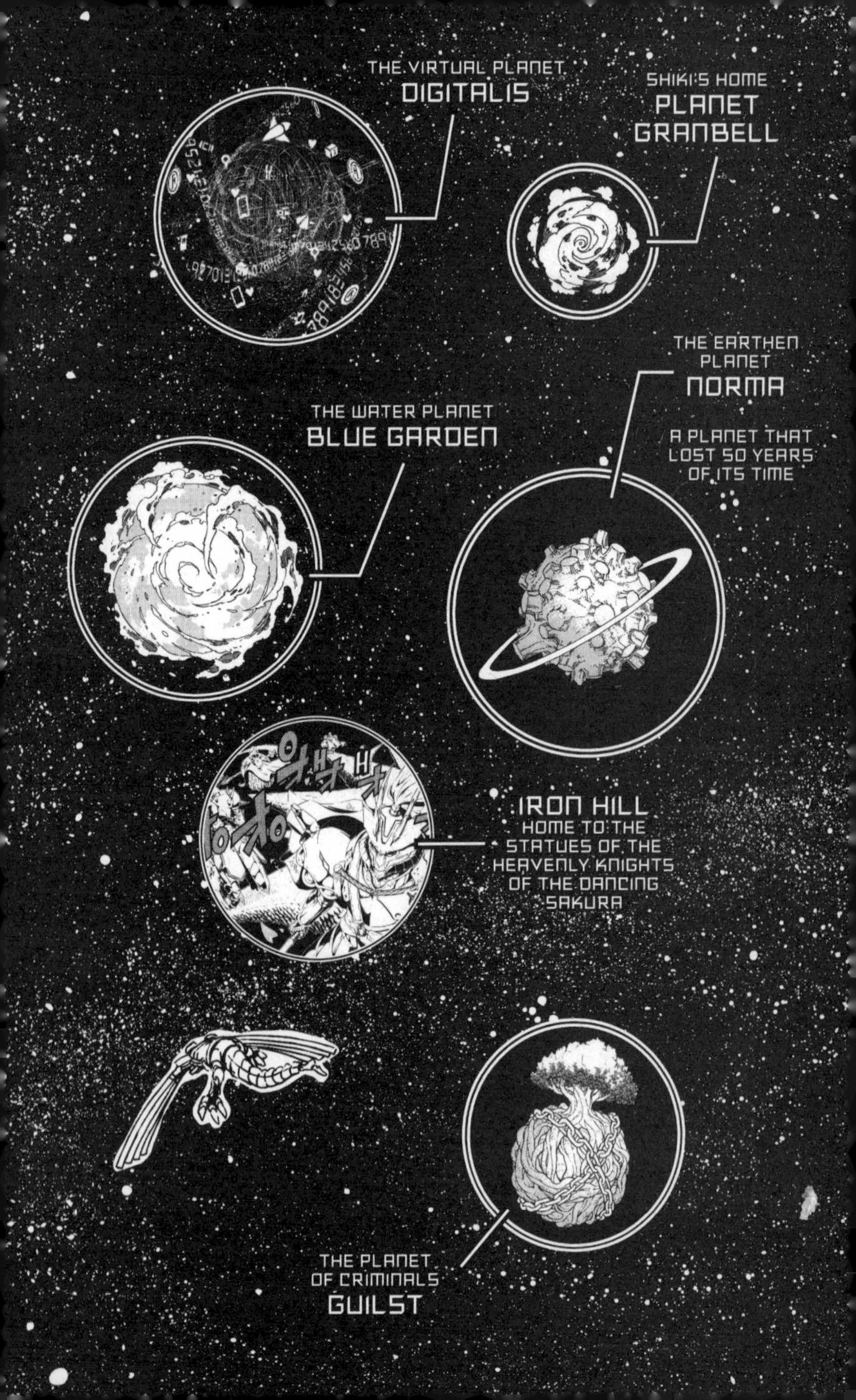
SHIKI'S HOME
PLANET GRANBELL
THE VIRTUAL PLANET
DIGITALIS
THE EARTHEN PLANET
NORMA
A PLANET THAT LOST 50 YEARS OF ITS TIME
THE WATER PLANET
BLUE GARDEN
IRON HILL
HOME TO THE STATUES OF THE HEAVENLY KNIGHTS OF THE DANCING SAKURA
THE PLANET OF CRIMINALS
GUILST

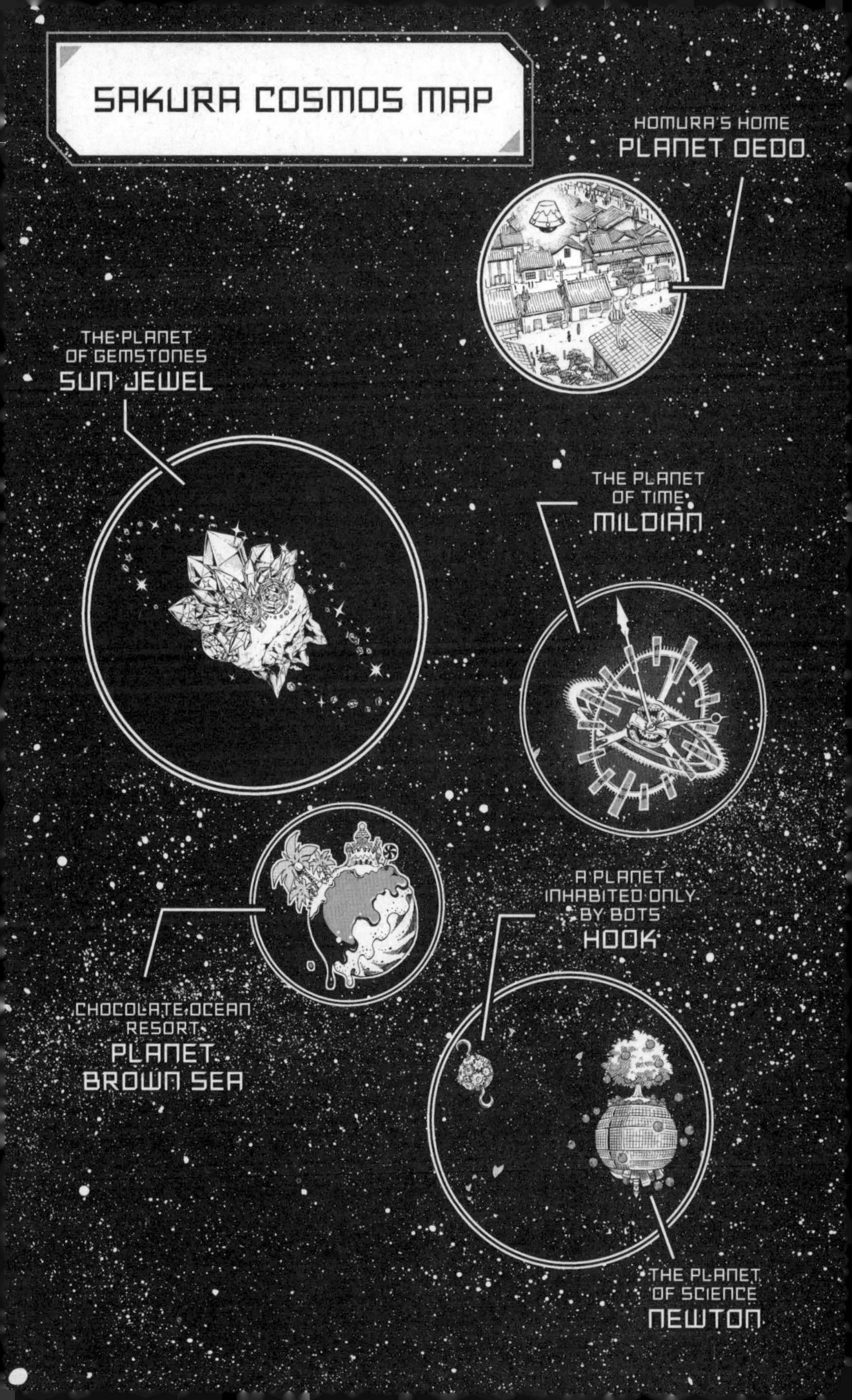
SAKURA COSMOS MAP
HOMURA'S HOME
PLANET OEDO
THE PLANET
OF GEMSTONES
SUN JEWEL
THE PLANET
OF TIME
MILDIAN
CHOCOLATE OCEAN
RESORT
PLANET
BROWN SEA
A PLANET
INHABITED ONLY
BY BOTS
HOOK
THE PLANET
OF SCIENCE
NEWTON

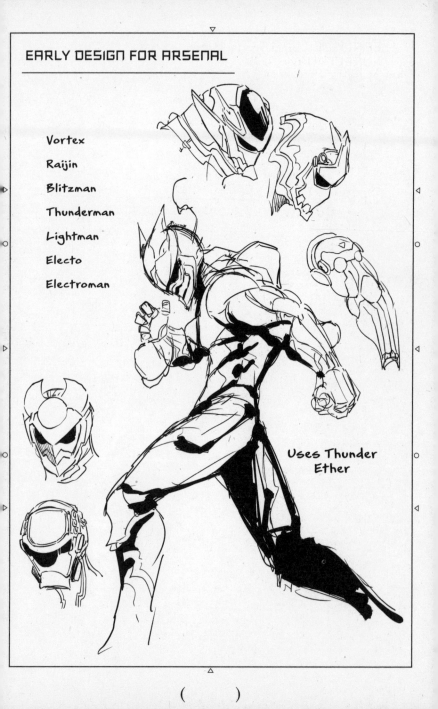

EARLY DESIGN FOR ARSENAL

Vortex
Raijin
Blitzman
Thunderman
Lightman
Electo
Electroman

Uses Thunder
Ether

( )

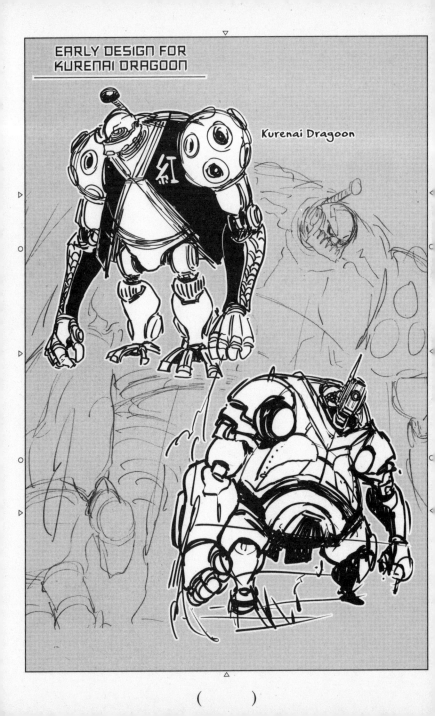

EARLY DESIGN FOR
KURENAI DRAGOON

Kurenai Dragoon

( )

WELCOME TO THE NEXT INSTALLMENT OF...

(AYAKO IMAMURA-SAN, TOKYO)

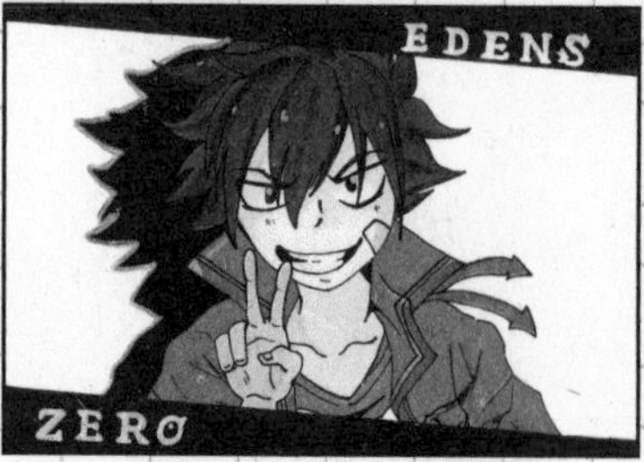
EDENS
ZERO

▲ THIS DRAWING WAS ACTUALLY DONE IN COLOR. I WONDER IF HE'S POSING FOR SOME KIND OF PHOTO SHOOT.

(RISA UEMURA-SAN, NARA)

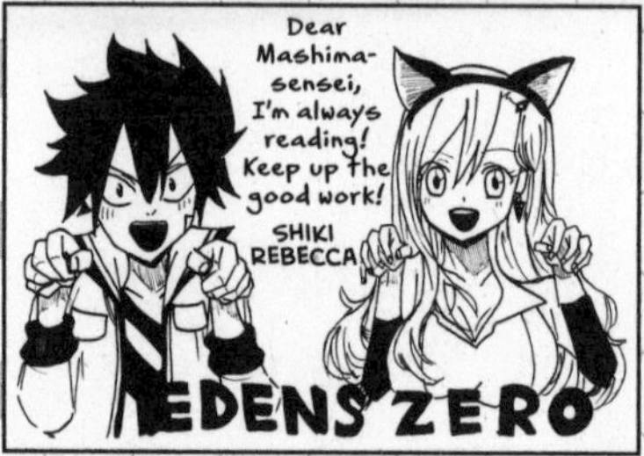
Dear Mashima-sensei, I'm always reading! Keep up the good work!
SHIKI
REBECCA
EDENS ZERO

▲ SHIKI'S DOING THE "MEOW-WOW," TOO. MAYBE THIS WILL DOUBLE HER VIEWERSHIP...?

MASHIMA'S ONE-HIT KO

(YUZUHO OGOSE-SAN, TOYAMA)

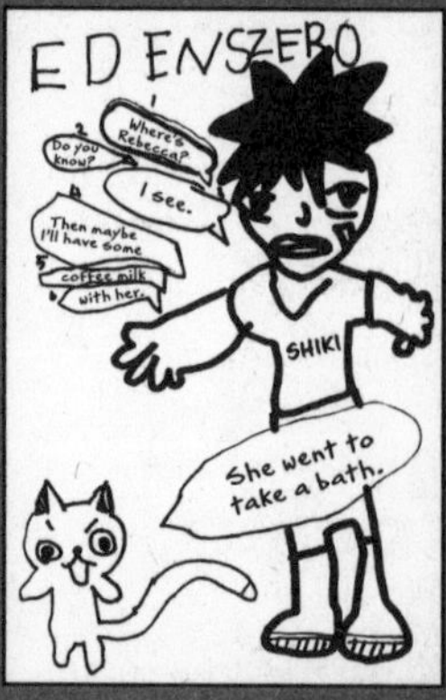
EDENSZERO
Where's Rebecca?
Do you know?
I see.
Then maybe I'll have some coffee milk with her.
SHIKI
She went to take a bath.

▲ YOU ALWAYS HAVE TO HAVE COFFEE MILK AFTER A BATH.

(FLASHY SOCKS-SAN, OSAKA)

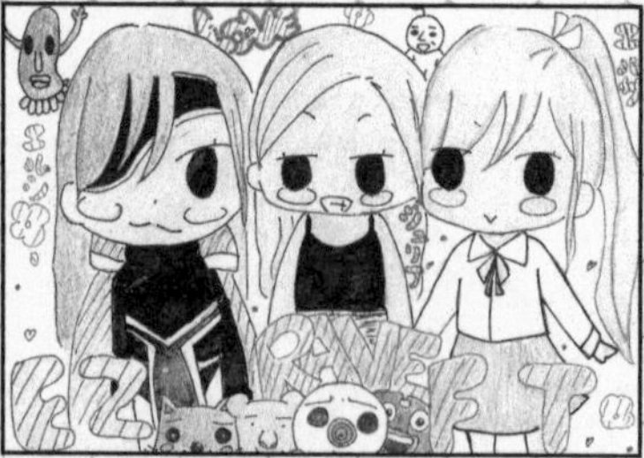

▲ THE SUPER TOUGH LADIES ARE LOOKING SUPER CUTE.

(HIMARI KAI-SAN, KANAGAWA)

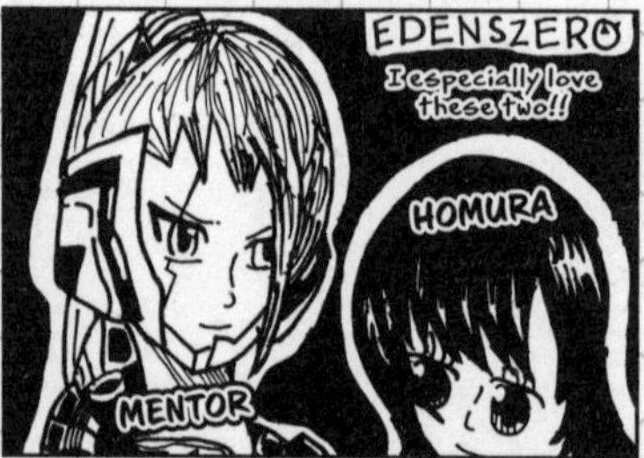
EDENSZERO
I especially love these two!!
HOMURA
MENTOR

▲ THE GREATEST MASTER AND STUDENT. THEIR BOND IS ETERNAL... NO ONE CAN BREAK IT.

EDITOR'S NOTE: SUBMISSIONS LIMITED TO JAPAN.

EZ DRAWING

(L-KICHI-SAN, KANAGAWA)

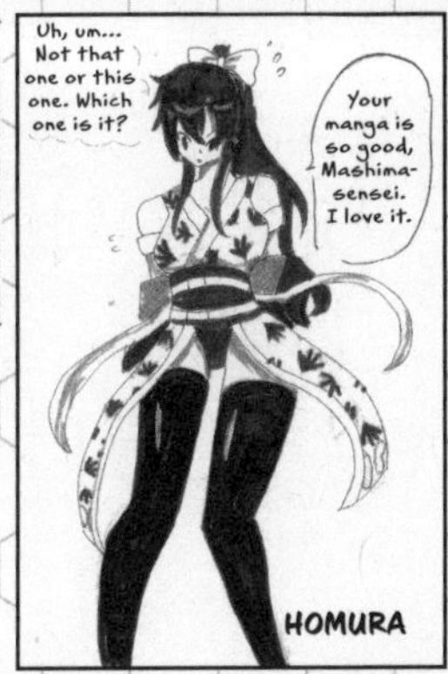

Your manga is so good, Mashima-sensei. I love it.
Uh, um... Not that one or this one. Which one is it?
HOMURA

▲ FOR BETTER OR WORSE, HOMURA CANNOT TELL A LIE. COULD SHE BE THE MOST HONEST PERSON IN THE COSMOS?

(HIIRO AIIRO-SAN, CHIBA)

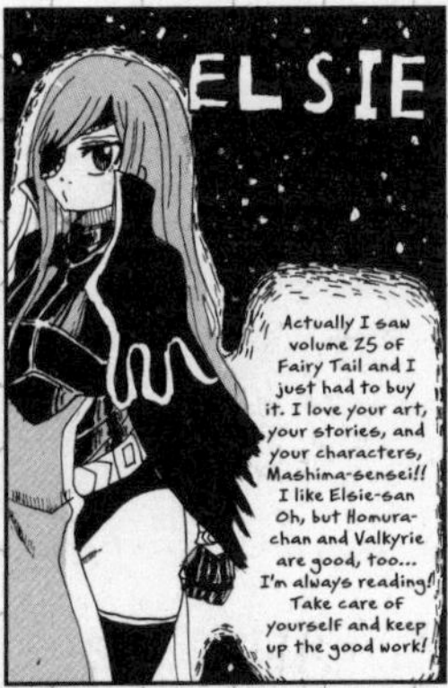

ELSIE
Actually I saw volume 25 of Fairy Tail and I just had to buy it. I love your art, your stories, and your characters, Mashima-sensei!! I like Elsie-san Oh, but Homura-chan and Valkyrie are good, too... I'm always reading!! Take care of yourself and keep up the good work!

▲ ELSIE, HOMURA, VALKYRIE....SO YOU'RE SAYING YOU LIKE STRONG WOMEN.

(YŪKI SUDŌ-SAN, TOKYO)

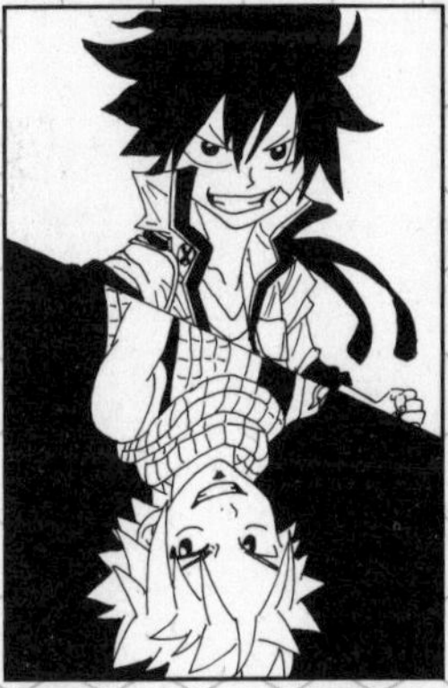

▲ BLACK AND WHITE, SHIKI AND NATSU. THANKS FOR CHECKING OUT *HERO'S*.*

(SHINKA-SAN, SAITAMA)

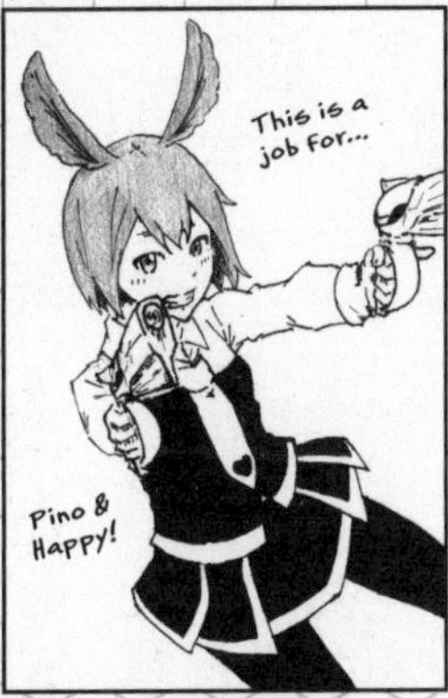

This is a job for...
Pino & Happy!

▲ PINO SEEMS LIKE SHE'D BE A GOOD MARKSWOMAN, SO THIS PAIRING MIGHT BE PRETTY SPOT-ON.

(SAYA-SAN, NAGANO)

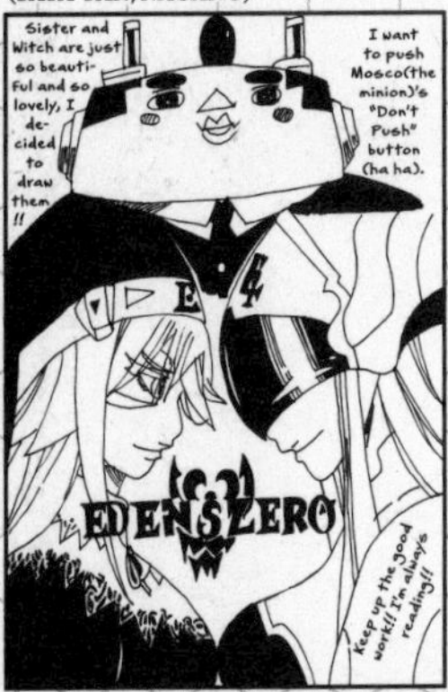

I want to push Mosco (the minion)'s "Don't Push" button (ha ha).
Sister and Witch are just so beautiful and so lovely, I decided to draw them!!
EDENS ZERO
Keep up the good work!! I'm always reading!!

▲ HUMAN OR ANDROID, IT DOESN'T MATTER. IF SOMEONE SAYS "DON'T PUSH," IT MAKES YOU WANT TO PUSH IT.

**HERO'S* is Hiro Mashima's most recent series: A crossover adventure featuring characters from *RAVE MASTER*, *FAIRY TAIL*, and *EDENS ZERO*! Available from Kodansha Comics in print and digital. See kodanshacomics.com for details!

The beloved characters from *Cardcaptor Sakura* return in a brand new, reimagined fantasy adventure!

"[*Tsubasa*] takes readers on a fantastic ride that only gets more exhilarating with each successive chapter." —Anime News Network

In the Kingdom of Clow, an archaeological dig unleashes an incredible power, causing Princess Sakura to lose her memories. To save her, her childhood friend Syaoran must follow the orders of the Dimension Witch and travel alongside Kurogane, an unrivaled warrior; Fai, a powerful magician; and Mokona, a curiously strange creature, to retrieve Sakura's dispersed memories!

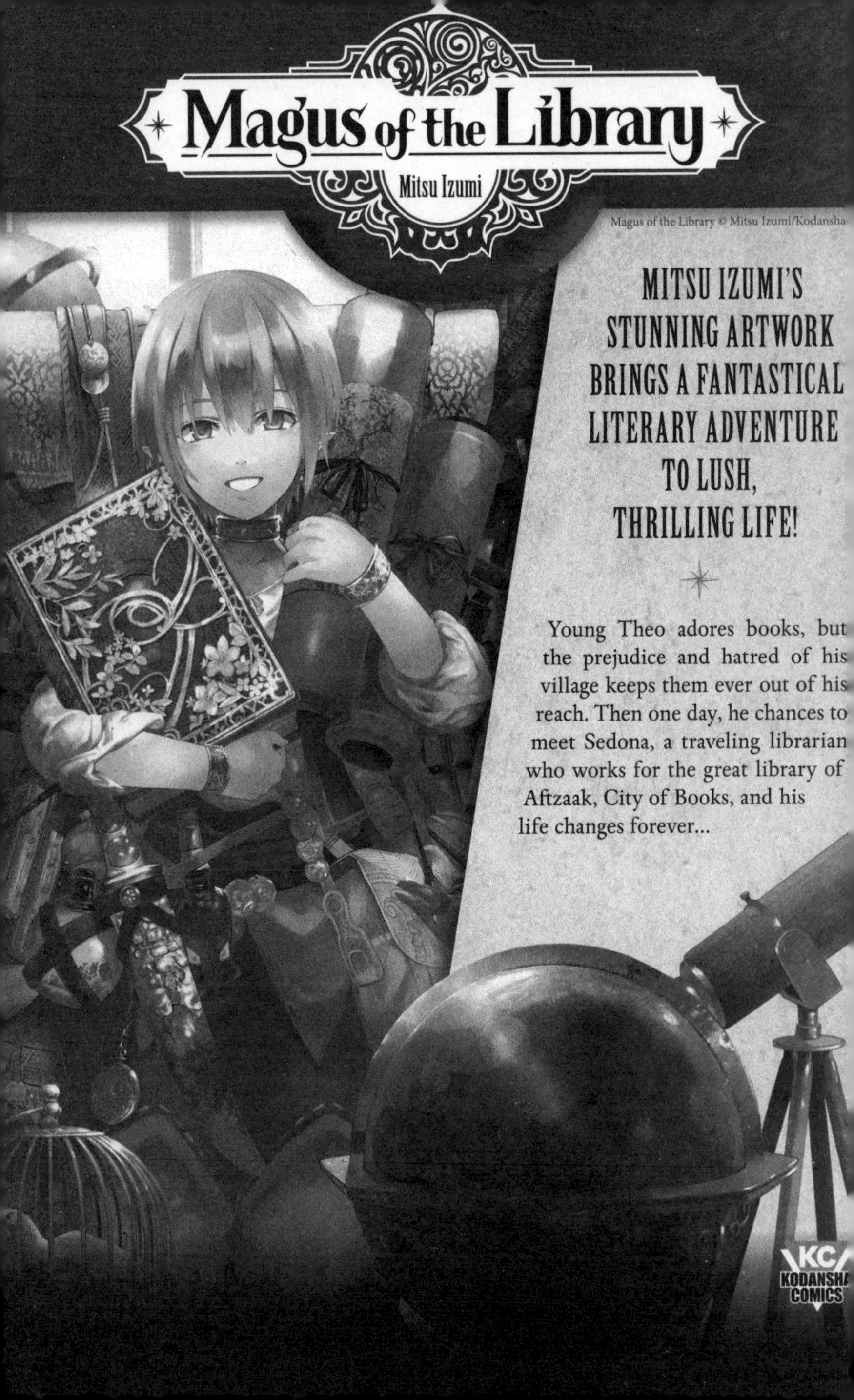
Magus of the Library
Mitsu Izumi
Magus of the Library © Mitsu Izumi/Kodansha
MITSU IZUMI'S STUNNING ARTWORK BRINGS A FANTASTICAL LITERARY ADVENTURE TO LUSH, THRILLING LIFE!
Young Theo adores books, but the prejudice and hatred of his village keeps them ever out of his reach. Then one day, he chances to meet Sedona, a traveling librarian who works for the great library of Aftzaak, City of Books, and his life changes forever...
KC KODANSHA COMICS

A Kodansha Comics Trade Paperback Original
EDENS ZERO 8 copyright © 2020 Hiro Mashima
English translation copyright © 2020 Hiro Mashima

All rights reserved.

Published in the United States by Kodansha Comics, an imprint of Kodansha USA Publishing, LLC, New York.

Publication rights for this English edition arranged through Kodansha Ltd., Tokyo.

First published in Japan in 2020 by Kodansha Ltd., Tokyo.

ISBN 978-1-63236-982-6

Original cover design by Narumi Miura (G x complex).

Printed in the United States of America.

www.kodanshacomics.com

9 8 7 6 5 4 3 2 1
Translation: Alethea Nibley & Athena Nibley
Lettering: AndWorld Design
Editing: Haruko Hashimoto
Kodansha Comics edition cover design by Phil Balsman

Publisher: Kiichiro Sugawara

Director of publishing services: Ben Applegate
Associate director of operations: Stephen Pakula
Publishing services managing editor: Noelle Webster
Assistant production manager: Emi Lotto, Angela Zurlo